FA Cup Non-League Giant-Killers Annual

1982 Edition

Goodall Publications Ltd
PO Box No. 201
12 Liverpool Street
London EC2M 7BS

01-283 5924

Copyright © 1982 by G. R. Goodall
Goodall Publications Ltd

Editor: G. R. (Bill) Goodall

Cover Design: Peter Gunthorpe

Front cover:
Graham Heathcote of Alliance Premier Leaguers Altrincham beating Liverpool and England goalkeeper Ray Clemence with a penalty goal during a Third Round tie at Anfield in January 1981. Liverpool won 4-1.
Copyright Photograph: *Cheshire County Newspapers*

Back cover:
Isthmian League Sutton United centre-half John Faulkner in action against Leeds and England striker Mick Jones during the U's dream Fourth Round tie in 1970 at Gander Green Lane against the First Division champions. Leeds won 6-0. Allan Clarke (left) scored four of the goals.
Copyright Photograph: *Sutton Herald*

ISBN 0 907579 0 19

Conditions of sale: This book is sold subject to the condition that it shall not, by way of trade or otherwise, be lent, re-sold, hired out, or otherwise circulated without the publisher's prior consent in any form of binding or cover other than that in which it is published and without a similar condition including this condition being imposed on the subsequent purchaser.

GOODALL PUBLICATIONS LTD
PO BOX NO 201,
12 LIVERPOOL STREET,
LONDON, EC2M 7BS
01-283 5924

Made and printed in Great Britain by
Hunt Barnard Printing Ltd., Aylesbury, Bucks.

CONTENTS

	Page
Foreword by Joe Mercer, O.B.E.	5
Editor's Note	6
ALTRINCHAM	8
BARNET	18
BATH CITY	29
BEDFORD TOWN	37
BISHOP AUCKLAND	47
BLYTH SPARTANS	56
BOSTON UNITED	67
CHELMSFORD CITY	76
COLCHESTER UNITED*	85
DAGENHAM	92
ENFIELD	97
GILLINGHAM*	108
GRAVESEND & NORTHFLEET	114
HARLOW TOWN	120
HASTINGS UNITED	127
HENDON	132
HEREFORD UNITED*	140
HILLINGDON BOROUGH	155
KETTERING TOWN	161
LEATHERHEAD	172
MACCLESFIELD TOWN	179
MAIDSTONE UNITED	185
NORTHWICH VICTORIA	192
NUNEATON	198
OXFORD UNITED*	206
PETERBOROUGH UNITED*	212
RHYL	225
RUNCORN	233
SCARBOROUGH	238

STAFFORD RANGERS	248
SUTTON UNITED	255
THANET UNITED	261
TOOTING AND MITCHAM UNITED	267
WALTHAMSTOW AVENUE	275
WEYMOUTH	284
WIGAN ATHLETIC*	297
WIMBLEDON*	308
WORCESTER CITY	320
WYCOMBE WANDERERS	327
YEOVIL TOWN	338

*Elected to the Football League

FOREWORD

by Joe Mercer, O.B.E.

The glorious uncertainty of the F.A. Cup makes it the greatest competition of the whole football world.

One of the main reasons for its popularity is that we start playing for it at the very beginning of the season with every team in the land competing – amateur and semi-pro killing themselves off until around the New Year when to a large extent only the professional League sides are still left in the hunt. Then the real 'giant-killing' begins and non-League history is often made.

I, like everyone else, have suffered humiliation from clubs from the lower regions of the game. I was in the Arsenal side when Third Division Bradford beat us 1–0 at Highbury. Incidentally Ron Greenwood was in that side!

I witnessed non-League Worcester City, inspired by Roy Paul, beating mighty Liverpool 2–1 when Phil Taylor left Billy Liddell out of a Liverpool Cup side for the first time.

I managed Manchester City when we were lucky to beat Wigan with a Colin Bell goal following a tragic mis-kick from Wigan's goalkeeper.

I marvelled in the late 'twenties when Walsall beat Herbert Chapman's Arsenal whose only excuse was that Alex James wasn't playing! And so we could go on and on recalling great 'giant-killing' feats.

I can remember a personal experience of playing for non-League Ellesmere Port against Northwich Victoria in an early round of the Cup. Not a nice experience – we were beaten 10–0!

Joe Mercer's Record . . .
Player
Everton, Arsenal and England
Manager
Sheffield United, Aston Villa, Manchester City and England
Director
Coventry City

EDITOR'S NOTE

This book records the thrilling post-war F.A. Cup deeds of the top non-League clubs. It includes the inspiring stories of clubs like Altrincham, Bedford, Harlow, Northwich Victoria, Worcester City and Yeovil as well as those who have since made the grade into the higher echelons (substantially as a result of their fairy-tale Cup successes), among them Hereford United, Oxford United (formerly Headington United), Peterborough United, Wimbledon and Wigan Athletic.

Every year when the Cup reaches the 1st, 2nd and 3rd Rounds, these Little Clubs, the relatively unknowns from outside League soccer, put in a brief but often scintillating 'giant-killing' appearance. It is one of the most fascinating phases of the F.A. Cup competition. These small clubs have won an affectionate place in the hearts of the British soccer supporter – indeed there are times when loyalties of League Club supporters are severely strained as they watch some tiny David doing battle on a First Division club's ground with the odds stacked against them.

Sir Matt Busby, the famous Manchester United and England manager, said of these Little Clubs when United were playing 5000-to-1 Cup outsiders Weymouth Town in 1950: 'Nothing appeals more to the sporting world than when one of these clubs comes along and beats one of the giants. The interest and appeal was never more fully demonstrated than by the remarkable attendance of over 80,000 spectators who turned up to see Yeovil play our lads at Maine Road. Yes, the success of one of the minnows has a wonderful attraction for the British sporting public'.

Non-League soccer is undoubtedly gaining stature. Most of the clubs in the Alliance Premier League have done enough to warrant inclusion in this book, a significant reminder of the underlying strength of this League and suggesting that its top clubs might well hold their own in the Fourth Division or alternatively that their aspirations might be met by the formation of a Fifth Division.

In recent years more non-League clubs that ever have reached the Third Round and beyond and although the last non-Leaguers to win the F.A. Cup were Spurs in 1901, three non-League sides have gained the rare distinction of having reached the Fifth Round (the last 16) – Colchester United (then in the Southern League) v Blackpool in 1948, Yeovil (then of the Southern League, now Alliance Premier) v Manchester United in the following season and more recently Blyth Spartans when they held Wrexham to a 1–1 draw in 1978 and then lost the replay by a narrow 1–0 margin. Thus the Spartans hold the honour of having progressed further in the F.A. Cup post-war than any other non-League club. And to Altrincham falls the honour of being the only non-League club to have reached the 3rd Round of the Cup in four consecutive seasons, 1978/9 – 1981/2. A presentation to mark this feat was made by the Alliance Premier League to the club during the A.P.L. Congress Week-end at Brighton on 12th June, 1982.

They are stirring stories and deserve to be read and re-read and not lie buried in the yellowing pages of the newspaper files. I am indebted in fact to those very files for fact and figure in those cases where I was not on the grounds covering the matches. I would also like to thank the clubs for having kindly checked my material at proof stage.

G. R. GOODALL

ALTRINCHAM

Founded: 1903

League: Alliance Premier

Ground: Moss Lane

Colours: Red and white shirts, black shorts

Although Altrincham made little impression in the F.A. Cup in the post-war years up to the mid-sixties their performance since, especially in some epic Third Round battles, have earned them the reputation of being one of the most formidable non-League Cup fighters in the country.

After an exciting Second Round result in the 1965/6 season when the part-timers beat Rochdale 3-1 on the League side's ground the Robins drew a Third Round tie at Molineux against Second Division Wolves, 30,000 spectators seeing the Robins beaten 5-0. The memory of this achievement has been dimmed somewhat by Altrincham's subsequent exploits — beginning in the 1974/5 season when they battled through to Round Three at Goodison Park on 4th January 1975 to hold mighty Everton to a 1-1 draw before a crowd of 34,509. At Old Trafford, where the replay was held before an even larger crowd (35,530) the part-timers went down 2-0 after a fantastic night of football.

Four seasons later the Robins again appeared in the Third Round draw having disposed of fellow non-Leaguers Southport and Droylsden to gain one of the finest Cup draws that soccer can offer — Spurs at White Hart Lane. A crowd of over 31,000 saw Spurs managing only a 1-1 draw, a penalty goal saving them from defeat. Spurs won the replay, staged at Maine Road, 3-0.

In the 1979/80 season Altrincham fought their way to the Third Round via the scalps of Fourth Division Crewe Alexandra and Third Division Rotherham United. The Third Round took Orient of the Second Division to Moss Lane and a 1-1 draw. At the replay at Brisbane Road Orient scraped through 2-1.

Cup glory came Robins way again in 1980/1 to enable them to celebrate the year of the 100th F.A. Cup competition. After defeating non-League opposition Burscough and Fourth Division Scunthorpe (after a replay) in the earlier rounds Altrincham drew a plum tie in the Third Round — mighty Liverpool at Anfield where the part-timers went down 4-1 after having made a terrific impression on Merseyside.

In the 1981/2 season the Robins were again on the Cup glory

trail, defeating Sheffield United and York City, both after replays, before going down 6-1 to Burnley away from home in the Third Round.

The Robins' first post-war First Round encounter was in 1963/4 against League opposition Third Division Wrexham at Moss Lane, three games being needed before Altrincham conceded defeat. The first contest had to be abandoned after 76 minutes because of fog, the restaged game ending in a blank scoresheet with the replay at Wrexham giving the League side a 3-0 win.

In 1965/6 the Robins were matched against Midland Leaguers Scarborough whom they beat 6-0. For the Second Round the Robins were drawn away against Fourth Division Rochdale, a crowd of over 8,000 at Spotland seeing the part-timers outmatch the League side to record a magnificent 3-1 victory and the reward of a Third Round tie against Second Division Wolves at Molineux.

This Third Round tie in January 1966 was one of the big events in Altrincham's Cup history. It was Wolves' biggest 'gate' of the season with over 30,000 on the ground including 10,000 Robins' supporters. The Robins had to bow to the inevitable as Wolves scored five without reply.

Altrincham: Smith, Brown, Forrester, Peters, Dewar, Halliwell, Taylor, Campbell, Connolly, Swindells, Colbridge.

Two seasons later, 1967/8, Altrincham were again in the First Round, drawn against fellow non-Leaguers Grantham away from home, the Robins bringing off a convincing 3-0 victory. For the Second Round tie the Robins drew Third Division Barrow at home. Altrincham opened the scoring but Barrow gained the upper hand and ran out 2-1 winners.

In the following season the Robins again had League opposition, Third Division Crewe Alexandra at Moss Lane and against the run of the play the visitors ran out 1-0 winners.

The Robins had to wait until 1971/2 before they were again in the First Round, this time against non-League opponents Rossendale United, the Cheshire League champions, away from home. The Robins lost 1-0.

The next season Altrincham had a home draw in the First

Round against League opposition, Notts County, Third Division, the League side scoring a late penalty to put the Robins out of the Cup.

In the following season, 1973/4, Altrincham added a further League scalp to their tally when they defeated Fourth Division Hartlepool United 2-0 in the First Round at Moss Lane. It was the third time in four seasons that Hartlepool had been defeated in the competition by a non-League club. For their Second Round tie the Robins were drawn against famous F.A. Cup fighters Blackburn Rovers, Third Division, away from home. A superbly organised Robins defence made Blackburn fight again after a goalless draw. At Moss Lane the Rovers kept tight control on Altrincham and ran out 2-0 winners.

The Robins began their historic 1974/5 season by drawing Scunthorpe, Fourth Division, away from home at the Old Show Ground. Although the non-Leaguers were a goal down in the 28th minute they drew level in the second half to make Scunthorpe fight again. The replay at Moss Lane drew a crowd of over 4,000 who, on a night of high excitement, saw the non-Leaguers run rings round their Fourth Division opponents to win 3-1.

The next round produced a home tie at Moss Lane against fellow non-Leaguers Gateshead, the Robins winning convincingly 3-0 to take them into the Third Round. Their reward was a money-spinning game against First Division Everton at Goodison Park. This memorable game, which resulted in a 1-1 draw, with a replay at Old Trafford where Altrincham went down 2-0 in glorious defeat, are both described in *Match Report*.

In the two following seasons Altrincham again arrived in the First Round and on both occasions drew League opposition away from home, in 1975/6 against Halifax Town who defeated them 3-1 and in 1976/7 when they sustained a heavy defeat 5-0 at the hands of Third Division Rotherham United.

Back in the First Round in 1978/9 the Robins had a home game against fellow Northern Premier Leaguers Southport. In a tense struggle the Robins scraped home by a 4-3 margin. For the Second Round Altrincham had to travel to meet Cheshire County League side Droylsden and their 2-0 win gave the Robins a fairy-tale draw in the Third Round against Spurs at White Hart Lane. The non-

Leaguers held the First Division side to a sensational 1-1 draw before going down 3-0 in the replay at Maine Road. Both matches are fully recorded in *Match Report*.

Altrincham began what was to be another fantastic Cup run in the 1979/80 season by meeting bottom of the Fourth Division side Crewe Alexandra in the First Round at home at Moss Lane. The Robins won 3-0 thus avenging the 1-0 defeat inflicted on them by Crewe in 1968. Altrincham's reward was an away tie in the Second Round against Rotherham United, midway in Division Three, who had inflicted such a heavy defeat on the part-timers three seasons previously. This time the Robins had their revenge with a fine 2-0 win to earn them the right to meet Orient at Moss Lane in the Third Round. Again Altrincham provided one of the Cup shocks of the day. With Alex Stepney, the former Manchester United star, in goal for the part-timers and giving an immaculate display, the Robins had little difficulty in curbing Orient's strikers and it was no surprise when the non-Leaguers took the lead in the 28th minute with a goal by Whitbread. It was not until the 80th minute that Orient equalised to keep their Cup hopes alive.

It was no different in the replay at Brisbane Road with Orient again finding they had a game on their hands against the battling non-Leaguers. There was little to choose between the two sides in the first-half, neither team being able to score. Within 45 seconds of the resumption Orient broke the deadlock, Stepney having blocked a sizzling shot from the on-form Coates, being beaten by Mayo who crashed in the rebound. Although Jennings scored number two for Orient the non-Leaguers were far from finished, Johnson pulling back a goal for the Robins in the closing minutes to make the final score 2-1.

Altrincham: Stepney, Allan, Davison, Bailey, Owens, King, Heathcote, Whitbread, Johnson, Rogers, Howard.

In the first game Barrow was in the Robins' line-up with Heathcote substitute.

The Robins' Cup legend continued in the following season, 1980/1, enabling the part-timers to play a fitting role in the centenary celebrations. In the First Round the Robins faced Cheshire County League side Burscough away from home, a hard match resulting in a 2-1 win for Altrincham. It was enough, however, to see the Robins safely through to the

Second Round, away from home against lowly-placed Fourth Division Scunthorpe United. The game was a triumph for Altrincham's defenders who successfully held their League opponents to a 0-0 draw to take them to Moss Lane for a replay. Altrincham began this second game in fine style and on the half-hour scoring the only goal of the match from a penalty. Robins' reward was a tie that every non-League side in the country dreams about – a Third Round encounter against Liverpool at Anfield, fully reported as a *Match Report*. It was the Robins third Third Round tie in successive seasons – a non-League record.

The 1981/2 competition was another great Cup season for the Robins when for the sixth time since the war they battled their way into the Third Round again to arouse speculation as to how long it would be before they were elected to the League. Their First Round tie was away at Bramall Lane against Fourth Division leaders Sheffield United, four times winners of the F.A. Cup. With Sheffield leading 1-0 at half-time the Alliance Premier League champions hit back when Rogers equalised immediately after the interval. United snatched back the lead in the 64th minute and Rogers, hitting his second six minutes from the end, again enabled the Robins to come from behind for the second time to earn a splendid draw. The 12,433 crowd was the largest Cup attendance of the day. The replay at Moss Lane produced a sensational 3-0 win for the non-Leaguers. After a goalless first-half the Robins rang rings round their League opponents, two goals by Howard and a cracker by Heathcote sending United reeling from the Cup.

The Robins' reward was a Second Round tie away against Fourth Division York City at Bootham Crescent which ended in a goalless draw. The replay at Moss Lane produced a ding-dong struggle and one of the upsets of the round. The Robins always had the better of their League opponents, leading 2-1 at half-time and winning a pulse-racing game 4-3, the Robins' goals being scored by Goulding, Rogers (2) and Whitbread.

The Robins were out of luck when they went to Turf Moor to do battle in the Third Round against Third Division Burnley. On a muddy pitch the League side dominated the game and ran out 6-1 winners, Altrincham's consolation goal coming from Howard.

MATCH REPORTS

THIRD ROUND F.A. CUP
4th January 1975
EVERTON 1   ALTRINCHAM 1

This was one of the greatest occasions in Altrincham's football history – meeting mighty Everton at Goodison Park before nearly 35,000 spectators in the Third Round of the Cup.

In the 30th minute of the game Goodison Park was stunned when the part-timers went ahead. While the Everton defence appealed for an off-side decision Heathcote moved the ball through to John HUGHES who, after quickly making sure that the referee was waving play on, coolly placed the ball past Davies from close in. Shortly afterwards Everton were back in the game with a header from Pearson when the ball went straight into the arms of Eales.

Half-time: Everton 0   Altrincham 1

For the second half Altrincham had substitute Windsor on in place of Dickinson who sustained concussion late in the first half. Without their captain Altrincham lost some of their rhythm but were still the superior side as they had been for most of the first half. Towards the end Everton moved into the attack and Eales in the Altrincham goal made a magnificent save when he tipped a Pearson shot over the bar.

In the 69th minute of the game Everton scored their equaliser through a penalty. This disaster for the Northern Premier Leaguers began when Casey made a bad pass across the 18 yard box and as Irving and Pearson broke through Allan brought down Irving. Referee Mr. R. Perkin immediately pointed to the spot and Dave CLEMENTS, who was skipper for the day and Everton's most accomplished player, strode up and fired the ball into the roof of the net.

Result: Everton 1   Altrincham 1

Teams:
Everton: Davies, Bernard, McLaughlan, Clements, McNaught, Lyons, Jones, Pearson, Irving, Latchford, Connolly. Sub: Telfer.
Altrincham: Eales, Allan, Crossley, Owens, Casey, Dickinson, Morris, Heathcote, Smith, Hughes, Davison. Sub: Windsor.
Referee: Mr. R. Perkin, (Staffordshire)
Attendance: 34,509

THIRD ROUND F.A. CUP REPLAY
7th January 1975
ALTRINCHAM 0   EVERTON 2
(At Old Trafford)

A 35,000 crowd was at Old Trafford for the exciting replay against the part-timers with thousands of Manchester United fans turning the Stretford end into a sea of red and white scarves in support of the Northern Premier Leaguers against United's old adversary, Everton.

The return to the Everton side of Martin Dobson, their skilful mid-field player, made a tremendous difference to the performance of the First Division side. Gary Jones who had been sent off during the previous encounter was Everton's man of the match and played a large part in Everton's ultimate victory.

After intense pressure it was no surprise when Everton opened the scoring. It was a tragedy for Altrincham as Graham Heathcote passed back to Eales from the edge of the penalty box when the ball stuck in the mud. LATCHFORD quickly ran up to steer the ball into the Altrincham net.

Half-time: Altrincham 0   Everton 1

After the restart Morris almost equalised for the Robins but he was late with his shot. In the 52nd minute, Everton put the game beyond recall when LYONS headed in a perfect second goal from a Telfer cross.

When the final whistle blew the crowd rose to acclaim Altrincham's tremendous effort and the team were congratulated by the Everton players as they went off the field.

Result: Altrincham 0   Everton 2

Teams:
Altrincham: Eales, Allan, Crossley, Owens, Casey, Dickinson, Morris, Heathcote, Smith, Hughes (J), Davison. Sub: Windsor.
Everton: Davies, Scott, McLaughlan, Clements, McNaught, Lyons, Jones, Dobson, Pearson, Latchford, Telfer. Sub: Marshall.
Referee: Mr. R. Perkin.
Attendance: 35,530

THIRD ROUND F.A. CUP
10th January 1979
TOTTENHAM HOTSPUR 1   ALTRINCHAM 1

Remembering Altrincham's classic display against First Division Everton three seasons previously, Spurs did not take their home draw against the Northern Premier League side lightly. On the great day there was a crowd of 31,081 to watch the minnows turn in a performance that could only be described as magic. Although for most of the first half Spurs had control of the midfield they were unable to penetrate a stubborn Altrincham defence.

The Robins had the misfortune to lose central defender, Malcolm Bailey, in the 20th minute with a dislocated collarbone. Three minutes later Spurs' goalkeeper Kendall had to palm a shot from Davison on to the bar and from the rebound Johnson only narrowly missed scoring. Then came misfortune for Altrincham as Ardiles was pulled down in the box, Peter TAYLOR opening Spurs account from the penalty.

Half-time: Tottenham 1   Altrincham 0

In the second half Spurs were unable to capitalise on their one goal lead and in the final twenty minutes of the game it was Altrincham's turn to throw everything into the attack. The Robins surged forward, and had their reward in the 84th minute when Jeff JOHNSON slotted the ball into the Spurs' net.

It was a tremendous performance by the non-Leaguers against the classy £2 million Spurs side – the total cost of Altrincham's team was £20,000, the precise amount they took home from the game!

Result: Tottenham 1   Altrincham 1

Teams:
Tottenham: Kendall, McAllister, Holmes, Villa, Lacy, Perryman, Pratt, Ardiles, Lee, Jones, Taylor. Sub: Armstrong.
Altrincham: Eales, Allan, Brooke, Bailey, Owens, Davison, King, Heathcote, Johnson, Rogers, Howard. Sub: Crossley.
Referee: Mr. C. Maskell, Cambs.
Attendance: 31,081

THIRD ROUND REPLAY F.A. CUP
16th January 1979
ALTRINCHAM 0   TOTTENHAM HOTSPUR 3
(at Maine Road)

There was a 'gate' of nearly 28,000 at Maine Road, Manchester, to watch brave Altrincham take on Spurs in this Third Round replay. As at White Hart Lane, Spurs began hesitantly against the part-timers and on a difficult pitch both Rogers and Heathcote had near misses and once Tottenham's new £100,000 signing from Luton, Aleksic, had to dash off his goal line to save from Howard.

Five minutes from the interval Spurs, who until then had rarely seemed like scoring, got a couple of goals in a vital four-minute spell. Spurs centre-forward Colin LEE scored both, the first during a goalmouth melee and the second two minutes later when he fired in a thunderous shot from a McAllister cross.

Half-time: Altrincham 0   Tottenham 2

After the interval Altrincham powered forward in an attempt to reduce the deficit but Spurs defence held firm with McAllister and Perryman playing resolutely in the heart of the visitors' defence. Altrincham never gave up and both Heathcote and Rogers had scoring chances.

Ten minutes from time LEE made the game safe for Spurs when he completed his hat-trick.

Result: Altrincham 0   Tottenham 3

Teams:
Altrincham: Eales, Crossley, Brooke, Allan, Owens, Davison, King, Heathcote, Johnson, Rogers, Howard. Sub: Tobin.
Tottenham: Aleksic, McAllister, Holmes, Villa, Lacy, Perryman, Pratt, Ardiles, Lee, Jones, Taylor. Sub: Naylor.
Referee: Mr. C. Maskell, Cambs.
Attendance: 27,878

THIRD ROUND F.A. CUP
3rd January 1981
LIVERPOOL 4   ALTRINCHAM 1

This was the game that every non-League club dreams about – a Third Round encounter at Anfield and in this case the champions of the Alliance Premier League facing the champions of England before a 37,000 crowd.

From the start Liverpool's pace and skill put the Robins' defences under severe pressure, David Johnson's lightning runs down the right flank, with Kenny Dalglish, Terry McDermott and Jimmy Case lurking in the middle and causing all kinds of problems. At the other end Robins' mid-fielder Graham Barrow produced a fine save from England's goalkeeper Ray Clemence when he hit a well-directed shot from 25 yards.

Altrincham fought back stubbornly and their defensive wall of white shirts, with their courageous goalkeeper John Connaughton in constant action, foiled attack after attack and this was interspersed with Altrincham forays into the Reds' territory.

Despite all the Liverpool pressure it was not until the 27th minute that the Reds broke down the Robins' defence, McDERMOTT taking a pass from Dalglish to hammer in a fine shot.

In the 39th minute Liverpool were 2-0 in the lead when DALGLISH completed a McDermott-Money move by heading in out of the reach of Connaughton.

Half-time: Liverpool 2   Altrincham 0

Altrincham had a slightly better second half, the pace having slackened and allowing the part-timers to play more composed football.

There was no stopping Liverpool however and in the 54th minute they went 3-0 in the lead from another cleverly-executed DALGLISH goal from close range. Altrincham were still showing plenty of fighting spirit and had their reward in the 71st minute. Clemence brought down Whitbread during a determined Altrincham attack and the referee had no hestitation in awarding a penalty. HEATHCOTE took the kick and blasted the ball past the England goalkeeper.

Towards the end Liverpool scored again when Ray KENNEDY beat Connaughton in the 88th minute with a glancing header.

Result: Liverpool 4   Altrincham 1

Teams:
Liverpool: Clemence, Neal, A. Kennedy, Irwin, R. Kennedy, Money, Dalglish, Lee, Johnson, McDermott, Case. Sub: Fairclough.
Altrincham: Connaughton, Allan, Davison, Bailey, Owens, King, Barrow, Heathcote, Johnson, Rogers, Howard. Sub: Whitbread.
Referee: Mr. T. Farley, Co. Durham.
Attendance: 37,170

CUP RUNS

1963/4
1st Round – *16th November*
Altrincham ....1 Wrexham 2
(abandoned after 76 minutes)

1st Round – *20th November*
Altrincham ....0 Wrexham 0

1st Round Replay – *26th November*
Wrexham ....3 Altrincham 0

1965/6
1st Round – *13th November*
Altrincham ....6 Scarborough 0

2nd Round – *8th December*
Rochdale ....1 Altrincham 3

3rd Round – *22nd January*
Wolves ....5 Altrincham 0

1967/8
1st Round – *9th December*
Grantham ....0 Altrincham 3

2nd Round – *6th January*
Altrincham ....1 Barrow 2

1968/9
1st Round – *16th November*
Altrincham ....0 Crewe Alex 1

1971/2
1st Round – *23rd November*
Rossendale ....1 Altrincham 0

1972/3
1st Round – *18th November*
Altrincham ....0 Notts County 1

1973/4
1st Round – *24th November*
Altrincham ....2 Hartlepool Utd .0

2nd Round – *15th December*
Blackburn Rov ..0 Altrincham 0

2nd Round Replay *19th December*
Altrincham ....0 Blackburn Rov .2

1974/5
1st Round – *23rd November*
Scunthorpe ....1 Altrincham 1

1st Round Replay – *25th November*
Altrincham ....3 Scunthorpe 1

2nd Round – *14th December*
Altrincham ....3 Gateshead 0

3rd Round – *4th January*
Everton ....1 Altrincham 1

3rd Round Replay – *7th January*
Altrincham ....0 Everton 2
(at Old Trafford)

1975/6
1st Round – *22nd November*
Halifax ....3 Altrincham 1

1976/7
1st Round – *20th November*
Rotherham ....5 Altrincham 0

1978/9
1st Round – *25th November*
Altrincham ....4 Southport 3

2nd Round – *16th December*
Droylsden ....0 Altrincham 2

3rd Round – *10th January*
Tottenham ....1 Altrincham 1

3rd Round Replay – *16th January*
Altrincham ....0 Tottenham 3
(at Maine Road)

1979/80
1st Round – *24th November*
Altrincham ....3 Crewe Alex 0

2nd Round – *15th December*
Rotherham ....0 Altrincham 2

3rd Round – *5th January*
Altrincham ....1 Orient 1

3rd Round Replay – *9th January*
Orient ....2 Altrincham 1

1980/81
1st Round – *22nd November*
Burscough ....1 Altrincham 2

2nd Round – *13th December*
Scunthorpe Utd .0 Altrincham 0

2nd Round Replay – *15th December*
Altrincham ....1 Scunthorpe Utd 0

3rd Round – *3rd January*
Liverpool ....4 Altrincham 1

1981/2
1st Round – *21st November*
Sheffield Utd .....2 Altrincham 2

1st Round Replay – *23rd November*
Altrincham ....3 Sheffield Utd ...0

2nd Round – *12th December*
York City ....0 Altrincham 0

2nd Round Replay – *2nd January*
Altrincham ....4 York City 3

3rd Round – *18th January*
Burnley ....6 Altrincham 1

BARNET

Founded: 1888

League: Alliance Premier

Ground: Underhill

Colours: Amber and black shirts; black shorts

Barnet, formerly of the Athenian and Southern Leagues, have firmly established themselves as post-war F.A. Cup 'giant-killers", having reached the Third Round on no fewer than four occasions and appearing on numerous occasions in the First and Second Rounds. Barnet's most memorable Cup performance to date was in the 1981/2 season when they were opposed by First Division Brighton at Underhill, adding a glory chapter to their history when they held the £3,000,000 side to a 0-0 draw, going down 3-1 in the replay (watched by 15,884) in a fighting display that kept the scoresheet clean until after half-time. Another notable Barnet performance was in the 1972/3 season when they were drawn against Queen's Park Rangers in a Third Round contest at Loftus Road, holding the Second Division side to a goalless draw in front of a crowd of nearly 14,000. In the replay at Underhill the League side was held for nearly 70 minutes before scoring and eventually running out 3-0 winners. Barnet had previously appeared in the Third Round in the 1964/5 season when they met Second Division Preston North End at Underhill, being narrowly defeated 3-2. The then Southern Leaguers were again in the Third Round in the 1970/1 season when they were defeated 1-0 at Underhill by Fourth Division Colchester United.

It was against Queen's Park Rangers in 1945/6, when the 'two-leg' system was in operation for one season, that Barnet began their many post-war appearances in the First Round. The first 'leg' was played at Underhill before a crowd of 8,060 when the Third Division side won 6-2. In the return 'leg' at Shepherds Bush before a 'gate' of 11,426 Rangers won 2-1 despite a sensational first minute goal by Barnet. QPR progressed into the next round on a 8-3 aggregate.

In the following season, when the competition returned to its original knockout form, Barnet drew a First Round home tie against Athenian League rivals Sutton United whom they dismissed 3–0. In the Second Round, which Barnet reached for the first time in the club's history, the then amateurs drew Southend United, Third Division South. Southend outplayed the part-timers and ran out 9–2 victors.

Barnet had the luck of the draw in the 1948/9 First Round contest, drawing Exeter City, Third Division South. Exeter's superior stamina triumphed and saw them to a 6–2 win.

Barnet were next in the First Round in the 1954/5 season when they were at home to Southampton, then Third Division South. Southampton had an easy 4–1 win helped by a Barnet 'own goal'.

Barnet had to wait until the 1959/60 season before next appearing in the First Round, their opponents being non-League Salisbury of the Western League away from home at the Victoria Park ground. Salisbury accounted for an off-form Barnet 1–0.

In the 1961/2 competition Barnet had to travel to face another non-League side in the First Round – Southern Leaguers Weymouth. A disputed penalty goal gave Weymouth a narrow 1–0 win.

Barnet had a difficult First Round tie in the 1963/4 season when they travelled to the west country to meet Fourth Division Torquay United at Plainmoor. A crowd of over 6,000 saw Torquay gain a comfortable 6–2 victory.

The following season, 1964/5, was to be a memorable one for Barnet when for the first time in the club's history they were to make headlines on reaching the Third Round. Their first hurdle was a First Round contest at Underhill against then Southern Leaguers Cambridge United, Barnet winning by a narrow 2–1 margin.

Barnet drew an away tie in the Second Round against fellow amateurs and neighbours Enfield Town, Isthmian League, recognised Cup-fighters in their own right. Enfield were three goals down within half an hour but levelled the score at 3–3 through Barnet defensive errors. Two more goals, one at each end, made the final scoreline 4–4. Barnet mastered the conditions at Underhill better than Enfield in the replay and gained an easy 3–0 win before a 9,000 crowd, their reward a Third Round contest at Underhill against Preston North End, the previous season's Cup finalists.

On the great day Preston, then in Division Two, came out on to Barnet's 8ft sloping pitch to the cheers of a crowd of over 10,000. The game was only 90 seconds old when Preston's right half, Kendall, who had appeared at Wembley the previous season, sent a cannonball shot into the back of the Barnet net from 30 yards and Godfrey scored another four minutes later to give Preston a 2-0 half-time lead. After the interval Figg reduced the deficit for Barnet within half a minute of the restart and in the 53rd minute the ground erupted when Whyte struck home the equaliser. Ten minutes from the end, with the amateurs looking set for a replay at Deepdale, Barnet defender Casey, attempting to head the ball away, put through his own goal to give Preston the match winner.

In the 1965/6 season Barnet were again in the First Round, at home against Dartford of the Premier Division, Southern League. Barnet's hopes of a Cup run were shattered, Dartford bringing off a 2-0 victory.

Barnet, now in the Southern League, had to wait until 1967/8 before they were again in the First Round, drawn against fellow Southern Leaguers Hereford United away from home. John Charles, former Welsh international, helped his side to a 3-2 win.

The next season Barnet were again in the First Round, drawn at home against fellow non-Leaguers Brentwood Town, also of the Southern League but a division below Barnet. The game ended in a 1-1 draw and the replay at Brentwood put Barnet out of the Cup by a 1-0 margin.

In 1969/70 Barnet drew an away game in the First Round against Isthmian Leaguers Walton & Hersham and beat the Swans by the only goal of the game. In the Second Round Barnet were matched against Athenian Leaguers Sutton United. Although Barnet had most of the game Sutton notched up a surprise 2-0 victory.

In the following season, 1970/1, Barnet achieved an outstanding Cup victory when in the First Round they decimated Newport County, Fourth Division 6-1 at Underhill, a game that is still talked about as one of the most impressive Cup wins ever by a non-League side over League opponents. Barnet's landslide victory equalled the previous record Cup wins by non-League sides against League opposition – Boston United's 6-1 against Derby County in 1955/6 and Hereford's 6-1 against QPR in 1957/8. Barnet's goals on this memorable occasion were scored by Rick George (3), Ferguson (o.g.), Powell and Adams.

For their Second Round tie Barnet were drawn against Slough, then in the Athenian League, away from home at Slough Stadium. Barnet scored the only goal of the match, a header from Eason who had scored 54 goals the previous season. Barnet went through to the Third Round for only the second time in the club's 82 years' history drawing a home game against Fourth Division Colchester United, themselves once Southern League 'giant-killers'.

Although Barnet had most of the play and mastered the Arctic conditions better than the professionals Barnet lost the game in the seventh minute when Mahon scored the only goal of the match from 35 yards. Barnet's outstanding performer was former Arsenal player Gordon Ferry.

Barnet: McClelland; Lye, Jenkins, Ward, Embery, King, Powell, Ferry, George, Eason and Adams.

After the Third Round excitement of the previous season Barnet were again in the First Round in 1971/2 drawn away from home against fellow Southern Leaguers Kettering. Kettering's biggest crowd of the season, nearly 4,000, was at Rockingham Road to see Barnet coast into the next round by a 4-2 margin. For the Second Round Barnet had home advantage against Third Division Torquay United and seemed set for another 'giant-killing' act when they scored two minutes after the kick-off. But Torquay settled down and won comfortably 4-1.

The following season Barnet were again in the First Round, drawing away to Banbury, from one of the lower divisions of the Southern League. Two second half goals put Barnet comfortably through to the next round. This Second Round tie was a home game against West Midlands side Bilston resulting in a 1-1 draw. There was another tough battle in the replay and it was not until the 70th minute that Barnet scored the match-winner to give the Southern Leaguers a money spinning tie against Queen's Park Rangers and a memorable replay at Underhill. Both games are described in full in *Match Report*.

Barnet were next in the First Round, after a break of several years, in the 1977/8 season when they were drawn at home against redoubtable Cup fighters Third Division Peterborough. The tie drew a 'gate' of over 4,000, some of whom were at Underhill to see fabulous 37-year-old Jimmy Greaves, England's former international and goal-scoring hero of Chelsea, Spurs, West Ham and A.C. Milan in Cup action once again. It was Jimmy's 80th Cup appearance in the competition proper, a career which saw him gain a F.A. Cup winners medal for Spurs in 1963 and 1967. Barnet were fielding a second player with a Cup winners' medal, Marvin Hinton, who got his when playing for Chelsea against Leeds in 1970. Peterborough scraped through with a 2-1 win.

For their First Round clash of 1978/9 Barnet drew Isthmian League Premier Division Woking for what turned out to be a marathon. The first incident-packed game took place at Underhill resulting in a 3-3 draw. The replay produced another battle royal, the result at 90 minutes being 2-2 and the game going into extra time. There was a goal at each end and the 3-3 stalemate again needed a further game to settle the issue.

When the two clubs met for the second replay on Brentford's ground the prize for the winners was a Second Round tie against Swansea. Woking ended the marathon with a 3-0 victory.

In the First Round in the 1980/1 season Barnet were hosts to Southern League opposition Minehead and did a houdini act to gain a 2-2 draw after trailing by two goals with only 17 minutes left. In the replay it was Minehead's turn to draw level after being 1-0 down but a second goal for Barnet in the closing stages secured them a place in the Second Round. This was at home against promotion-chasing Fourth Division Peterborough. The League side's class told and the Alliance Premier Leaguers went out 1-0.

Again in the First Round in the 1981/2 season Barnet had an away draw against fellow non-League Cup heroes Harlow Town of the Isthmian League. The game ended in a goalless draw but a sixth minute Barnet goal in the replay at Underhill gave the Alliance Premier Leaguers the chance of a tilt against Isthmian Leaguers Wycombe Wanderers. Played at Underhill. Barnet surged ahead in the 25th minute and made the game safe two minutes from the end to give them the right to meet First Division draw specialists Brighton & Hove Albion in the Third Round. The epic games against Brighton are fully described in *Match Report*.

MATCH REPORTS

THIRD ROUND F.A. CUP
13th January 1973
QUEEN'S PARK RANGERS 0   BARNET 0

Holding high-flying Second Division Q.P.R., who at the end of the season were promoted to the First Division, to a 0–0 draw at Loftus Road was one of the most memorable exploits in the history of the Southern Leaguers. Barnet's manager, Tom Coleman, decided on an aggressive 4-2-4 formation against the high-scoring £500,000 Q.P.R. attack. Jack McClelland, the former Arsenal goalkeeper capped by Northern Ireland, played an inspired game in the Barnet goal; equally solid in defence was Joe Fascione, the former Chelsea winger, playing a mid-field role.

Although Barnet had to absorb a good deal of Q.P.R. pressure they were often dangerous in break-outs, led by their most effective forward Colin Powell, who throughout the match was an impressive figure as he rampaged down the right flank.

Half-time: Queen's Park Rangers 0   Barnet 0

After the interval Barnet continued to worry Rangers with their occasional sorties into the Q.P.R. goal area.

Eason, taking advantage of a defensive error, went close with a shot that could have taken the part-timers into the Fourth Round. In the last ten minutes Powell nearly won the game for Barnet when he hammered in a fierce shot that struck the bar with Parkes beaten.

When the final whistle blew the crowd rose to acclaim one of the finest Cup performances ever given by a non-League side.

Result: Barnet 0   Queen's Park Rangers 0

Teams:
Queen's Park Rangers: Parkes, Hazell, Clement, Leach, Mancini, Hunt, Ferguson, Salvage, Thomas, Bowles, Givens.
Barnet: McClelland, Lye, Plume, Fascione, Tom, Godfrey, Powell, Ferry, Embery, Davies, Eason.
Referee: Mr. W. J. Gow (Swansea).
Attendance: 13,626

THIRD ROUND F.A. CUP REPLAY
16th January 1973
BARNET 0   QUEEN'S PARK RANGERS 3

Before the biggest crowd at Underhill for many years Barnet effectively marshalled their defence and for 70 minutes withstood a continuous series of attacks by Rangers. Jack McClelland, who had so magnificently blunted Rangers' attacks during the first game, was ruled out because of a leg infection. In his place came Wilf Woodend, a 26-year-old Army sapper who previously had had only one game for Barnet, but in the finality Woodend played a hero's game in the Barnet goal. Rangers also made team changes, the most significant of which was the return of Gerry Francis, whose absence from the Rangers mid-field trio in the previous game was greatly missed.

Despite their persistent pressure Rangers had fewer scoring opportunities than on the previous occasion. Former Arsenal defender, Gordon Ferry, again played an outstanding game as he marshalled the Barnet defence in a valiant effort to stem Rangers' attack. As the first half came to a close Rangers built up even more pressure and a terrific drive from Clement struck the foot of the post.

Half-time: Barnet 0   Q.P.R. 0

Shortly after the interval Dave Thomas, who played an outstanding game for Q.P.R. hit the outside of the post and in the 70th minute Q.P.R., held up for 160 minutes by the non-Leaguers, finally ended the deadlock through LEACH from a Dave Thomas corner. Five minutes later BOWLES hammered a shot under Woodend's body to settle the issue and the final goal, in the 81st minute, again came from a Thomas corner and was slotted in by MANCINI.

It was the end of the brave Barnet challenge to the powerful Second Division club and as the team left the field the crowd rose in tribute to the part-timers.

Result: Barnet 0   Q.P.R. 3

Teams:
Barnet: Woodend, Lye, Plume, Fascione, Tom, Godfrey, Powell, Ferry, Embery, Davies, Eason.
Queen's Park Rangers: Parkes, Watson, Clement, Hazell, Mancini, Thomas, Bowles, Givens, Leach, Ferguson, Francis.
Referee: Mr. G. Kew (Amersham)
Attendance: 10,919

THIRD ROUND F.A. CUP
2nd January 1982
BARNET 0   BRIGHTON & HOVE ALBION 0

Brighton of the First Division meeting Premier Alliance Leaguers Barnet at Underhill – this was the fairy-tale draw which nearly caused the football upset of the year and which was to provide the non-Leaguers with another magnificent chapter in their Cup history. Brighton's star-studded side included four full internationals – Sammy Nelson, ex-Arsenal defender and Northern Ireland international, Republic of Ireland international Tony Grealish, Welsh international Mike Thomas, formerly of Everton and another Republic of Ireland international Michael Robinson, ex-Manchester City. Also in the line-up were such famous names as Jimmy Case, the former Liverpool midfield player and Andy Ritchie, Manchester United's former high-scoring star.

Twice in the opening quarter of an hour headers from Gary

Sargent brought splendid saves from Brighton's goalkeeper Graham Moseley and it soon became apparent that on the day Barnet's team of part-timers were every bit as good as their celebrated opponents from the First Division. Barnet's policy of all-out attack almost bore fruit in the 40th minute when Colin Barnes got the ball in the Brighton net but the cheers died when the referee disallowed the 'goal' because Barnes had handled.

After a goalless 45 minutes Barnet went in to a well-deserved ovation, a tribute to the non-Leaguers' battling spirit against First Division opponents.

Half-time: Barnet 0   Brighton & Hove Albion 0

After the interval Barnes' intelligent prompting almost brought a goal for the non-Leaguers when from a clever pass to Russell Townsend, the Barnet midfield player sent a rasping shot from 20 yards just wide of the far post. Barnet goalkeeper, Gary Phillips, who had made several spectacular saves in the first-half continued with the good work as the part-timers began to wilt under the pressure, a reflex action save from substitute Stevens being of international class. This must have given immense pleasure to Phillips who at one stage was with Brighton but was released from their squad.

Such was the quality of Barnet's defence, in which Phillips, Campbell, Millett and Pearce were outstanding, that with ten minutes to go Brighton appeared to be prepared to settle for a draw and thus to emphasise their reputation as draw specialists. The moral victory lay with the non-Leaguers who had given their manager Barry Fry a highly satisfactory performance.

Result: Barnet 0   Brighton & Hove Albion 0

Teams:
Barnet: Phillips, Robinson, Millett, Campbell, Pearce, Watson, Pittaway, Townsend, Barnes, Sargent, Westwood. Sub: Voyce.
Brighton: Moseley, Shanks, Gatting, Foster, Nelson, Case, McNab, Grealish, Thomas, Ritchie, Robinson. Sub: Stevens.
Referee: Mr. A. Glasson (Salisbury)
Attendance: 3,842

THIRD ROUND F.A. CUP REPLAY
5th January 1982
BRIGHTON & HOVE ALBION 3   BARNET 1

There was a crowd of nearly 16,000 at the Goldstone ground to see the part-timers put up another fighting display against their First Division opponents. Brighton set up an all-out attack in an attempt to secure an early goal and with Barnet's defence unsettled in the early stages the non-Leaguers' goalkeeper Gary Phillips was soon in action with some acrobatic saves. On the half-hour Mike Robinson, the ex-Manchester City striker and Irish Republic international, had to go off with a recurrence of an old injury and was replaced by Foster.

Brighton kept up their barrage and Andy Ritchie missed two scoring chances. Barnet also had their moments, Watson in particular trying to break through as the non-Leaguers' counter-attacks momentarily relieved their hard-pressed defenders. Minutes before half-time, both Campbell and Millett made valiant clearances to keep the Barnet goal intact.

Again the non-Leaguers received a well-deserved ovation as they went in at half-time with the not inconsiderable achievement of having once more held off the Brighton attack.

Half-time: Brighton & Hove Albion 0   Barnet 0

Brighton opened strongly after the interval and within a minute were a goal up, a clearance by Townsend striking Mickey THOMAS on the head before the ball flew into the net to give the Welsh international his first goal since joining the club from Everton. Bad finishing in the box prevented Brighton, whose record against non-League clubs in the Cup has been somewhat mediocre, from capitalising on this success until the 66th minute. Then a 15-yards drive by Jimmy CASE struck Millett before entering the net to give the First Division side their second deflected goal.

Even this setback did not deter the part-timers who picked themselves up to score the best goal of the game in the 75th minute when Gary SARGENT sent in a piledriver from 25 yards. Brighton restored their lead within three minutes when Millett was penalised for allegedly pushing over Ritchie in the box. Most observers regarded it as a particularly harsh decision. McNAB scored from the spot. Until this incident Barnet still had hopes of retrieving the situation.

When the whistle blew the crowd gave the part-timers another great ovation in appreciation of their fighting performance. It signalled the end of another great glory game by the part-timers.

Result: Brighton & Hove Albion 3   Barnet 1

Teams:
Brighton: Moseley, Shanks, Nelson, Grealish, Foster, Gatting, Case, Ritchie, M. Robinson, McNab, Thomas. Sub. Ryan.
Barnet: Phillips, Pittaway, Pearce, Millett, Campbell, Townsend, S. Robinson, Watson, Sargent, Barnes, Westwood. Sub: Voyce.
Referee: Mr. A. Glasson, Salisbury.
Attendance: 15,884.

CUP RUNS

1945/6
1st Round (1st leg) *17th November*
Barnet ....2 QPR 6
1st Round (2nd leg) – *24th November*
QPR ....2 Barnet 1
(QPR won on aggregate 8–3)

1946/7
1st Round – *30th November*
Barnet ....3 Sutton United ...0
2nd Round – *14th December*
Barnet ....2 Southend 9

1948/9
1st Round *4th December*
Barnet ....2 Exeter City 6

1954/5
1st Round *20th November*
Barnet ....1 Southampton 4

1959/60
1st Round *14th November*
Salisbury ....1 Barnet 0

1961/2
1st Round *4th November*
Weymouth ....1 Barnet 0

1963/4
1st Round – *16th November*
Torquay Utd .....6 Barnet 2

1964/5
1st Round *14th November*
Barnet ....2 Cambridge Utd .1
2nd Round *5th December*
Enfield ....4 Barnet 4
2nd Round Replay *8th December*
Barnet ....3 Enfield 0
3rd Round *9th January*
Barnet ....2 Preston 3

1965/6
1st Round *13th November*
Barnet ....0 Dartford 2

1967/8
1st Round *13th December*
Hereford Utd ....3 Barnet 2

1968/9
1st Round – *16th November*
Barnet ....1 Brentwood 1
1st Round Replay – *18th November*
Brentwood ....1 Barnet 0

1969/70
1st Round – *15th November*
Walton & H ......0 Barnet 1
2nd Round – *6th December*
Barnet ....0 Sutton United ...2

1970/71
1st Round – *21st November*
Barnet ....6 Newport C 1
2nd Round – *11th December*
Slough ....0 Barnet 1
3rd Round – *5th January*
Barnet ....0 Colchester Utd ..1

1971/2
1st Round *20th November*
Kettering Tn ......2 Barnet 4
2nd Round – *11th December*
Barnet ....1 Torquay Utd......4

1972/3
1st Round *18th November*
Banbury ....0 Barnet 2
2nd Round – *9th December*
Barnet ....1 Bilston 1
2nd Round Replay *12th December*
Bilston ....0 Barnet 1
3rd Round *13th January*
QPR ....0 Barnet 0
3rd Round Replay *16th January*
Barnet ....0 QPR 3

1977/8
1st Round *26th November*
Barnet ....1 Peterborough 2

1978/9
1st Round – *25th November*
Barnet ....3 Woking 3
1st Round Replay *28th November*
Woking ....3 Barnet 3
(After extra time score at 90 mins: 2 2)
1st Round 2nd Replay *5th Dec.*
Barnet ....0 Woking 3

Cup Runs - Barnet (Contd)

1980/1

1st Round - *22nd November*
Barnet 2   Minehead 2

1st Round Replay *25th November*
Minehead 1   Barnet 2

2nd Round - *13th December*
Barnet 0   Peterborough 1

1981/2

1st Round - *21st November*
Harlow 0   Barnet 0

1st Round Replay - 24th November
Barnet 1   Harlow 0

2nd Round - *15th December*
Barnet 2   Wycombe W 0

3rd Round - *2nd January*
Barnet 0   Brighton 0

3rd Round Replay - *5th January*
Brighton 3   Barnet 1

BATH CITY

Founded: 1889

League: Alliance Premier

Ground: Twerton Park

Colours: White shirts, black trim; black shorts, white trim

Alliance Premier Leaguers Bath City have been distinguished performers in the F.A. Cup in the post-war years. City's name appears regularly in the First Round ties and since the 1945/6 season they have appeared seven times in the Second Round and twice in the Third Round. Their first post-war appearance in the Third Round was in the 1959/60 season when they were defeated by a lone goal by Second Division Brighton at Twerton Park and their most remarkable performance of all was on 4th January 1964 when, again on their own ground they held mighty First Division opponents Bolton Wanderers to a Third Round 1-1 draw, losing the replay at Bolton 3-0. Several League clubs have been put out of the Cup by City, their post-war scalps including Southend United, Exeter City, Millwall, Notts County (a great performance away from home in the Second Round of the 1959/60 competition) and Newport County.

City's first post-war appearance in the First Round of the Cup was in 1945/6 when the two-leg system was in vogue for that season only. Bath drew fellow Southern Leaguers Cheltenham Town and the first leg, played at Twerton Park, resulted in a 3-2 win for City. In the second leg at Cheltenham Bath had a convincing 2-0 win thus going into the next round with a comfortable 5-2 aggregate. Their opponents in the Second Round were the Welsh part-timers Lovell's, also playing in the Southern League. This time City's run came to an end with a 7-3 aggregate defeat.

It was not until the 1952/3 season that Bath were again in the First Round. Their opponents were Third Division Southend United, City having the luck of the draw with a home tie. Cup fever gripped Bath and before the game there were hopes that the Twerton Park record – 17,300 for a war-time game against Aston Villa – might be broken. It was 19 years previously that a League side – Crystal Palace – had last visited Twerton Park when the part-timers claimed a remarkable victory. In the event 10,005 spectators were on City's ground to watch the tie against Southend and to see the semi-professionals record a memorable 3–1 victory. City were in the Second Round for the first time for 21 years drawn against Grimsby, Third Division North, away from home. Grimsby, at the time Third Division North leaders, were a tough proposition but City's defence held out until the 83rd minute when Grimsby scored the only goal of the game. The 'gate' was 15,244.

In 1953/4, for the second year in succession, Bath faced League opposition at Twerton Park in the First Round – against Third Division Walsall. The League side had a tradition to maintain – for only once in the previous 32 years had a non-League side knocked them out of the Cup, in 1926–7 when the Corinthians inflicted a 4–0 defeat. The Saddlers, although lowly placed in the Third Division, comfortably held their record, defeating City 3–0. The 'gate' was 10,700, a post-war record.

In the 1957/8 competition Bath, who had not reached the First Round for four seasons, were drawn at home against Third Division Exeter City. A crowd of 9,300 saw Bath go into a 11th minute lead and although Exeter equalised, Cup glory came to Bath 15 minutes from the end when the Southern Leaguers' centre-forward Pickard scored the winner. In the Second Round City drew a difficult tie away from home against Southern League rivals Yeovil on the famous slope and before a crowd of 11,700 went down 2–0.

For the First Round of the 1958/9 competition Bath were drawn away to Third Division Colchester United at the Layer Road ground. The 10,636 crowd on the ground saw the League side generally in command with two goals, one in each half, putting an end to City's Cup aspirations for that season.

The 1959/60 season was to prove a memorable one for City and which was to see them reaching the Third Round for the first time in the post-war era. In the First Round City were drawn at home to Fourth Division Millwall and notched up a thrilling 3–1 victory, one of the shock results of the day. For the Second Round, City were drawn away from home against Fourth Division Notts County, the oldest side in the League, who frequently find themselves opposed by non-League opposition. Bath's tactics were all-out attack and three minutes after the interval City scored the only goal of the match through O'Neil. County, who had won their previous nine home games, flung everything into an attempt to retrieve the situation but Ian Black, ex-Scotland and Fulham, kept them out. At the end of the game Black and the City captain ex-Scotland and Sunderland 'Cannonball' Fleming were carried off the pitch by their jubilant supporters.

This sensational away victory gave City their first postwar Third Round contest – against Second Division Brighton at Twerton Park.

The game attracted 18,020 spectators, a ground record, and a great ovation greeted Charlie 'Cannonball' Fleming as he led out City's team. Half-time came with a blank scoresheet with City having had the lion's share of the play. In the second half Brighton's goalkeeper Hollins saved the day several times for the Second Division side as Bath kept up the pressure. Then misfortune struck City. Owing to a misunderstanding in the box Brighton striker Tiddy was able to lash the ball from 30 yards into an empty net to score the only goal of the match.

Bath: Black, Book, MacFarlane, Hale, Scott, Meadows, Thomas, Fleming, Wilshire, O'Neil, Wring.
Brighton: Hollins, Bissett, Little, Bertolini, Jennings, Burtenshaw, Tiddy, McNeill, Curry, Thorne, Jones.

Again in the First Round of the 1960/61 competition Bath were drawn away from home against Third Division Swindon Town, doughty Cup fighters themselves, and put up a competent performance to earn a 2–2 draw, Swindon having drawn level in the closing stages. A titanic struggle developed in the replay at Twerton Park, the 12,000 spectators rewarded with a goal feast as the game ebbed and flowed. With only 25 minutes left and Swindon leading 4–1, Tony Book, who was later to gain fame with Manchester City, reduced the deficit only for Swindon to score again and go into a 5–2 lead. Then the game took a dramatic turn with two sensational goals by Bath and the final outcome in the balance. With the crowd roaring for the equaliser Swindon added a further goal to make the final score 6–4.

Bath were not seen again in the First Round until the

1963/4 season when they had a momentous Cup run culminating in forcing a draw against First Division Bolton Wanderers at Twerton Park, their first ever Cup clash with a First Division side, before going down in the replay 3–0. This outstanding season began for City when they drew an away tie against Athenian Leaguers Maidenhead United and won 2–0. This gave Bath a Second Round away tie against then Isthmian Leaguers and Amateur Cup holders Wimbledon and a dour struggle, watched by 7,500, resulted in a 2–2 draw. The replay at Twerton Park saw City move comfortably into the Third Round with a 4–0 win to make club history when they were set to meet famous Cup battlers First Division Bolton Wanderers. The first game at Twerton Park and the replay at Burnden Park are fully recorded as *Match Reports*.

In the 1964/5 season City were matched in the First Round against Third Division Queen's Park Rangers away from home at Loftus Road, the League side getting the better of the non-Leaguers by a 2–0 margin.

In the First round in the following season Bath drew a home tie against Fourth Division Newport County, so often the Cup victims of non-League sides. This time was no exception. A crowd of over 7,000 at Twerton Park saw City engage in some exciting Cup football with honours even at half-time, two second-half goals sinking the League side. It was one of the shock results of the First Round. Next City were drawn away from home against Bournemouth, Third Division, before a 9,000 plus crowd at Dean Court. Although the Cherries scored first City equalised and then went into a 2–1 lead. It was a game of fluctuating fortunes Boscombe going in at half-time with a 3–2 lead, adding two further goals after the interval and City pulling one back four minutes from time. Final score: 5–3.

In the First Round again in 1966/7 Bath drew a home tie against Isthmian Leaguers Sutton United. In a closely contested game Bath scored the only goal of the game in the 65th minute. For the Second Round Bath again had the luck to be drawn at home – against Third Division Brighton who in 1960 had defeated City by an only goal. History repeated itself, a top-form Brighton hustling City out of the Cup 5–0.

Seven seasons elapsed before City again fought their way to the First Round, in 1974/5, away to Southern Leaguers Wimbledon whose Cup exploits were making them the toast of non-League soccer. It was a ding-dong struggle and when it seemed Bath had earned a replay Mahon sent in a pile-driver from 35 yards to give Wimbledon a 1-0 victory.

City were next in contention for Cup honours in 1977/8 when they were drawn in the First Round against Third Division Plymouth Argyle. There was a 'gate' of nearly 8,000 to watch the Southern Leaguers fight out a battle royal against their League opponents and to emerge at the end with a blank scoresheet. In the replay at Plymouth, Argyle proved too much for City, putting them out of the Cup 2-0.

MATCH REPORTS
THIRD ROUND F.A. CUP
4th January 1964
BATH CITY 1   BOLTON WANDERERS 1

This was one of the greatest Cup feats ever recorded by a non-League side – Bath City, for over 40 years a Southern League club taking on four times Cup winners, First Division Bolton Wanderers, and leading 1–0 until the 79th minute when only a penalty goal kept the Lancastrians in the Cup.

Over 12,000 spectators were at Twerton Park to see the David and Goliath encounter and gave Tony Book a tremendous ovation as he led the Southern Leaguers on to the field.

Bolton were first to attack but City were no respecters of reputations and began to build up pressure in the Bolton goal area. Right winger Owens had a hard shot smothered by Bolton's international goalkeeper Eddie Hopkinson and a shot from Bath's former Scottish international Fleming scorched over the cross-bar.

Play switched from end to end although the Southern Leaguers had rather the better of the first half exchanges. Both goalkeepers, Drinkwater for Bath and Hopkinson for Bolton, were in brilliant form. Once Hopkinson swept the ball off Sanderson's toe to save what appeared to be a certain goal. Hopkinson almost immediately repeated the technique against Fleming and then saved an Owens breakthrough. Walker, on City's left wing, was prominent in building up City attacks but just as readily dropped back in defence during the Bolton attacks.

Half-time: Bath City 0   Bolton Wanderers 0

In the 73rd minute Bath had their reward for their persistent attacking football. Fleming, who had previously seen a hard shot hit the side netting, rounded Hopkinson who had to leave his goal to intercept and slipped a pass for Ken OWENS to head into the empty Bolton net.

In the 79th minute Bath's luck changed. The visitors were awarded a penalty for hands when it seemed that City defenders had matters under control. LEE scored from the spot. Bath tried to snatch the winner in the closing minutes but were caught in Bolton's offside trap.

Result: Bath City 1   Bolton Wanderers 1

Teams:
Bath City: Drinkwater, Book, Gough, Phillips, MacFarlane, Carter, Owens, Fleming Cartwright, Sanderson, Walker.
Bolton Wanderers: Hopkinson, Hartle, Farrimond, Hatton, Edwards, Lennard, Davison, Lee, Davies, Deakin, Hill.
Referee: Mr. K. Stokes, (Newark)
Attendance: 12,779

THIRD ROUND F.A. CUP REPLAY
8th January 1964
BOLTON WANDERERS 3   BATH CITY 0

This great Third Round replay at Burden Park was another epic for Bath City. Although they were defeated 3–0 City gave a great display of teamwork and method. Veteran internationals Len Phillips and 'Cannonball' Fleming dominated the midfield play and left-winger Walker was an extra man in defence. One northern newspaper correspondent referred to City's performance as 'equalling anything we see from the Wanderers' First Division opponents at Burnden Park'.

Bath were by no means over-awed by the Burnden Park lights and the 26,000 crowd and despite adopting a defensive pattern in the early stages – Phillips, MacFarlane and Carter were able to master the Bolton front line – a series of dangerous attacks were mounted on the Bolton goal. Eddie Hopkinson had to deal with a hard drive from Phillips and both Owens and Sanderson went near to scoring.

Half-time: Bolton Wanderers 0   Bath City 0

After the interval Bath carried on with their attacking policy. Fleming delivered one of his 'specials' which hit a defender and Sanderson slammed in a shot on the rebound which Hopkinson was lucky to save. Later Fleming, a consistent raider, Walker, Owens and Sanderson all tried shots at the Bolton goal.

In the 59th minute Bolton, marginally against the run of the play, opened the scoring when 18-years-old reserve player TAYLOR caught Drinkwater unawares with an acute-angled shot.

Bolton went into a 2–0 lead in the 80th minute with a penalty goal. Wanderers' inside-right Frank LEE, who had saved the First Division side in the first encounter with a penalty goal, again scored from the spot.

This set-back unsettled the City and Wanderers scored again in the closing stages through centre-forward DAVIES.

Result: Bolton Wanderers 3   Bath City 0

Teams:
Bolton Wanderers: Hopkinson, Hartle, Farrimond, Hatton, Edwards, Lennard, Taylor, Lee, Davies, Deakin, Hill.
Bath City: Drinkwater, Book, Gough, Phillips, MacFarlane, Carter, Owens, Fleming, Cartwright, Sanderson, Walker.
Referee: Mr. K. Stokes, (Newark).
Attendance: 26,983

Bath (Contd)   CUP RUNS

1945/6

1st Round (First Leg) – *17th November*
Bath 3   Cheltenham 2

1st Round (Second Leg) – *24th Nov.*
Cheltenham 0   Bath 2
(Bath won 5–2 on agg.)

2nd Round (First Leg) – *8th December*
Lovell's 2   Bath 1

2nd Round (Second Leg) – *15th Dec.*
Bath 2   Lovell's 5
(Lovell's won 7–3 on agg.)

1952/3

1st Round – *22nd November*
Bath 3   Southend 1

2nd Round – *6th December*
Grimsby 1   Bath 0

1953/4

1st Round – *21st November*
Bath 0   Walsall 3

1957/8

1st Round – *16th November*
Bath 2   Exeter City 1

2nd Round – *7th December*
Yeovil 2   Bath 0

1958/9

1st Round – *15th November*
Colchester Utd ... 2   Bath 0

1959/60

1st Round – *14th November*
Bath 3   Millwall 1

2nd Round – *5th December*
Notts County 0   Bath 1

3rd Round – *9th January*
Bath 0   Brighton 1

1960/1

1st Round – *5th November*
Swindon 2   Bath 2

1st Round Replay – *10th November*
Bath 4   Swindon 6

1963/4

1st Round – *16th November*
Maidenhead 0   Bath 2

2nd Round – *7th December*
Wimbledon 2   Bath 2

2nd Round Replay – *12th December*
Bath 4   Wimbledon 0

3rd Round – *4th January*
Bath 1   Bolton 1

3rd Round Replay – *8th January*
Bolton 3   Bath 0

1964/5

1st Round – *14th November*
QPR 2   Bath 0

1965/6

1st Round – *13th November*
Bath 2   Newport County 0

2nd Round – *4th December*
Bournemouth 5   Bath 3

1966/7

1st Round – *26th November*
Bath 1   Sutton Utd 0

2nd Round – *7th January*
Bath 0   Brighton 5

1974/5

1st Round – *23rd November*
Wimbledon 1   Bath 0

1977/8

1st Round – *26th November*
Bath 0   Plymouth A. 0

1st Round Replay – *29th November*
Plymouth A. 2   Bath 0

BEDFORD TOWN

Founded: 1908

League: Southern, Midland Division

Ground: The Eyrie

Colours: Blue shirts, white shorts

Bedford Town, one of the most redoubtable non-League Cup-fighting sides in the country, did not appear in the post-war First Round Cup struggles until 1951/2 but since then they have frequently sent pulses racing as they have challenged the elite of the Football League in epic Cup tussles. During two memorable seasons the Eagles battled their way through to the Fourth Round and on two other occasions fought their way to the Third Round before defeat. In the 1963/4 season they went out in the Fourth Round at home at the Eyrie to Carlisle United after sensationally beating Newcastle United in the previous round at St. James's Park. In the 1965/6 season they were defeated 3-0 in the Fourth Round at home to First Division Everton who went on to win the Cup. One of their greatest achievements was in the 1955/6 season when they held mighty Arsenal at Highbury in the Third Round and lost the replay at Bedford 2-1 after extra time. In the 1966/7 season the name of Bedford again appeared among the elite in the Third Round when they were opposed at the Eyrie by another famous Cup-fighting side, Peterborough United, and although defeated 6-2 none the less enhanced their reputation as a Cup force to be reckoned with.

Bedford's first post-war First Round encounter was in the 1951/2 season when they had to travel to oppose Third Division Swindon Town. It was the first time that the Eagles had encountered a Football League side in the Cup. Although Swindon won 2–0 Ronnie Rooke, hero of many an Arsenal victory, inspired the Eagles to a great second-half rally and only Swindon's Irish international goalkeeper Pritchard kept out the part-timers. The 'gate' was 15,899.

Two seasons later, in 1953/4, Bedford again reached the First Round and drew fellow Southern Leaguers Weymouth away from home, losing 2–0. The following season was something of a repetition. This time the opposition was Western League side Dorchester and again the Eagles lost 2-0.

The following season, 1955/6, was a history-making one for the Eagles and one that was to see them in the Third Round and facing mighty Arsenal. This memorable season began with the Eagles drawing Leyton, an Athenian League amateur side, in the First Round and among a number of 'firsts' to be created was that this was the first time in the post-war era that a First Round tie had been played at The Eyrie. Bedford cruised comfortably into the Second Round for the first time in the club's history with a 3-0 win.

The Eagles were rewarded with League opposition at home in the shape of Watford Town, Third Division South. It was the first Cup visit of a Third Division side to Bedford in the club's history. A record crowd of 13,150 watched the part-timers gain a dramatic 3-2 victory. After opening the scoring in the 33rd minute, the Eagles conceded an 'own goal' and then went into a 3-1 lead when Staroscik scored twice. Watford managed a further goal late in the game.

Bedford's reward was the draw of draws - an away Third Round tie against Arsenal at Highbury. Before over 55,000 spectators the gallant Southern Leaguers held the First Division side to a 2-2 draw and were unlucky not to have won. They were even more unlucky not to have won the replay at the Eyrie where they went down 2-1 after extra time. Both these exciting games are fully recorded as *Match Reports*.

In the following season Bedford were again among the 'giant-killers' - defeating Norwich City, Third Division South 4-2 in the First Round away from home at Carrow Road. A crowd of 14,530 saw Norwich go ahead mid-way through the half. Bedford equalised from the penalty spot and then took the lead for the first time. Just before the interval Norwich brought the score level at 2-2. In the second half the Eagles scored twice to record a brilliant 4-2 victory. For the Second Round, against Reading, Third Division South, away at Elm Park twice the normal crowd, 23,895, saw the League side scrape through by a lone goal. The Eagles had a 'goal' disallowed.

In the 1959/60 season Bedford were again in the First Round, drawn at home to Fourth Division Gillingham but suffered a 4-0 defeat.

Three seasons later Bedford were matched in the First Round at home against fellow Southern Leaguers Cambridge United whom they narrowly defeated 2–1. For the Second Round the Eagles were drawn away from home at Priestfield Stadium against Fourth Division Gillingham, their opponents of the 1959/60 season and again the part-timers were out of luck, losing 3–0.

Bedford began their memorable 1963/4 Cup run with an away First Round tie against fellow Southern Leaguers Weymouth, a hard-fought contest resulting in a 1–1 draw. At the replay at The Eyrie the Eagles scraped through to the next round with a lone goal. In the Second Round the Eagles again drew Southern League opposition, Chelmsford City away at the Stadium ground. The game was only nine minutes old when Bedford scored the only goal of the match. Bedford's reward was a plum draw against famous Cup fighters Second Division Newcastle United away from home at St. James's Park, producing the Cup shock of the day, Bedford winning 2–1, fully described in *Match Report*.

As a result of this famous victory the Eagles were in the Fourth Round for the first time in the club's history, drawing well-placed Fourth Division Carlisle United at The Eyrie.

The game attracted a record crowd of nearly 18,000 reflecting the tremendous pre-match build-up. A great roar went up as the Bedford captain, David Coney, led the Eagles on to the field. Just before half-time Carlisle went ahead with a goal by Kirkup. The turning point of the game came in the 57th minute when Heckman hammered the ball home for Bedford but the referee disallowed the 'goal' resulting in a pitch invasion. After this incident Carlisle appeared to take command and Bedford's goalkeeper Wallace had to produce some international-class saves. Livingstone scored Carlisle's second and Davies added another from the penalty spot. Thus ended Bedford's electrifying Cup run that had been the talk of the soccer world.

Teams:
Bedford: Wallace, Coney, Avis, Goundry, Collins, Anderson, Lovell, Sturrock, Fahy, Heckman, Miles.
Carlisle: Ross, Neil, Caldwell, Thompson, Passmoor, McConnell, Taylor, Livingstone, McIlmoyle, Davies, Kirkup.

Bedford's next appearance in the First Round was in the

1965/6 competition, which was to prove another unforgettable season, the Southern Leaguers drawing an away First Round tie against Exeter City at St. James's Park. The Eagles, playing the better football, overcame a mediocre Exeter side to win 2-1, one of the shock results of the day. Exeter had not been beaten in the Cup by a non-League side since Southern Leaguers Bath City had lowered their colours some 43 years previously. For the Second Round Bedford were once again drawn away from home – against Third Division Brighton who had put out Southern Leaguers Wisbech in the previous round 10-1. There was a crowd of nearly 17,000, the second biggest of the season, at Goldstone to see all Brighton's first-half attacks fail with the scoresheet blank at half-time. Three minutes after the resumption Bedford went ahead and again got the ball in the net – in the 80th minute – but the 'goal' was disallowed. It looked like a certain shock victory for the Eagles but Albion scored a face-saving equaliser in the third minute of injury time. There was a crowd of 11,500 at The Eyrie to watch an action-packed replay. Brighton opened the scoring with a first-half 'own goal' but the Eagles equalised in the 72nd minute. Minutes later the crowds rushed on to the field – for the second time – as Bedford inside-right ex-Hearts player Paton swerved through a packed Brighton defence to steer the ball into the Albion net to give the Eagles a dramatic 2-1 win.

Bedford had the luck of the draw for their Third Round tie – a home game against fellow Southern Leaguers Hereford United. This clash of two top Southern League sides on a snow-covered pitch at The Eyrie attracted a crowd of over 13,000 to see the Eagles go into the Fourth Round with a well-deserved 2-1 win. Hereford got the ball in the net in the 10th minute but the 'goal' was disallowed. Bedford scored a few minutes later through Hall and made it 2-0 shortly after the interval with Hall again the scorer. Fogg reduced the deficit for Hereford two minutes from the end but it was too late for the visitors to retrieve the situation. The Eagles had thus emulated their 1963/4 performance in reaching the Fourth Round.

Bedford: Collier, Morgan, Skinn, Wright, Collins, Bailey, Benning, Paton, Brown, Hall, Sturrock.

The Eagles were drawn against mighty First Division

Everton in the Fourth Round at The Eyrie and a record crowd of 18,407 saw the eventual Cup winners defeat the Southern Leaguers 3-0. The game is fully described in *Match Report*.

After their Cup triumphs of the previous season the Eagles were again in the First Round line-up in 1966/7 when they were drawn against Isthmian League amateurs Wycombe Wanderers away from home at Loakes Park. A crowd of nearly 8,000 saw a thrilling game result in a 1-1 draw. The two sides met in the replay at The Eyrie and with three goals each after extra time the tie was still undecided. Wycombe won the toss for the venue for the next encounter and there was a crowd of nearly 9,000 to watch the marathon continue. At the end of 90 minutes the sides were still level at 1-1 and with conditions worsening the referee abandoned the game at the start of extra time. The last phase of the marathon was played out at The Eyrie when Bedford triumphed 3-2 after 6½ hours' play watched by over 32,000 spectators.

Bedford lost ground advantage in the Second Round being drawn away against Third Division Oxford United, themselves once famous Southern League 'giantkillers'. A crowd of 11,949 at Manor Park saw Oxford in the ascendency for most of the game yet the Southern Leaguers were able to hold the League side to a 1-1 draw to force a replay at The Eyrie. Bedford managed a handful more spectators than saw the game at Manor Park – 11,953 – to see the Eagles put out their League opponents by an only goal to reach the Third Round for the third time in four years, a tremendous record for a non-League club. Bedford's goal came after Fogg had been brought down in the penalty area resulting in an indirect free kick from which Sturrock scored the vital goal. 'Eagles, Eagles' chanted the happy home crowd.

In the Third Round Bedford were drawn at home against another famous Cup fighting side – Peterborough United, Third Division, a game that attracted a 'gate' of over 14,000 to see Posh, for many years football's famous outsiders and 'giantkillers' in their own right. Up to half-time there was little to choose between the two sides who went in 1-1. After the interval the Eagles' right-half had to go off injured and the reorganised Bedford side were unable to withstand the Peterborough pressure, the League side piling on five more goals with a further goal for Bedford to make the final score 6–2.

Bedford: Collier, Morgan, Skinn, Wright, Collins, Cooley, Benning, Sturrock, Fogg, Pygall, Paton.

Bedford had to wait a long time before reappearing in the First Round – until the 1975/6 season when they were drawn against their old Isthmian League adversaries Wycombe Wanderers and incredibly another marathon developed but not with such a happy ending as before for the Eagles. Although Wycombe had the better of the exchanges at Loakes Park the game ended in a goalless draw. At The Eyrie Bedford were in command in the early stages leading by two clear goals but Wycombe managed to draw level and the game went into extra time without result. In the second encounter at Loakes Park there was a goalless first half with Wycombe eventually edging into the next round with two second half goals and only a consolation goal to show for the Eagles' endeavours.

Bedford were out of the Cup headlines for several more seasons before reappearing in the First Round in the 1981/2 season when they drew a home tie against Third Division Wimbledon. After the Dons had gone a goal up in the early stages the Eagles had to rearrange their side after being beset by injuries. A second-half goal gave Wimbledon a failry easy 2–0 passage into the next Round, Bedford's compensation being a 'gate' of 4,000.

MATCH REPORTS

THIRD ROUND F.A. CUP
7th January 1956
ARSENAL 2   BEDFORD TOWN 2

This Third Round tie at Highbury, a David and Goliath encounter, turned out to be one of Bedford's finest hours.

Before a crowd of over 55,000 Arsenal began in fine style and within five minutes TAPSCOTT had notched Arsenal's first. The Eagles' centre-half Craig and his two backs Cooke and Quinn applied themselves to the task of keeping out the Arsenal strikers whilst the Bedford goalkeeper Pope had a splendid game.

Half-time: Arsenal 1   Bedford Town 0

Five minutes after the interval Arsenal scored their second, a splendidly hit goal taken on the volley by centre-forward GROVES.

There were only 13 minutes of play left and the Gunners were still coasting along when Bedford set the game alight STEEL racing along the right wing to send a cross-shot streaking past the Arsenal goalkeeper. A mighty roar broke out under the floodlights as the crowd suddenly realised that Bedford were fighting back. The Bedford line swept into the attack and with only five minutes left the part-timers sensationally equalised when from an Adey cross Eagles' inside-right Yates tipped the ball over the outstretched hands of Sullivan for MOORE to score.

With a minute to go Arsenal were all but bundled out of the Cup. A cleverly-directed centre from Steel looked as if it was heading for the back of the net when Arsenal pivot Fotheringham struck out a leg and diverted the ball into the side netting.

Result: Arsenal 2   Bedford Town 2

Teams:
Arsenal: Sullivan, Charlton, Evans, Goring, Fotheringham, Holton, Clapton, Tapscott, Groves, Bloomfield, Tiddy.
Bedford Town: Pope, Cooke, Quinn, Farquhar, Craig, Garwood, Steel, Yates, More, Adey, Staroscik.
Referee: Mr. L. Callaghan, (Methyr Tydfil).
Attendance: 55,178

THIRD ROUND F.A. CUP REPLAY
12th January 1956
BEDFORD TOWN 1   ARSENAL 2

In this sensational replay on the Eagles' ground Bedford were leading mighty Arsenal until four minutes from time when the 15,000 crowd saw Arsenal equalise.

The Bedford inside trio Yates, Moore and Adey, often had the Arsenal defenders in difficulties and on the wings Steel and

Staroscik, well supplied with passes by the hard-working half-back line, Farquhar, Craig and Garwood, were a constant threat.

At the end of the first 45 minutes the Southern Leaguers were well satisfied at having curbed the Arsenal goal scoring machine.

Half-time: Bedford Town 0   Arsenal 0

Within the first minute of resuming The Eyrie erupted when Bedford opened the scoring, YATES having taken advantage of an Arsenal defensive lapse to volley the ball past Kelsey. With 30 minutes left for play Moore slipped a pass to Steel whose cross was blocked inside the post; the ball ran loose and Yates was again on hand to prod the ball into goal. Alas for Bedford and the wildly excited crowd it was no goal, the referee disallowing the point because of offside.

Four minutes from the end, when Bedford looked poised for a sensational victory, a GROVES header saved Arsenal.

The game went into extra time and within three minutes Arsenal took the lead when TAPSCOTT sent in a flying header.

In the fading minutes of extra time former Polish international Staroscik steered the ball into the net. Again the referee disallowed a goal and again on grounds of offside.

These two great games against Arsenal had earned a place for the Eagles among the immortals of the non-League world.

Result: Bedford Town 1   Arsenal 2

Teams:
Bedford Town: Pope, Cooke, Quinn, Farquhar, Craig, Garwood, Steel, Yates, Moore, Adey, Staroscik.
Arsenal: Kelsey, Charlton, Evans, Goring Fotheringham, Holton, Groves, Tapscott, Roper, Bloomfield, Tiddy.
Referee: Mr. L. Callaghan, (Merthyr Tydfil).
Attendance: 15,000

THIRD ROUND F.A. CUP
4th January 1964
NEWCASTLE UNITED 1   BEDFORD TOWN 2

A crowd of over 34,000 at St. James's Park saw famous Cup fighters Newcastle United humbled by Southern Leaguers Bedford Town in the biggest Cup shock of the day – a 2-1 defeat for United.

The Eagles soon began to attack, and in the 27th minute Fahy beat Marshall in the air and got the ball in the net but the centre-forward had handled and the referee ordered a free kick.

In the 29th minute Bedford split open the United defence and sensationally opened the scoring when FAHY beat Marshall with a header.

In the 42nd minute the Eagles scored again, the turning point of the game, and a disaster for Newcastle. Bedford outside-right Lovell sent a cross into United's penalty area and in attempting to clear Newcastle right-back McKINNEY put the ball into his own net.

Half-time: Newcastle United 0   Bedford Town 2

After the interval the Southern Leaguers continued to attack and twice Heckman tested Marshall with power drives.

A minute from time Newcastle reduced the arrears when ANDERSON eluded two Bedford defenders and scored with a left-footed shot. After a shaky start the Eagles had taken control and had held the might of Newcastle on their own ground. It was one of the greatest-ever Cup triumphs for a non-League side.

Result: Newcastle United 1   Bedford Town 2

Teams:
Newcastle United: Marshall, McKinney, Dalton, Anderson (S), McGrath, Iley, Hockey, Hilley, Thomas, Penman, Suddick.
Bedford Town: Wallace, Coney, Avis, Goundry, Collins, Anderson (R), Lovell, Sturrock, Fahy, Heckman, Miles.
Referee: Mr. E. Crawford, (Doncaster).
Attendance: 34,542

FOURTH ROUND F.A. CUP
12th February, 1964
BEDFORD TOWN 0   EVERTON 3

A record crowd of over 18,000 at The Eyrie saw the Fourth Round clash with Everton. The First Division club began at a terrific pace and the Eagles had no alternative but to fall back on defence.

On the rare occasions that the Bedford line advanced the Everton half-back line, Gabriel, Labone and Harris were waiting to intercept and farther back England left-back Wilson seldom gave the Eagles any latitude.

In the 38th minute Everton opened the scoring following a Temple-Scott movement, TEMPLE nodding the ball over the line.

Five minutes later Everton went further into the lead when TEMPLE scored again.

Half-time: Bedford Town 0   Everton 2

In the second half Everton lost some of the urgency that had been evident in the opening phases and allowed Bedford a little more of the game. Eleven minutes from the end Everton made it 3-0 when England leader PICKERING scored with a glancing header.

Result: Bedford Town 0   Everton 3

Teams:
Bedford Town: Collier, Morgan, Skinn, Wright (A), Collins, Bailey, Benning, Paton, Brown, Hall, Sturrock.
Everton: West, Wright (T), Wilson, Gabriel, Labone, Harris, Scott, Young, Pickering, Harvey, Temple.
Referee: Mr. A. W. Sparling, (Grimsby).
Attendance: 18,407

Bedford (Contd)   CUP RUNS

1951/2
1st Round – *24th November*
Swindon 2   Bedford 0

1953/4
1st Round – *21st November*
Weymouth 2   Bedford 0

1954/5
1st Round – *20th November*
Dorchester 2   Bedford 0

1955/6
1st Round – *19th November*
Bedford 3   Leyton 0

2nd Round *10th December*
Bedford 3   Watford 2

3rd Round – *7th January*
Arsenal 2   Bedford 2

3rd Round Replay – *12th January*
Bedford 1   Arsenal 2
(after extra time)

1956/7
1st Round – *17th November*
Norwich City 2   Bedford 4

2nd Round – *8th December*
Reading 1   Bedford 0

1959/60
1st Round – *14th November*
Bedford 0   Gillingham 4

1962/3
1st Round – *3rd November*
Bedford 2   Cambridge Utd .. 1

2nd Round – *24th November*
Gillingham 3   Bedford 0

1963/4
1st Round – *16th November*
Weymouth 1   Bedford 1

1st Round Replay – *21st November*
Bedford 1   Weymouth 0

2nd Round – *7th December*
Chelmsford 0   Bedford 1

3rd Round – *4th January*
Newcastle Utd .. 1   Bedford 2

4th Round – *25th January*
Bedford 0   Carlisle Utd 3

1965/6
1st Round – *13th November*
Exeter City 1   Bedford 2

2nd Round – *4th December*
Brighton 1   Bedford 1

2nd Round Replay – *6th December*
Bedford 2   Brighton 1

3rd Round – *22nd January*
Bedford 2   Hereford 1

4th Round – *12th February*
Bedford 0   Everton 3

1966/7
1st Round – *26th November*
Wycombe W 1   Bedford 1

1st Round Replay – *5th December*
Bedford 3   Wycombe W 3
(after extra time. Score at 90 mins: 2–2)

1st Round, 2nd Replay – *5th December*
Wycombe W 1   Bedford 1
(Abandoned after 90 mins. Ground unfit)

1st Round, 3rd Replay – *8th December*
Bedford 3   Wycombe W 2

2nd Round – *11th January 1967*
Oxford U 1   Bedford 1

2nd Round Replay – *16th January*
Bedford 1   Oxford U 0

3rd Round – *26th January*
Bedford 2   Peterborough 6

1975/6
1st Round – *22nd November*
Wycombe W 0   Bedford 0

1st Round Replay – *24th November*
Bedford 2   Wycombe W 2
(After extra time)

1st Round 2nd Replay – *1st December*
Wycombe W 2   Bedford 1

1981/2
1st Round – *21st November*
Bedford 0   Wimbledon 2

BISHOP AUCKLAND

Founded: 1886

League: Northern

Ground: Kingsway

Colours: Light blue shirts, dark blue shorts

Bishop Auckland, one of the most illustrious Cup-fighting non-League sides in the country, have a fine record of challenging football's Goliaths. The Bishops have appeared in the First Round no fewer than 15 times since the war and in their outstanding 1954/5 season they disposed of Crystal Palace away from home in the Second Round and Ipswich (after a replay) in the Third before being defeated in the Fourth Round 3-1 by York City after a great struggle.

The Bishops began their post-war First Round encounters with a convincing 5-0 win over fellow Northern Leaguers Willington away from home in the first leg of the two-leg competition operating in 1945/6. In the second leg, on their own ground, Willington ran out 2-0 winners, although the Bishops went into the next round on a 5-2 aggregate. In the Second Round the Bishops were drawn against Third Division York City, the first leg being played at Kingsway, the League side scraping through 2-1. Before a 'gate' of nearly 9,000 at York for the return bout the League side had a clear-cut 3-0 victory to put the Bishops out on a 5-1 aggregate.

In the following two seasons the Bishops were out of luck although they managed to get through to the First Round. In the 1946/7 season they were drawn against Rochdale, Third Division North, away from home and got a 6-1 drubbing. The following year the Bishops were drawn away from home – against Chester, Third Division North, at the Stadium ground. Taking due note of the Bishops' Cup fighting exploits – seven times winners of the Amateur Cup – Chester never relaxed and ran out 3-1 winners.

Two seasons elapsed before the Bishops again appeared in the First Round – at home to York City in the 1950/1 season. Before a 'gate' of 10,500 Auckland kept the Third Division opposition at full stretch and earned a creditable 2-2 draw. For the replay at Bootham Crescent Auckland did well to hold the League side to a goalless first half. Then York scored twice although the Bishops pulled one back two minutes from time to make the final score 2-1.

The next season the Bishops met fellow non-Leaguers Blyth Spartans away from home in the First Round at Croft Park and before a record 'gate' of 9,468 were defeated 2-1. In the following season 1952/3, Auckland, again in the First Round, made amends by beating Yorkshire League side Selby away from home 5-1. The Bishops received Coventry City, Third Division South, in the Second Round and set up a ground record of 16,319. Guests of honour at the match were four Auckland players, E. Proud, K. Rudd, J. Allan and F. Hopper, who met Coventry in a F.A. Cup-tie at Highfield Park in 1907. The Bishops were no match for a quick-thinking Coventry side and lost 4-1.

Bishops greatest-ever F.A. Cup season to date, 1954/5, began well for Auckland when they entertained Southern League Kettering Town at home in the First Round and gave a below-par Poppies side a 5-1 beating. The Bishops were a big attraction at Selhurst Park where Crystal Palace, Third Division South, entertained the famous amateurs in the Second Round before a crowd of over 20,000. Despite Auckland having the better of the early exchanges Palace were first to score and although Edwards equalised for the Bishops Palace scored again to go in at half-time with a 2-1 lead. After the interval the amateurs overran Palace and a hat-trick by amateur international Major gave Auckland a thrilling 4-2 victory.

The Bishops went on to even greater fame; in the Third Round they held Second Division Ipswich Town to a 2-2 draw at Portman Road and then caused a Cup sensation by defeating them 3-0 in the replay at Kingsway. In the Fourth Round Auckland were drawn at home to York City, Third Division North and must have fancied their chances but the 15,000 crowd saw the amateurs go down 3-1 after a thrilling game. These three exciting encounters are recorded as *Match Reports*.

The following season saw the Bishops hitting the Cup trail

again and began well by defeating Northern League Durham City 3-1 at home in the First Round. The Bishops had seven amateur internationals in their side. In the Second Round Auckland again had the luck of the draw – at home against Scunthorpe, Third Division North. The game resulted in a goalless draw, Scunthorpe missing a penalty. In the replay at the Old Showground Auckland were on top in the early stages with Scunthorpe gradually taking command and winning 2-0. Scunthorpe's second goal was an oddity. Auckland's goalkeeper ran to the touchline to take a throw-in himself but before he could get back to his goal-line Scunthorpe striker Hubbard had seized the ball and hammered it into the back of the net from 30 yards.

Again in the First Round in the 1956/7 season the Bishops were drawn against Tranmere Rovers, Third Division North. Although Auckland were below strength, the amateurs were mainly in command and pulled off a tremendous 2-1 victory. For the next round the Bishops were drawn against Cheshire County League side Rhyl. The Bishops had a surprise waiting for them for a top-form Rhyl beat them 3-1.

Bury, Third Division North, were the Bishops' next League opponents in the First Round in 1957/8 at home at Kingsway. The Shakers put on an indifferent performance and Auckland were unlucky not to have won. In the closing minutes of the game Auckland almost grabbed the winner but had to be content with a goalless draw. In the replay at Bury, before a crowd of 21,347, the League side celebrated their lucky let-off at Kingsway with a comfortable 4-1 victory.

In a First Round encounter in the 1958/9 season the Bishops were drawn away against Third Division Tranmere Rovers, the League side extracting full revenge for their previous defeat by the amateurs, Auckland getting a 8-1 drubbing.

Auckland returned to the First Round in 1960/1 when they secured a home tie against Bridlington Town of the Yorkshire League. At the end of a closely contested game Auckland ran out winners 3-2, the Bishops decider coming 15 minutes from the end. In the next round the Bishops drew Fourth Division Stockport County away at Edgeley Park, two opportunist goals by County giving them a comfortable win over the non-Leaguers.

In the 1966/7 season the Bishops made up for their several seasons' absence from First Round cup duty by celebrating with a long running duel with old Cup adversaries Blyth Spartans, fellow Northern Leaguers. In the first contest, at Kingsway, the Bishops could only manage a 1-1 draw. The first of three replays, at Blyth, ended in a blank scoresheet after 120 minutes play, including extra time. The second replay took place at Roker Park, Sunderland before a sparse attendance with the two clubs fighting to a standstill to record a 3-3 draw after extra time. Replay number three also took place at Roker Park. The Bishops took control of the game and won 4-1 despite Blyth having taken the lead.

Auckland's reward was a home game in the Second Round against Fourth Division Halifax where, on an icebound pitch, a thrilling duel with the Shaymen ended in a 0-0 draw. It was a different story in the replay at Halifax where the Bishops encountered an on-form League side and were demolished 7-0. The Bishops' reward was a share in the 14,297 'gate', the best at Halifax for years.

Auckland were to be absent for seven seasons before they again won through to the First Round, in 1974/5, when they celebrated by trouncing Northern Premier Leaguers Morecambe 5-0 at Kingsway. The Second Round saw the Bishops again at home and entertaining famous Cup fighters from Division Three Preston North End. The non-Leaguers went in at half-time with the scoresheet blank having kept Preston's fire-power, including that of Bobby Charlton, at bay. But within seconds of the resumption Charlton unleashed one of his 'specials' from 20 yards that finished in the back of the net and with thirteen minutes to go Preston scored again to make the final score 2-0.

After an absence of several seasons the Bishops were again in the First Round in the 1981/2 season when they drew a home game against fellow non-Leaguers Nuneaton Borough of the Alliance Premier League. On-form Bishops went into a 1-0 half-time lead and although Nuneaton equalised early in the second half Auckland went on a late goal spree, the game ending in a 4-1 win for the Northern Leaguers with Kevin Cross notching a hat-trick.

For their Second Round encounter the Bishops drew a difficult away tie against high-riding Third Division Carlisle United. The game was played on a quagmire of a pitch and after a goalless first-half the referee decided to abandon proceedings in the 70th minute. Eventually the tie was played at Workington. The non-Leaguers had a splendid game against the formidable Third Division side, the Bishops' goalkeeper Phil Owers being in superb form. After a goalless first-half the Bishops' defenders continued to hold out and it looked odds-on that Auckland would be fighting out a replay at Kingsway. But 11 minutes from the end following a free kick Carlisle's Bob Lee sent a powerful header past Owers to put the Bishops out of the Cup.

MATCH REPORTS
THIRD ROUND F.A. CUP
8th January 1955
IPSWICH TOWN 2   BISHOP AUCKLAND 2

Before a near 16,000 crowd at Portman Road the Second Division side opened strongly and in the second minute GARNEYS put them in the lead. Auckland were always dangerous and seven minutes after Town's shock goal they were on terms when OLIVER, the Bishops' centre-forward, headed in.

Auckland, undaunted by the Second Division opposition, continued to take the game into their opponent's half and their aggressive policy paid off two minutes from half-time when outside-right McKENNA put the amateurs in front.

Half-time: Ipswich Town 1   Bishop Auckland 2

Throughout most of the second half Ipswich had to fight a goal down although they had somewhat the better of the exchanges.

In the closing stages of the game Ipswich made desperate efforts to grab the equaliser but it did not come until seven minutes from the end. Reed, the Ipswich right-winger, headed towards goal and Auckland centre-half CRESSWELL, in attempting to intercept hooked the ball into his own net.

Result: Ipswich Town 2   Bishop Auckland 2

Ipswich Town:	Parry, Malcolm, Feeney, Fletcher, Rees, Parker, Reed, Grant, Garneys, Phillips, McLuckie.
Bishop Auckland:	Sharratt, Marshall, Stewart, Hardisty, Cresswell, Nimmins, McKenna, Lewin, Oliver, Major, Edwards.
Referee:	Mr. G. McCabe, (Sheffield).
Attendance:	15,974

THIRD ROUND F.A. CUP REPLAY
12th January 1955
BISHOP AUCKLAND 3   IPSWICH TOWN 0

Two inches of snow covered the pitch at the kick-off and the players also had to contend with a high wind. In the 22nd minute the League side were presented with a gilt-edged chance which they failed to take. Although Sharratt won a race for the ball with the Ipswich leader Grant, the Auckland goalkeeper was only able to make a partial clearance and Grant regained possession. Cresswell, the Bishops' centre-half, thrust himself at the ball to clear and thus made amends for his 'own goal' at Portman Road,

Half-time: Bishop Auckland 0   Ipswich Town 0

After the interval Ipswich attacked strongly and appeared to be taking control. But they received a blow in the 63rd minute when

Auckland outside-right McKENNA headed in for the amateurs. Spurred on by this success the Bishops went all out and McKENNA scored a second. The crowd urged on the amateurs to even greater efforts and amid great excitement MAJOR crashed in a pile-driver from 20 yards.

The League side realised that they were well beaten and their efforts to pull back a goal and thus present a more respectable score were checked by a well-drilled Auckland defence.

Result: Bishop Auckland 3 Ipswich Town 0

Teams:
Bishop Auckland: Sharratt; Marshall, Stewart, Hardisty, Cresswell, Nimmins, McKenna, Lewin, Oliver, Major, Edwards.
Ipswich Town: Parry, Malcolm, Feeney, Myles, Rees, Parker, Reed, Crowe, Grant, Callaghan (W), McLuckie.
Referee: Mr. G. McCabe, (Sheffield).
Attendance: 9,000

FOURTH ROUND F.A. CUP
29th January, 1955
BISHOP AUCKLAND 1 YORK CITY 3

After having disposed of Second Division Ipswich Town and Crystal Palace, Third Division South, the Bishops were drawn at home in the Fourth Round against York City, Third Division North. At Kingsway a crowd of 15,000 saw the fighting amateurs hold the League side to a 1-1 draw for over 70 minutes.

Auckland had a fair share of the game during the early exchanges but gave away a goal after six minutes as a result of a defensive lapse which let in City's inside-left STOREY. This early reverse did little to upset Auckland's confidence and immediately after the kick-off the amateurs' outside-left Benny EDWARDS equalised with a powerful shot.

Half-time: Bishop Auckland 1 York City 1

In the 75th minute, as the Bishops' stamina gave way, BOTTOM scored to give City a 2-1 lead. The League side pressed Auckland back in their own half and Stewart gave away a penalty in the closing stages. BOTTOM scored from the spot kick to gain his second and to give York a 3-1 victory.

Result: Bishop Auckland 1 York City 3

Teams:
Bishop Auckland: Sharratt, Marshall, Stewart, Hardisty, Cresswell, Nimmins, McKenna, Lewin, Oliver, Major, Edwards.
York City: Forgan, Phillips, Howe, Brown, Stewart (A), Spence, Hughes, Bottom, Wilkinson, Storey, Fenton.
Referee: Mr. T. Jepson, (Mansfield).
Attendance: 15,000

Bishop Auckland (Contd)

CUP RUNS

1945/6

1st Round (1st leg) – *17th November*
Willington 0   Bishop A 5

1st Round (2nd leg) – *24th November*
Bishop A. 0   Willington 2
(Bishop Auckland won on 5-2 aggregate)

2nd Round (1st leg) – *8th December*
Bishop A. 1   York 2

2nd Round (2nd leg) – *15th December*
York 3   Bishop A. 0
(York won on 5-1 aggregate)

1946/7

1st Round – *30th November*
Rochdale 6   Bishop A. 1

1947/8

1st Round – *29th November*
Chester 3   Bishop A. 1

1950/1

1st Round – *25th November*
Bishop A. 2   York 2

1st Round Replay – *29th November 1950*
York 2   Bishop A. 1

1951/2

1st Round – *24th November*
Blyth Spartans .. 2   Bishop A. 1

1952/3

1st Round – *22nd November*
Selby 1   Bishop A. 5

2nd Round – *6th December*
Bishop A. 1   Coventry 4

1954/5

1st Round – *20th November*
Bishop A. 5   Kettering 1

2nd Round – *11th December*
Crystal Palace ... 2   Bishop A. 4

3rd Round – *8th January*
Ipswich Town ... 2   Bishop A. 2

3rd Round Replay – *12th January*
Bishop A. 3   Ipswich Town ... 0

4th Round – *29th January*
Bishop A. 1   York City 3

1955/6

1st Round – *19th November*
Bishop A. 3   Durham City 1

2nd Round – *10th December*
Bishop A. 0   Scunthorpe 0

2nd Round Replay – *15th December*
Scunthorpe 2   Bishop A. 0

1956/7

1st Round – *17th November*
Bishop A. 2   Tranmere R. 1

2nd Round – *8th December*
Rhyl 3   Bishop A. 1

1957/8

1st Round – *16th November*
Bishop A. 0   Bury 0

1st Round Replay – *19th November*
Bury 4   Bishop A. 1

1958/9

1st Round – *15th November*
Tranmere R. 8   Bishop A. 1

1960/1

1st Round – *5th November*
Bishop A. 3   Bridlington 2

2nd Round – *26th November*
Stockport 2   Bishop A. 0

1966/7

1st Round – *26th November*
Bishop A. 1   Blyth Spartans .. 1

1st Round Replay – *30th November*
Blyth Spartans .. 0   Bishop A. 0
(after extra time)

1st Round, 2nd Replay – *5th December*
Bishop A. 3   Blyth Spartans .. 3
(score after 90 mins: 3-3)
At Roker Park, Sunderland

1st Round, 3rd Replay – *8th December*
Blyth Spartans .. 1   Bishop A. 4
(at Roker Park, Sunderland)

2nd Round – *7th January*
Bishop A. 0   Halifax 0

2nd Round Replay – *10th January*
Halifax 7   Bishop A. 0

1974/5

1st Round – *23rd November*
Bishop A. 5   Morecambe 0

2nd Round – *14th December*
Bishop A. 0   Preston N E 2

1981/2

1st Round – *21st November*
Bishop A............ 4   Nuneaton 1

2nd Round – *2nd January*
Carlisle 0   Bishop A. 0
(abandoned after 70 mins – pitch waterlogged)

2nd Round – *9th January*
Carlisle 1   Bishop A. 0
(at Workington)

BLYTH SPARTANS

Founded: **1946**

League: **Northern**

Ground: **Croft Park**

Colours: **Green and white striped shirts; white or black shorts**

Blyth Spartans, formerly of the North Eastern and Midland Leagues and now in the Northern, is one of the most famous of the non-League Cup fighting sides, having made history in the 1977/8 season when they took Third Division Wrexham to a Fifth Round replay, the furthest any non-League club has progressed in the F.A. Cup since the war. In their first Fifth Round encounter with Wrexham the Spartans were but two minutes away from history-making when the League side equalised to prevent Blyth from becoming the first non-League team since the war to secure a place in the quarter finals.

The Spartans' series of post-war Cup runs began in 1951/2 when they entertained famous Amateur Cup fighters Bishop Auckland at Croft Park before a crowd of 9,468, a ground record. A 2-1 victory gave them an away draw against Third Division Tranmere Rovers. The Spartans gave a creditable performance to emerge with a 1-1 draw before a near 10,000 crowd. The part-timers mustered a 'gate' of 9,388 for the return game at Croft Park and with the score at 1-1 at 90 minutes the referee abandoned the game a quarter of an hour into extra time because of bad light.

The second replay was played on Carlisle's ground and again resulted in stalemate – a 2-2 draw, Blyth having equalised 12 minutes from time. The last chapter of the long duel was played out at Goodison Park before a 'gate' of over 25,000 and ended in a convincing win for Rovers 5-1.

Blyth were again drawn against a League side in 1953/4 when they entertained Accrington Stanley, Third Division North, in the First Round. Accrington scraped through with a single goal.

The Spartans again fought their way to the First Round in the following season. Their opponents, away from home, were fellow Midland Leaguers Boston Utd, a 1-1 draw producing a thrilling replay at Croft Park between the two part-timers, Blyth eventually running out 5-4 winners. The Second Round brought Third Division South Torquay United to Croft Park, a crowd of 8,717 seeing Blyth defeated 3-1.

Two seasons later, in 1956/7, Blyth drew Ilkeston Town of the Central Alliance League in the First Round away from home and the Spartans saw off the opposition 5-1. They themselves were defeated 1-0 in the Second Round at Croft Park by Hartlepool United Third Division North. In the First Round of the 1958/9 season Spartans were drawn away to Lancashire Combination side Morecambe and snatched a 2-1 win. In the Second Round Spartans drew a home tie against Third Division Stockport County, County winning 4-3.

In the following three seasons Blyth again advanced to the First Round but no further. In 1959/60 Wrexham were hosts to the Spartans, the League club winning 2-1; the following year they were again drawn away from home – against Fourth Division Mansfield Town who triumphed 3-1; and in 1961/2 Spartans again had to travel – to Hartlepool United who registered a 5-1 win against an off-form Blyth.

Blyth had more luck the following season, drawing a home game in the First Round against Lancashire Combination champions Morecambe. A hard game resulted in a win for Spartans 2-1. In the Second Round Blyth drew a home game against Third Division side Carlisle United. The League side ran out 2-0 winners.

In the First Round of the 1963/4 competition the Spartans drew an away game against Fourth Division Chester. When the League side had gone into a 3-0 half-time lead it looked like a walkover but Spartans pulled back two goals.

Blyth were next in the First Round in 1966/7 and celebrated their return to the headlines with a marathon tussle with fellow amateurs Bishop Auckland. The first of four encounters was played away from home at the Kingsway Ground, the scoreline being 1-1, Auckland doing well to retain their unbeaten record. The return bout at Croft Park ran into extra time but both defences were unyielding and neither side succeeded in scoring. The next instalment was fought out at Sunderland's Roker Park under floodlights. A tense game ended all square at 3-3 after extra time. The seven hour marathon concluded - again at Roker - when The Bishops ran out 4-1 winners.

Four seasons elapsed before the Spartans again fought their way to the First Round, in the 1971/2 season, when they,drew an away game against Fourth Division strugglers Crewe Alexandra at Gresty Road. Spartans went one up in the 12th minute and clung on to their lead until the final whistle to chalk up a notable victory. Their reward was a home tie in the Second Round against Fourth Division Stockport County and Spartans were set to avenge Cup defeats by County in 1934 and 1958. Before 5,800 cheering fans Blyth bundled Stockport out of the Cup with a 32nd minute goal - and put Spartans in the Third Round for the first time since the war and the second time in the club's history.

Spartans were disappointed with their Third Round draw - against another Fourth Division side Reading but luckily at Croft Park. Spartans were trailing 2-0 for most of the game but came from behind to score two goals in the last 13 minutes as well as having a 'goal' disallowed in the 81st minute. Unfortunately the replay at Elm Park did not go well for Spartans, Reading running up a 3-0 lead at half-time and going on to beat the part-timers 6-1.

Spartans were next in the First Round in 1973/4 when they drew an away tie against Midland League side Alfreton Town. Neither side were able to score and the two teams met again at Croft Park, Blyth winning 2-1, Spartans winning goal coming from their popular player-coach Eddie Alder. Blyth's reward was an away tie in the Second Round against Third Division Grimsby Town. The parttimers scored in the second minute and although Grimsby equalised later in the first half they were at full stretch to contain the Spartans. Luck deserted the Spartans in the replay at Croft Park, Grimsby running out 2-0 winners.

In the following season the Spartans were again in the First Round, drawing a home tie against famous Cup fighters Third Division Preston North End. There was a crowd of over 8,000 at Croft Park for the game with special interest centred on former England international Bobby Charlton and other former England internationals Nobby

Stiles and David Sadler. Blyth had a fairy-tale start with a goal in the first three minutes but 18 minutes from the end Preston snatched the equaliser. It was a different story at Deepdale where the game had attracted an attendance of 10,101. The part-timers were defeated 5–1, Holden getting four of the Preston goals.

In 1977/8 Blyth were to have their finest Cup run ever culminating in a Fifth Round appearance against Wrexham away from home and producing a shock 1–1 draw before going down 2–1 at Newcastle in the replay. Blyth's First Round opponents were another non-League outfit, Burscough of the Cheshire County League, whom the Spartans defeated at Croft Park by a narrow 1–0 margin. The Spartans again had the luck of the draw in the Second Round – a home tie against Third Division Chesterfield. Again there was a shock result, the 3,700 'gate' seeing Blyth take the lead on the half-hour with Chesterfield unable to secure the equaliser.

For their Third Round encounter Blyth again had a home draw – against Isthmian Leaguers Enfield. The Spartans were hit by injuries and a rearranged side included Alan Shoulder, later transferred to Newcastle United, playing in his first Cup tie for the club. Spartans were faced with an Enfield side unbeaten in 32 games and although initially they fell back under the Enfield onslaught Shoulder soon developed an understanding with Ron Guthrie who had seen previous F.A. Cup glory as left-back in Sunderland's winning side at Wembley in 1973. It was Shoulder who scored the only goal of the match to put the Spartans in the Fourth Round, an away tie against Second Division Stoke City. A report of this match and the two Fifth Round encounters against Wrexham appear in *Match Report*.

Again in the First Round in the 1978/9 season the Spartans took 2,000 fans to Fourth Division York City where a ding-dong struggle resulted in a 1–1 draw. York scored first against the run of the play but Blyth equalised with a penalty. The replay at Croft Park, before a crowd of 3,500, had all the ingredients of Cup football, two Alan Shoulder penalties and a Blyth 'own goal' contributing some of the elements of a thrilling game that produced a 3–3 draw at 90 minutes. Two City goals in extra time gave the League side a 5–3 win.

The Spartans were again in the First Round of the

1979/80 competition, drawing a home game against Mansfield Town, then in the lower regions of Division Three. It was one of Spartans less convincing Cup performances, Mansfield going into a 2-0 half-time lead and then shutting up shop.

In 1980/81 Blyth had home advantage in their First Round tussle with Northern Premier Leaguers Burton Albion. The score was level at 1-1 at half-time but Spartans managed a second goal after the interval to edge into the Second Round.

Spartans luck deserted them in the Second Round draw, away to Third Division Hull City. A crowd of over 6,000 at Boothferry Park saw Spartans put up a stirring display despite being a goal down in the 9th minute. Spartans, had a 'goal' disallowed and then lost one of their midfield men carried off. It came right in the 80th minute when Mutrie equalised.

In the replay at Croft Park the Spartans came within inches of again getting a place in the Third Round. Spartans opened the scoring and although Hull got an equaliser Blyth made the score 2-1 and it looked odds-on on the part-timers going through until five minutes from the end when City again drew level.

Fighting the second replay at Elland Road, the Spartans laid siege to City's goal and were unfortunate to be a goal down midway through the second half. Five minutes from time Mutrie redeemed a penalty miss in the previous game by equalising with a twice-taken penalty kick. In the 26th minute of extra time Hull won the tie with a further goal.

In the First Round of the 1981/2 competition the Spartans drew a home game against high-riding Third Division Walsall. Blyth were under pressure for most of the first half and only a brilliant performance by the part-timers' ex-Newcastle goalkeeper Clarke kept Walsall's half-time lead down to 1-0. Eleven minutes from the end Spartans equalised with only three minutes left. With the non-Leaguers in sight of a replay, Walsall scored again to make the final score 2-1.

MATCH REPORTS

THIRD ROUND F.A. CUP
7th January 1978
BLYTH SPARTANS 1   ENFIELD 0

Although Enfield were disappointed that their Third Round encounter had not produced First Division opposition they went north to Croft Park to meet Blyth Spartans feeling confident of entering the Fourth Round for the first time in the club's history.

Injury-hit Spartans had to concede territorial advantage in the early stages to Enfield, who in the sixth minute almost took the lead when Tony Bass fired in a shot that was deflected for a corner.

Enfield continued to exert pressure and twice Derek Baker missed clear-cut chances to put the Isthmian Leaguers ahead. Tony Bass, after eluding the Blyth defenders, fired in a shot that hit the post and bounced back into play.

Half-time: Blyth Spartans 0   Enfield 0

Midway through the half Enfield midfield player O'Sullivan was sent off and weakened the Enfield side when it looked as if it was only a question of time before the Blyth defence surrendered.

Blyth began to look more confident and in a goalmouth melee Johnson, the former Newcastle striker, almost put the Northern Premier Leaguers into the lead.

Blyth were not to be denied, however, and 13 minutes from time Jimmy SHOULDER scored the winner when Varty flicked the ball to the Blyth striker who headed a magnificent goal.

Result: Blyth Spartans 1   Enfield 0

Blyth Spartans:	Clarke, Waterson, Guthrie, Varty, Scott, Dixon, Shoulder, Johnson, Mutrie, Houghton, R. Carney. Sub: S. Carney.
Enfield:	Moore, Wright, Tone, Jennings, Elley, Howell, O'Sullivan, Baker, Bass, Searle, Bishop. Sub: Knapman.
Referee:	Mr. K. Walmsley, (Blackpool).
Attendance:	5,800

FOURTH ROUND F.A. CUP
6th February 1978
STOKE CITY 2   BLYTH SPARTANS 3

There was a crowd of over 18,000 at the Victoria Ground Stoke to watch this tie turn into a fairy-tale win for the non-Leaguers to enable them to make Cup history by going into the Fifth Round, the third non-League club in more than half a century to advance so far and joining Colchester (then in the Southern League) who accomplished this feat in 1947/8 and Yeovil also of the Southern League in the following year.

Stoke began promisingly enough with centre-forward Viv Busby immediately racing through evading, Dave Clarke's tackle to hammer in a shot that hit the side netting. Spartans quickly got into the game, however, and Rob Carney had a shot at goal but his effort went wide.

Then came a sensational moment, in the 10th minute, when the Spartans went ahead. Spartans gained a corner and the cross from Carney was badly taken by Stoke's goalkeeper, Jones. The ball ran to Terry JOHNSON, Spartans centre-forward (who had joined Blyth at the start of the season from Fourth Division Brentford) who slotted the ball home from point-blank range.

Half-time: Stoke City 0   Blyth Spartans 1

As the second half began Stoke piled into the attack and scored two goals within two minutes. The equaliser came in the 57th minute when BUSBY, always prominent in the City's attacks beat Clarke with a well-directed shot. This had an adverse effect on the Spartans and two minutes later the Second Division side were ahead after Stoke had gained a corner. From Conroy's cross the ball was headed on by Busby for CROOKS to score with a diving header.

The Spartans summoned up all their reserves after visibly tiring and in the 80th minute gained a fantastic equaliser. Ron Guthrie, who played the game of his life, took a free-kick and his powerful shot hit the Stoke defensive wall and was deflected against the right-hand post. Alan Shoulder headed the ball against the opposite post and it fell right for Steve CARNEY to slot it home from close range.

Visibly tiring after such a tremendous duel Spartans still had sufficient energy to mount a last attack and with only seconds left before the final whistle scored a sensational goal to put them into the Fifth Round. Awarded a free-kick, which was taken by John Waterson, the ball ran clear and Terry JOHNSON moved smartly forward to smash the ball past Jones.

Result: Stoke City 2   Blyth Spartans 3

Stoke City:	Jones, Marsh, Lindsay, Kendall, Dodd, Bloor, Waddington, Scott G, Busby, Conroy. (Sub: Cook). Crooks.
Blyth Spartans:	Clarke, Waterson, Guthrie, Alder, Scott R, Dixon, Shoulder, Houghton, Johnson, Carney S, Carney R. (Sub: Varty).
Referee:	Mr. G. Nolan (Stockport).
Attendance:	18,765

FIFTH ROUND F.A. CUP
18th February 1978
WREXHAM 1   BLYTH SPARTANS 1

Watched by a crowd of nearly 20,000 on Wrexham's bone-hard Racecourse Ground the Spartans attempted to make history by being the first non-League club post-war to reach the quarter finals – and they came within two minutes of doing so.

Wrexham decided to move the ball quickly in an attempt to secure an early goal and they would have done so had it not been for two spectacular saves by Dave Clarke in the Blyth goal. The Northern Premier Leaguers, far from being over-awed by their League opponents, moved into the attack and in the 11th minute gained a shock lead. The move started with Bobby Carney setting up an attack on the left and the threat seemed to have petered out when the ball was collected by Wrexham full-back, Hill, who turned the ball back to his goalkeeper. It was a weak pass, however, and Terry JOHNSON nipped in to round the goalkeeper to put the Spartans one up.

Half-time: Wrexham 0   Blyth Spartans 1

After the resumption Wrexham continued their bombardment of Spartans goal with Clarke in constant action whereas his opposite number Davies, the Welsh international goalkeeper, had little to do. As the minutes ticked by the 4,000 Spartan supporters on the ground began to sense victory. With only two minutes left for the final whistle Spartans' luck ran out. The League side had been awarded a corner which Cartwright took on the left wing. Dave Clarke came off his goal-line and caught the ball comfortably but the referee, observing that the corner flag had fallen down, ordered the kick to be retaken. This time McNEIL rushed in to head the ball over Clarke's outstretched arms to maintain his record of a goal in every Round.

Although not a match that produced particularly high-quality football it was, in a sense, a game between two Cup-fighting giants.

Result: Wrexham 1   Blyth Spartans 1

Teams:
Wrexham: Davies, Hill, Dwyer, Evans, Roberts, Thomas, Shinton, Sutton, McNeil, Whittle, Cartwright. (Sub: Lyons).
Blyth Spartans: Clarke, Waterson, Guthrie, Alder, Scott, Dixon, Shoulder, Houghton, Johnson, Carney S, Carney B.
Referee: Mr. A. W. Grey, (Great Yarmouth).
Attendance: 19,935

FIFTH ROUND F.A. CUP REPLAY
27th February 1978
BLYTH SPARTANS 1   WREXHAM 2
(at Newcastle Utd.)

There was the biggest crowd of the season at St. James's Park, Newcastle for the replay – 42,157 – to watch Spartans continue the battle against Third Division Wrexham who had removed First Division opposition Bristol City and Newcastle United in previous Rounds. A good half of Blyth were on the ground and substantial support came from Newcastle supporters who were hopeful of seeing Spartans turn the tables on Wrexham. There were at least ten thousand Blyth supporters outside the ground when the match began – the crowd was double Newcastle's 'gate' of the previous Saturday.

As before the game was a hard fought encounter with cut and thrust on both sides. In the ninth minute Wrexham took the lead with a highly disputed penalty. Referee Alf Grey, gave a penalty against the Spartans for alleged pushing by Ronnie Scott on Dixie McNeil. Graham WHITTLE easily scored from the spot kick. Ten minutes later Wrexham scored again, Gareth Davis swinging the ball over from the right to be met with a tremendous shot on the volley from McNEIL, giving Clarke no chance.

Half-time: Blyth Spartans 0   Wrexham 2

After the resumption Blyth went bravely forward and in the first minute a cross from Varty just eluded both Carney and Johnson lurking in the penalty area. The crowd continued to lift Spartans and in the 83rd minute the non-Leaguers got a goal back, Whittle losing possession near the Wrexham goal. Terry JOHNSON was on hand to force the ball past Davies. Spartans threw everything into the closing minutes but were unable to snatch the equaliser. Their luck had run out on the St. James's Park pitch but it was a near thing and their great Cup battle which nearly brought them into the Sixth Round, will never be forgotten.

Result: Blyth Spartans 1   Wrexham 2

Teams:
Blyth Spartans: Clarke, Waterson, Guthrie, Varty, Scott, Dixon, Shoulder, Houghton, Johnson, Carney S, Carney R. (Sub: Mutrie).
Wrexham: Davies, Evans, Dwyer, Davis, Roberts, Thomas, Shinton, Sutton, McNeil, Whittle, Cartwright. (Sub: Hill).
Referee: Mr. A. W. Grey, (Great Yarmouth).
Attendance: 42,157

CUP RUNS

1951/2

1st Round – *24th November*
Blyth Spartans ..2   Bishop A. 1

2nd Round – *15th December*
Tranmere R. 1   Blyth Spartans ..1

2nd Round Replay – *19th December*
Blyth Spartans ..1   Tranmere R. 1
(aban. after 15 minutes of extra time)

2nd Round, 2nd Replay – *3rd January*
Tranmere R. 2   Blyth Spartans ..2
(at Carlisle, after extra time)

2nd Round, 3rd Replay – *7th January*
Blyth Spartans ..1   Tranmere R. 5
(at Goodison Park)

1953/4

1st Round – *21st November*
Blyth Spartans ..0   Accrington 1

1954/5

1st Round – *20th November*
Boston United ..1   Blyth Spartans ..1

1st Round Replay – *24th November*
Blyth Spartans ..5   Boston United ..4

2nd Round – *11th December*
Blyth Spartans ..1   Torquay Utd. 3

1956/7

1st Round – *17th November*
Ilkeston Town ..1   Blyth Spartans ..5

2nd Round – *8th December*
Blyth Spartans ..0   Hartlepool Utd ..1

1958/9

1st Round – *15th November*
Morecambe 1   Blyth Spartans ..2

2nd Round – *6th December*
Blyth Spartans .3   Stockport C. 4

1959/60

1st Round – *14th November*
Wrexham 2   Blyth Spartans ..1

1960/1

1st Round – *5th November*
Mansfield Town 3   Blyth Spartans ..1

1961/2

1st Round – *4th November*
Hartlepool Utd ..5   Blyth Spartans ..1

1962/3

1st Round – *3rd November*
Blyth Spartans ..2   Morecambe 1

2nd Round – *24th November*
Blyth Spartans ..0   Carlisle Utd 2

1963/4

1st Round – *16th November*
Chester 3   Blyth Spartans ..2

1966/7

1st Round – *26th November*
Bishop A. 1   Blyth Spartans ..1

1st Round Replay – *30th November*
Blyth Spartans ..0   Bishop A. 0
(after extra time)

1st Round, 2nd Replay – *5th December*
Bishop A. 3   Blyth Spartans ..3
(score after 90 mins: 3–3)
At Roker Park Sunderland

1st Round, 3rd Replay – *8th December*
Blyth Spartans ..1   Bishop A. 4
(At Roker Park, Sunderland)

1971/2

1st Round – *20th November*
Crewe Alex 0   Blyth Spartans ..1

2nd Round – *11th December*
Blyth Spartans ..1   Stockport Cty ...0

3rd Round – *15th January*
Blyth Spartans ..2   Reading 2

3rd Round Replay – *19th January*
Reading 6   Blyth Spartans ..1

1973/4

1st Round – *24th November*
Alfreton 0   Blyth Spartans ..0

1st Round Replay – *28th November*
Blyth Spartans ..2   Alfreton 1

2nd Round – *15th December*
Grimsby Town ..1   Blyth Spartans ..1

2nd Round Replay – *19th December*
Blyth Spartans ..0   Grimsby Town ..2

1974/5

1st Round – *23rd November*
Blyth Spartans ..1   Preston NE 1

1st Round Replay – *26th November*
Preston NE 5   Blyth Spartans ..1

Blyth Spartans (Contd)

1977/8

1st Round – *26th November*
Blyth Spartans ..1   Burscough 0

2nd Round – *17th December*
Blyth Spartans ..1   Chesterfield 0

3rd Round – *7th January*
Blyth Spartans ..1   Enfield 0

4th Round – *6th February*
Stoke City 2   Blyth Spartans ..3

5th Round – *18th February*
Wrexham 1   Blyth Spartans ..1

5th Round Replay – *27th February*
Blyth Spartans ..1   Wrexham 2
   (at St. James's Park, Newcastle)

1978/9

1st Round – *25th November*
York City 1   Blyth Spartans ..1

1st Round Replay – *28th November*
Blyth Spartans ..3   York City 5
(after extra time. Score at 90 mins: 3-3)

1979 80

1st Round – *24th November*
Blyth Spartans ..0   Mansfield 2

1980/1

1st Round – *22nd November*
Blyth Spartans ..2   Burton Albion ..1

2nd Round – *13th December*
Hull City 1   Blyth Spartans ..1

2nd Round Replay – *16th December*
Blyth Spartans ..2   Hull City 2
   (After extra time. Score at 90 mins)

2nd Round 2nd Replay – *22nd December*
Hull City 2   Blyth Spartans ..1
(After extra time. Score at 90 mins 1-1)
      (At Elland Road, Leeds)

1981/2

1st Round – *21st November*
Blyth Spartans ..1   Walsall 2

BOSTON UNITED

Founded: 1935

League: Alliance Premier

Ground: York Street

Colours: Black and amber

Boston United have made several notable contributions to non-League F.A. Cup history including the never-to-be-forgotten appearance at White Hart Lane in 1956 in the Third Round when United went down in glorious defeat 4-0 at the hands of Spurs. The previous time United had appeared in the final stages of the Cup was in 1926 when they visited Sunderland and were beaten 8-1.

The Second Round away tie against Derby County in the 1955/6 season, the passport to White Hart Lane, produced one of the most sensational results ever achieved by a non-League side against Football League opposition in the Cup – the Third Division side was trounced 6-1, to this day one of the highest scores ever recorded by part-timers against League opponents.

Boston have despatched various League sides from the Cup, Southport in 1970, Hartlepool United the following year and appeared in the Third Round for the second time since the war in 1972 when they were narrowly defeated by Second Division Portsmouth by a lone goal at York Street.

Again in the Third Round in the 1973/4 season United drew their League opponents of 18 years previously – Derby County but in 1955 enjoying First Division status. At the Baseball Ground Boston held their distinguished opponents to a shock 0-0 draw – in the replay Derby defeated United 6-1, by an amazing coincidence the same score as Boston had inflicted on County in 1955.

It was in the 1952/3 season that United began their post-war First Round appearances in the Cup when they entertained Third Division Oldham Athletic at home, being narrowly defeated 2-1. United were again in the First Round in the following season when they were matched against Third Division Scunthorpe away from home and had the humiliating experience of being overrun to the extent of 9-0.

Boston were again in contention in the First Round of the

1954/5 season drawing a home game against North Eastern Leaguers Blyth Spartans, and managing a 1-1 draw before a crowd of over 8,000. The replay at Blyth brought Spartans a remarkable 5-4 victory. Although Boston were holding a 4-2 lead well into the second half Spartans staged a tremendous rally in the closing stages and hit the last of three late goals 45 seconds from the end to gain a thrilling victory.

It was in the 1955/6 season when Boston began to make Cup history, fighting their way to the Third Round and to a memorable appearance at White Hart Lane. The First Round draw was modest enough, a home game against Cheshire League side Northwich Victoria which United did well to win 3-2.

In the Second Round Boston staggered the football world by thrashing Derby County, then in Third Division North, 6-1 away from home, still one of the greatest Cup triumphs ever achieved by a non-League side over League opponents. This success was followed by a Third Round appearance at White Hart Lane where, before a crowd of 46,000, Spurs defeated the gallant non-Leaguers 4-0. Both these memorable games are fully recorded in *Match Report*.

After their glorious 1955/6 season United were again in the First Round the following year when they were drawn at home against Third Division Bradford Park Avenue, the League side gaining a 2-0 win against an off-form United.

In the First Round of the 1957/8 competition United had a home game against Billingham S.R., then Northern League champions, United comfortably overcoming the opposition 5-2. Boston's centre forward, ex-Lincoln City Andy Graver, scored four of United's goals. In the Second Round United drew Darlington, Third Division North, away from home at Feethams. History repeated itself for in 1932 United went out to Darlington 1-0 in the Cup and again the League side triumphed, the part-timers going down 5-3 before a crowd of 10,017.

In the following season United were drawn away from home against Fourth Division Chester, the League side gaining a narrow 3-2 victory. Boston missed a penalty.

Boston drew a home game in the First Round of the 1962/3 competition against Southern Leaguers King's Lynn who won 2-1 after being presented with two gift goals by United. Boston's misfortune was compounded by having a 'goal' disallowed.

Round Boston drew an attractive home game against lowly-placed Third Division Orient and after an exciting game held the League side to a 1–1 draw. At Brisbane Road in the replay Orient just managed to overcome their non-League opponents by a narrow 2–1 margin.

United reappeared in the First Round in the 1970/1 season when they were drawn away against Fourth Division Southport. Boston made short work of the League opposition, their 2–0 win scarcely indicating the constant bombardment the Southport goal endured throughout the game. In the Second Round Boston found themselves faced with much tougher opposition – renowned Cup fighters Fourth Division York City but with ground advantage. It turned out to be one of the most dramatic Cup ties ever seen by United supporters. York, who had gone 22 games without defeat, were a goal down in the 16th minute Brian Bates being the marksman – and the non-Leaguers held their lead until 10 minutes from the end when City equalised. Then, in the fading minutes, York were awarded a penalty after a goalmouth incident and this they converted to gain a narrow 2–1 victory.

United again forced their way into the First Round in 1971/2 when they were drawn away from home against Northern Premier League rivals Ellesmere Port Town. It was the start of another incredibly successful Cup season. After disposing of their fellow non-Leaguers 3–0 United were matched in the Second Round against bottom of the Fourth Division Hartlepool United. Boston were trying to beat a hoodoo of not having beaten a League side on their home ground since 1925/6. The part-timers led 2–0 up to the closing stages and although Hartlepool managed to get a goal back to provide an exciting climax United were well-satisfied with their 2–1 win.

In the Third Round for the second time since the war Boston drew home advantage against Second Division Portsmouth who had never previously drawn non-League opposition in the Cup. Among the top drawer in the Portsmouth side were captain and Eire international Eoin Hand; a new signing from Spurs, Don Collins, and under-23 international Norman Piper, a £40,000 signing from Plymouth. From the beginning of the game Boston took the attack into the Portsmouth half and Pompey were lucky to survive a non-stop bombardment. Twice United's appeal for

Boston's next appearance in the First Round was delayed until the 1967/8 season when they were drawn away against Southern Leaguers Corby Town. United mastered the conditions on a snowbound pitch better than their opponents and came away with a 3-0 win. For the Second a penalty were dismissed by the referee. The interval arrived with Jim Smith, Boston's man of the match, blasting a free kick only inches over the Portsmouth crossbar. The part-timers were unlucky to go in at half-time without a goal to their credit. In the second half Portsmouth were more in command and in the 53rd minute scored the only goal of the match through Jennings. It had been an inspiring display by the non-Leaguers who enhanced their reputation in the football world.

Boston: White, Lakin, Pilgrim, Smith, Bate, Howells, Hughes, Svarc, Froggatt, Coates, Wilkinson. Sub: Wright. Portsmouth: Milkins, Smith, Collins, Piper, Hand, Blant, Jennings, Reynolds, Hiron, Ley, McCann. Sub: Trebilcock.

After their exciting Third Round encounter against Portsmouth, United were again in the First Round in the following season, 1972/3, when they drew a home game against Lancaster City, at that point bottom of the Northern Premier League. An off-form United were surprisingly beaten 2-1.

United were again in the First Round in the following season 1973/4 when they drew a home tie against Isthmian League amateurs Hayes to begin another fabulous Cup run. The amateurs allowed United little scope and the 0-0 draw was a fair result. There was plenty of drama in the replay at Hayes. A blank scoresheet at half-time, United missing a penalty in the 60th minute, a goal each in one four minute spell and United winning in extra time with a goal by John Froggatt. For their Second Round encounter Boston again had the luck of the draw, a home game against Isthmian Leaguers Hitchin. There was little to choose between the two sides, United scoring the only goal of the game in the second half. Boston's reward was a fairy-tale Third Round encounter against Derby County, their 1955 opponents but now in the First Division, at the Baseball Ground. The game which ended in a 0-0 draw is fully described as a *Match Report*.

The result of the replay at York Street before a crowd of

12,000 provided an incredible coincidence – Derby overwhelming the non-Leaguers by precisely the same score-line, 6-1, that Boston notched up when they shocked the soccer world 18 years' previously when the Rams were put out in the Second Round. From the kick-off Derby turned in a thoroughly professional performance, their goals coming from Archie Gemmill (3), Bourne (2) and Nish whilst Conde netted United's consolation goal. It had to be conceded that on the day Boston were outclassed by the international-studded Derby side.

The next season United had little luck. A difficult draw in the First Round saw them away to Third Division Chesterfield at the Saltergate ground, losing 3-1.

In 1975/6 United had home advantage when they drew Fourth Division pace-setters Lincoln City in the First Round. There was plenty of Cup-tie atmosphere for this local derby which Boston dominated for the first half although there was no scoring. In the second half Lincoln had more of the game and scored the only goal.

Boston missed two seasons before they again appeared in the First Round in 1978/9 drawn away to lowly-placed Third Division Tranmere Rovers. Despite early Boston attacks Tranmere were two goals up at half time although the non-Leaguers made a game of it with a second half consolation goal.

Boston were next in the First Round in the 1980/1 season when they drew a home game against Third Division Rotherham United. A 6,004 crowd saw Boston concede a goal within ten minutes but the League side had to wait until early in the second half before increasing their score. Rotherham made the final tally 4-0 with two late goals.

Boston again made a First Round appearance in the following season, 1981/2, when they drew a home tie against fellow Alliance Premier Leaguers Kettering. The visitors had the better of the first half and had the ball in the net in the 19th minute but the 'goal' was disallowed. Kettering scored the only goal of the game in the 60th minute.

MATCH REPORTS

SECOND ROUND F.A. CUP
10th December 1955
DERBY COUNTY 1   BOSTON UNITED 6

This was the greatest hour in the history of Boston United – an almost unbelievable 6–1 win over Third Division (North) Derby County at the Baseball Ground, a sensational result that reverberated throughout the football world. It was a scoreline that has been accomplished only twice since – by Hereford Utd. and Barnet, both having beaten League opponents by the same score.

There was a crowd of over 23,000 at the Baseball Ground to watch the then Midland Leaguers take on the Third Division side. No fewer than six ex-Rams were in the Boston team, thus earning them the nickname of 'Derby County Old Boys'. There were the two Hazledene brothers, Ray Wilkins, Reg Harrison (who was in the Derby side at Wembley in 1946), Dave Miller and goalkeeper Ray Middleton.

In the opening minutes Derby pressed hard and Boston's goalkeeper was soon in action. But the non-Leaguers retaliated and opened the scoring in the 26th minute when centre-forward WILKINS rushed in to net as the ball skimmed across the Derby goalmouth.

Nine minutes later Webster, in the County goal, let the ball slip out of his hands and Geoff HAZLEDENE was on hand to score United's second.

Derby hit back in the 36th minute when Jesse PYE, County's famous striker (ex-England, Wolves and Luton – he led Wolves F.A. Cup winning team in 1949) scored from the penalty spot. Minutes later Boston restored their lead when inside-left BIRKBECK netted following a defensive lapse. It was a double misfortune for Derby, McDonnell, who was injured trying to stop Birbeck, having to be carried off.

Half-time: Derby County 1   Boston United 3

After the resumption the non-Leaguers ran away with the game. In the 61st minute Geoff HAZLEDENE made it 4–1. The non-Leaguers continued on the rampage and six minutes later Geoff HAZLEDENE, who was having a field day, completed his hat-trick. In the 78th minute WILKINS scored again to make the final tally 6–1 in this exhilarating win for the underdogs. Captain and right-half Don Hazledene had a splendid game and was a tower of strength. It was one of the greatest Cup performances ever put up by a non-League side against League opposition.

Result: Derby County 1   Boston United 6

Teams:
Derby County: Webster, Barrowcliffe, Upton, Mays, McDonnell, Ryan, Cresswell, Parry, Todd, Pye, Powell.
Boston United: Middleston, Robinson, Snade, Hazledene (D), Miller, Lowder, Harrison, Hazledene (G), Wilkins, Birkbeck, Howlett.
Referee: Mr. E. T. Jennings, (Stourbridge).
Attendance: 23,757

THIRD ROUND F.A. CUP
7th January 1956
TOTTENHAM HOTSPUR 4   BOSTON UNITED 0

Thousands of Boston United supporters were at White Hart Lane to cheer on the Midland Leaguers after their 6-1 trouncing of Derby County in the previous Round. In the Spurs side at centre-half was Harry Clarke, an ex-Southern Leaguer from Lovell's Athletic.

During one early Boston attack left-winger Howlett let fly and only a superb flying leap by Reynolds saved a certain Boston goal.

Spurs opened the scoring with a goal by SMITH after his first shot had rebounded from a post.

Spurs' second goal came just before half-time as a result of a move by Robb who evaded right-back Robinson to enable DUQUEMIN to run on to a through pass and score. There was little to choose between the two teams and Spurs 2-0 half-time lead was scarcely a true reflection of the play.

Half-time: Spurs 2   Boston United 0

Boston pressed strongly after the interval but could not get the goals. Spurs further increased their lead with a goal by SMITH who headed in following a Dulin cross via a Blanchflower free-kick. Spurs' fourth and final goal came as a result of a Duquemin pass to ROBB who headed past Middleton.

Boston played a valiant game against Spurs' efficient goal-scoring machine although the Division One side was somewhat flattered by the result. The Boston defence emerged with flying colours, the back division Robinson and Snade giving a particularly creditable performance in containing the Tottenham inside trio Brooks, Duquemin and Smith for long periods of the game.

Result: Tottenham Hotspur 4   Boston United 0

Teams:
Tottenham: Reynolds, Norman, Hopkins, Blanchflower, Clarke, Marchi, Dulin, Brooks, Duquemin, Smith, Robb.
Boston United: Middleton, Robinson, Snade, Hazeldine (D), Miller, Lowder, Harrison, Hazeldine (G), Wilkins, Birbeck, Howlett.
Referee: Mr. N. C. Taylor, (Wiltshire).
Attendance: 46,185

THIRD ROUND F.A. CUP
6th January 1974
DERBY COUNTY 0   BOSTON UNITED 0

This great David and Goliath encounter at the Baseball Ground was the glamour tie of the Third Round, Northern Premier League semi-professionals pitting themselves against fabulous Derby County managed by Dave Mackay. There were no fewer than six internationals on view in the Derby side to meet the part-timers, skipper Roy McFarland, Archie Gemmill, Colin Todd, Kevin Hector, Rod Thomas and Alan Hinton. Derby County, one of the elite of the First Division, champions in 1972 and European Cup semi-finalists in 1973 were matching their professional skills against the part-timers. Derby had four corners in the first five minutes of the game bringing Simpson quickly into action. After about ten minutes United settled down and began to play more controlled football.

One of the Derby players attempting to pierce the Boston defences was Steve Powell, whose father had been one of the Rams' players in the Derby side which was humiliated 6-1 by Boston in 1955. In the 34th minute Derby skipper McFarland had to go off the field with a limp and was replaced by substitute Daniel.

Half-time: Derby County 0   Boston United 0

Derby put on some sustained pressure after the interval in order to try to break the deadlock whilst taking care to keep Webster, Daniel, Todd and Thomas in the rear to deal with Boston's occasional breakaways.

In the 71st minute Boston almost made football history. Froggatt moved the ball down the left, played back to Wilkinson whose fine centre found Tewley unmarked in the Derby penalty area. Tewley leapt in and headed the ball fast and low and beat Boulton all ends up only to hit the inside of the post, the ball rolling along the goal line for Thomas to clear.

It was a memorable game which will go down in the annals of Boston United as one of their greatest F.A. Cup performances. The team received a standing ovation from the Derby crowd as they left the field.

Result: Derby County 0   Boston United 0

Teams:
Derby County: Boulton, Webster, Thomas, Newton, McFarland, Todd, Powell, Gemmill, Bourne, Hector, Hinton.
Boston United: Simpson, Lakin, Waller, Moyes, Bate, Howells, Wright, Tewley, Froggatt, Conde, Wilkinson.
Referee: Mr. D. Turner.
Attendance: 25,788

CUP RUNS

1952/3

1st Round – *22nd November*
Boston United . 1   Oldham Ath. . . . 2

1953/4

1st Round – *21st November*
Scunthorpe 9   Boston United . 0

1954/5

1st Round – *20th November*
Boston United . 1   Blyth Spartans   1

1st Round Replay – *24th November*
Blyth Spartans . 5   Boston United . 4

1955/6

1st Round – *19th November*
Boston United . 3   Northwich Vic. 2

2nd Round – *10th December*
Derby County . 1   Boston United . 6

3rd Round – *7th January*
Tottenham H. . 4   Boston United . 0

1956/7

1st Round – *17th November*
Boston United . 0   Bradford 2

1957/8

1st Round – *16th November*
Boston United . 5   Billingham S.R. 2

2nd Round – *7th December*
Darlington 5   Boston United . 3

1958/9

1st Round   *15th November*
Chester 3   Boston United . 2

1962/3

1st Round – *3rd November*
Boston United . 1   King's Lynn . . . 2

1967/8

1st Round   *9th December*
Corby 0   Boston United . 3

2nd Round – *6th January*
Boston United . 1   Orient 1

2nd Round Replay – *15th January*
Orient 2   Boston United . 1

1970/1

1st Round – *21st November*
Southport 0   Boston United . 2

2nd Round – *11th December*
Boston United . 1   York City 2

1971/2

1st Round – *20th November*
Ellesmere Port . 0   Boston United . 3

2nd Round – *11th December*
Boston United . 2   Hartlepool Utd 1

3rd Round – *15th January*
Boston United . 0   Portsmouth . . . 1

1972/3

1st Round – *18th November*
Boston United . 1   Lancaster 2

1973/4

1st Round – *24th November*
Boston United . 0   Hayes 0

1st Round Replay – *28th November*
Hayes 1   Boston United . 2

2nd Round – *15th December*
Boston United . 1   Hitchin 0

3rd Round – *6th January*
Derby County . 0   Boston United . 0

3rd Round Replay – *9th January*
Boston United . 1   Derby County . 6

1974/5

1st Round   *23rd November*
Chesterfield . . . 3   Boston United . 1

1975/6

1st Round – *22nd November*
Boston United . 0   Lincoln City . . 1

1978/9

1st Round   *25th November*
Tranmere 2   Boston United . 1

1980/1

1st Round   *22nd November*
Boston United . 0   Rotherham 4

1981/2

1st Round   *21st November*
Boston United . 0   Kettering 1

75

CHELSMFORD CITY

Founded: 1938

League: Southern (Premier Division)

Ground: New Writtle Street

Colours: Claret and white

Chelmsford had a dazzling start in their first full season following formation in 1938 when they were beaten in the Fourth Round by Birmingham after having disposed of League clubs Darlington and Southampton on the way. In the post-war years Chelmsford have appeared regularly in the First and Second Round ties and in an outstanding 1972/3 season entertained First Division Ipswich Town at New Writtle Street in the Third Round. City's League opponents in the Second Round have included Ipswich Town (in the 1949/50 season when Ipswich were in the Third Division South), Mansfield Town, Colchester United and Torquay United. League opposition in First Round contests have included Northampton, Aldershot, Crystal Palace, Port Vale, Shrewsbury, Notts County, Oxford United, Brentford, Watford and Charlton Athletic.

Chelmsford's first post-war appearance in the First Round was in the 1945/6 season when they were drawn against Northampton Town, Division Three South. This was the season when the two-leg system was in operation and City were badly beaten 10–1 on aggregate.

Chelmsford were next in the First Round in 1948/9 season when they had a difficult away game against then Western League side Weymouth and were beaten 2–1, a Chelmsford 'goal' minutes from time being disallowed.

Chelmsford's Cup run in the following season, 1949/50, took them into the Second Round. In the First Round they drew an away game against Isthmian League amateurs Leytonstone. A crowd of 9,732, four short of the ground record, saw a goalless first half, Chelmsford scoring two second half goals to put them into the next Round despite a last minute Stones goal.

In the Second Round Chelmsford had the luck of a home tie against Ipswich Town, Third Division South and held them to a one-all draw at the New Writtle Stadium. The game is fully described as a *Match Report*.

There was a 'gate' of over 10,000, fewer than at City's ground, at Portman Road to watch the continuation of the battle between City and their Third Division opponents. The interval came with a blank scoresheet but with the Southern Leaguers taking the credit of holding up a Third Division side on their own ground. But with City only five minutes away from taking their opponents into extra time Ipswich scored the only goal of the game.

Again on the First Round battlefront in the following season, 1950/1, Chelmsford had the luck of a home draw against fellow Southern Leaguers Tonbridge resulting in a 2-2 draw. A ding-dong struggle developed in the replay at Tonbridge and at the end of 90 minutes the scoresheet was blank. With only six minutes of extra time remaining City scored the decisive goal that was to give them a Second Round contest at home against Mansfield Town, Third Division North, led by Freddie Steele, formerly of Stoke City and England. The Southern Leaguers were off form in this game and the Stags built up a 4-0 lead – all Chelmsford could manage was a second-half consolation goal.

Several seasons elapsed before Chelmsford again appeared in the First Round. Drawn away to Aldershot, Third Division South, in the 1954/5 season, City were three goals behind before a defensive error gave Chelmsford the chance to pull a goal back to make the final score 3-1.

Chelmsford did not reach the First Round again until the 1958/9 season when they were drawn at home to fellow Southern Leaguers Worcester City. Over 5,000 spectators saw a goalless draw in which Worcester had the edge in the first half but were forced on the defensive in the closing stages. At the replay at Worcester the home side were one up at half time as a result of a remarkable goal scored when everyone else on the field had stopped playing, believing that the referee had blown up for a foul. Chelmsford equalised in the 72nd minute but Worcester added two late goals to make the final score 3-1.

In the following season Chelmsford, drawn away to Fourth Division Crystal Palace, went to Selhurst Park having lost their previous four Southern League games. City went down 5-1 before the second biggest Cup crowd of the day – 17,249.

Chelmsford had better luck in the 1960/1 season when they were drawn at home against Third Division Port Vale, founder members of the Second Division in 1892. On a heavy ground Vale went into a 3-0 lead but City staged a glorious rally and scored twice to get back into the game. Then came a disputed 'goal', Taylor appearing to have got the equaliser but his effort was disallowed.

The following season, 1961/2, Chelmsford seemed to have an easier task, drawn at home in the First Round against lowly-placed fellow Southern Leaguers King's Lynn. Although Chelmsford gained a 1-0 half time lead Lynn improved after the interval, scoring the equaliser and in the last 30 seconds of the game grabbed the winner.

Chelmsford were back in the First Round in the 1962/3 season on their own ground but their side had had to be re-arranged and they were decisively beaten 6-2 by Third Division Shrewsbury Town. Chelmsford fans saw Arthur Rowley, Shrewsbury's famous player-manager, whose goal tally when the game began was 422, score one of his side's goals. Irish international McLaughlin scored four.

In 1963/4 Chelmsford were drawn away to fellow Southern Leaguers Cambridge United and a 'gate' of over 7,000 at the Abbey Stadium saw City win the tie with a lone goal scored two minutes after the interval. For the Second Round Chelmsford found themselves facing more Southern League opposition – Bedford Town at home. A 9,000 crowd saw Bedford score the match-winner in the ninth minute.

In the First Round of the 1964/5 competition City had interesting League opponents in Fourth Division Notts County, the oldest club in the Football League, away from home at the Meadow Lane ground. Although City held out until the interval County increased the pressure in the second half and scored two late goals.

There was a crowd of over 8,000 at Griffin Park to watch Fourth Division Brentford play City in the First Round of the 1966/7 competition. There were two John Docherty's on the field, one on each side and both were concerned with the only goal of the match – in the eighth minute Chelmsford's John Docherty handled and Brentford's John Docherty scored from the spot. It was enough to continue the non-Leaguers' hoodoo at Griffin Park – in F.A. Cup games with non-League sides since the war, none up to that point had managed to lower Brentford's colours. But it was a situation that was to change!

Chelmsford were next in the First Round in the following season, 1967/8, when there was a battle royal with Oxford United, pace setters in the Third Division, eventually winning through to the Second Round. Chelmsford's first encounter with United was a home game at New Writtle Street where a 'gate' of nearly 7,000 saw United force a 3-3 draw after three times trailing behind Chelmsford. In the replay at Oxford Chelmsford showed tenacious spirit when they came back after being 3-1 down midway through the second half to equalise 3-3 with a last-fling goal seconds from the final whistle. There were no further goals in extra time.

The second replay took place at Griffin Park, Brentford where a crowd of 4,350 saw Chelmsford make a remarkable start. Straight from the kick-off, after the Oxford defence had been spread-eagled, Cassidy scored with a powerful header. It turned out to be the only goal of the match and City's supporters had to endure an agonising 89 minutes before they knew that their team had again reached the Second Round. Their opponents, at New Writtle Street, were neighbours Fourth Division Colchester United who defeated the part-timers 2-0.

In 1968/9 Chelmsford were drawn away from home against Midland League side Grantham and although City led at half time through a penalty goal Grantham scored twice in the second half to deny Chelmsford any further interest in the Cup.

In the First Round in 1969/70 Chelmsford drew a home game against highly-placed fellow Southern Leaguers and redoubtable Cup fighters Hereford United. Although City took the lead with a penalty goal, Hereford, led by John Charles, the famous former Welsh international, equalised and midway through the second half scored the winner.

The following season saw Chelmsford draw an away game against Crawley, also of the Southern League but from a lower division. First Crawley had a 'goal' disallowed and then took the lead but towards the end increasing City pressure produced the equaliser. The replay at New Writtle Street was a nightmare for Crawley who were trounced 6-1. Chelmsford had the luck of the draw in the Second Round when they were opposed at home by well-placed Third Division Torquay United. The 8,000 plus crowd watched

City hold their League opponents to a 0–0 draw at half time but on the hour Torquay scored the only goal of the match.

Chelmsford had to wait until the 1972/3 season before they made another appearance in the First Round, drawn at home against fellow Southern Leaguers Hillingdon Borough. It was a modest enough start to a run that was to end with Third Round honours, the prize a visit of a First Division club to New Writtle Street. The all Southern League clash resulted in a 2–0 win for City. In the Second Round Chelmsford again had the luck of the draw, matched against another Southern League side Telford United who got a 5–0 thrashing at the hands of City. Thus Chelmsford went into the Third Round for the first time in 34 years, drawing a fairy-tale tie at home against legendary Cup fighters First Division Ipswich Town, a game fully described in *Match Report*.

Chelmsford were again on First Round Cup duty in the following season, 1973/4, when they drew an away tie against Third Division Watford. The League side scored the only goal of the match just before half-time.

In 1974/5 Chelmsford were drawn at home in the First Round against Third Division Charlton Athletic. The League side had two 'goals' disallowed before they scored the only goal of the match in the 37th minute to maintain their record of never having been beaten by a non-League club in the Cup.

MATCH REPORTS
SECOND ROUND F.A. CUP
10th December 1949
CHELMSFORD CITY 1   IPSWICH TOWN 1

Bad weather affected the 'gate' for this Second Round tie at the New Writtle Street ground against Ipswich Town, Third Division South. The attendance was 11,327 whereas over 20,000 had been expected. The game was a hard, fast Cup battle but City had several scoring opportunities that should have made a replay unnecessary. McCormack and Plunkett both went near when well placed early in the half and towards the interval the Ipswich goal had several narrow escapes as Chelmsford consistently attacked.

Although Ipswich had their share of the attacking Chelmsford had more scoring chances.

Half-time: Chelmsford City 0   Ipswich 0

After the interval the League side had a slight edge over the Southern Leaguers and in the 53rd minute BROWN (J) put Ipswich ahead. Ipswich tried to increase their lead but good defensive work by the Southern Leaguers prevented them going further ahead. The non-Leaguers took the attack to the Ipswich end and Gowers and Suttle on the wings frequently had the Ipswich defenders in difficulties. Ten minutes from the end Chelmsford had their reward when HURST scored during a goalmouth scramble.

Result: Chelmsford City 1   Ipswich Town 1

Teams:
Chelmsford: Crozier, Hutton, Bidewell, Hurst, Wicks, Lane, Gowers, Hold, Plunkett, McCormack, Suttle.
Ipswich: Brown (T), Bell, Mitchell, Baird, Clark (G), Parker (T), Brown (J), Parker (S), Gibbons, Little, O'Brien.
Referee: Mr. F. S. Fiander, (High Wycombe).
Attendance: 11,327

THIRD ROUND F.A. CUP
13th January 1973
CHELMSFORD 1   IPSWICH TOWN 3

Ipswich Town, City's Third Round opponents, had once before met the Southern Leaguers in the Cup – 24 years previously when Chelmsford held the League side to a draw in a Second Round tie and then went out 1-0 in the replay at Portman Road. This time, however, there was a substantial difference. Whereas previously Ipswich were a Third Division South side they had now progressed to a dominating position in the First Division. Chelmsford equally had made progress. Nurtured by experienced manager Dave Bumpstead, the former Bristol Rovers and Millwall wing half,

Chelmsford were playing good football in the Southern League and for this tie fielded only two players without Football League experience although one of them Eddie Dilsworth from Sierra Leone, had played at Wembley in 1966 in the Amateur Cup final before a crowd of 45,000.

Leading Chelmsford's attack was Roy Woolcott, a former Spurs player, together with Frank Peterson, the talented City striker who had previously played League football with Millwall. When the game began it became evident that Chelmsford had a struggle on their hands facing an unchanged international-studded Ipswich side. City were forced to play a defensive 4-4-2 combination which allowed Ipswich to take the initiative. In the ninth minute the League side opened their account when Taylor, the Chelmsford goalkeeper, unfortunately carried the ball out of the area. From the resulting free-kick Morris slid the ball to Colin HARPER who unleashed a power drive to give Taylor no chance.

Ipswich twin-strikers Dave Johnson and Trevor Whymark posed a constant threat to City but they were well held throughout most of the 90 minutes by Tommy Coakley and Mick Loughton. In the 35th minute Chelmsford gave away a corner which led to the League side's second goal. After Lambert's cross had been palmed away by Laurie Taylor, Ipswich defender Alan Taylor headed the ball back into the goalmouth for JOHNSON to flick it into the back of the net with a well-taken header.

Half-time: Chelmsford City 0   Ipswich Town 2

After half time Chelmsford attempted to reduce the arrears with their left wing of Dilsworth and Peterson causing the League side a fair amount of trouble.

Ipswich were coasting to an easy victory and in the 75th minute scored again. Mills had picked up a loose ball, pushed it through to Whymark who got round Delea for HAMILTON to slip the ball into the net. A minute from time Chelmsford pulled back a goal. From Thornley's corner WOOLCOTT rose high over the Ipswich defenders, headed over Best and the ball went over the line as Mills tried to scramble it out. It was a fine performance by the Southern Leaguers even though they were outclassed by a superior First Division side.

Result: Chelmsford City 1   Ipswich Town 3

Chelmsford: Taylor, Coakley, Gomersall, Delea, Loughton, Tomkins, Lewis, Price, Woolcott, Peterson, Dilsworth.
Ipswich: Best, Mills, Harper, Morris, Hunter, Peddelty, Hamilton, Viljoen, Johnson, Whymark, Lambert.
Referee: Mr. Iowerth Jones, (Glamorgan).
Attendance: 15,557

CUP RUNS

1945/6

1st Round (1st leg) – *17th November*
Northampton 5   Chelmsford 1

1st Round (2nd leg) – *24th November*
Chelmsford 0   Northampton 5
(Northampton won on 10-1 aggregate)

1948/9

1st Round – *27th November*
Weymouth 2   Chelmsford 1

1949/50

1st Round – *26th November*
Leytonstone 1   Chelmsford 2

2nd Round – *10th December*
Chelmsford 1   Ipswich Town ... 1

2nd Round Replay – *14th December*
Ipswich Town ... 1   Chelmsford 0

1950/1

1st Round – *25th November*
Chelmsford 2   Tonbridge 2

1st Round Replay – *29th November*
Tonbridge 0   Chelmsford 1
(after extra time   score at 90 mins 0-0)

2nd Round   *9th December*
Chelmsford 1   Mansfield Town 4

1954/5

1st Round – *20th November*
Aldershot 3   Chelmsford 1

1958/9

1st Round   *15th November*
Chelmsford 0   Worcester City .. 0

1st Round Replay   *20th November*
Worcester City .. 3   Chelmsford 1

1959/60

1st Round   *14th November*
Crystal Palace ... 5   Chelmsford 1

1960/1

1st Round   *5th November*
Chelmsford 2   Port Vale 3

1961/2

1st Round   *4th November*
Chelmsford 1   King's Lynn 2

1962/3

1st Round   *3rd November*
Chelmsford 2   Shrewsbury 6

1963/4

1st Round – *16th November*
Cambridge Utd .. 0   Chelmsford 1

2nd Round – *7th December*
Chelmsford 0   Bedford Tn. 1

1964/5

1st Round – *14th November*
Notts County 2   Chelmsford 0

1966/7

1st Round   *26th November*
Brentford 1   Chelmsford 0

1967/8

1st Round – *9th December*
Chelmsford 3   Oxford United .. 3

1st Round Replay   *13th December*
Oxford United .. 3   Chelmsford 3
(after extra time. Score at 90 mins: 3 3)

1st Round Second Replay – *18th Dec.*
Chelmsford 1   Oxford United .. 0
(at Brentford)

2nd Round   *6th January*
Chelmsford 0   Colchester Utd .. 2

1968/9

1st Round   *16th November*
Grantham 2   Chelmsford 1

1969/70

1st Round   *15th November*
Chelmsford 1   Hereford Utd 2

1970/71

1st Round – *21st November*
Crawley 1   Chelmsford 1

1st Round Replay   *23rd November*
Chelmsford 6   Crawley 1

2nd Round – *11th December*
Chelmsford 0   Torquay Utd 1

1972/3

1st Round   *18th November*
Chelmsford 2   Hillingdon 0

Chelmsford (Contd)

1972/3

2nd Round - *9th December*
Chelmsford 5   Telford 0

3rd Round - *13th January*
Chelmsford 1   Ipswich Town ... 3

1973/4
1st Round - *24th November*
Watford 1   Chelmsford 0

1974/5
1st Round - *23rd November*
Chelmsford 0   Charlton 1

COLCHESTER UNITED

Founded: 1937

League: Formerly Southern (now Fourth Division)

Ground: Layer Road

Colours: Blue and white vertical stripes; blue shorts

Before Colchester United were elected to the Football League in 1950/51 they had some memorable moments in the Cup rounds whilst members of the Southern League and undoubtedly it was their Cup feats that proved their fitness for being elevated into football's big time. Colchester had a never-to-be-forgotten Cup run in the 1947/8 season when they reached the Fifth Round, one of only three non-League clubs (the other two being Yeovil and Blyth Spartans) to have made the last 16 since the war. To reach the Fifth Round in that fantastic season United had first to beat Banbury Spencer and Third Division North, Wrexham in the first two rounds, then caused a sensational upset by beating First Division Huddersfield 1-0 in the Third Round, disposed of Second Division Bradford City 3-2 in the Fourth Round before finally going down 5-0 to First Division Blackpool in the Fifth Round. In between times Colchester were drawn against Reading, Third Division South and were beaten on both occasions.

Colchester's first post-war First Round contest was in the 1946/7 season when they were drawn away against Reading, Third Division South. Over 13,000 spectators were at Elm Park to see Reading master the heavy conditions and win 5-0. Arthur Turner, the former Charlton Athletic amateur centre-forward, who had appeared in the Charlton v Derby County final at Wembley the previous season, played for Colchester.

United's sensational 1947/8 Cup run began at Layer Road when the Southern Leaguers drew a First Round tie against Birmingham Combination side Banbury Spencer. An off-form United made hard work of disposing of Banbury and only just scraped through by a 2-1 margin.

The Second Round brought Colchester a home tie against highly-placed Wrexham, Third Division North. The 10,642 crowd saw one of the most exciting F.A. Cup tussles ever seen at Layer Road. The game resulted in a memorable 1–0 win for the Southern Leaguers and at the end there were unprecedented scenes as the fans surged on to the pitch. After Curry had scored U's lone goal in the 27th minute of the second half a tense situation developed when one of the Wrexham strikers was brought down in the penalty area. U's had a lucky let-off when the ball went straight into the goalkeeper's arms. Then in the closing minutes it was Colchester's turn for a penalty but the Wrexham goalkepper brought off a magnificent save for the second penalty miss of the game.

The luck of the draw was still with Colchester when the names came out of the hat for the Third Round, the non-Leaguers securing a home game against First Division Huddersfield Town. The story of Colchester's famous victory against the First Division club, their subsequent win against Bradford in the Fourth Round and the team's finest hour when they appeared in the Fifth Round against First Division Blackpool are described in *Match Report*.

After the stirring deeds of the previous season Colchester were again in action in the First Round of the 1948/9 season, drawing old Cup adversaries Reading at Layer Road. There was a record crowd, 19,072 to see the non-Leaguers score the first goal. In the 29th minute, as fog began to encompass the ground, Reading equalised and six minutes later the referee abandoned the game.

There was another good gate, over 13,000, for the resumed game when Reading, on top form, dismissed the Southern Leaguers 4–2. Up to a late stage Reading were 4–0 in the lead and then the U's put on a great rally in the last 15 minutes, scoring two goals and still attacking at the final whistle. It was a fitting end to Colchester's Cup exploits as non-Leaguers for 1950 saw them elected to the Third Division South.

MATCH REPORTS

THIRD ROUND F.A. CUP
10th January 1948
COLCHESTER UNITED 1   HUDDERSFIELD TOWN 0

Several incidents when Colchester went close in the first quarter of an hour in this Third Round tie gave a hint that there was an even chance of the non-Leaguers accounting for their distinguished First Division opponents.

United were quick to attack and Hesford in the Huddersfield goal had to dive full length to save a Turner 'special'. Shortly afterwards an overhead kick from the Colchester centre-forward went just wide with Hesford beaten.

The Colchester fans among the 16,000 crowd at Layer Road began to sense that the unbelievable might happen as United continued to attack and Peter Doherty, Huddersfield's famous Irish international inside-left, was kept under tight control. Ted Fenton not only subdued Doherty but he also went into the attack himself, moving up for corner kicks and on one occasion going close with a header from a Cater cross.

In addition to Fenton, Kettle, Allen and ex-Chelsea Bearryman kept a close watch on the Huddersfield front line. Half-time came with no score, a highly creditable performance for the Southern Leaguers.

Half-time: Colchester United 0   Huddersfield Town 0

After the interval Metcalfe, Huddersfield's left-winger, almost scored when his shot skimmed the bar. In these early stages of the second half Huddersfield had more of the play and again had a good scoring chance when Whittingham eluded Fenton and raced for goal. United's goalkeeper Wright brought off a brilliant save as he dived at the centre-forward's feet.

In the 24th minute of the second half came the goal that was to make Cup history. Kettle, the "U's" right-back, gathered the ball and ran the length of the field and when a few yards short of the penalty area was upended.

Left-back Allen went up to take the free kick and to try a shot for goal. Hesford could only make a partial clearance and CURRY, lurking in the penalty area, seized on the ball and drove it into the net. Pandemonium broke out as the United fans realised that unbelievably the Southern Leaguers were on top.

Colchester turned on the heat and both Cater and Turner nearly added to the score. Huddersfield had a last chance to equalise when Metcalfe gained possession but the winger shot wide.

Colchester thus gained a great team victory over a First Division side which had £50,000 worth of footballing talent in its ranks. Inspired throughout by Fenton, the Huddersfield defence never succeeded in taming the eager Colchester forwards. The result was a classic win for the little club, rank outsiders against such glittering First Division opposition, and their victory has been writ large in F.A. Cup history.

Result: Colchester United 1   Huddersfield Town 0

Teams:
Colchester United: Wright, Kettle, Allen, Bearryman, Fenton, Brown, Hillman, Curry, Turner, Cutting, Cater.
Huddersfield Town: Hesford, Hayes, Barker, Smith (L), Hepplewhite, Boot, Smith (C), Glazzard, Whittingham, Doherty, Metcalfe.
Referee: Mr. G. Reader.
Attendance: 16,000

FOURTH ROUND F.A. CUP
24th January 1948
COLCHESTER UNITED 3   BRADFORD CITY 2

Cup interest continued at fever pitch at Layer Road for the visit of Second Division Bradford who had conquered mighty Arsenal in the previous Round. It was the fifth Cup game in a row that United had been drawn at home. Before 17,000 spectators the "U's" flung themselves into battle confident that they would be able to account for yet another League side from Yorkshire.

In the opening minutes the game fluctuated from end to end and set the pattern for a tremendous Cup thriller. For a while neither side was able to gain an advantage but in the 13th minute Bradford scored through ELLIOTT. City's joy was short-lived for three minutes later CURRY sent the crowd wild when he headed a Cater pass past Bradford's goalkeeper Farr.

Within three minutes of the restart the "U's" went into the lead for the first time when Turner slipped a pass to CURRY for the inside forward to score from 12 yards.

In the 28th minute Bradford scored the equaliser through centre-forward AINSLEY. Bradford had two menacing wingers in Elliott and Smith and United's defence were at full stretch in attempting to hold them. Just before half-time a shot from Smith struck the crossbar with Wright beaten.

Half-time: Colchester United 2   Bradford City 2

On the resumption the crowd were on their toes when "U's" inside-left Cutting raced through. Goalkeeper Farr came out, the ball hit Turner and rebounded into goal. The cheers were cut short however when the referee disallowed the 'goal'.

Amid tremendous excitement Colchester scored the match-winner when CUTTING moved on to an upfield pass from Kettle and slammed the ball into the net. More excitement was to follow as a 'goal' by Curry was disallowed (the second time in the game that the "U's" had had the disappointment of a 'no-goal') and Bradford all but equalised in the last three minutes when Wright saved magnificently from Ainsley.

The excitement was so great in the final stages that the crowd, anticipating the final whistle, invaded the pitch. As soon as the game ended the crowd jumped the barriers and chaired the players off the field.

Up to that moment it was only the second occasion this century that a non-League side had entered the last 16, the previous side to do so being Darlington (then in the North Eastern League) in 1911.

Result: Colchester United 3   Bradford City 2

Teams:
Colchester United: Wright, Kettle, Allen, Bearryman, Fenton, Brown, Hillman, Curry, Turner, Cutting, Cater.
Bradford: Farr, Hepworth, Farrell, White, Greenwood, Deplidge, Smith, Henry, Ainsley, Downie, Elliott.
Referee: Mr. G. Clark, (London).

FIFTH ROUND F.A. CUP
7th February 1948
BLACKPOOL 5   COLCHESTER UNITED 0

Colchester United, 'giantkillers' of the 1947/8 season, took 4,000 fans to Blackpool for their encounter with the First Division side in this historic Cup-tie at Bloomfield Road. There was a civic welcome for the non-Leaguers and after the game the Mayor of Blackpool entertained the two teams to dinner and the ball was presented to United's captain, Bob Curry.

Ted Fenton had spent some pre-match time endeavouring to work out an 'M' plan to outwit the Matthews-Mortensen combination but there was no formula to be found; in the early minutes of the game the legendary Stan Matthews sent over a flagkick from which MUNRO scored the first goal.

The 30,000 crowd at Bloomfield Road saw United fight back and Curry nearly equalised in the 14th minute when the "U's" captain flashed the ball just wide of the post. Curry repeated the performance shortly afterwards when Robinson, the Blackpool goalkeeper, had to go full-length to save.

After 30 minutes' play Blackpool went into a 2–0 lead through McINTOSH after the Blackpool forwards had given the Colchester goal a battering.

Half-time: Blackpool 2   Colchester United 0

Soon after the restart Colchester were forced back on the defensive and in the second minute MORTENSEN dribbled through from the touch-line to score number three. A minute later MORTENSEN scored again to give Blackpool a 4–0 lead. Almost from the kick-off McINTOSH scored again to complete a shattering five minutes for Colchester. In addition the "U's" narrowly missed having a penalty awarded against them when Matthews was brought down.

Five minutes from the end "U's" goalkeeper Wright was temporarily knocked out when he made a daring save from Dick.

Although the Southern Leaguers had been outplayed by the clever First Division side they will be remembered for having given a fighting display against heavy odds and of having the honour of being in the last 16 out of an original 500. At that time still only the first non-League side to have reached the Fifth Round since the war Colchester have a special niche in the history of the F.A. Cup.

Result: Blackpool 5   Colchester United 0

Teams:
Blackpool: Robinson, Shimwell, Suart, Johnston, Hayward, Kelly, Matthews, Mortensen, McIntosh, Dick, Munro.
Colchester United: Wright, Kettle, Allen, Brown, Fenton, Bearryman, Hillman, Curry, Turner, Cutting, Cater.
Referee: Mr. H. W. Moore, (North Riding).
Attendance: 30,000

CUP RUNS

1946/7
1st Round – *30th November*
Reading 5   Colchester 0

1947/8
1st Round – *29th November*
Colchester 2   Banbury S 1

2nd Round – *13th December*
Colchester 1   Wrexham 0

3rd Round – *10th January*
Colchester 1   Huddersfield 0

4th Round – *24th January*
Colchester 3   Bradford 2

5th Round – *7th February*
Blackpool 5   Colchester 0

1948/9
1st Round – *27th November*
Colchester 1   Reading 1
(abandoned after 35 minutes)

1st Round Replay – *4th December*
Colchester 2   Reading 4

ELECTED TO THIRD
DIVISION SOUTH – 1950/51

DAGENHAM

Founded: 1949

League: Alliance Premier

Ground: Victoria Road

Colours: Red shirts, red shorts

It is only in recent years that Dagenham have made any significant impact in the Cup, their first appearance at First Round level coming in the 1967/8 season when after beating Southern Leaguers Tonbridge they entered the Second Round to meet Third Division Reading away at Elm Park. For many years non-League sides have found Reading hard to beat in the Cup and it was a splendid performance by the Daggers when they held the League side to a 1-1 draw. With high hopes of success in the replay at Victoria Road the non-Leaguers were unable to complete the task so ably begun at Elm Park and the professionals went through to the next round with a slim 1-0 victory.

Since then the Daggers have reached the Second Round on two further occasions, in 1970/1, when they were beaten by a lone goal by Fourth Division Southend United and in 1981/2 when Third Division Millwall won 2-1 and have also faced other League opponents in the Cup including Walsall (twice), Aldershot, Watford and Gillingham.

In their First Round encounter in the 1967/8 season Dagenham had ground advantage when they drew Southern Leaguers Tonbridge. On a treacherous pitch the Daggers scored midway through the first-half and retained their lead until the final whistle to put them in the Second Round for the first time. This gave the then Athenian Leaguers an away game against high-riding Third Division Reading, a bumper crowd of over 12,000 seeing the amateurs put up what is arguably their finest Cup performance to date by holding the professionals to a 1-1 draw and making them replay at Victoria Road. The game is fully described in *Match Report*.

In the exciting but finally disappointing Second Round replay before a crowd of 8,100 the amateurs were removed from the Cup by an 11th minute 'gift' goal scored by ex-Spurs striker and former Dagenham supporter John Sainty.

In the closing minutes the part-timers forced five corners in an unsuccessful attempt to grab the equaliser.

After missing a season Dagenham were again on First Round duty in the 1969/70 season when they drew a home game against fellow amateurs Isthmian Leaguers Sutton United, redoubtable Cup fighters themselves. After taking a 16th minute lead Sutton hung on to emerge 1–0 victors to deny the Daggers another Second Round appearance.

In the 1970/1 competition Dagenham once more had a successful Cup run. Drawn at home in the First Round against fellow part-timers Margate of the Southern League the Daggers turned on a brilliant first-half display that quickly yielded two goals and thereafter were content to keep their opponents at bay. Dagenham drew a difficult away tie in the Second Round, matched against Fourth Division Southend at Roots Hall, often the graveyard of the non-Leaguers. It was lucky for the League side that they snatched a goal in the 13th minute that in the end was to win the match for them. For most of the rest of the game belonged to Dagenham, especially the second half during which the amateurs laid siege to the Southend goal saved only by a courageous display by the League side's Welsh under-23 international goalkeeper Brian Lloyd.

In the following season, 1971/2, the Daggers were again in the First Round draw, having to travel to meet Third Division Walsall. The Saddlers went into the lead mid-way through the first-half and there was no further scoring before the break. In the first minute of the second half Walsall went into a 2–0 lead and it was at that point that the Daggers began to pressurise their professional opponents, getting a goal back in the 53rd minute from a penalty. Walsall took command scoring two late goals to run out 4–1 winners.

It was in the 1973/4 season that the Daggers next appeared in the First Round, again drawing League opposition, Third Division Aldershot, at home at Victoria Road. The Daggers could make little impression against a skilful and determined League side who built up a 3–0 half-time lead and made the final tally 4–0 with a further goal scored late in the second half.

The Daggers did not reappear in the First Round until four seasons later, in 1977/8, when they faced former Cup opponents Third Division Walsall away from home at Fellows Park. Dagenham greatly improved on their 4–1 defeat in 1971 and although they lost by a lone goal scored in the 16th minute it was a close-run affair. Although Walsall were in control in the first-half the Daggers later piled on the pressure in an unsuccessful attempt to gain the equaliser.

In the following season, 1978/9, the Daggers drew a hard tie, away from home, against Third Division Watford at Vicarage Road. Watford invariably play above themselves in the Cup and this game was no exception, the League side controlling the game from the start and running out 3-0 winners with a Ross Jenkins hat-trick.

After missing a season Dagenham were again in the First Round in the 1980/1 competition but had to travel to the Priestfield Stadium to meet Third Division Gillingham. A controversial goal for the Gills in the 21st minute and a second from a deflection seven minutes later put the League side 2-0 in the lead but this did not deter the Daggers who fought back desperately to pull a goal back before half-time. After the interval Dagenham had most of the play as Gillingham fiercely defended their narrow lead.

Again in the following season 1981/2 the Daggers won their 4th qualifying round tie to secure a place in the First Round, drawn at home to formidable Cup fighters, fellow Alliance Premier Leaguers Yeovil. Yeovil laid siege to the Daggers' goal, went into a 1-0 half-time lead and then struck again a minute after half-time. To almost any other club this would have been the finish against Cup opponents of the calibre of Yeovil but in the case of the Daggers it was a clarion call to action and Dagenham made an almost unbelievable comeback to score twice – both through Burton – to give the Essex club another chance. The replay at Huish was fought out in the same tenacious fashion as the first encounter, neither defence yielding and the game going into extra time. Malcolm Stewart scored the winner for the Daggers in the 114th minute to give the Londoners a tilt at high-riding Third Division Millwall at home in the Second Round. Before a crowd of 4,825 the Daggers gave an heroic performance, for most of the first half in command of the game with Millwall forced back on the defensive. On the half hour Dagenham went into the lead when Stein scored from a corner kick. Millwall managed to retrieve the situation just before half-time and in a closely contested second half the League side scored again to gain a narrow 2-1 victory. It was vintage Cup football that did the non-Leaguers proud.

MATCH REPORT

SECOND ROUND F.A. CUP
6th January 1968
READING 1   DAGENHAM 1

The greatest day to date in Dagenham's short history as the non-Leaguers held high-riding Third Division Reading to a 1-1 draw away at Elm Park before a crowd of 12,445.

From the outset the Athenian League amateurs established midfield control and in the early exchanges outshone their League opponents, Reading goalkeeper Mike Dixon being constantly under pressure. Gradually Reading settled down and the two Dagenham-born players, ex-Spurs John Saintly and Dennis Allen began to show their class. But ironically as Reading for the first time in the game began to look dangerous Dagenham struck. After a clearance by Daniels following a Reading attack Peter Green took the ball upfield and after eluding two Reading defenders passed to Dave MORRISS who volleyed the ball into the back of the net giving Dixon no chance.

Towards the end of the first-half Reading pressed strongly but with the Daggers' goalkeeper Huttley in splendid form, were unable to capitalise on their chances.

Half-time: Reading 0   Dagenham 1

Reading opened the second-half in attacking mood, mounting raid after raid on the Daggers' goal but without success as the Dagenham rearguard, with Huttley outstanding, stood firm. Both the Reading full backs, Yard and Spiers joined in the onslaught but everything was repulsed until the 56th minute. Then George HARRIS, Reading's best forward, eluded the defence to head in the equaliser.

In the closing stages the Daggers regained the initiative but finally had to settle for a draw. It was a magnificent result for the non-Leaguers against a side notoriously difficult to beat on their own ground in the Cup.

Result: Reading 1   Dagenham 1

Teams:
Reading: Dixon, Yard, Spiers, Meldrum, Bayliss, Allen, Foster, Smee, Collins, Sainty, Harris.
Dagenham: Huttley, Smith, Dudley, Daniels, Willingham, Moore, Drake, Greene, Bass, Morris, Pudney.
Referee: Mr. P. Bye.
Attendance: 12,445

Dagenham (Contd) CUP RUNS

1967/8

1st Round – *9th December*
Dagenham 1   Tonbridge 0

2nd Round – *6th January*
Reading 1   Dagenham 1

2nd Round Replay – *15th January*
Dagenham 0   Reading 1

1969/70

1st Round – *15th November*
Dagenham 0   Sutton United ... 1

1970/1

1st Round – *21st November*
Dagenham 2   Margate 0

2nd Round – *11th December*
Southend Utd ... 1   Dagenham 0

1971/2

1st Round – *20th November*
Walsall 4   Dagenham 1

1973/4

1st Round – *24th November*
Dagenham 0   Aldershot 4

1977/8

1st Round – *26th November*
Walsall 1   Dagenham 0

1978/9

1st Round – *25th November*
Watford 3   Dagenham 0

1980/1

1st Round – *22nd November*
Gillingham 2   Dagenham 1

1981/2

1st Round – *21st November*
Dagenham 2   Yeovil 2

1st Round Replay – *25th November*
Yeovil 0   Dagenham 1
(after extra time)

2nd Round – *30th December*
Dagenham 1   Millwall 2

ENFIELD

Founded: 1900

League: Alliance Premier

Ground: The Stadium, Southbury Road

Colours: White shirts with blue trim; blue shorts

Former Isthmian League amateurs Enfield (now Alliance Premier League) did not join the post-war First Round Cup hunt until the 1959/60 season. Since then they have regularly hit the headlines following tussles with the League clubs and the semi-professionals culminating in the magical 1980/81 run when after beating non-League Wembley, Hereford Utd and Port Vale (after a replay) they went out gloriously at White Hart Lane in the Fourth Round against Third Division Barnsley, again after a replay, before a fantastic 'gate' of over 35,000. Enfield have survived until the Second Round on no fewer than seven occasions since the war and have reached the Third Round heights three times — in 1977/8, when they went out by a lone goal away from home against fellow non-Leaguers Blyth Spartans; in 1980/81 when they first drew 1-1 away at Port Vale and then had a comfortable 3-0 win over the League side in the replay (this gave them entry into the dizzy strata of the Fourth Round and the memorable games against Barnsley); and in 1981/2 when they were beaten 3-2 at home by Second Division Crystal Palace.

When Enfield fought their way to the First Round in 1959/60, matched against Southern Leaguers Headington United (now Third Division Oxford Utd) it was the first time that they had progressed so far in the Cup since the 1930's. It was tough opposition, Headington, managed by former Birmingham City player Arthur Turner, having gone 13 games without defeat. Enfield were to change all that – the 5,000 crowd seeing the amateurs leading 4-0 with only 25 minutes play left. But the Isthmian Leaguers had a player ordered off and Headington were able to score three in a remarkable recovery in the closing stages. Enfield held on to win 4-3. In the Second Round for the first time since the club's formation the amateurs again had the luck of the draw, a home game against Third Division Bournemouth at The Stadium. The amateurs made a fight of it but went down 5-1.

Again in the First Round in the 1962/3 competition the amateurs drew what turned out to be a high-scoring tie against Southern Leaguers Cheltenham Town away from home, Enfield winning an exciting contest 6-3. Enfield had no luck with the draw for the Second Round away from home against powerful Cup fighters Third Division Peterborough United. Enfield's unyielding defence kept out the Peterborough strikers until after half-time when in the 75th minute Posh scored the only goal of the game.

In the First Round in the 1963/4 season the amateurs were again unlucky with the draw – away from home against Third Division Reading at Elm Park. A crowd of over 10,000 saw Enfield go into a 1-0 lead which they held up to half-time and then unbelievably go 2-0 in the lead. But both sides then had a player ordered off and with Enfield's loss the greater Reading pulled back two goals to make the final score 2-2. After their great performance at Elm Park the amateurs resumed battle before a 7,000 crowd and intent on preserving their home record stretching back over 41 games. The story was the reverse of what had happened at Elm Park, the League side going into a first-half 1-0 lead and scoring again soon after the second half had begun. It was Enfield's turn to battle for the equaliser, pulling one back in the 63rd minute and getting the second almost on time. In extra time the gallant Enfield defence gave out and Reading won 4-2.

In the following season, 1964/5, Enfield drew an away First Round with semi-professionals Romford of the Southern League to begin what turned out to be a marathon. Although Enfield had the ball in the net the referee disallowed the 'goal' and the game finished a goalless draw. When the teams reassembled at The Stadium there was a near-record crowd and shortly after the game had begun the main gate collapsed under the weight of supporters trying to get in. Again there were no goals, the game going into extra time without result. The marathon continued at Highbury before a crowd of 9,000 where Enfield decisively ended matters 4-2. For the Second Round Enfield drew a home game against fellow amateurs Barnet of the Athenian League. Although within half an hour Enfield were 3-0 down they made a good recovery and an exciting game ended all-square 4-4. The replay at Underhill saw Barnet move comfortably into the next round with a 3-0 win.

Enfield next appeared in the First Round in the 1966/7 season when they drew a home tie against Chesham United, Athenian League amateurs. Enfield, who had five amateur internationals in their side, won convincingly 6-0 to earn a home tie in the Second Round against Third Division Watford. There was a 'gate' of over 7,000 at The Stadium to watch the Isthmian Leaguers challenge their League opponents, an interesting first-half struggle producing two goals apiece. But in the second half Watford scored two more to make the final tally 4-2.

In the 1967/8 season Enfield, then Amateur Cup holders, drew an away game against Fourth Division Swansea Town at Vetch Field, a daunting task for a non-League side. A solid Enfield defence kept out the Swans during the first half but two second half goals put the League side into the next round.

Enfield missed a season before they were next in a First Round contest, in 1969/70 when they faced Third Division Brighton at the Goldstone Ground. With Enfield fielding eight amateur internationals Albion were made to fight hard before the 11,276 crowd and just edged into the next round on a 2-1 margin. Enfield scored first from a penalty.

In the following season, 1970/1, Enfield were again on First Round duty having drawn a home game against Fourth Division Cambridge United. Cambridge scored the only goal of the match as a result of an Enfield defensive error.

Enfield were given a boost when they drew fellow Isthmian League amateurs Maidenhead United at The Stadium in the following season. With Maidenhead having to field a rearranged side Enfield moved smoothly into the next round on a 2-0 margin. This turned out to be an away contest against renowned Cup fighters Peterborough United who had knocked out the amateurs ten years previously. Enfield had no better luck, going down 4-0.

In 1972/3 Enfield again fought their way to the First Round being host to fellow amateurs Bishop's Stortford. The first clash produced a 1-1 draw with Stortford winning the replay 1-0 to enter the Second Round for the first time in their 98-year history.

It was not until the 1976/7 season that Enfield were again in the First Round drawn at home against fellow non-Leaguers Harwich and Parkeston. The first encounter ended in a goalless draw but in the replay Enfield were clearly superior and won 3-0 to earn the right to visit Crystal Palace in the Second Round.

It was decided to transfer the tie from Enfield's tiny Southbury Road ground to Selhurst Park – a wise decision since 13,670 spectators were drawn to the game. The Isthmian Leaguers were generally outclassed by Palace who were three goals to the good before half time. Palace scored again in the 82nd minute to make the final score 4-0.

Enfield had a good run in the 1977/8 season when they began with a First Round encounter at home against Fourth Division strugglers Wimbledon, once the pride of the Southern League. On this occasion the boot was on the other foot with the powerful Isthmian League champions, with an unbeaten run of 25 games, seeking the cup glory. Enfield were one up in the 37th minute and half-time arrived with the amateurs still holding their 1-0 lead. In the second half Enfield again had most of the play, scoring again in the 75th minute and adding a further goal ten minutes later to make the final score 3-0. It was a magnificent display by the non-Leaguers who gained their first League scalp in the club's history.

Enfield's reward was a Second Round encounter away from home against Fourth Division Northampton Town. In a closely-contested game the Cobblers' defence concentrated on marking Tony Bass out of the game but this gave extra freedom to Keith Searle whose two headed goals, in the 23rd and 74th minutes, gave the amateurs a well-deserved 2-0 victory. The measure of Enfield success was that Northampton had lost only two home games that season. Enfield were looking forward to meeting a glamour club in the Third Round but instead drew an away tie against dangerous Northern League Cup fighters Blyth Spartans.

Enfield went north full of confidence – unbeaten in 32 games, bidding for the Isthmian League championship for the third time running and with a redoubtable defence that had given away only one goal in the six Cup rounds the club had played. The interval arrived with the scoresheet blank. After the break the Isthmian Leaguers continued on the offensive but in the closing stages Blyth improved and 13 minutes from time snatched the match-winner when Shoulder, who was later transferred to Newcastle United, scored with an unstoppable header.

Enfield were back in the First Round in the 1978/9 season when Southern Leaguers Wealdstone put up a dismal performance on their own ground against the Isthmian Leaguers. Two-thirds of the way through the first half Enfield went 1-0 in the lead but, with Wealdstone having lost a man sent off, ran riot in the second half adding four more goals to make the final score 5-0. In the Second Round Enfield faced leading Third Division side Swindon Town away at the County Ground. The Isthmian League champions held up the League side for over an hour before Swindon finally scored in the 61st minute and then proceeded to add a further two to make it a 3-0 victory.

In the following season, 1979/80 Enfield had an unenviable draw even though with ground advantage – famous F.A. Cup fighters Yeovil Town from the Alliance Premier League. Yeovil snatched the winning goal in the 61st minute.

Then came the 1980/81 season which turned out to be the greatest Cup season in Enfield's history, fighting their way through to the Fourth Round and hitting the national headlines in a never-to-be-forgotten replay at White Hart Lane before a crowd of over 35,000. The Cup run started on fairly modest lines – Wembley from the First Division of the Isthmian League at The Stadium. Enfield notched up a comfortable 3-0 win – two goals ahead at half-time, a penalty miss and a third goal 12 minutes from time. This gave Enfield the right of another tilt at a League club in the Second Round – struggling Fourth Division Hereford United who had made Cup history as 'giantkillers' in their Southern League days. This time it was Enfield's turn to do the giant-killing, two goals by Peter Burton, one in the first half and the other late in a second half that had been completely dominated by Enfield, was enough to once again get the Isthmian Leaguers into the magical Third Round.

Once again a big name eluded the little club, their opponents being lowly-placed Fourth Division Port Vale, away at Vale Park. Vale's rearranged side made little impression with Enfield looking by far the more dangerous. In the 41st minute Johnny Bishop swept the ball into the Port Vale net from close range from a corner – Enfield's first – taken by Steve King. In the second half Enfield continued to pressurise Vale although more action came from the League side towards the end. Vale equalised in the 70th minute and also had a 'goal' disallowed.

Enfield's sensational 3-0 win against Vale in the replay and their two fabulous games against Barnsley in the Fourth Round are fully recorded in *Match Report*.

Again in the First Round in the 1981/2 season Enfield were drawn at home against Southern Leaguers Hastings United and won a hard-fought tie 2-0. In the Second Round Enfield again had the luck of the draw, being set to entertain Wimbledon, at the bottom of the Third Division, at Southbury Road. Enfield found themselves trailing 1-0 at half-time through a penalty but discovered their form after the interval and equalised on the hour through Turner. In a hectic scoring spree in the last half hour further goals for Enfield from Ironton, Oliver and Waite gave the non-Leaguers a shattering 4-1 win.

Enfield's Cup luck continued when they were drawn at home in the Third round against Second Division Crystal Palace to make it the third occasion since the war that the club had reached an advanced stage in the Cup. Enfield began the game with tremendous enthusiasm and were unlucky to be a goal down in the 13th minute when, against the run of the play, David Price, who had played in three F.A. Cup Finals and a European Cup Winners Cup Final whilst with Arsenal, slotted in number one. Nine minutes later Palace were two up when after a fine run by Eire international Jerry Murphy, Vince Hilaire completed the move. Far from being disheartened Enfield pulled out the stops and in the 34th minute Nicky Ironton put Enfield back in the game. Midway through the second half Hilaire scored his second to restore Palace's lead. But the non-Leaguers, summoning up their remaining reserves of strength, again reduced the arrears with a header from Oliver. This was the signal for an all-out attack on the Palace goal but although the League side were staggering towards the end the equaliser eluded the part-timers. Result: Enfield 2 Crystal Palace 3. Attendance 3,467. Enfield: Jacobs, Barrett, Tone, Jennings, Waite, Ironton, Ashford, Taylor, Holmes, Oliver, King. Crystal Palace: Barron; Hinshelwood, Boulter, Murphy, Wicks, Cannon, Price, Smillie, Walsh, Mabbutt, Hilaire.

MATCH REPORTS
THIRD ROUND F.A. CUP REPLAY
6th January 1981
ENFIELD 3   PORT VALE 0

This was one of the most impressive Cup results in non-League Cup history as the joint Isthmian League champions Enfield registered a comprehensive victory over Fourth Division Port Vale in this Third Round replay.

From the kick-off the part-timers set about the task of demolishing Port Vale in the same way as they had threatened to do at Vale. On a treacherous pitch, watched by a record crowd of over 6,000, Enfield took the attack to their opponents' half from the outset. The part-timers forced three quick corners as the Vale defenders retreated with goalkeeper Cherry, the former England youth international on loan from Derby, having to make a diving save to prevent Burton from scoring. This attacking style of football soon paid off. In the fifth minute Enfield opened their account when Wade placed the ball for BISHOP to head in.

In the 39th minute Enfield went further ahead. During a determined attack on the Vale goal Cherry rushed out of his area to try to connect with a long through ball, miskicked and KING had the easiest of tasks to collect the ball and stroke it into the net.

Half-time: Enfield 2   Port Vale 0

After the interval Enfield continued as they had started, making dangerous raids into Vale's penalty area and completely dominating the midfield. In an isolated Vale attack Miller shot an indirect kick into Enfield's goal but the point was disallowed.

Ten minutes from the end Enfield put the matter beyond doubt. Alan King produced another defence-splitting run before passing the ball to HOWELL who thumped it into the back of the net.

Enfield, the last non-League side left in the 1980/1 competition, did not get the glamour tie they were hoping for in the Fourth Round – they had to be content with away game against Norman Hunter's high-riding Third Division Barnsley.

Result: Enfield 3   Port Vale 0

Teams:
Enfield: Jacobs, Wade, Tone, Jennings, Oliver, Howell, Ashford, Barrett, Burton, Bishop, King. Sub: Holmes.
Port Vale: Cherry, Griffiths, Miller, Beach, Bowles, Sproson, Farrell, Jones, Chamberlain N, Chamberlain M, Bromage. Sub: Elsby.
Referee: Mr. K. W. Baker, Rugby.
Attendance: 6,449

FOURTH ROUND F.A. CUP
24th January 1981
BARNSLEY 1   ENFIELD 1

This great Cup-tie, played before a crowd of over 24,000, Barnsley's highest of the season, gave the fans everything expected from a David and Goliath encounter – the Isthmian Leaguers in the Fourth Round for the first time in their 81 years' history facing a Barnsley side with an unbeaten Cup and League run of 16 games, three disallowed 'goals' (two that finished up in the Barnsley net) and a sensational 89th equaliser that made Barnsley fight again.

Barnsley's early attacks looked dangerous, Parker smashing a header on to the crossbar. As Enfield got over their nerves they began to play composed football and to attack the Barnsley goal to good effect but no reward. First Oliver had the ball in the net but the 'goal' was disallowed for offside and then London taxi driver Bishop beat the Barnsley goalkeeper but he too was ruled offside.

Then came a cruel blow for Enfield just on half-time. Jacobs was penalised for handling outside his area and from the free kick Glavin struck a post and AYLOTT scored from the rebound.

Half-time: Barnsley 1   Enfield 0

In the early stages of the second-half Barnsley had more of the attack, Aylott missed an open goal and Parker had the ball in the net but the 'goal' was disallowed, another offside decision.

Ten minutes from the end the non-Leaguers staged a grandstand finish. Throwing men forward Eddie McCluskey's team raised their game as they struggled to get on terms. Then a minute from time Oliver began the move that led to 29-year-old P.E. teacher Peter BURTON, who was born near Barnsley, heading in to score the dramatic equaliser.

Result: Barnsley 1   Enfield 1

Teams:
Barnsley: New, Joyce, Chambers, Glavin, Banks, McCarthy, Evans, Parker, Aylott, Lester, Downes.
Enfield: Jacobs, Wade, Tone, Jennings, Barrett, Howell, Ashford, Bishop, Burton, Oliver, King.
Referee: Mr. P. Willis, (Co. Durham).
Attendance: 24,251

FOURTH ROUND F.A. CUP REPLAY
28th January 1981
ENFIELD 0   BARNSLEY 3
(at White Hart Lane)

This was the greatest night in Enfield's history – under the floodlights at White Hart Lane before a crowd of over 35,000 (with more still trying to get in half an hour after the game had begun) to resume battle against high-riding Barnsley.

Enfield had a fantastic welcome as they stepped out on to the White Hart Lane pitch with 30,000 North London supporters all set to cheer them on to victory.

The Isthmian Leaguers soon showed that they intended to commit themselves to attack and after ten minutes all but scored when New pushed a well-directed header from Oliver over the bar. Oliver then went even nearer, hitting the bar with a powerful header as the Barnsley defenders got themselves into a tangle.

Just after half an hour Barnsley snatched a goal against the run of the play, AYLOTT floating in a cross out of the reach of Jacobs.

Half-time: Enfield 0   Barnsley 1

Enfield came out for the second half with another great roar echoing in their ears. The non-Leaguers quickly took the game into the Barnsley half and it was this commitment to attack that eventually lost them the game. In the 59th minute Barnsley broke out of the grip of the ceaseless Enfield attacks and former Scottish international GLAVIN scored number two. Back on the attack Enfield had two near misses when both Barrett and King hit the woodwork.

In the last minute of the game AYLOTT headed Barnsley's third.

Result: Enfield 0   Barnsley 3

Teams:
Enfield: Jacobs, Wade, Tone, Jennings, Barrett, Howell, Ashford, Bishop, Burton, Oliver, King.
Barnsley: New, Joyce, Chambers, Glavin, Banks, McCarthy, Evans, Parker, Aylott, Lester, Downes.
Referee: Mr. A. Gunn, Sussex.
Attendance: 35,244

Enfield (Contd) — CUP RUNS

1959/60
1st Round – *14th November*
Enfield 4   Headington Utd 3

2nd Round – *5th December*
Enfield 1   Bournemouth 5

1962/3
1st Round – *3rd November*
Cheltenham 3   Enfield 6

2nd Round – *24th November*
Peterborough 1   Enfield 0

1963/4
1st Round – *16th November*
Reading 2   Enfield 2

1st Round Replay – *19th November*
Enfield 2   Reading 4
(after extra time: score at 90 mins. 2–2)

1964/5
1st Round – *14th November*
Romford 0   Enfield 0

1st Round Replay – *17th November*
Enfield 0   Romford 0
(after extra time)

1st Round 2nd Replay – *23rd November*
Enfield 4   Romford 2
(at Highbury)

2nd Round – *5th December*
Enfield 4   Barnet 4

2nd Round replay – *8th December*
Barnet 3   Enfield 0

1966/7
1st Round – *26th November*
Enfield 6   Chesham Utd 0

2nd Round – *7th January*
Enfield 2   Watford 4

1967/8
1st Round – *18th December*
Swansea Town .. 2   Enfield 0

1969/70
1st Round – *15th November*
Brighton 2   Enfield 1

1970/71
1st Round – *21st November*
Enfield 0   Cambridge Utd .1

1971/2
1st Round – *20th November*
Enfield 2   Maidenhead 0

2nd Round – *11th December*
Peterborough 4   Enfield 0

1972/3
1st Round – *18th November*
Enfield 1   Bishops Stortfd. 1

1st Round Replay – *21st November*
Bishops Stortfd. 1   Enfield 0

1976/7
1st Round – *20th November*
Enfield 0   Harwich and P .0

1st Round Replay – *23rd November*
Harwich and P .0   Enfield 3

2nd Round – *11th December*
Enfield 0   Crystal Palace ...4
(at Selhurst Park)

1977/8
1st Round – *26th November*
Enfield 3   Wimbledon 0

2nd Round – *17th December*
Northampton 0   Enfield 2

3rd Round – *7th January*
Blyth Spartans .. 1   Enfield 0

1978/9
1st Round – *25th November*
Wealdstone 0   Enfield 5

2nd Round – *16th December*
Swindon 3   Enfield 0

1979/80
1st Round – *24th November*
Enfield 0   Yeovil 1

1980/81
1st Round – *22nd November*
Enfield 3   Wembley 0

2nd Round – *13th December*
Enfield 2   Hereford Utd 0

3rd Round – *3rd January*
Port Vale 1   Enfield 1

3rd Round Replay – *6th January*
Enfield 3   Port Vale 0

4th Round – *24th January*
Barnsley 1   Enfield 1

4th Round Replay – *28th January*
Enfield 0   Barnsley 3
   (at Tottenham Hotspur)

1981/2
1st Round – *21st November*
Enfield 2   Hastings Utd 0

2nd Round – *15th December*
Enfield 4   Wimbledon 1

3rd Round – *2nd January*
Enfield 2   Crystal Palace ... 3

GILLINGHAM

Founded: 1893

League: Formerly Southern, now Division Three

Ground: Priestfield Stadium

Colours: Blue shirts, white shorts

Gillingham, a Southern League club before being reintroduced to League football in 1950 — they lost their League status in 1938 — had a short but interesting post-war Cup run before rejoining the elite. Both in the 1946/7 and 1947/8 seasons they reached the Third Round and in the 1949/50 season got as far as the Second Round before being overtaken by famous non-League Cup fighters Yeovil. Undoubtedly Gillingham's swift return to League football can be partly attributed to the fame they achieved as non-Leaguers in their Third Round Cup battles against Swansea and Queen's Park Rangers.

Gillingham's First Round opponents in the 1946/7 season were fellow Southern Leaguers Gravesend who had to travel to Priestfield Road. A crowd of over 10,000 saw the Gills give Gravesend a football lesson to gain an easy 4–1 victory. Gillingham's opponents in the Second Round were Bristol City, Third Division South, at Ashton Gate where Arsenal scouts were among the 22,000 crowd. City found it difficult to adapt to the sticky conditions and the Gills had the better of a goalless first half. In the 52nd minute Gillingham suffered a reverse when City were awarded a penalty. Collins, the Gills goalkeeper, made a magnificent diving save from City leader Don Clark but the Bristol striker followed up to score the first goal of the match. This unexpected turn of events produced a fighting response from the 'giant-killers' who within two minutes were on level terms through a Wilson header. Towards the end Gillingham added to their Cup history when Russell got the match-winner to put the Gills in the Third Round for the first time since 1928.

Archie Clark's side, anxious to regain their League status, journeyed confidently to Swansea to meet the lowly-placed

Second Division team in the Third Round – but met an on-form Swans side and were defeated 4–1. Cup fever gripped Swansea for the visit of the Southern League part-timers and there was a 'gate' of over 30,000. In the Gills team were three Servicemen, three paper mill operatives, a welder, two engineers and two dockyard staff whereas Swansea's side opposing the non-League challenge included five internationals. It would have been six except that Ford, the Swans' international centre-forward, had departed for Villa Park on the eve of the tie. There was not a great deal of difference between the two sides up to half-time when the score stood at one all, a seven minute goal by Swansea's McCrory being neutralised by the Gills' inside-right Wilson. After the interval Swansea took command and ran up a 4–1 win through further goals by Payne, Squires and Jones. Gillingham: Collins; Marks, Poole; Boswell, Kingsnorth, Piper; Akers, Wilson, Russell, Briggs, Warsap.

After this splendid Cup campaign Gillingham began the 1947/8 season with great confidence and again fought their way to the Third Round after some electrifying games involving League opposition. Gills' first victim, in the First Round, was Leyton Orient at home at Priestfield Road. A 15,517 'gate' saw Akers score the only goal of the match in the 16th minute to give Gillingham a Second Round away game against Rochdale, Third Division North. The part-timers again showed their Cup fighting qualities by holding the League side to a 1–1 draw after extra time. The Gills led 1–0 at half-time through a 26th minute Russell header, Rochdale's second-half equaliser coming from Hugh O'Donnell who had won a Wembley medal with Preston North End in 1928.

Cup fever gripped the Medway town for the replay, over 17,000 spectators turning up at Priestfield Road – only heavy rain prevented the ground record (19,472 versus Cardiff City in a Cup replay in 1924) being beaten. Gillingham put on a brilliant display of Cup football and their superiority was never in doubt despite a Rochdale second-half revival. A first-half goal by Forrester followed by two more in the second-half by Wilson and Briggs saw the Southern Leaguers safely into the Third Round where they were matched against then Third Division South, Queen's Park Rangers at Priestfield Road. This game, which ended in a 1–1 draw after extra time and the subsequent replay which the Gills lost 3-1, are fully described in *Match Report*.

In the 1949/50 season the Gills took on fellow Southern Leaguers Hastings United away in the First Round and before a record 'gate' of over 9,000 notched up a clear-cut 3-1 win. In what was their last Cup game as non-Leaguers before re-election to the Football League Gillingham went to Yeovil for the Second Round to fight the 'battle of the slope' against their fellow Southern Leaguers. The Gills fared no better or worse than many teams before and since, going down 3-1, Gillingham's only goal coming from a penalty, scored by Russell.

MATCH REPORTS

THIRD ROUND F.A. CUP
10th January 1948
GILLINGHAM 1   QUEEN'S PARK RANGERS 1
(after extra time)

With a record crowd at Priestfield Stadium urging on the Southern Leaguers, the Gills began their hard task of trying to eliminate Third Division South leaders, Queen's Park Rangers, from the Cup.

Rangers had other ideas however and in the ninth minute of the game went ahead through centre-forward BOXSHALL who had been put in possession after a Gillingham defensive mix-up.

The Gills fought back with great spirit, on one occasion Russell delivering one of his 'specials' that Allen was fortunate to hold. Ten minutes after QPR had opened the scoring Gillingham were on terms. From an Akers centre Forrester sent a neat pass to RUSSELL who hammered the ball into the back of the net. On half time Gillingham nearly scored again when Russell, shooting on the turn, put his shot just wide of the post.

Half-time: Gillingham 1   Queen's Park Rangers 1

Both sides threw in everything in the second half. In the 87th minute Briggs went through for Gillingham after a Rangers' defensive blunder but his shot went straight at Allen who turned the ball round the post. When the game went into extra time left winger Forrester almost got the winner for Gillingham with a great volley that was held by Allen in masterly fashion.

Result: Gillingham 1   Queen's Park Rangers 1

Teams:
Gillingham: Burke, Dorling, Poole, Boswell, Kingsnorth, Piper, Akers, Wilson, Russell, Briggs, Forrester.
QPR: Allen, G. Powell, Jefferson, I. Powell, G. Smith, Daniels, McEwan, Ramscar, Boxshall, Hatton, Pattison.
Attendance: 23,002 (ground record)   Receipts: £2,095.

THIRD ROUND F.A. CUP REPLAY
17th January 1948
QUEEN'S PARK RANGERS 3   GILLINGHAM 1

Despite gloomy weather over 27,000 fans made their way to the Loftus Road ground for the second instalment of this Cup thriller. On the heavy pitch Gillingham sustained a number of casualties – Forrester and Russell, both lame and Briggs badly shaken. None the less the Southern Leaguers gave a first-class exhibition of never-say-die Cup football. Gillingham took the lead in the eighth minute when WARSAP got a splendid header past QPR goalkeeper Allen. The Loftus Road crowd had some anxious moments before HARTBURN netted the equaliser shortly before half time.

Half-time: Queen's Park Rangers 1   Gillingham 1

After the change of ends Rangers threw everything into attack. In the 63rd minute QPR took the lead through HATTON who scored an easy goal after a Gillingham defensive lapse. Gillingham's attack was at a standstill and the Gills defence came in for a hammering. With sweeping passes to the wings QPR split open the Gillingham defence and in the 71st minute McEWAN made the game safe for Rangers. It was an honourable defeat for the Gills who once again had proved themselves worthy opposition for a Third Division club.

Result: Queen's Park Rangers 3   Gillingham 1

Teams:
QPR: Allen, G. Powell, Jefferson, I. Powell, G. Smith, Daniels, McEwan, Ramscar, Boxshall, Hatton, Hartburn.
Gillingham: Burke, Dorling, Poole, Boswell, Kingsnorth, Piper, Wilson, Forrester, Russell, Briggs, Warsap.
Attendance: 27,550 (£2,322)

CUP RUNS

1946/7

1st Round – *30th November*
Gillingham 4   Gravesend 1

2nd Round – *14th December*
Bristol City 1   Gillingham 2

3rd Round – *11th January*
Swansea 4   Gillingham 1

1947/8

1st Round – *29th November*
Gillingham 1   Leyton Orient ...0

2nd Round – *13th December*
Rochdale 1   Gillingham 1
(after extra time)

2nd Round Replay – *20th December*
Gillingham 3   Rochdale 0

3rd Round – *10th January*
Gillingham 1   QPR 1
(after extra time. Score at 90 mins: 1-1)

3rd Round Replay – *17th January*
QPR 3   Gillingham 1

1949/50

1st Round – *26th November*
Hastings United 1   Gillingham 3

2nd Round – *10th December*
Yeovil 3   Gillingham 1

RE-ELECTED TO THE
FOOTBALL LEAGUE 1950/51

GRAVESEND AND NORTHFLEET

Founded: 1946/7

League: Southern (Premier Division)

Ground: Stonebridge Road

Colours: Red shirts, white shorts

Until their epic performances in the 1962/3 season when they reached the Fourth Round and took on and drew with mighty Sunderland Gravesend had made no real impact in the F.A. Cup. Their first appearance in the post-war First Round contests was in 1946/7 when they went out against then Southern League Gillingham. The 1962/3 heroics were to change all that as the non-Leaguers vanquished Exeter City and Carlisle before drawing 1-1 at home against Sunderland and then fighting a great rearguard action at Roker Park where they went down 5-2. Gravesend have been in contention in the Cup with League sides Torquay United (twice), Brentford, Bournemouth and Wimbledon (after a previous encounter when the Dons were in the Southern League).

When Gravesend went to Priestfield Road to meet Gillingham in the First Round of the 1946/7 competition they had an unbeaten away record in the Kent League in their first season of senior football but the Southern Leaguers lowered their colours to win convincingly 4-1.

Gravesend had to wait until the 1949/50 season before they were again in the First Round, entertaining Third Division South, Torquay at Stonebridge Road. It was a history-making occasion for Gravesend as it marked the first time that the club had opposed a League outfit. Although Gravesend scored first Torquay equalised and added two further goals in the closing stages to end the part-timers' dreams for that season.

Gravesend's great Cup run in 1962/3 began auspiciously on their own ground when they entertained Fourth Division Exeter City in the First Round. The League side, leading by two goals in the 50th minute looked as if they were heading for an easy victory. But the fortunes of the non-Leaguers changed dramatically as first they pulled a goal back and then with the Exeter goalkeeper off injured and Carter, who had scored both City's goals donning his jersey, the part-timers scored twice to gain an exciting 3-2 victory.

The non-Leaguers again had ground advantage in the Second Round (which they reached for the first time since the club was formed) when they beat Isthmian League amateurs Wycombe Wanderers 3-1 to join football's elite in the Third Round. Gravesend, the last surviving non-League club, had to travel 300 miles to meet Third Division Carlisle United against whom non-Leaguers have enjoyed precious little success. Although Carlisle mounted attack after attack in the early stages of the game ex-West Ham goalkeeper Peter Reader foiled every raid. Ten of the Gravesend players had had League experience and marshalling all their skills the Southern Leaguers began to attack and Sitford rocketed the ball into the Carlisle net from 20 yards. In the later stages of the game Carlisle got the ball in the net but the 'goal' was disallowed. In the closing minutes Carlisle stormed into the Gravesend penalty area to try to save the game but the Southern Leaguers pulled back every man and succeeded in keeping their goal intact. It was the shock win of the round and one of the greatest Cup victories ever recorded by a non-League side.

Gravesend became the toast of the soccer world when they drew 1-1 against mighty Second Division Sunderland at Stonebridge Road and then went out fighting 5-2 in the replay at Roker Park. Both these epic games are fully described in *Match Report*.

In the First Round of the 1963/4 contest Gravesend were drawn away from home against amateurs Tooting and Mitcham of the Isthmian League, themselves established 'giantkillers'. A tightly-contested game resulted in a win for Gravesend by a narrow 2-1 margin. Gravesend's reward was a Second Round tie against Third Division Brentford at Griffin Park, so often the graveyard of the non-Leaguers in the Cup. This was to be no exception although the Southern Leaguers made a great fight of it, the Bees winning by the only goal of the match scored 20 minutes from time due to a defensive error. The 'gate' was 11,850.

A veil is best drawn over Gravesend's next foray into the First Round. Drawn against Third Division Bournemouth in the 1964/5 season away at Dean Court the Southern

Leaguers were overwhelmed and took a 7–0 hammering.

Gravesend again got to the First Round in the following season when they drew an away game against fellow Southern Leaguers and noted Cup fighters Wimbledon. In an incident-packed game Wimbledon had the better of the exchanges, coasting to a 4–1 victory.

This signalled the end of Gravesend's Cup aspirations for a number of years and it was not until the 1978/9 season that they reappeared in the First Round, drawn against old Cup adversaries Wimbledon with the notable difference that the Dons' Cup exploits had put them into higher company. At the time of this encounter Wimbledon were Fourth Division leaders. They were not good enough however to get the better of Gravesend at the first try and the Southern Leaguers were unlucky when they had a first-half disallowed 'goal'. Smelt, the Gravesend goalkeeper, became the hero of the day when he brought off a spectacular one-handed save from a penalty only for the penalty to be retaken because of an infringement. Again Smelt saved and the game ended 0–0. At the replay at Plough Lane the Dons just managed to edge into the next round with a lone goal.

Gravesend were again in the First Round in the following season, 1979/80 when they attracted Fourth Division Torquay United to Stonebridge Road. As expected this was a hard match, Gravesend having a 'goal' disallowed in the sixth minute, Torquay netting the only goal of the game ten minutes later against the run of the play.

Gravesend were drawn at home against Isthmian Leaguers St. Albans in the 1980/1 First Round draw. After a goalless first-half the Saints went into a two goal lead with two penalties, the second four minutes from time and although the Southern Leaguers pulled back a goal immediately afterwards time had run out for a bid for the equaliser. Their 2–1 win put St. Albans in the Second Round for the first time in the club's history.

MATCH REPORTS

FOURTH ROUND F.A. CUP
12th February 1963
GRAVESEND & NORTHFLEET 1   SUNDERLAND 1

This was undoubtedly Gravesend's finest hour. A winter's night 12,032 spectators (a ground record), and Gravesend's team of part-timers facing the might of Sunderland – seven internationals and soccer talent worth £200,000 in transfer fees. This was the stage set for the slaying of giants – and it very nearly came off.

Gravesend were the last of the little clubs left in the Cup and their Southern League record was unenviable – second from the bottom of the table. But this night they fought like tigers and with utter disregard for Sunderland's skill and elite position in the soccer world.

When the game started it looked very much as if Sunderland would run up a cricket score. It was all Sunderland as their power-packed forward line ran rings round the Gravesend defence. In the first five minutes Sunderland had forced three corners. Only six minutes had elapsed before Eire international Ambrose Fogarty tested Gravesend's 'keeper, Peter Reader, one of the heroes of the night, with one of his 'specials'. Then his save from a Crossan 'thunderbolt' at point-blank range was of international class, repeated a few seconds later when he pulled off a magnificent save from a Hurley header. In the 12th minute, however, Fleet's defence let in Sunderland's Scottish international, George MULHALL, whose first time shot put Sunderland in the lead. The home side's first real threat came when Johnny Sanchez, playing his farewell game before leaving for Australia, connected with a centre by Easton and produced a brilliant save from Sunderland goalkeeper Montgomery.

Half-time: Gravesend & Northfleet 0   Sunderland 1

After the interval the pattern was much as before, Sunderland combining well on the muddy ground and Gravesend's defenders desperately trying to prevent the Wearsiders increasing their score. Then came the unbelievable. Outside left Easton raced down the wing, shot at Montgomery who failed to hold the ball and let it run loose. Centre forward Brian SKINGLEY pounced and in the 72nd minute hammered it in to score an historic goal for the Fleet. Stonebridge Road erupted as Skingley was mobbed by his team mates.

Sensing a possible victory Gravesend attacked vigorously and Stonebridge Road could easily have become a Sunderland graveyard as Yeovil's sloping ground did in 1949 when the Southern

Leaguers beat the Wearsiders. There was no further score however and Gravesend had to be content with their history-making draw.

Result: Gravesend & Northfleet 1   Sunderland 1

Teams:
Gravesend: Reader, McNicol, McDonald, Walley, Newcombe, Sanchez, Williams, Cameron, Skingley, Sitford, Easton.
Sunderland: Montgomery, Nelson, Ashurst, Harvey, Hurley, McNab, Herd, Fogarty, Sharkey, Crossan, Mulhall.
Referee: Mr. L. W. Faulkner, (Liverpool).
Attendance: 12,032 (receipts: £2,345)

FOURTH ROUND F.A. CUP
18th February 1963
SUNDERLAND 5   GRAVESEND & NORTHFLEET 2

Gravesend's reward for their fine Cup run – a replay at Roker Park before a 29,659 'gate'. With centre forward Skingley injured and Sanchez having left for Australia, Gravesend had to face the handicap of four positional changes. Sunderland fielded an unchanged side. From the kick-off Sunderland soon had the Southern Leaguers in difficulties, shots from Fogarty and Sharkey going close.

With the Gravesend harassed defence keeping an anxious eye on Hurley and the other Sunderland forwards poised in the penalty area, FINCH in the 9th minute, trying to effect a clearance, put into his own goal. CROSSAN added number two five minutes later (his first goal since leaving Belgian Club Standard Liege) with the Gravesend defence spreadeagled. After 18 minutes FOGARTY, collected a loose ball just outside the penalty area to score number three. Almost on half time CROSSAN increased the lead to 4–0. Gravesend could only manage sporadic attacks.

Half-time: Sunderland 4   Gravesend & Northfleet 0

After the interval Sunderland were content to relax and thus enabled the Southern Leaguers to go over to the attack, Easton crashed a shot against the bar and after 67 minutes skipper Bob McNICOL scored with a well taken header. Eight minutes later, after Cameron had found a gap in the Sunderland defence, SITFORD scored a second. But in the closing minutes SHARKEY scored a fifth for Sunderland. At the final whistle the Roker Park crowd cheered gallant Gravesend off the park.

Result: Sunderland 5   Gravesend & Northfleet 2

Teams:
Sunderland: Montgomery, Nelson, Ashurst, Harvey, Hurley, McNab, Herd, Fogarty, Sharkey, Crossan, Mulhall,
Gravesend: Reader, McNicol, McDonald, Walley, Newcombe, Finch, Golding, Cameron, Williams, Sitford, Easton.
Referee: Mr. L. W. Faulkner (Liverpool)
Attendance: 29,659 (receipts: £5,620)

CUP RUNS

1946/7
1st Round – *30th November*
Gillingham 4   Gravesend 1

1949/50
1st Round – *26th November*
Gravesend 1   Torquay 3

1962/3
1st Round – *3rd November*
Gravesend 3   Exeter 2

2nd Round – *24th November*
Gravesend 3   Wycombe W. 1

3rd Round – *29th January*
Carlisle 0   Gravesend 1

4th Round – *12th February*
Gravesend 1   Sunderland 1

4th Round Replay – *18th February*
Sunderland 5   Gravesend 2

1963/4
1st Round – *16th November*
Tooting & M. ... 1   Gravesend 2

2nd Round – *7th December*
Brentford 1   Gravesend 0

1964/5
1st Round – *14th November*
Bournemouth 7   Gravesend 0

1965/6
1st Round – *13th November*
Wimbledon 4   Gravesend 1

1978/9
1st Round – *25th November*
Gravesend 0   Wimbledon 0

1st Round Replay – *28th November*
Wimbledon 1   Gravesend 0

1979/80
1st Round – *24th November*
Gravesend 0   Torquay Utd. 1

1980/1
1st Round   *22nd November*
Gravesend 1   St. Albans 2

HARLOW TOWN

Founded: 1879

League: Isthmian, Premier Division

Ground: Sportcentre

Colours: Red shirts, white shorts

In all their 100 years of history Harlow Town had not appeared in the First Round of the F.A. Cup until their centenary year in 1979 when they had a sensational run which will be talked about in the soccer world as long as football exists. Not only did they appear in the First Round for the first time when they beat fellow Isthmian Leaguers Leytonstone by a narrow 2-1 margin but they went on to Cup glory by putting out Third Division Southend United 1-0 at the Sportcentre after having held the League side to a 1-1 draw on their own ground. The amateurs then accomplished the near impossible in the Third Round by first of all holding Second Division Leicester City to a 1-1 draw at Filbert Street. Then came the night of all nights when at the Sportcentre, this minnow of the football world achieved lasting fame when they disposed of their distinguished opponents 1-0 to go on to further glory in the Fourth Round. This was at Vicarage Road, Watford, when they gave their Second Division opponents a nasty shock, fighting back from 4-1 down to lose by the narrowest of margins 4-3 to make it the most exciting game of the round and one that will always be remembered when League versus non-League Cup games are recounted.

To begin their magical Cup run after fighting their way through the qualifying rounds Harlow drew a First Round tie against Isthmian League neighbours Leytonstone and before a crowd of 1,800 at the Sportcentre won a hard game by a 2–1 margin. It earned the Owls a Second Round tie away from home against Third Division Southend United.

Riding on the crest of a wave Harlow took hundreds of supporters to Southend. Already having made history by appearing in the First Round for the first time Harlow had reached another milestone – their first encounter ever with a League club. It was expected to be a hard game since

Southend are no mean performers in Cup games and already that season had removed First Division Bolton Wanderers from the League Cup.

Harlow returned from Roots Hall with an almost unbelievable result – a 1-1 draw to force Southend to a replay at the Sportcentre. Southend must have imagined that they had the game in their pocket when they went ahead in the 15th minute and at half-time were retaining their 1-0 lead. But for Harlow the all-important goal came in the 51st minute when the Owls equalised with a goal by Neil Prosser who was playing his first game for two months.

Celebrating the first visit of a League club to the Sportcentre it became a night for champagne when at the end of an exciting 90 minutes Harlow had defeated Southend by a narrow 1-0 margin. As in the previous game Southend had the better of the early exchanges but their finishing was poor. The part-timers' central defenders held their League opponents in a fairly tight grip and it was no surprise when half-time arrived with a blank scoresheet. Then in the 61st minute Mickey Mann put the finishing touch to a glory night when he shot the Owls into a 1-0 lead. It was a great night for the part-timers who earned themselves a plum away tie in the Third Round against Second Division Leicester City. It was a great achievement for Owls' manager Ian Wolstenholme, the former Enfield and England amateur goalkeeper in his third season with the Essex club.

Harlow's deeds in the Third Round, when they drew and then subsequently defeated Leicester City and were narrowly defeated 4-3 by Watford in the Fourth Round, were Cup magic and these great games are fully recorded as *Match Reports*.

In the 1980/81 First Round Harlow had home advantage when they were drawn against highly-placed Third Division Charlton Athletic. Alas no Cup glory was to come Harlow's way. Although the Owls put in some lively attacks, particularly in the first half, it was Athletic who opened the scoring on the half hour and Harlow's joy ten minutes later when they thought they had equalised turned to bitter disappointment when the 'goal' was disallowed. Charlton followed up with a further goal in first half injury time and held their 2-0 lead until the final whistle. Attendance – over 6,000.

Town again found themselves in the First Round in the 1981/2 season but were unable to repeat the fabulous success of 1979/80. Drawn at home against non-League opposition, Alliance Premier Leaguers Barnet, Harlow were unable to take advantage of their chances and the game finished a goalless draw. In the replay at Underhill the Alliance Premier Leaguers had the edge and scored the only goal of the match in the sixth minute. Harlow had slightly the better of the second half.

MATCH REPORTS
THIRD ROUND F.A. CUP
5th January 1980
LEICESTER CITY 1   HARLOW TOWN 1

This was the fairytale draw – with a fairytale ending – in Harlow's centenary year when they journeyed to Filbert Street to take on Second Division Leicester City before a crowd of over 21,000.

In the first half it was all Leicester, keeping up a constant bombardment of the Isthmian Leaguers goal but to no effect. The part-timers were fortunate in having captain Tony Gough as well as central defender Micky Mann in superb form. The Leicester bombardment went on until the 26th minute of the game when HENDERSON capitalized on one of Kitson's few errors and put the League side in the lead.

Half-time: Leicester City 1   Harlow Town 0

In the second half Harlow appeared to improve, the moves from midfield being more studied and the tackling less frantic. It was just into injury time when the part-timers set the game alight. After having defied everything that the professionals could throw at them for most of the 90 minutes history was suddenly made. Totally unexpectedly, with the crowd waiting for the final whistle to blow, 22-year-old Neil PROSSER who was recovering from a cartilage operation, was put clear by Peter Twigg and moving out of the way of defender May calmly pushed the ball past Leicester City goalkeeper Wallington.

Result: Leicester City 1   Harlow Town 1

Teams:
Leicester City: Wallington, Williams, Byrne, Goodwin, May, O'Neill, Byrne, Henderson, Young, Kelly, Smith.
Harlow Town: Kitson, Wickenden, Flack, Gough, Clarke, Adnams, Mackenzie, Mann, Prosser, Twigg, Griffiths. (Sub: Austin).
Referee: Mr. A. Robinson, (Waterlooville).
Attendance: 21,302

THIRD ROUND REPLAY F.A. CUP
8th January 1980
HARLOW TOWN 1   LEICESTER CITY 0

This is the game that will be remembered in Harlow for all time as the Cup heroes of the Isthmian Legue fought on equal terms with their Second Division opponents and at the end of the night saw them off to claim their second League scalp. There were the best part of 10,000 fans crammed in Harlow's tiny Sportcentre to watch the well-organised Isthmian Leaguers give City a night that they will wish to forget. It was in the 43rd minute of the game that 25-

year-old John MACKENZIE, a company accountant, scored his never-to-be-forgotten goal, taking another Micky Mann free kick into the penalty area and smashing it into the Leicester goal through a crowd of players past a stranded Wallington. The Sportcentre erupted as the Harlow fans realised that they were watching what was to be the first major Cup giant-killing act of the season.

Half-time: Harlow Town 1   Leicester City 0

In the second half Harlow continued to contain the professionals and the only tense moment for Paul Kitson was in the 67th minute when he was hard pressed to save from Alan Young. As the game wore on Harlow's defence became even more confident and the final whistle blew amidst amazing scenes as the crowd erupted.

Result: Harlow Town 1   Leicester City 0

Teams:
Harlow Town: Kitson, Wickenden, Flack, Gough, Clarke, Adnams, Mackenzie, Mann, Prosser, Twigg, Austin.
Leicester City: Wallington, Williams, Rofe, Goodwin, May, O'Neill, Lineker, Henderson, Young, Kelly, Smith.
Referee: Mr. A. Robinson, (Waterlooville).
Attendance: 9,723

FOURTH ROUND F.A. CUP
26th January 1980
WATFORD 4   HARLOW TOWN 3

This Fourth Round Cup tie at Vicarage Road against Second Division Watford will probably be the most remembered game in the 1979/80 season other than the Cup final itself. For here in front of a Watford crowd swollen from its normal 15,000 or 16,000 to nearly 25,000 saw Ian Wostenholme's Owls put up an incredible performance to go out of the Cup by a sensational 4-3 margin after being 4-1 down. It was a brave performance, highly appropriate to the celebrations going on around Harlow's centenary year. As one newspaper said at the time "no wonder the F.A. Cup will never lose its glamour and romanticism".

In the early stages of the game it was end-to-end football and difficult to decide which was the League side and which were the part-timers. Watford had several chances which they squandered and it was no surprise when the Isthmian Leaguers went into the lead in the 38th minute. It was after Harlow's first corner of the game which Mann pushed towards the far post where PROSSER was on hand to flick the ball past the stranded Watford goalkeeper Steele. Despite Watford's protests both the referee and the linesmen ruled that the ball had entered the net. Ten thousand Harlow fans gathered at the Rookery end erupted as they foresaw another sensational Cup upset in prospect. Although up to that stage Watford had looked a very ordinary side they reacted strongly, Simms twice heading over the bar and Poskett having a try but still could not make any impression on the well-drilled Harlow defence.

Half-time: Watford 0   Harlow Town 1

Watford manager Graham Taylor's half time talk had an immediate effect for in the 48th minute POSKETT scored the equaliser, his first goal since being signed from Brighton. Four minutes later following three corners within a minute with the Harlow defence at sixes and sevens Martin PATCHING dived on to a corner by Jenkins and headed past Kitson to make the score 2-1. Three minutes later with Harlow still reeling under the Watford pressure PATCHING scored again after a goalmouth scramble.

Nothing seemed to go right for the part-timers at this stage of the game and in the 63rd minute Watford made the score 4-1 when Ian BOLTON smashed in a free kick from 25 yards.

Then came Harlow's finest hour as they staged a miraculous comeback in the 65th minute. Still going for the Watford goal Clarke headed on to John MACKENZIE, a piratical looking figure with his head swathed in bandages as a result of an earlier injury, who drove in from 12 yards to make the score 4-2.

MACKENZIE had refused to go off and he got a further reward in the 84th minute when he latched on to a cross by Twigg and from 30 yards sent in a 'thunderbolt' which Steele never saw to make the score 4-3.

In the final minutes of the game there were dramatic scenes as the part-timers raced for the Watford goal with the Harlow fans willing them on to score the equaliser. But it was not to be and the final whistle blew with the non-Leaguers out of the Cup after their epic battle.

As the Harlow players went over to the Rookery end to salute their fans the Watford side, headed by their manager Graham Taylor lined up to salute the part-timers as they left the field weary but proud of their performance.

Result: Watford 4   Harlow Town 3

Teams:
Watford: Steele, Henderson, Harrison, Patching, Sims, Bolton, Blisset, Poskett, Jenkins, Train, Rostron.
Harlow Town: Kitson, Wickenden, Flack, Gough, Clarke, Adnams, Mann, Mackenzie, Twigg, Prosser, Griffiths.
Referee: Mr. N. Midgley, (Salford).
Attendance: 24,586

Harlow Town (Contd)

CUP RUNS

1979/80

1st Round - *24th November*
Harlow Town ...2   Leytonstone 1

2nd Round - *15th December*
Southend Utd ...1   Harlow Town ...1

2nd Round Replay - *18th December*
Harlow Town ...1   Southend Utd ...0

3rd Round - *5th January*
Leicester City 1   Harlow Town ...1

3rd Round Replay - *8th January*
Harlow Town ...1   Leicester City 0

4th Round - *26th January*
Watford Town ..4   Harlow Town ...3

1980/81

1st Round - *22nd November*
Harlow Town ...0   Charlton Ath 2

1981/2

1st Round - *21st November*
Harlow Town ...0   Barnet 0

1st Round Replay - *24th November*
Barnet 1   Harlow Town ...0

HASTINGS UNITED

Founded: 1948

League: Southern (Premier Division)

Ground: Pilot Field

Colours: All white shirts and shorts with claret and blue stripe

Although Hastings have not been consistent performers in the post-war First Round contests they have several outstanding Cup runs to their credit. The first of two great seasons was in 1953/4 when they advanced as far as the Third Round for the first time in the club's history. Having disposed of Swindon, Third Division South, in the Second Round by a handsome 4–1 margin they received Third Division South leaders Norwich City at Pilot Field and before a record crowd of over 12,000 held the League side to a 3-3 draw after an exciting contest. Although Hastings lost 3-0 in the replay at Carrow Road they had done enough to make their name known in the higher echelons of the football world. The following season, 1954/5, was another record-making year for United when, after beating two non-League clubs on the way, they again arrived in the Third Round to be drawn away at Hillsborough against First Division Sheffield Wednesday. A crowd of nearly 26,000 saw the non-Leaguers narrowly beaten 2-1. Other League opposition that Hastings have encountered in their Cup games have included Northampton (twice), Ipswich and Notts County.

For their first post-war First Round appearance Hastings had the luck to draw a home game at Pilot Field against fellow Southern Leaguers Gillingham and although the match drew a record crowd of 9,150 United were unable to hold the Gills who won 3–1.

Hastings' record-breaking 1953/4 season began modestly enough with a home game against fellow Southern Leaguers Guildford City, United winning by a lone goal to put them in the Second Round for the first time in their history.

Hastings had home advantage when they drew Third Division South, Swindon Town in the Second Round, the attendance of 9,917 being a ground record. Swindon, hit by injuries, had to field a reshuffled team and were outplayed from the start. Within two minutes Hastings were one up as a result of an 'own goal', Huckstepp scored another in the 13th minute and five minutes later the ground erupted when Asher made it 3-0. Over half an hour went by before the Hastings goalkeeper got a touch of the ball. Although Swindon scored a consolation goal early in the second half Hillman crashed in a power drive in the 70th minute to give the Southern Leaguers a sensational 4-1 victory. It was the first time since the war that Swindon had been beaten by a non-League side.

Hastings: Ball; Crapper, Thompson; Peacock, Griffiths, Barr; Hillman, Huckstepp, Asher, Parks, Girling.

For their history-making Third Round tie Hastings again had the benefit of a home game, set to entertain Norwich City, Third Division South leaders, at Pilot Field. Hastings again played with the determination that had characterised the game against Swindon and within four minutes were one up when Parks hooked the ball past the Norwich goalkeeper. Half way through the first half Brennan put Norwich level and as the game began to swing in the Canaries' favour Hansell put the League side into a 2-1 half-time lead. United came out for the second half full of fight, and Parks headed in the equaliser. When it seemed that the Norwich defence was completely overwhelmed and against the run of the play Gavin again put the League side in the lead. But the 'giantkillers', who had completely dominated the second half were not finished and justice was done when Girling grabbed the equaliser to make the final score 3-3. The ground record at Pilot Field was again broken, 12,527 going through the turnstiles. The replay at Carrow Road, watched by a crowd of 17,027, was this time dominated by a top-form Norwich and on the rare occasions when Hastings threatened the Canaries quickly fell back and put up a brickwall defence. Norwich gained a clear-cut 3-0 victory.

In the following season, 1954/5, Hastings had another fine Cup run culminating in a Third Round encounter with then First Division Sheffield Wednesday at Hillsborough. United reached the heights following two wins against non-League opposition in the First and Second Rounds. Firstly, an away game against then Corinthian League side Hounslow gave Hastings a comfortable 4-2 win. In the

Second Round Hastings were drawn away against Selby Town, Yorkshire League champions. It was the first time that a Yorkshire League side had appeared in the Second Round. United clung to a 40th minute lead until three minutes before the end when they scored again to make the game safe. This gave them a memorable Third Round tie against First Division Sheffield Wednesday which they lost by a narrow 2-1 margin. The game is fully reported in *Match Report*.

Hastings were again in the First Round draw in the 1955/6 season when they entertained non-League Southall at the Pilot Field and overran the amateurs 6-1. United had the tables turned on them in the Second Round when, drawn away from home against pace-setters Third Division South Northampton Town, they went down 4-1. A crowd of 15,510 watched the game.

Again in the First Round in the following season United drew an attractive away game against high-riding Third Division South Ipswich Town. A 'gate' of 13,486 saw Ipswich give Hastings a hammering to the tune of 4-0.

United had to wait until the 1959/60 season before their next appearance in the First Round when they were drawn at home against Fourth Division Notts County, the oldest club in the Football League. Although the Southern Leaguers held the League side to a goalless first half and scored first in the 55th minute County dominated most of the second half scoring twice to put Hastings out of the Cup for another season.

Undaunted United again fought their way through the qualifying rounds in the following season 1960/1 to find themselves in the First Round drawn away against old League adversaries Fourth Division Northampton. This time, opposed by an on-form United who included in their side ex-Spurs striker Len Duquemin, the Cobblers found their task none too easy and were glad to settle for a narrow 2-1 victory.

Hastings made a welcome reappearance in the First Round in the 1981/2 season after their long absence, drawn away against formidable Alliance Premier League Cup fighters Enfield. There was little difference between the two sides in the first-half and Enfield were fortunate to go into a 1-0 lead in the 34th minute. Despite Hastings' efforts to equalise in a rousing second-half Enfield succeeded in snatching a 'soft' goal in the 66th minute to make the score 2-0.

MATCH REPORT
THIRD ROUND F.A. CUP
8th January 1955
SHEFFIELD WEDNESDAY 2   HASTINGS UNITED 1

This was one of the greatest days in the Cup history of the 'giant-killers' from the Southern League – matched against redoubtable First Division Sheffield Wednesday at the famous Hillsborough stadium and watched by a crowd of nearly 26,000. Wednesday had a long injury list and as a consequence were languishing at the foot of Division One when the tie was played. Jack Sewell and Alan Finney were among the Wednesday stars on the injured list.

United began well, showing no trace of nerves and soon settling down to playing some constructive football. The reshuffled Wednesday side could not get going and passes went astray. Sheffield's defence looked suspect against the bustling United attack in which Alan Burgess was prominent; twice the Hastings striker went close. United often looked extremely dangerous, an incredible situation as the Southern Leaguers looked as if they might overwhelm their distinguished First Division opponents.

In the 25th minute United took a well-deserved lead. The Hastings captain and centre-half, Bill Griffiths, intercepted a Wednesday attack, took the ball down the field and gave a deft pass to Robinson. The Hastings winger slipped the ball to Parks, storming into the area and ASHER completed the move with a magnificent goal. It was a moment to be savoured as the non-Leaguers went into the lead. The sporting Sheffield crowd joined in the cheers and suddenly Wednesday realised that they had a game on their hands.

Half-time: Sheffield Wednesday 0   Hasting United 1

In the second half Wednesday threw everything into attack and in the 15th minute after the interval centre-forward SHAW equalised.

In the final three minutes Wednesday stormed into the Hastings half and scored the match-winner with a hotly disputed goal. In this final despairing attack the Wednesday strikers hammered shot after shot into the Hastings penalty area and during the onslaught the referee judged that GREENSMITH had got the ball over the line.

Result: Sheffield Wednesday 2   Hastings United 1

Teams:
Sheffield Wednesday: McIntosh, Conwell, Curtis, Gannon, McEvoy, Turley, Marriott, Quixall, Shaw, McAnearney, Greensmith.
Hastings United: Ball, Crapper, Chadwick, Peacock, Griffiths, Girling, Hillman, Burgess, Asher, Parks, Robinson.
Referee: Mr. T. L. Wood.
Attendance: 25,965

CUP RUNS

1949/50

1st Round *26th November*
Hastings 1   Gillingham 3

1953/4

1st Round *21st November*
Hastings 1   Guildford 0

2nd Round *12th December*
Hastings 4   Swindon 1

3rd Round *9th January*
Hastings 3   Norwich 3

3rd Round Replay *13th January*
Norwich 3   Hastings 0

1954/5

1st Round *20th November*
Hounslow 2   Hastings 4

2nd Round *11th December*
Selby 0   Hastings 2

3rd Round *8th January*
Sheffield Wed ... 2   Hastings 1

1955/6

1st Round *19th November*
Hastings 6   Southall 1

2nd Round *10th December*
Northampton 4   Hastings 1

1956/7

1st Round *17th November*
Ipswich 4   Hastings 0

1959/60

1st Round *14th November*
Hastings 1   Notts County 2

1960/1

1st Round *5th November*
Northampton 2   Hastings 1

1981/2

1st Round *21st November*
Enfield 2   Hastings 0

HENDON

Founded: 1908

League: Isthmian

Ground: Claremont Road

Colours: Green shirts; white shorts

Hendon have been prominent in post-war F.A. Cup battles ever since the 1952/3 season when they held Northampton Town, Third Division South to a 0-0 draw at Claremont Road and then went out 2-0 in the replay. Their most glorious chapter was the 1973/4 season when they reached the Third Round via the scalps of two non-Leaguers in the earlier rounds and then made history at St. James's Park where they held mighty First Division Newcastle United to a 1-1 draw before a crowd of over 31,000. Although Hendon lost the replay, played at Vicarage Road, Watford, by 4-0 the name of this 'giant-killer' is now write large in the annals of the F.A. Cup. On three other post-war occasions Hendon have fought their way to the Second Round only to fail at that stage at the hands of Exeter City, non-League Brentwood and Swindon Town. Other League clubs who have been paired with Hendon in Cup battles include Port Vale, Reading (twice), Aldershot, Plymouth and Watford.

When Hendon began their post-war Cup runs in the 1952/3 season they were in the Athenian League and their performance in holding high-scoring Northampton to a goalless draw at Claremont Road was a fine achievement. In the replay at the County Ground a solid Hendon defence denied the Cobblers in the first-half although the League side had a 'goal' disallowed. The game appeared to be heading for extra time when Northampton scored twice five minutes before the end.

Hendon were next in the First Round in the 1955/6 season when they were drawn away from home against semi-professionals Halesowen of the Birmingham and District League. On Halesowen's tilted pitch Hendon took the lead in the 24th minute, Halesowen equalised three minutes before half-time and the amateurs regained the lead a minute later to establish a 2-1 half-time lead. Although shortly after the restart Halesowen were on terms the Athenian Leaguers added two more goals to win 4-2 and to make history by reaching the Second Round for the first time. Drawn away from home to Exeter City at St. James's Park Hendon were heavily defeated 6-2 by their League opponents.

In the 1960/1 season, Hendon, Amateur Cup winners, again reached the First Round to be faced at Claremont Road by Southern League Oxford United, top of the Premier Division with an unbeaten League record. Although Oxford took a five minute lead the exchanges were fairly even and the final scoreline 2-2 was a fair reflection of the game, United having equalised in the closing stages. In the replay at the Manor Ground before a record-breaking crowd of 10,600 two shock goals in the first-half, one an 'own goal', put Oxford into a 2-0 lead. Defensive errors after the restart gave Oxford another goal although before the end the amateurs scored twice to make the final tally 3-2.

Now in the Isthmian League Hendon drew a First Round tie in the 1964/5 season against Third Division Port Vale away from home at Vale Park. Vale were one up at half-time and increased their lead shortly after the resumption. Although Hendon pulled back a goal in the closing stages they were unable to force a replay.

Again in the First Round in the following season, 1965/6, Hendon found themselves matched against fellow non-Leaguers Grantham, Midland League, away from home. The Gingerbreads, who had built up a 3-0 half-time lead, went futher ahead after the restart whilst all that Hendon could manage was a consolation goal three minutes from the end.

Hendon managed to get another crack at a League side in the 1966/7 season when they entertained Third Division Reading at Claremont Road. Reading were 3-0 in the lead at half-time. Hendon scored a consolation goal in the 49th minute to make the final score 3-1.

Hendon missed two seasons before they were again in the First Round, in 1969/70, when they had a home game against fellow non-Leaguers Carshalton Athletic of the Athenian League. A Hendon goal blitz in the first 12 minutes produced three goals. Hendon added two further goals to their scoreline before half-time with Carshalton taking advantage of a poor back pass to get on the scoresheet to make the half-time total 5-1. Injuries to Hendon in the second half reduced their impetus and enabled the Athenians to score two more and to make the final tally a respectable 5-3.

The amateurs drew semi-professionals Brentwood Town, Premier Division, Southern League, for their Second Round clash and again had home advantage. Although Hendon had the best of the first-half they failed to score and Brentwood took over after the interval. In a three-minute inspired spell they scored twice to put the amateurs out of the Cup.

Again fighting their way to the First Round in the following season, 1970/1, Hendon were opposed by Fourth Division Aldershot, the amateurs again having the luck to come out of the hat first. Hendon kept the League side at bay until just before half-time when Aldershot went 1-0 in the lead. The pattern was the same in the second half, Hendon attacking strongly for a time but the League side generally in command and scoring again in injury time.

After missing a season Hendon were back on First Round duty in 1972/3 when they had an interesting away tie against Third Division Plymouth Argyle at Home Park. Hendon put up a gallant performance, a stout-hearted defence keeping out the Argyle strikers, almost scoring themselves just before half-time which was reached with the scoresheet blank. In the second-half Hendon's defenders, including goalkeeper Swannell, acquitted themselves magnificently and it was bad luck for the amateurs when Plymouth scored a soft goal two minutes from the end to deny the Isthmian Leaguers the chance of a replay.

The next season, 1973/4, saw Hendon covering themselves with glory when they went through to the Third Round to take on mighty Newcastle United. But before taking their place among the elite Hendon had more down to earth opposition to take care of in the First Round – fellow Isthmian Leaguers Leytonstone at Claremont Road. It was a fairly easy task for Hendon who led 1-0 at half time and then scored two more after the restart. For their Second Round tie Hendon had to travel to Wales to meet Southern Leaguers Merthyr Tydfil at Penydarren Park where the great Welsh international John Charles was in action. But the Welshmen were no match for a lively Hendon side who, as in the previous round, were one up at the break and scored two more in the second-half to complete a fine 3–0 away win. This gave Hendon entry into the Third Round for the first time in the club's history and provided them with a glamour tie against First Division Newcastle United at St. James's Park. The sensational 1–1 draw against United and the subsequent replay on Watford's ground are fully recorded in *Match Report*.

Hendon pulled off one of the First Round Cup shocks of the season when they received Fourth Division Reading in 1975/6. The only goal of the match came in the 40th minute through Alan Phillips and despite all-out Reading pressure after the interval the Hendon defenders held firm and survived until the final whistle. This was a particularly fine achievement considering Reading's reputation for vanquishing non-League sides in the Cup. Hendon: Dalrymple; J. Field, Hand, Yerby, Philips, Haider, A. Field, Metchick, Childs, Baker, Jefferies. Sub. Coombs.

The Second Round brought another home game – against lowly-placed Third Division Swindon. The League side were unable to stamp their authority on the game and half-time arrived with the scoresheet blank. In the end Swindon scraped through with a late penalty.

The next season was a blank so far as a First Round appearance was concerned but in 1977/8 Hendon popped up again in the First Round to take on Fourth Division leaders Watford at Vicarage Road. In the Hendon side were Rod Haider, Deadman and Butterfield who between them had won no fewer than 124 England international amateur caps. The 12,000 crowd saw Hendon put up a spirited fight but were unable to prevent Watford taking a 31st minute lead. Watford clinched the issue late in the game to win 2–0.

In the First Round in 1981/2 and making their first appearance at that stage for four seasons Hendon drew a home game against fellow Isthmian Leaguers and experienced Cup fighters Wycombe Wanderers. In a stern battle Wycombe took a 21st minute lead and had the better of the first half. After the interval it was a different story, Hendon turning on the heat and equalising in the 66th minute to force a replay. Injury-hit Hendon had to field a rearranged side for the replay against an on-form Wycombe. Hendon's hard-working defence kept out the opposition until after the interval, just failing to score themselves almost on half-time. Two Wycombe second half goals clinched the issue.

MATCH REPORTS
THIRD ROUND F.A. CUP
5th January 1974
NEWCASTLE UNITED 1   HENDON 1

This was the finest hour in the history of the Isthmian League champions battling it out with the mighty First Division side at St. James's Park before a crowd of nearly 32,000. Newcastle have a poor home record against non-League sides in the Cup and this encounter again highlighted United's traditional weakness against opposition from the lower echelons.

Newcastle started as if they meant to annihilate the amateurs, sweeping dangerously into the Hendon penalty area without being able to get the ball in the net. Malcolm Macdonald was prominent in these early raids and in the 11th minute Craig had a bad miss when he crashed the ball against the woodwork from eight yards out.

As Hendon began to recover from their early nerves and as Newcastle's fire waned the amateurs posed problems for the First Division side. On the half hour Hendon had settled down and were beginning to test United, Ian McFaul, Newcastle's Northern Ireland goalkeeper doing well to push a hard shot from Fry over the bar in the 38th minute.

But it was Newcastle who took the lead three minutes before the interval to ease their fans' worries. Macdonald made one of his celebrated long throws from the touchline to place the ball for central defender Pat HOWARD to race through to head the ball into the net out of the reach of Hendon's goalkeeper John Swannell.

Half-time: Newcastle United 1   Hendon 0

The second half belonged to the non-Leaguers who began to probe Newcastle's defences in search of the equaliser. In the 62nd minute they almost got it, a superb header from Derek Baker producing a fine reflex save from McFaul. The equaliser was only delayed, however, for six minutes later Hendon scored the goal that put their name in the history books. From a free kick from the half-way line the ball went to Baker, standing just inside the Newcastle penalty area, who nodded it to the Hendon captain Rod HAIDER who slammed the ball into the Magpies' net past McFaul. It was a superb goal, the result of a well-performed set piece, and put the Hendon contingent in fine fettle.

As Newcastle fought back to prevent a replay Hendon's back four putting up a great rearguard fight, culminating in a heart-stopping moment in the closing seconds when Deadman cleared off the line from McDermott. Hendon's achievement in holding mighty Newcastle, six times winners of the Cup, on their own ground at St. James's Park was rightly regarded as the shock result of the day and a moment that will be savoured for ever by Hendon supporters.

Result: Newcastle United 1   Hendon 1

Teams:
Newcastle: McFaul, Craig, Kennedy, McDermott, Howard, Clark, Gibb, Smith, Macdonald, Tudor, Hibbitt.
Hendon: Swannell, Jennings, Hand, Deadman, Phillips, Haider, Baker, D. Childs, Baker, J. Somers, Fry.
Referee: Mr. P. Baldwin, (Redcar).
Attendance: 31,606

THIRD ROUND F.A. CUP REPLAY
9th January 1974
HENDON 0   NEWCASTLE UNITED 4
(at Watford)

To accommodate the 15,000 crowd, twice as many as could have squeezed into Hendon's tiny ground, the Isthmian Leaguers elected to hold the replay at Watford's Vicarage Road ground. When they kicked off the amateurs had the satisfaction of knowing that their name had gone into the draw for the Fourth Round for the first time in the club's 66-year history and that if they beat United they would be paired with either Scunthorpe or Millwall.

Hendon fielded an unchanged side although they moved amateur international Roger Connell, recovered from injury, to the substitutes' bench. Joe Harvey, Newcastle's manager, made one change from the side so nearly humiliated at St. James's Park. The amateurs opened brightly, moving deep into the Newcastle half in search of an early goal.

Hendon's hopes of moving into the next round received a blow when United took the lead in the 14th minute with a hotly-disputed goal. After moving on to a long clearance MACDONALD carved his way past two defenders and slammed the ball into the Hendon net whilst a linesman was flagging for offside. But the referee ignored strong Hendon protests and the goal stood.

Half-time: Hendon 0   Newcastle United 1

There was nearly a sensational equaliser when the second half began, McFaul punching a clearance straight to Fry who rocketed in a first-time shot with the goalkeeper beaten, only for defender Howard to pop up on the line to head the ball clear. The dose was repeated minutes later when Somers sent a powerful header flashing past the wrong side of the post.

Then came the cruel finale. In the 64th minute, with Newcastle struggling back to life, HIBBITT lashed in United's second and minutes later the First Division side went into a 3-0 lead when McDERMOTT scored from a penalty after a Hendon defender had handled. Twelve minutes from the end TUDOR made it number four for Newcastle and a gallant Hendon, finally beaten by superior class and stamina, went off the field after a highly creditable performance.

Result: Hendon 0   Newcastle United 4

Teams:
Hendon: Swannell, Jennings, Hand, Deadman, Phillips, Haider, Baker, D., Childs, Baker, J., Somers, Fry. (Sub: Connell).
Newcastle: McFaul, Craig, Kennedy, McDermott, Howard, Clark, Gibb, Cassidy, Macdonald, Tudor, Hibbitt. (Sub: Barrowclough).
Referee: Mr. R. C. Challis, (Tonbridge).
Attendance: 15,385

CUP RUNS

1952/3

1st Round – *22nd November*
Hendon 0   Northampton 0

1st Round Replay – *27th November*
Northampton 2   Hendon 0

1955/6

1st Round – *19th November*
Halesowen 2   Hendon 4

2nd Round – *10th December*
Exeter City 6   Hendon 2

1960/1

1st Round – *5th November*
Hendon 2   Oxford United .. 2

1st Round Replay – *9th November*
Oxford United .. 3   Hendon 2

1964/5

1st Round – *14th November*
Port Vale 2   Hendon 1

1965/6

1st Round – *13th November*
Grantham 4   Hendon 1

1966/7

1st Round – *26th November*
Hendon 1   Reading 3

1969/70

1st Round – *15th November*
Hendon 5   Carshalton 3

2nd Round – *6th December*
Hendon 0   Brentwood 2

1970/1

1st Round – *21st November*
Hendon 0   Aldershot 2

1972/3

1st Round – *18th November*
Plymouth 1   Hendon 0

1973/4

1st Round – *24th November*
Hendon 3   Leytonstone 0

2nd Round – *15th December*
Merthyr 0   Hendon 3

3rd Round – *5th January*
Newcastle Utd .. 1   Hendon 1

3rd Round Replay – *9th January*
Hendon 0   Newcastle Utd .. 4
(Played at Watford)

1975/6

1st Round – *22nd November*
Hendon 1   Reading 0

2nd Round – *13th December*
Hendon 0   Swindon 1

1977/8

1st Round – *26th November*
Watford 2   Hendon 0

1981/2

1st Round – *21st November*
Hendon 1   Wycombe W 1

1st Round Replay – *24th November*
Wycombe W 2   Hendon 0

HEREFORD UNITED

Founded: 1924

League: Fourth Division

Ground: Edgar Street

Colours: White shirts with red and black trim; black shorts

As a Southern League club Hereford United were one of the lengendary non-Leaguers whose Cup battles against the League giants have gone into the history books, exploits that rightly gained them the reward of League status in May, 1972. Their post-war record in the Cup was fabulous — 13 times in the Second Round, three times in the Third and once in the Fourth, effectively establishing them as one of the greatest non-League sides in the country.

In their numerous First Round battles Hereford claimed the League scalps of Exeter, Aldershot and Northampton and in exciting Second Round clashes United met a succession of League clubs including Newport County, their bogey side (twice), Scunthorpe (which went to a replay) Southend United, Queen's Park Rangers, who suffered an incredible 6-1 defeat at the hands of the part-timers, Millwall (whose colours were lowered 1-0), Watford, Brighton and Northampton (beaten in extra time in the second replay).

Hereford first achieved the triumph of a Third Round tie in the 1957/8 season when they were beaten at home 3-0 by First Division Sheffield Wednesday and again in 1965/6 when they were beaten 2-1 away by another Southern League club Bedford Town. But the real glory was reserved for their last season in the Southern League when in the Third Round they held mighty First Division Newcastle United to a 2-2 draw at St. James's Park and then went on to gain an incredible 2-1 victory at Edgar Street in the replay after extra time. Even greater glory was to come in the Fourth Round, the part-timers holding Cup giants First Division West Ham United to a 0-0 draw at Edgar Street before bowing out 3-1 at Upton Park before a crowd of only 51 below the ground record. Such was the Southern Leaguers' drawing power.

Making their first post-war appearance in the First Round in 1948/9 Hereford celebrated their Silver Jubilee season by comprehensively defeating Southern League rivals Kidderminster Harriers 3-0 away from home to go into the Second Round hat for the first time in their history. Drawing Exeter City, Third Division South away the Southern Leaguers were defeated by the odd goal in three.

In the following season 1949/50 Hereford were again on the Wembley trail when they beat fellow non-Leaguers Bromsgrove Rovers at home 3-0 to appear once again in the Second Round. They had to be content with an away fixture against fellow Southern Leaguers Weymouth who dismissed them 2-1.

Again in the First Round in the following season 1950/1 United again found themselves opposed by Bromsgrove Rovers, this time away from home but the result again going in Hereford's favour 3-1. The Second Round gave Hereford a home tie against Newport County, Third Division South, the first of a succession of Cup ties against the Welsh club which always ended in defeat making Newport Hereford's 'bogey' team. In the first of these encounters Newport ran out easy 3-0 winners before a 'gate' of 15,526.

Keeping up their First Round appearance record in the following season 1951/2 Hereford received a 4-1 shock away defeat at the hands of fellow non-Leaguers Guildford.

Undeterred Hereford fought their way to the First Round in the next season 1952/3 and had a better run, being held to a 0-0 draw away by Athenian Leaguers Leyton before beating them 3-2 in the replay. This led to a Second Round home encounter against Third Division North, Scunthorpe. Although the Southern Leaguers forced a 0-0 draw they had two 'goals' disallowed. A 10,631 'gate' at Scunthorpe for the replay saw Hereford put out 2-1.

Faced in the following season, 1953/4, with old Cup opponents Exeter City, Third Division South, at St. James Park Hereford were to begin making post-war Cup history. In a tough battle the Southern Leaguers forced a 1-1 draw to make their League opponents replay at Edgar Street where United chalked up a splendid 2-0 win, their first post-war victory over League opponents. Once again in the Second Round they were matched away against Lancashire Combination side Wigan Athletic, a tie that drew a crowd of 24,526, a record for two non-League sides in the F.A. Cup. Wigan were the faster side, winning comfortably 4-1.

Hereford only failed to reach the First Round once in 24 years between 1948 and 1972 when they were elected to

141

the Football League. That was in the 1954/5 season when they lost 3-2 to Birmingham League Nuneaton in the 4th Qualifying Round. But a few days before they entertained West Bromwich Albion who had earlier in the year won the F.A. Cup (beating Preston N.E. 3 2 in the Final) in a floodlit friendly. Hereford gained an incredible 10 5 win over the Cupholders. Back in the First Round in the 1955/6 season Hereford lost 4-0 away to Swindon, Third Division South.

Hereford again distinguished themselves in the First Round of the 1956/7 competition by disposing of Aldershot, Division Three South, 3-2. This led to the appearance at Edgar Street of Southend United, Third Division South, in the Second Round. A crowd of nearly 11,000 saw an exciting game, Hereford gaining a 1-0 half-time lead, four goals being scored in the second half, Southend netting in the last two minutes to gain a narrow 3-2 win.

In the following season 1957/8 United had to travel to the Isle of Wight to meet Hampshire League side Newport whom they had no difficulty in beating by a 3-0 margin. This brought them a Second Round home tie against Queen's Park Rangers, Third Division South, when over 10,000 Hereford fans saw the League side overwhelmed 6-1, one of the heaviest Cup defeats ever recorded against a team from the higher echelons. It was the same margin by which Derby were k.o.-ed by Boston United in December 1955 although in the case of Q.P.R. they suffered the disadvantage of losing their 'keeper Springett injured in the 13th minute. Hereford were two up by half-time and piled on the pressure after the interval to bring their tally to six. In 1970/1 Barnet beat Newport County by the same margin, 6 1.

Hereford had a splendid reward for this success, a Third Round encounter at Edgar Street with First Division Sheffield Wednesday fully reported in *Match Report.*

In the First Round in the following season, 1958/9, Hereford were back in their own class, an away game against fellow Southern Leaguers Guildford City whom they managed to beat 2-1. This led to another confrontation at home in the Second Round, with United's 'bogey' team Newport. A 12,000 crowd gave United a terrific reception as the team ran on to the pitch. Although United lost their goalkeeper injured on the half hour the Southern Leaguers held their own and it looked as if Hereford might force a draw but County scored twice in the closing minutes.

Hereford must have thought their luck had run out when in the next season, 1959/60, lo and behold their 'bogey' team reappeared – Third Division Newport County away from home. Although Hereford battled hard and managed to score twice Newport had the upper hand and gained an easy 4-2 victory. In the 1960/1 season Hereford fared little better when they might have expected a change in fortune. Drawn away against Western League side Bridgwater Town they were unexpectedly defeated 3-0.

The next season, 1961/2, gave Hereford a more satisfactory Cup run. Drawn away to Third Division Bristol City in the First Round the tie attracted a crowd of 13,000 to Ashton Gate. Hereford had a great start scoring in the 14th minute holding their lead until after half-time when City levelled the score in the 55th minute. In the return game at Edgar Street City ran out clear-cut 5-2 winners.

In the 1962/3 season United were again removed in the First Round, this time by Third Division Crystal Palace. A crowd of 15,317 at Selhurst Park saw Hereford have slightly more of the game in the first-half although it was in that period that Palace scored the two goals that settled the game. In Hereford's side were three former Arsenal stars Tony Biggs, Don Bennett and Gordon Nutt.

Hereford were again in the First Round in the following season, 1963/4, and out of the hat once again came their 'bogey' side, Fourth Division Newport County but with Hereford having ground advantage. This fourth encounter in the Cup between these two sides since the war drew a crowd of over 6,000 to Edgar Street to see Hereford put on a fine display. After a goalless draw County went ahead in the 60th minute against the run of play, Peter Isaac in United's goal who had a great game saved a penalty and Hereford equalised in the 75th minute amid great excitement. Newport, as expected, won the replay at Somerton Park by a 4-0 margin.

In the First Round of the 1964/5 competition United had to travel to meet Third Division Oldham Athletic. A crowd of 11,789 saw a five-man Oldham attack too much for the Southern Leaguers who lost 4-0.

The following season, 1965/6 Hereford again had an away tie in the First Round – against Isthmian League amateurs Leytonstone. Just before half-time Hereford took the lead which they held to the end to win 1-0, having a second half 'goal' disallowed. United's next Cup battle, in the Second Round, was at home against Third Division leaders Millwall, a game that attracted a 'gate' of 11,940 to Edgar Street. From the start Hereford dominated the game, Millwall's goalkeeper Alex Stepney having to make several spectacular saves to keep out the Southern Leaguers. After a goalless first half Hereford continued to attack and were rewarded in the 61st minute when Fogg scored the only goal of the match, thus putting the Southern Leaguers into the Third Round for the second time in their history. Millwall, beaten in previous years by Southern League sides Bath, Worcester and Kettering, had once again been vanquished by a Southern League club.

Hereford's Third Round opponents were fellow Southern Leaguers Bedford Town, away at The Eyrie. This clash of these two formidable Southern League Cup-fighting sides drew a crowd of 13,245 to see The Eagles edge into the Fourth Round by a narrow 2-1 margin. In the early stages United had the better of the exchanges and Fogg had the ball in the net in the 10th minute but the 'goal' was disallowed. Once they had settled down Bedford began to look dangerous and in the 17th minute took the lead when Hall scored with a flying header. Bedford held on to their lead to half-time and after the interval, still dominating the game, went into a 2-0 lead, Hall again being the scorer. United mounted a strong challenge in the closing stages and Fogg reduced the deficit two minutes from the end. Hereford attacked furiously in an attempt to save the game but the Bedford defenders held out to gain a Fourth Round tie against Everton. Teams:- Bedford Town: Collier; Morgan, Skinn; Wright, Collins, Bailey; Benning, Paton, Brown, Hall, Sturrock. Hereford: Isaac; Vale, Timms; McCall, Daniel, McIntosh; Punter, Rodgerson, Fogg, Derrick, Jones. Referee: Mr. T.W. Dawes, Norwich.

United drew an attractive away tie in the First Round of the 1966/7 competition against Third Division Peterborough United, one-time non-League 'giantkillers' whose exploits as Midland Leaguers are still well remembered. The tie drew Peterborough's highest 'gate' of the season, 12,218. Posh were in no mood to allow of any giantkilling to remind them of the past and were in control for most of the game running out easy 4-1 winners despite the promptings of John

Charles, United's Welsh international.

Continuing their long sequence of First Round appearances Hereford had ground advantage in the 1967/8 season when they were matched against fellow Southern Leaguers Barnet. A hotly-contested game resulted in Hereford gaining a narrow 3-2 victory.

This success led United to the Vicarage Road ground to take on Third Division Watford in the Second Round. Although Hereford were fielding their strongest side, which included their two ex-Middlesborough players Bob Appleby and Eddie Holiday, David Dodson formerly of Arsenal and Portsmouth and led by the redoubtable John Charles, the former Welsh, Leeds and Juventus centre-forward, the Southern Leaguers were no match for their League opponents and went down 3-0.

Again in the hat for the First Round in the following season, 1968/9, Hereford were drawn at home against Third Division Torquay United. Both sets of defence were well-organised and although Hereford put on a grandstand finish the game ended in a goalless draw. The man in the middle was famous international referee Clive Thomas. Although Hereford scored first in the replay at Plainmoor Torquay soon hit back, equalised before the interval and went on to win 4-2.

Hereford's First Round opponents in the 1969/70 competition were fellow Southern Leaguers Chelmsford City away from home and a tense game ended in a narrow 2-1 win for United. In the Second Round for the 11th time since 1948 the Southern Leaguers once again drew their 'bogey' team Fourth Division Newport County and although Hereford made a fight of it the League side brought off their inevitable victory although this time by only a narrow 2-1 margin.

In the 1970/1 season, Hereford again among the Southern Leaguers in the First Round drew a home game against high-riding Fourth Division Northampton Town. There was a crowd of 10,401 at Edgar Street to see the Cobblers take a 2-0 interval lead against the run of the play and then to glory in United's second half revival when they reduced the arrears in the 57th minute and equalised three minutes from time.

Hereford made history in the replay at the County Ground. United began the game with a flurry of attacks on the Northampton goal and with the Cobblers reeling scored twice in the first 14 minutes. Northampton were unable to get their game together and Hereford easily held their lead up to half-time. Although Northampton got a goal back in the 59th minute United managed to hold on to record their first away victory over a League club in 15 attempts.

Hereford's reward for this splendid performance was a home game in the Second Round against Third Division Brighton. A 13,000 crowd saw some tense end-to-end football with Hereford's defenders in good form. Half-time arrived with the scoresheet blank and after the interval, in the 62nd minute, the crowd went wild as John Charles scored for the Southern League leaders with a brilliant header. But the euphoria did not last long, Brighton equalising three minutes later and with a further late goal squeezed through into the next round on a slender 2-1 margin.

This brought Hereford to the 1971/2 competition, their glory season and as it turned out their last in the Southern League. Their First Round encounter was an away game against fellow Southern Leaguers King's Lynn. Although United had most of the play and hit the woodwork several times the Linnets' defence held firm and the game ended a goalless draw. A stern battle developed at Edgar Street in the replay but a Hereford goal in the 27th minute was enough to gain them entry into the Second Round for the 13th time since the war.

Hereford savoured the draw for their Second Round tie, finding themselves at home against their old adversary Northampton Town whom they beat in a First Round replay in 1970/1. The game developed into a dour struggle and although both sides had chances the defences gave little away and the match ended a goalless draw. An exciting replay at the County Ground ended all-square with the score 2-2 after extra time. Hereford held a 1-0 lead at half-time through a 27th minute goal but in a dramatic second half Northampton equalised, United went ahead again only for Town to draw level seven minutes from time. There was no further scoring in extra time.

The Hawthorns was the scene of the second replay on a night made for giantkilling. When Northampton scored in the fourth minute a victory for the League side seemed on the cards. But that would not have taken account of Hereford's skill and tenacity, the Southern Leaguers mounting attack after attack that often had the League side reeling. It was a near thing for United however for they did not equalise until the second minute of injury time. Hereford shone in extra time and scored the vital goal to make the final score 2-1 and with it the distinction of having put Northampton out of the Cup for the second season in succession.

This success brought Hereford once again into the hat for the Third Round with the chance of meeting a glamour club – and this came their way in drawing mighty First Division Newcastle United, six times winners of the F.A. Cup, at St. James's Park. There was a crowd of 39,300 at the twice-postponed tie to watch the Southern Leaguers give a sparkling display of controlled, attacking football that belied their lowly position in the football hierarchy. In less than a minute Hereford caused a mighty sensation when they went into the lead, Owen volleying in from 15 yards past the astonished Newcastle goalkeeper McFaul. But only minutes later Newcastle were level. Burly centre-forward Malcolm Macdonald was brought down in the area as he was going through and the Magpies' striker took the penalty himself and scored. Intense Newcastle pressure put the Hereford defenders in momentary disarray and in the 23rd minute Tudor put the First Division side in the lead. But not for long as Hereford counter-attacked strongly and were on level terms within two minutes when Colin Addison, seeing goalkeeper McFaul off his line, sent a powerful 25 yards shot crashing into the back of the net. In the second half Hereford put up a defensive wall in front of their goal and all Newcastle's frantic efforts to snatch the winner came to nought. In this battle royal, which ended so magnificently for the non-Leaguers, Potter in the Hereford goal gave a great display as did fellow defenders McLaughlin and Jones, strikers Owen and Tyler were always in the picture and a consummate performance came from Addison. It was a great night for the underdogs. Hereford:- Potter; Griffiths, Mallender, Jones, McLaughlin, Addison, Gough, Tyler, Meadows, Owen, Radford. Sub. George.

The stories of United's fantastic win over Newcastle in the replay, their epic draw at Edgar Street against First Division West Ham in the Fourth Round and their bowing out 3-1 after a memorable performance at Upton Park are fully recorded as *Match Reports*. It was a magnificent ending to a tremendous season for United with, finally, the accolade of membership of the Fourth Division.

MATCH REPORTS
THIRD ROUND F.A. CUP
4th January 1958
HEREFORD UNITED 0 SHEFFIELD WEDNESDAY 3

The largest 'gate' to assemble at Edgar Street to date, over 18,000, including one party of Hereford fans that travelled from Pembrokeshire, saw the gallant Southern League side hold First Division Sheffield Wednesday to three goals. Niblett and Beech passed fitness tests whilst Joe Wade, the Hereford skipper, had to have an injection immediately before the match to kill the pain from a boil. Reggie Bowen, who broke his leg in the previous match, had to watch the game from the trainer's bench.

The Wednesday won the toss and Hereford kicked off and at once went into the attack, with two Fidler headers bringing Ryalls quickly into action. Hereford were evidently adopting a policy of not letting Wednesday settle down; twice the pressure on the Sheffield goal was relieved by back passes to the goalkeeper and a snap shot by Horton produced a good save from Ryalls. Then Williams was fouled but McEvoy cleared and sent Quixall away to test the Hereford defence.

Play was end to end, the game being fought out at a terrific pace. Sewell did well to hold a Quixall drive from 30 yards whilst at the other end Beech drove inches wide. United almost scored when a Williams shot was stopped on the goal-line by the sawdust!

Wednesday began to come more into the game and some clever Shiner and Quixall inter-passing produced a few ominous gaps in the United defence. Tomkins checked Finney as the Sheffield outside-left was going through and during another dangerous Sheffield attack Sewell punched the ball off Shiner's head. Although Hereford were at this stage of the game under considerable pressure the defence held together and managed to keep the Wednesday forwards out. Five minutes before half-time FROGGATT scored from a Shiner pass. For Hereford Beech was only a fraction wide with a good header.

Half-time: Hereford 0 Sheffield Wednesday 1

After the interval Sheffied were again on the attack and in a mix-up in the Hereford goal O'Donnell came near to scoring. Froggatt and Finney were a handful for the United defence but it was SHINER who notched Wednesday's second goal in the 53rd minute, after a goalmouth mix-up. Both Shiner and Finney were prominent in further Wednesday attack, with the Hereford forwards falling back to help out a hard-pressed defence. Hereford still had plenty of fight.left and in sporadic attacks Beech twice went close. Horton who was struck in the face by the ball had to leave the field and during his absence FROGGATT notched Wednesday's third, seven minutes from time.

Result: Hereford United 0   Sheffield Wednesday 3

Teams:
Hereford United: Sewell, Tomkins, Wade, Masters, Niblett, Horton, Jones, Clayton, Fidler, Williams, Beech.
Sheffield Wednesday: Ryalls, Martin, Curtis, McAenarney, McEvoy, O'Donnell, Wilkinson, Quixall, Shiner, Froggatt, Finney.
Referee: Mr. W. Hickson, (Wigan).
Attendance: 18,114

THIRD ROUND REPLAY F.A. CUP
5th February 1972
HEREFORD UNITED 2   NEWCASTLE UNITED 1

After their tremendous performance in holding mighty Newcastle United at St. James's Park the Southern Leaguers went on to make history in the replay at Edgar Street by defeating their illustrious opponents 2-1 to become the first non-League side for 23 years to lower the colours of a First Division side in the Cup.

Newcastle set about their task confidently, soon having Hereford on the defensive with shots from Tudor and Hibbett striking the bar and forcing six corners as the Southern Leaguers reeled under the barrage. Malcolm Macdonald missed a chance of putting the Tynesiders in the lead but after these near-misses the edge wore off the Newcastle attack. Hereford began to assert themselves urged on by player-manager Colin Addison and Newcastle were looking decidedly irresolute as the interval approached but neither side could break the deadlock.

Half-time: Hereford United 0   Newcastle United 0

After the interval Hereford unbelievably began to get the upper hand over their First Division opponents, Dudley Tyler putting in two shots that brought the best out of Newcastle's goalkeeper McFaul. At the heart of the Hereford defence McLaughlin and Mallender were in superb form while Potter in goal was playing the game of his life. Then in the 82nd minute against the run of the play Newcastle went one up, a Vic Busby cross reaching the head of MACDONALD for the centre-forward to deflect the ball past Potter. For most part-timers this would have spelled defeat but not for the Southern Leaguers who tore into the Newcastle defence. Four minutes from the end the tireless RADFORD scored one of the most spectacular goals of his career to secure a heart-stopping equaliser; latching on to the ball from at least 40 yards out he crashed his shot past McFaul to score the goal of a life-time. Hereford raised their game again in extra time harrying Newcastle unmercifully and showing themselves easily the fitter team. In the 12th minute of the first period of extra time Hereford got their reward when Ricky GEORGE, who had come on as substitute, scored the winner, hitting the ball past McFaul from 10 yards to bring the fans surging on to the field. It was curtains for Newcastle as Hereford held out until the final whistle for the Southern Leaguers to record one of the most exciting Cup wins in the history of the competition.

Result: Hereford United 2   Newcastle United 1

Teams:
Hereford: Potter, Griffiths, Mallender, Jones, McLaughlin, Addison, Gough, Tyler, Meadows, Owen, Radford. (Sub: George).
Newcastle: McFaul, Craig, Clark, Nattrass, Howard, Moncur, Busby, Green, Macdonald, Tudor, Reid.
Referee: Mr. D. Turner, (Cannock).
Attendance: 15,000

FOURTH ROUND F.A. CUP
9th February 1972
HEREFORD UNITED 0   WEST HAM UNITED 0

Another capacity crowd at Edgar Street saw the Southern Leaguers in action against First Division opponents for the second time in four days. This time it was the Hammers who had to brave the onslaught of the part-timers and to marvel at the skill and talent of men whose football is essentially of the week-end variety. In the Fourth Round for the first time in their history the Southern Leaguers quickly took control of the midfield with Colin Addison, George and Radford generally getting the better of the West Ham attack.

Under the floodlights on this fairy-tale night Hereford played with tremendous jest, doing a splendid levelling job and at times looking more like a First Division side than their distinguished opponents. It was a night fit for heroes. As Hereford made one dangerous thrust after another into the Hammers' area West Ham were lucky in having the coolness and anticipation of Bobby Moore to rely on. He was well supported by Taylor, McDowell and Ferguson and it was only the tenacity of these defenders that denied Hereford a first-half goal that they richly deserved.

Half-time: Hereford United 0   West Ham United 0

On resuming Hereford put up another splendid display, continually exerting pressure on the West Ham defence with goalkeeper Ferguson making some outstanding saves, Meadows and Owen giving the hard-pressed Hammers little rest. Determined clearances by Taylor and McDowell saved the Hammers time after time although once Radford broke through to send a tremendous header skimming over the bar. At the other end West Ham were rarely in the picture and when the final whistle blew Hereford could count themselves unlucky not to have won. Although a goalless draw it was a memorable game for the Southern Leaguers who added to their growing reputation as one of the greatest giant-killing sides of the century.

Result: Hereford United 0   West Ham United 0

Teams:
Hereford United: Potter, Gough, Mallender, Jones, McLaughlin, Addison, George, Tyler, Meadows, Owen, Radford.
West Ham United: Ferguson, McDowell, Lampard, Bonds, Taylor, Redknapp, Best, Hurst, Brooking, Robson.
Referee: Mr. Ray Tinkler, (Boston).
Attendance: 14,819

FOURTH ROUND F.A. CUP REPLAY
14th February 1972
WEST HAM UNITED 3   HEREFORD UNITED 1

This was the game that captured the imagination of football fans everywhere – the Cup magic of non-League Hereford pitted against the might of First Division West Ham drawing a fantastic mid-week attendance of 42,271, only 51 below the ground record with thousands of supporters locked outside.

It was a very different West Ham to the one that had performed so uninspiringly in the first game. Quickly gaining midfield control, the Hammers were soon pounding away at Hereford's goal and the Southern Leaguers goalkeeper Potter was at action stations within the first few minutes – cheered generously by the West Ham fans as he produced one spectacular save after another. Jones and McLoughlin were outstanding in defence for Hereford and helped to deny the West Ham attackers the goal they deserved. Both Hurst and Robson missed chances and the scoresheet was blank until two minutes from the interval. Then Clyde Best ran down the left flank for Geoff HURST to score the first of his three. Hereford's best chance came on the half hour when George shot wide with Ferguson beaten.

Half-time: West Ham United 1   Hereford United 0

After the resumption West Ham continued to press forward, Potter producing one fine save from Best which prompted the Hammers' striker to continue running forward to congratulate the Hereford goalkeeper. In the 52nd minute West Ham began to make the game look safe when HURST scored his second, collecting a Brooking pass and, eluding McLoughlin, smashed the ball into the roof of the net.

Hereford refused to lie down and pressed forward, fighting every inch of the way as they had done in over 15 hours of Cup football. Ferguson had to pull out the stops to push a hard shot from Meadows over the bar, a header from Owen again had Ferguson in action and then Meadows sent a first-time volley screaming towards goal but just off target. But it was West Ham who had the finishing touch, HURST completing his hat-trick in the 74th minute to put the game beyond recall.

Still Hereford refused to give up and a minute from time the Southern Leaguers had their reward when centre-forward MEADOWS scored a much-deserved consolation goal. That was the end of the scoring and when the whistle blew Hereford went out on a glory note to the thunderous cheers of the home crowd with the West Ham team sportingly lined up as the part-timers trooped off the field. Undeterred by the huge home crowd, by the internationals facing them, the part-timers had put up a courageous effort and a few months later their worth was recognised when they were deservedly elected to the Football League.

Result: West Ham United 3   Hereford United 1

Teams:
West Ham United: Ferguson, McDowell, Lampard, Bonds, Taylor, Moore, Redknapp, Best, Hurst, Brooking, Robson.
Hereford United: Potter, Gough, Mallender, Jones, McLaughlin, Addison, George, Tyler, Meadows, Owens, Radford.
Referee: Mr. Ray Tinkler, (Boston).
Attendance: 42,271

CUP RUNS

1948/9
1st Round – *27th November*
Kidderminster ...0 Hereford 3

2nd Round – *11th December*
Exeter ....2 Hereford 1

1949/50
1st Round – *26th November*
Hereford ....3 Bromsgrove 0

2nd Round – *10th December*
Weymouth ....2 Hereford 1

1950/1
1st Round – *25th November*
Bromsgrove R. ..1 Hereford 3

2nd Round – *9th December*
Hereford ....0 Newport 3

1951/2
1st Round – *24th November*
Guildford ....4 Hereford 1

1952/3
1st Round – *22nd November*
Leyton ....0 Hereford 0

1st Round Replay – *27th November*
Hereford ....3 Leyton 2

2nd Round – *6th December*
Hereford ....0 Scunthorpe 0

2nd Round Replay – *11th December*
Scunthorpe ....2 Hereford 1

1953/4
1st Round – *21st November*
Exeter ....1 Hereford 1

1st Round Replay – *26th November*
Hereford ....2 Exeter 0

2nd Round – *12th December*
Wigan ....4 Hereford 1

1955/6
1st Round – *19th November*
Swindon ....4 Hereford 0

1956/7
1st Round – *17th November*
Hereford ....3 Aldershot 2

2nd Round – *8th December*
Hereford ....2 Southend 3

1957/8
1st Round – *16th November*
Newport ....0 Hereford 3
(I. of W.)

2nd Round – *7th December*
Hereford ....6 QPR 1

3rd Round – *4th January*
Hereford ....0 Sheffield Wed ...3

1958/9
1st Round – *15th November*
Guildford ....1 Hereford 2

2nd Round – *6th December*
Hereford ....0 Newport 2

1959/60
1st Round – *14th November*
Newport ....4 Hereford 2

1960/1
1st Round – *5th November*
Bridgwater ....3 Hereford 0

1961/2
1st Round – *4th November*
Bristol City ....1 Hereford 1

1st Round Replay – *8th November*
Hereford ....2 Bristol City 5

1962/3
1st Round – *3rd November*
Crystal Palace ...2 Hereford 0

1963/4
1st Round – *16th November*
Hereford ....1 Newport Co. 1

1st Round Replay – *18th November*
Newport Co. .....4 Hereford 0

1964/5
1st Round – *14th November*
Oldham Ath. .....4 Hereford 0

1965/6
1st Round – *13th November*
Leytonstone ......0 Hereford 1

2nd Round – *4th December*
Hereford ....1 Millwall 0

3rd Round – *22nd January*
Bedford Town ..2 Hereford 1

Hereford Utd (Contd)

1966/7

1st Round - *26th November*
Peterborough 4   Hereford 1

1967/8

1st Round - *13th December*
Hereford 3   Barnet 2

2nd Round - *6th January*
Watford 3   Hereford 0

1968/9

1st Round - *16th November*
Hereford 0   Torquay Utd 0

1st Round Replay - *20th November*
Torquay Utd 4   Hereford 2

1969/70

1st Round - *15th November*
Chelmsford City 1   Hereford 2

2nd Round - *6th December*
Newport C. 2   Hereford 1

1970/1

1st Round - *21st November*
Hereford 2   Northampton 2

1st Round Replay - *24th November*
Northampton 1   Hereford 2

2nd Round - *11th December*
Hereford 1   Brighton 2

1971/2

1st Round - *20th November*
King's Lynn 0   Hereford 0

1st Round Replay - *24th November*
Hereford 1   King's Lynn 0

2nd Round - *11th December*
Hereford 0   Northampton 0

2nd Round Replay - *14th December*
Northampton 2   Hereford 2
(After extra time)
Score at 90 mins 2-2

2nd Round, 2nd Replay - *20th Dec.*
Hereford 2   Northampton 1
At West Bromwich
(After extra time. Score at 90 mins 1-1)

3rd Round - *24th January*
Newcastle Utd .. 2   Hereford 2

3rd Round Replay - *5th February*
Hereford 2   Newcastle Utd .. 1
(After extra time. Score at 90 mins 1-1)

4th Round - *9th February*
Hereford 0   West Ham Utd .0

4th Round Replay - *14th February*
West Ham Utd .3   Hereford 1

MAY 1972 ELECTED TO FOURTH
DIVISION, FOOTBALL LEAGUE

HILLINGDON BOROUGH
(formerly Yiewsley)

Founded: 1872

League: Southern (Southern Division)

Ground: Leas Stadium

Colours: White with light and dark blue hoops

Hillingdon Borough, which up to the 1969/70 season played under the name of Yiewsley, a suburb of Uxbridge, as amateurs in the Corinthian League, made their first post-war First Round Cup appearance in the 1956/7 season. They were matched against Gillingham, Third Division South, at the Leas Stadium and did well to hold the professionals to a 2-2 draw before going out 2-0 in the replay. In 1958 the club turned professional under the managership of former Fulham and England player Jim Taylor but Cup success eluded the side until their best run to date — in the 1969/70 season when, on their way to the Third Round, they defeated Third Division leaders Luton Town 2-1. Their Third Round opponents were Isthmian Leaguers Sutton United and although Boro' managed to hold the amateurs to a goalless draw at the Leas Stadium they made little impression in the replay which Sutton won 4-1. Hillingdon have since appeared sporadically in the First Round, not with any great success except in the 1976/7 season when they beat Torquay on United's ground 2-1. Since Torquay usually see off non-League sides in the Cup this was a considerable achievement. Hillingdon have also met Brighton and Swansea in the Cup.

In their First Round encounter in the 1956/7 season at home against Gillingham, Third Division South, Yiewsley made history for it was the first time that the club had reached this level in the Cup. It was an exciting game with the Gills going ahead in the 28th minute, Yiewsley getting the equaliser five minutes before the interval to put the teams on equal terms. The second half opened sensationally with the amateurs taking the lead, Gillingham fighting back desperately and scoring the equaliser only seconds before the final whistle. Yiewsley had to take a weakened side to Gillingham, the League side scoring twice within 15 minutes to win 2–0.

Boro' had a long wait for their next appearance in the First Round, in the 1969/70 season, their most successful Cup run to date. As Hillingdon Borough of the Southern League they drew a First Round tie at home at Leas Stadium against fellow Southern Leaguers Wimbledon. Key man in the Hillingdon side was 37-years-old player-manager Jimmy Langley, three times an England international and formerly with Leeds, Brighton, Fulham and Queen's Park Rangers, and having played in two F.A. Cup semi-finals and ending his Football League career on a high note when he helped Q.P.R. to win the 1967 League Cup. The game against the Dons was goalless at half-time but Hillingdon scored twice in the closing stages to go forward into the next Round. This was a never-to-be-forgotten home game against Third Division pace-setters Luton Town whom the Boro' dramatically beat 2-1, the game being fully described in *Match Report*.

As a result of this great win Hillingdon found themselves in the Third Round for the first time in their history, their opponents being fellow non-Leaguers from the Isthmian League, Sutton United, at home at the Leas Stadium. The game had had to be postponed because of bad weather and when the teams eventually met it was known that the winners would be at home to mighty Leeds and Don Revie was on the Hillingdon ground to check over the two sides. In arctic conditions an exciting game ended in a goalless draw with Boro' having to make a trip to Sutton for the replay. At the last minute it was revealed that Jimmy Langley could not play because of injury. Although Sutton had the ball in the net within nine minutes the 'goal' was disallowed and the teams went off the field at half-time with a blank scoresheet. Boro' had a nightmare second half. Sutton took a 48th minute lead and in the 70th minute went two up. Five minutes later a Terry goal gave Boro' heart but they were eclipsed in the closing stages when Howard and Bladon added further goals to make the final score 4-1. Hillingdon: Lowe; Batt, Watson; Reeve, Newcombe, Moore; Fairchild, Cozens; Terry, Carter, Vafiadis. Sub. Townend.

Boro' had to wait until the 1971/2 season before they were again in the First Round, drawn against Third Division Brighton and Hove Albion away at the Goldstone ground. A crowd of nearly 10,000 saw Brighton pile up a 7-1 victory.

In the First Round again in the following season, 1972/3,

Hillingdon found themselves matched against fellow non-Leaguers Chelmsford City away from home. Although Boro' had plenty of chances they were a goal down midway through the first half with a second Chelmsford goal three minutes from time giving their opponents a comfortable victory.

Hillingdon's appearances in the First Round continued in the next season, 1973/4, when they were again drawn against non-League opposition, fellow Southern Leaguers Grantham at the Leas Stadium. Hillingdon fared badly against the high-riding Gingerbreads, down 3-0 at half time and finally going out by four clear goals.

Hillingdon's Cup fortunes changed in the 1976/7 season when they handed out the Cup shock of the day beating Fourth Division Torquay United 2-1 away at Plainmoor. An evenly-contested first-half produced a 0-0 stalemate but after the interval Hillingdon turned on the heat and scored twice, the first from Metchick in the 60th minute and a second from Smith five minutes later. Torquay gained a consolation goal a minute from time.

The Second Round gave Boro' ground advantage, their visitors being near neighbours Fourth Division Watford. The game had its bizarre touches. The match was well under way before anyone realised that the referee was not taking part, having had to go to the Boro' goalkeeper to complain about an illegal mark on the six yard line. The game had to be restarted and Boro' were one up within a minute. It was a fluctuating affair the score standing at 2-2 until three minutes from the end when Watford scored again to emerge 3-2 winners.

Hillingdon were again in the First Round in the 1978/9 season when they drew an attractive away game against Third Division promotion candidates Swansea City. The Swans went into a 2-0 interval lead with the final score 4-1, Boro's consolation goal coming from an 'own goal'.

MATCH REPORT
SECOND ROUND F.A. CUP
6th December 1969
HILLINGDON BOROUGH 2   LUTON TOWN 1

Luton were riding high at the top of the Third Division when they were at the receiving end of this 'giantkilling' performance by the Southern Leaguers, the best Cup victory ever seen at the Leas Stadium. Apart from giving Boro' the chance of gaining a place in the Third Round, the tie was of exceptional local interest. It was Alec Stock, Luton's manager, who persuaded Jimmy Langley to take over the player-managership of Boro' and Stock himself is perhaps best remembered for his brilliant managership of Yeovil in the historic season when they defeated Bury and Sunderland to go on to a never-to-be-forgotten Fifth Round tie at Old Trafford.

Then there was the magic of Jimmy Langley, a revered name in the football world, a product of the nearby Evelyns secondary school and at 14 one of the youngest-ever players to appear for Yiewsley, then in the Great Western Combination. After rejoining Yiewsley after the war and a brief spell with Guildford he went on to League football to gain honours with Fulham and QPR. There were two other players on view who were to make their mark later on – Malcolm MacDonald, playing in a striker's role for Luton, who was to achieve fame and fortune with Newcastle United and John Cozens, Boro's inside-right, who was to score many future goals for Peterborough United.

At the start of the game Boro' were forced back on defence and in the ninth minute Luton went ahead. Boro's defenders were having difficulty in dealing with the speed of French on the left wing and when he was obstructed going through the resultant free-kick led to Luton taking the lead. French took the free-kick himself finding the head of centre-forward TEES who headed past Lowe.

In the 25th minute Carter, one of Boro's front men, pulled a muscle and was replaced by Gary Townend who had seen League football with Millwall. Two minutes before the interval Boro gained their reward when following a Fairchild corner and a loose clearance REEVE raced through to score.

Half-time: Hillingdon Borough 1   Luton Town 1

After the interval the Southern Leaguers continued to harry their League opponents, skipper Dickie Moore and Jimmy Langley urging on their side to great deeds. And it came in the 53rd minute to set Boro' on the glory trail. Full back Vic Batt, who had seen League service with Reading, cut out a Luton attack, then got Fairchild and Cozens moving down the right wing, Fairchild crossing for TOWNEND to prod the ball home via the goalkeeper's legs. It was only in the closing stages, when Luton threw everyone forward, that Hillingdon were forced on the defensive. As David

Lacy in the *Guardian* graphically put it: "Admitted there was a moment near the end when, with a tumble of bodies in the goalmouth, Hillingdon seemed intent on closing up the walls with their English dead but this was the only time in the game when they betrayed their humble leanings".

Result: Hillingdon Borough 2   Luton Town 1

Teams:
Hillingdon: Lowe, Batt, Langley, Reeve, Newcombe, Moore, Fairchild, Cozens, Terry, Carter, Vafiadis. (Sub: Townend).
Luton: Davie, Ryan, Bannister, Keen, Nichol, Slough, Collins, MacDonald, Tees, Allen, French, (Sub: Harrison).
Referee: Mr. P. K. Byford, (Essex).
Attendance: 9,333

Hillingdon (Contd)

CUP RUNS

As Yiewsley

1956/7
1st Round – *17th November*
Yiewsley ....2 Gillingham 2

1st Round Replay – *21st November 1956*
Gillingham ....2 Yiewsley 0

As Hillingdon Borough

1969/70
1st Round – *15th November*
Hillingdon ....2 Wimbledon 0
2nd Round – *6th December*
Hillingdon ....2 Luton Town 1
3rd Round – *6th January*
Hillingdon ....0 Sutton Utd 0
3rd Round Replay – *12th January*
Sutton Utd ....4 Hillingdon 1

1971/2
1st Round – *20th November*
Brighton ....7 Hillingdon 1

1972/3
1st Round – *18th November*
Chelmsford ....2 Hillingdon 0

1973/4
1st Round – *24th November*
Hillingdon ....0 Grantham 4

1976/7
1st Round – *20th November*
Torquay Utd .....1 Hillingdon 2
2nd Round – *11th December*
Hillingdon ....2 Watford 3

1978/9
1st Round – *25th November*
Swansea ....4 Hillingdon 1

KETTERING TOWN

Founded: 1876

League: Alliance Premier

Ground: Rockingham Road

Colours: Red shirts, white shorts

Kettering have always been a non-League force to be reckoned with in the Cup. The Poppies have appeared consistently in the First Round draw, frequently being matched against League sides, and having the scalps of Swindon, Millwall, Swansea and Oxford United under their belts. Twice since the war they have reached the Third Round — in 1968/9 when after beating two non-League sides in the earlier rounds, Waterlooville and Dartford they held Bristol Rovers to a 1-1 draw at Eastville before being defeated 2-1 in the replay at home; again in 1976/7 when after beating Third Division Oxford United (after a replay) and non-Leaguers Tooting they were put out of the Cup at home 3-2 by Fourth Division Colchester United.

The Poppies began their post-war Cup runs in the 1945/6 season when the two leg system was in operation, going out 7-3 on aggregate against Midland League Grantham.

The Poppies were not seen again in the First Round until the 1951/2 season when they were drawn away to Third Division Bristol Rovers who had reached the last 16 in the previous season. In the first half hour Rovers built up a 3-0 lead which they held to the end, the Poppies having a 'goal' disallowed.

Two seasons later the Poppies were again in the First Round, gaining an attractive away tie against Third Division Leyton Orient before a crowd of 15,048, Kettering again losing by a clear-cut 3-0.

In the following season, 1954/5, the Poppies found themselves in a First Round contest away from home against redoubtable Cup fighters amateurs Bishop Auckland of the Northern League. The Poppies found Auckland in peak form and were hustled out of the Cup 5-1.

Four seasons later, in 1958/9, the Poppies were again in

the First Round opposed to old rivals Peterborough United, then in the Midland League and who had faced each other seven times since the war in the qualifying rounds. 'Posh' had ground advantage and a large crowd of 17,800 saw a hard fought game result in a 2-2 draw. Kettering were without their player-manager Jack Froggatt. In the replay at Rockingham Road Kettering built up a 2-0 lead, 'Posh' pulled one back and five minutes from time Poppies put through their own goal. Peterborough scored in extra time to make the result 3-2.

Kettering continued their First Round appearances in the following season, 1959/60, when they received Southern Leaguers Margate at Rockingham Road. The game resulted in a 1-1 draw with Margate winning a keenly contested replay 3-2.

In a First Round tie in the 1960/1 season the Poppies drew a difficult away tie against Isthmian League amateurs Wycombe Wanderers. Kettering won 2-1 to go into the Second Round for the first time in the club's history. Kettering had to visit Elm Park to play Third Division Reading and found themselves 4-1 down at the interval, Reading centre-forward Lacey scoring a hat-trick. Although the Poppies reduced the gap to 4-2 in the second-half the well-drilled Reading defence prevented any further scoring.

The following season, 1961/2, Kettering were drawn away in the First Round against Third Division Swindon Town. In a 75 minute battering of the Kettering goal Swindon went into a comfortable 2-0 lead but in the last quarter of an hour the tide turned dramatically, Kettering pulling a goal back and then gaining a dramatic equaliser with a penalty in the closing stages. In the replay at Rockingham Road Kettering made football history with a glorious 3-0 win over the League side, fully described in *Match Report*.

Their success over Swindon gave the Poppies an away game in the Second Round against local rivals, highly placed Third Division Northampton Town. The Cobblers were superior in all departments and went into a 3-0 half-time lead, all the goals being scored by Holton, the former Arsenal forward. Kettering were unable to mount a second-half challenge and the Cobblers were content to hold their three nil lead. The tie drew 18,825, the biggest 'gate' of the Second Round.

Kettering entertained Third Division Millwall at Rockingham Road in a First Round tie in the 1963/4 competition. Millwall, often unlucky against non-League sides in the Cup, had to defend strongly against early Kettering attacks although the League side scored first. Kettering equalised ten minutes from the end to force a replay at The Den. This game produced a dramatic 3-2 win under the floodlights for the part-timers, level 1-1 at half-time and the Poppies scoring the decider ten minutes from time.

In the Second Round Kettering had to travel to meet Fourth Division Oxford United before a 10,000 crowd at Manor Road. The League side scraped through 2-1, Kettering having an 80th minute 'goal' disallowed.

In the First Round again in the 1964/5 season Kettering were once again paired with Millwall, away from home and the League side gained a 2-0 revenge for their defeat at the hands of the non-Leaguers the previous season.

The Poppies' next appearance in the First Round was delayed until the 1968/9 season when Kettering had two splendid wins to take them into a history-making Third Round tie. In the First Round they were drawn away to Southern Leaguers Waterlooville whom they narrowly defeated 2-1 and in the Second Round had a more comfortable passage when they overwhelmed fellow Southern Leaguers Dartford 5-0 at Rockingham Road. The Poppies drew a money-spinning tie in the Third Round (which they reached for the first time in their history) against Third Division Bristol Rovers at Eastville. After a great battle the Southern Leaguers held the League side to a 1-1 draw, the game being fully described in *Match Report*.

For the Third Round replay at Rockingham Road a crowd of over 10,000 saw the Poppies resume where they had left off, strongly attacking in the Rovers' half and getting their reward ten minutes before half-time when Daldy gave the Southern Leaguers a 1-0 lead. After the interval Kettering were awarded a penalty but the Rovers' goalkeeper saved. Misfortune struck Kettering ten minutes from the end, Rovers getting the equaliser through S. Taylor and almost on time the Poppies captain Gammon turned the ball into his own net to make the final score 2-1 in the League side's favour. Kettering: Harvey; Ashby, Needham, Gammon, Reed, Evans, Daldy, Gully, Smith, Goodall, Walden.

After their thrilling performances of the previous season the Poppies were again in the Cup hunt in the 1969/70 season when they drew a First Round tie at home against Fourth Division Swansea, going down 2-0. Swansea had Welsh internationals Mel Nurse and Len Allchurch in their team.

After failing to qualify the next season Kettering were next in the First Round in 1971/2 opposed to fellow Southern Leaguers Barnet at Rockingham Road. Although Kettering kept the score level 1-1 at half-time the second half belonged to Barnet who won 4-2. Kettering's first-half goal was an extraordinary 'own goal', King crashing the ball into his own net from 35 yards.

The following season Kettering drew an away game in the First Round against Third Division Walsall at Fellows Park, an incident-packed game ending in a 3-3 draw. The Poppies were 3-1 down at one stage, scored again to get back into the game and drew level seven minutes from the end after a solo effort by Ron Clayton, Kettering's £8,000 signing from Oxford United. One writer described this goal as 'a jewel of a moment, shining radiantly through the Staffordshire gloom'. In the replay at Rockingham Road the Poppies had high hopes of continuing where they had left off but the 9,000 plus crowd saw Walsall run out 2-1 victors.

It was not until the 1974/5 season that the Poppies had a further chance of showing their mettle when they were drawn away in the First Round against old Cup opponents Fourth Division Swansea. The Poppies adapted better to the muddy conditions and went into the lead in the 21st minute, Swansea having to wait until early in the second-half before drawing level. In the replay at Rockingham Road Kettering delighted the home supporters with a fine display of attacking football and were rewarded with goals by Pawley (17th minute), Ashby, penalty (53rd minute) and Clayton (87th minute) with Swansea only managing a consolation goal. This splendid 3-1 win for the Southern Leaguers was one of the most memorable of Kettering's Cup runs.
Kettering: Livesey, Ashby, Goodall, Myton, Suddards, Rathbone, Large, Atkinson, Conde, Clayton, Pawley. (Sub: Loughlan).

In the Second Round draw Kettering were paired with fellow Southern Leaguers Wimbledon away at Plough Lane where a crowd of nearly 6,000, the highest for 11 years, saw the Dons win 2-0 to give them a Third Round tie against First Division Burnley.

The Poppies were next in the First Round in 1976/7, a memorable season in which they were again to reach the Third Round and to go out fighting against Fourth Division Colchester United. Their opponents in the First Round were Third Division Oxford United at Rockingham Road. Oxford went into a 1–0 first-half lead, had a second-half 'goal' disallowed but allowed the Southern Leaguers to get back into the game to score the equaliser. There was a crowd of nearly 6,000 at the Manor Ground for the replay to see the Southern Leaguers triumph 1–0 to gain a place in the Second Round. Derek Dougan, the former Wolves and Northern Ireland striker and Kettering's chief executive, who had been substitute in the first game, was included in the team and scored the vital goal in the 72nd minute. Kettering were drawn at home in the Second Round against Isthmian Leaguers Tooting. Although the visitors packed their goal in the hope of a replay Kettering managed to score the match-winner nine minutes from the end.

The Southern Leaguers found themselves in the Third Round for the second time since the war drawn at home against Fourth Division Colchester United. The Poppies were entirely out of luck in this key game having two 'goals' disallowed, were involved in several breathtaking goal-line clearances in the Colchester goalmouth and had a penalty appeal turned down. Meanwhile Colchester built up a 3–0 lead with two goals in the first half and the third in the 60th minute. But brave Kettering were not finished and in a grandstand finish, which enhanced their Cup fighting reputation, scored two in the last ten minutes.

Kettering: Livesey, Lucas, Merrick, Mortimer, Dixey, Ashby, Faulkner, Glover, Kellock, Clayton, Phipps. (Sub: Wood).

Colchester: Walker, Cook, Williams, Leslie, Smith, Dowman, Garwood, Gough, Froggatt, Bunkell, Dyer. (Sub: Allison).

Kettering's next appearance in the First Round was in the following season, 1977/8, when they drew an away game against Isthmian Leaguers Tilbury. It was a game that went down in soccer history for when 15-year-old Scott Endersby, a fifth-former at a Wellingborough school, turned out in the Kettering goal he became the youngest player ever to appear in the First Round of the F.A. Cup. In a hard game Kettering snatched a 1–0 half-time lead which they retained until the end. It seemed that Tilbury were out of the Cup but a sensational turn of events were to prove otherwise. Tilbury appealed to the F.A. that Len Glover, who had played only for ten minutes in the game, was ineligible and following an enquiry the F.A. ordered a replay. This produced a 2-2 draw and at the replay at Rockingham Road, after the Poppies had gone into a 2-0 lead, the Isthmian Leaguers drew level and in the second half scored again to win 3-2.

Kettering missed a season before again seeking Cup honours in the First Round in 1979/80, drawn away against Third Division Reading at Elm Park. Kettering, now in the Alliance Premier League, tore into Reading and opened the scoring in the 10th minute. Reading hit back to level the score but before half-time Kettering had scored again to put them into a 2-1 lead. In the second half Reading turned the tables in a five minute goal spree in which they scored three times to make the final result 4-2. This was exactly the same result that was recorded at Elm Park 19 years previously when the two teams last met.

Kettering had a fight on their hands when they drew fellow Alliance Premier Leaguers Maidstone in the First Round of the 1980/1 season at home at Rockingham Road. Although the Poppies had the best of the first-half Maidstone were in control for most of the remaining 45 minutes, scored soon after the resumption and the Poppies were hard pressed to gain a late equaliser. A dour encounter in the replay produced a goalless draw after extra time and the two teams had to line up again at Maidstone for a second replay. On the night the game went Maidstone's way but a note of piquancy was introduced into the affair when, with Maidstone leading 2-1 with five minutes left, the notorious Stones lights failed. After a 25 minutes' wait for repairs the game was resumed and Maidstone scored again to make the final score 3-1.

The Poppies again fought their way through to the First Round in the 1981/2 season drawing fellow Alliance Premier Leaguers Boston United away from home. The Poppies scored the only goal of the game in the 60th minute. Kettering drew a home game in the Second Round against Fourth Division Blackpool and although the Poppies had their chances the League side went in at half-time a goal to the good. Despite a fighting second-half display by the non-Leaguers Blackpool added two further goals to make the final score 3-0.

MATCH REPORTS
FIRST ROUND F.A. CUP REPLAY
8th November 1961
KETTERING TOWN 3   SWINDON TOWN 0

This was Kettering's red letter day. After narrowly forcing a replay with two late goals against Swindon on the League club's ground in the first encounter the Southern Leaguers settled down in the replay at Rockingham Road. It was a closely-contested first half with honours fairly even. Jack Froggatt, the former England centre-half, kept a close watch on Ernie Hunt, the Swindon marksman, and exerted a steadying influence on the team.

Kettering's two backs, Maurice Marston and Norman Lawson, gave an impeccable performance, Marston once blocking a fierce shot from Ernie Hunt on the goal-line to prevent what had seemed a certain goal.

Half-time: Kettering 0   Swindon 0

It was second-half glory for Kettering who opened up the game to gain a sensational win over their League opponents. In the 61st minute, after the Swindon defence had been split up, Golding was impeded in the penalty area by the Swindon goalkeeper. Terry CURRAN, who had scored the vital equaliser in the first game, took the spot kick and netted easily.

The Poppies decided to continue to attack rather than fall back to defend their lead. In the 77th minute CURRAN scored again after another Golding defence-splitting run.

Swindon tried hard to get back into the game but the non-League defenders stood firm. There was another shock in store for the League side. First Golding had a 'goal' disallowed for impeding the Swindon goalkeeper. Then Kettering scored number three to add to the glory. Golding, again in the picture, slipped a perfect pass to centre-forward RITCHIE who hammered the ball in.

The whole of the Kettering team had raised their game and contributed to a distinguished performance.

Result: Kettering 3   Swindon 0

Teams:
Kettering: Smethurst, Marston, Lawson, Shaw, Froggatt, Armour, Morrow, Morris, Ritchie, Curran, Golding.
Swindon: Burton, Jones, Trollope, Morgan, Owen, Woodruff, Summberbee, E. Hunt, McPherson, R. Hunt, Jackson.
Referee: Mr. E. P. Clarke, (Coventry).
Attendance: 8,385

THIRD ROUND F.A. CUP
4th January 1969
BRISTOL ROVERS 1   KETTERING 1

In the Third Round of the Cup for the first time in the club's history and the last remaining non-League side in the Cup, the team had a rousing reception from the 12,000 crowd when they came out on the Eastville park. There were over 1,000 Kettering supporters present, accompanied by their traditional mascot. Rovers won the toss and decided to kick towards the Muller Road end. Although the Poppies were quick to attack Rovers soon got into their stride and Brian Harvey, the most experienced player in the Poppies' side, having played First Division football for Newcastle, Blackpool and Northampton, carried out several fine saves.

Shortly after the start Mabbutt was penalised for a foul on Gully and Poppies' player-manager, Steve Gammon, who had had his career at Cardiff wrecked by three leg fractures, sent a high ball into the Rovers penalty area. Laurie Taylor had to be quick off his line to stop the onrushing Goodall.

A goal always seemed on the cards as Rovers' pressure built up and it came in the 17th minute, Jarman sending over a cross that was headed down by Bobby Jones for Ray GRAYDON to slot the ball into the net.

In the 35th minute, Kettering gained the equaliser. Gully had outwitted two defenders to pass to Walden whose shot was turned round the post by Laurie Taylor for a corner. Walden took the flag kick and the ball went to Mick REED standing on the edge of the box and the centre-half promptly squeezed the ball into the back of the net.

Rovers surged into the attack to try to regain the advantage and Bobby Jones twice missed chances with the Poppies' defence spread-eagled. Just before the interval Kettering's goalkeeper Harvey produced a class save, going full-length across his area to prevent Wayne Jones from scoring.

Half-time: Bristol Rovers 1   Kettering 1

After the interval Rovers settled down to an all-out attack on the Kettering goal and the part-timers' defence had to work overtime. In the closing stages of the game the Poppies fought a tremendous rearguard action, surviving a series of free kicks and constant pressure in the goalmouth.

By a miracle Kettering's packed defence survived and frustration mounted for Rovers. In the 65th minute Poppies nearly took a shock lead when Goodall broke through with only the goal-keeper to beat but Taylor moved off his line to narrow the angle. Against the odds the part-timers survived to take the League side to a replay at Rockingham Road. The game had been a classic in unyielding defensive play and the Poppies earned a roaring cheer as they left the pitch.

Result: Bristol Rovers 1   Kettering 1

Teams:
Bristol Rovers: L. Taylor, Parsons, Stanton, S. Taylor, Lloys, Petts, Graydon, S. Jones, Mabbutt, W. Jones, Jarman. (Sub: Ronaldson).
Kettering: Harvey, Ashby, Needham, Gammon, Reed, Evans, Daldy, Gully, Smith, Goodall, Walden, (Sub: R. Webster).
Referee: Mr. I. P. Jones, (Trelewis).
Attendance: 12,230

Kettering (Contd)
CUP RUNS

1945/6

1st Round (1st leg) *17th November*
Kettering ...... 1 Grantham 5

1st Round (2nd leg) *24th November*
Grantham ..... 2 Kettering 2
  (Grantham won on 7-3 aggregate)

1951/2

1st Round – *24th November*
Bristol Rovers . 3 Kettering 0

1953/4

1st Round – *21st November*
Leyton Orient . 3 Kettering 0

1954/5

1st Round – *20th November*
Bishop Auck. .. 5 Kettering 1

1958/9

1st Round – *15th November*
Peterborough .. 2 Kettering 2

1st Round Replay *20th November*
Kettering ...... 2 Peterborough .. 3

1959/60

1st Round *14th November*
Kettering ...... 1 Margate 1

1st Round Replay *19th November*
Margate ...... 3 Kettering 2

1960/1

1st Round – *5th November*
Wycombe W. .. 1 Kettering 2

2nd Round *26th November*
Reading .... 4 Kettering 2

1961/2

1st Round *4th November*
Swindon ...... 2 Kettering 2

1st Round Replay *8th November*
Kettering ...... 3 Swindon 0

2nd Round *25th November*
Northampton .. 3 Kettering 0

1963/4

1st Round – *16th November*
Kettering ...... 1 Millwall 1

1st Round Replay *25th November*
Millwall .... 2 Kettering 3

1964/5

1st Round – *14th November*
Millwall .... 2 Kettering 0

1968/9

1st Round – *16th November*
Waterlooville .. 1 Kettering 2

2nd Round – *7th December*
Kettering ...... 5 Dartford 0

3rd Round – *4th January*
Bristol Rovers . 1 Kettering 1

3rd Round Replay – *8th January*
Kettering ...... 1 Bristol Rovers . 2

1969/70

1st Round – *15th November*
Kettering ...... 0 Swansea 2

1971/2

1st Round *20th November*
Kettering ...... 2 Barnet 4

1972/3

1st Round *18th November*
Walsall .... 3 Kettering 3

1st Round Replay *22nd November*
Kettering ...... 1 Walsall 2

1974/5

1st Round *26th November*
Swansea ...... 1 Kettering 1

1st Round Replay – *2nd December*
Kettering ...... 3 Swansea 1

2nd Round *14th December*
Wimbledon .... 2 Kettering 0

1976/7

1st Round *20th November*
Kettering ...... 1 Oxford Utd. .. 1

1st Round Replay – *23rd November*
Oxford Utd ... 0 Kettering 1

2nd Round *11th December*
Kettering ...... 1 Tooting 0

3rd Round *8th January*
Kettering ...... 2 Colchester Utd 3

1977/8

1st Round *26th November*
Tilbury 0   Kettering 1
(Kettering ordered to replay tie because of ineligible player)

1st Round (replayed) *5th December*
Tilbury 2   Kettering 2

1st Round Replay *7th December*
Kettering 2   Tilbury 3

1979/80

1st Round *24th November*
Reading 4   Kettering 2

1980/1

1st Round *22nd November*
Kettering 1   Maidstone 1

1st Round Replay *26th November*
Maidstone 0   Kettering 0
(after extra time)

1st Round 2nd Replay *1st December*
Maidstone 3   Kettering 1

1981/2

1st Round *21st November*
Boston Utd 0   Kettering 1

2nd Round *2nd January*
Kettering 0   Blackpool 3

LEATHERHEAD

Founded: 1946

League: Isthmian

Ground: Fetcham Grove

Colours: Green shirts, black shorts

Although Leatherhead were late entrants in the post-war F.A. Cup First Round stakes—their first appearance was in the 1974/5 season — they amply made up for it by being one of the few non-League clubs in the country to have reached the Fourth Round. This was on 25th January, 1975 when, even though conceding ground advantage to their opponents Leicester City of the First Division, they were squeezed out of the Cup by a narrow 3-2 margin after being in the lead 2-0 at half-time.

In the following season 1975/6 Leatherhead carried on where they had left off by defeating Fourth Division Cambridge United in the First Round 2-0, eventually being put out by fellow Isthmian Leaguers Tooting and Mitcham 2-1 after extra time in a Second Round replay.

The pattern was repeated in the 1976/7 First Round Cup tie when the Tanners despatched Northampton 2-0 but were put out in the Second Round by renowned non-League Cup fighters Wimbledon then of the Southern League. Other League sides whom the Tanners have met in the Cup include Colchester Utd., Swansea and Exeter.

The Tanners had most of the game in the First Round tie in the 1974/5 season away from home at the Rhodes Avenue ground when they faced fellow amateurs Bishops Stortford but the tie ended in a goalless draw.

The replay at Fetcham Grove attracted the best 'gate' of the season, 1,775, to see the Tanners turn in a commendable 2–0 victory to earn them a home game in the Second Round against Third Division, Colchester United, the first time that Leatherhead had met a League club in the F.A. Cup.

The Tanners were on top form when they met their Third Division opponents at Fetcham Grove before a 3,500 crowd. Unbeaten Leatherhead secured early control of the midfield and it was no surprise when in the 19th minute the non-Leaguers took the lead when Johnny Doyle slotted in a shot from 12 yards. It was the only goal of the game and took the non-Leaguers into the Third Round.

Leatherhead's 'giant-killing' saga continued in the Third Round when Third Division Brighton were the next League club to bite the dust – losing 1-0 on their own ground at Goldstone. This put the Tanners into a history-making Fourth Round clash with First Division Leicester City – although they had conceded ground advantage for the bigger 'gate' the Tanners were two goals in the lead at half-time with City coming back in the second-half to score three and edge the amateurs out of the Cup. Both these glory games are fully described in *Match Report*.

Back in the First Round in the following season, 1975/6, Leatherhead were again matched against a League side, home to Fourth Division Cambridge United before a 3,000 crowd at Fetcham Grove. Chris Kelly, back in the side after illness and a brief stay at Millwall, made the two first-half goals that swept Cambridge out of the Cup and mesmerising United with his own special brand of football.

For their Second Round encounter the Tanners drew a home tie against fellow Isthmian Leaguers Tooting and Mitcham. Defences were on top and the game resulted in a goalless draw. This drew Leatherhead to Sandy Lane for the replay played on a frostbound pitch, the referee abandoning proceedings in the 57th minute with the score standing at 1-1. Starting again from scratch with the prize of a Third Round tie against Swindon at stake, a hard-fought game ended 1-1 at 90 minutes. In extra time Tooting scored the vital goal that denied the Tanners further Third Round glory that season.

Leatherhead duly appeared in the First Round in the 1976/7 season with the luck of a home game against Fourth Division Northampton Town. The Tanners dominated the game, defeating their League opponents 2-0.

For their Second Round tie the Tanners again had the luck of ground advantage, drawn against then Southern League champions Wimbledon. The Dons led 1-0 at half-time, and went into the next round with a 3-1 win.

Leatherhead again saw First Round Cup action in the 1977/8 season when they faced Fourth Division Swansea City at home before a 3,000 crowd. Leatherhead were at full strength against a weakened City side, and the Swans were glad to settle for a goalless draw.

A crowd of over 7,000 watched the replay with the Swans having to pull out all the stops in order to overcome their non-League opponents. City made a nervous start against the Tanners with a treacherous pitch neutralising Swansea's professional advantage. City gradually built up their confidence and were one up at half time through a Jeremy Charles header and in the 54th minute scored again. The Tanners stormed back and John Baker reduced the deficit but the equaliser eluded them.

The following season, 1978/9, Leatherhead again fought their way through to the First Round, drawn at home against fellow non-Leaguers Merthyr Tydfil of the Southern League. After going two goals in the lead Leatherhead had a fight on their hands as the Welshmen pulled a goal back.

Leatherhead's opponents at Fetcham Grove in the Second Round were Third Division Colchester United whom the Tanners had narrowly beaten in 1974. The first-half belonged to Colchester who went into the lead on the half hour and the Tanners spent most of the time defending. In the second-half Leatherhead had more of the game and in the 73rd minute Chris Kelly, so often the hero of Leatherhead's Cup exploits, jinxed his way through to equalise and force a replay.

At Layer Road the Isthmian Leaguers found themselves faced with a difficult task and although they kept out their League opponents for most of the first-half Colchester went in at half-time a goal to the good. In the second half Colchester overwhelmed the amateurs to gain a comfortable 4–0 win.

The Tanners missed a season before reappearing in the First Round in 1980/1 when they had to travel to St. James's Park to meet Third Division Exeter City. It was an unhappy day for the Tanners, two down at half-time, including an 'own goal', Kelly injured and then having to suffer the indignity of three more Exeter goals in the second half, the second week in succession that City had scored five.

MATCH REPORTS
THIRD ROUND F.A. CUP
4th January 1975
BRIGHTON 0   LEATHERHEAD 1

The feat of this part-time Isthmian League team in taking on Third Division Brighton on their own ground at Goldstone in the Third Round and emerging with a 1-0 victory under their belts to take them into the Fourth Round is the stuff that F.A. Cup dreams are made of.

In this history-making tie the Tanners made their intentions clear from the start, attacking strongly and playing controlled, skilful football. Leatherhead's side was strengthened by the return of Chris Kelly, wearing the No 9 shirt, after several weeks' absence following a cartilage operation.

The Tanners controlled the midfield from the outset and in defence played with great composure.

Kelly, displaying his famous shuffle, had the beating of Brighton's defenders and once tried an overhead kick that, fortunately for the home side, flew over the bar.

There were some tense moments at both ends but half-time arrived with the scoresheet blank.

Half-time: Brighton 0   Leatherhead 0

After the interval Brighton managed their first real shot at goal but John Swannell, the Tanners' goalkeeper, dealt with it comfortably.

In the 65th minute came the move that led to the match-winning goal. Leatherhead defender John Cooper moved the ball upfield to McGillicuddy on the left who quickly passed it to Chris Kelly lurking in the centre of the field. KELLY raced over 40 yards down the middle, jinxed past two defenders and calmly slotted the ball past goalkeeper Grummitt. It was a fantastic goal and provided the club with one of the greatest moments in its history.

Tension mounted as Brighton fought for the equaliser. Brighton made a substitution to give more urgency to their front line and in the course of a gallant defence the Tanners' resolute centre-half Reid went down injured although he was able to carry on. Not only that he took time off from defending to join the Leatherhead attack and managed a header that almost beat Grummitt.

In the closing stages Leatherhead mounted yet another attack that ended when Doyle's shot was blocked. At the other end two back passes to Swannell almost had disastrous results for the part-timers. but the Isthmian Leaguers held out until the final whistle when their fans saluted a famous victory.

Result: Brighton 0   Leatherhead 1

Teams:
Brighton: Grummitt; Tiler, Wilson, Mason, Piper, Winstanley, Towner,

	O'Sullivan, Binney, Mellor, Walker. (Sub: Marlowe).
Leatherhead:	Swannell; Sargent, Webb, Cooper, Reid, McGillicuddy, Woffinden, Lavers, Kelly, Smith, Doyle. (Sub: Wells).
Referee:	Mr. R. C. Challis, (Kent).
Attendance:	20,491

FOURTH ROUND F.A. CUP
25th January 1975
LEATHERHEAD 2   LEICESTER CITY 3
(at Leicester)

This was Leatherhead's finest hour – after switching this Fourth Round tie from Fetcham Grove to Filbert Street for the bigger 'gate' – to find themselves 2–0 in the lead at half-time against their First Division opponents and then finally going down to a glorious 3–2 defeat after a desperate City rally.

Among the 32,000 spectators in this 'big time' atmosphere were 5,000 Leatherhead fans who gave enormous vocal support to the amateurs.

The game had not been in progress long before Leatherhead took a sensational lead. After Lavers had made ground and survived several tackles from Leicester defenders his pass found Chris Kelly who promptly squared the ball to McGILLICUDDY who had an easy task in flicking it into the City net.

This fine start inspired the Tanners who began to pressurise the stunned Leicester defenders. But City came back and Webb, playing a fine game in the Tanners' defence, was lucky not to have scored an 'own goal' when his header flew the wrong way towards his own net, calling for a smart save from Swannell.

In the 27th minute Leatherhead went further ahead with a dramatic goal by Chris KELLY. After Munro had fouled McGillicuddy the resultant free-kick was floated into City's area by Webb and Kelly was on hand to put a fantastic back-header well out of the reach of goalkeeper Wallington.

The Tanners, cool, composed, and playing skilful football continued on the attack as their delirious supporters were chanting, "Easy, Easy". Leicester were glad to hear the half-time whistle.

Half-time: Leatherhead 2   Leicester City 0

Only minutes after the resumption the Tanners were within an ace of scoring a third. After Cross had stumbled to let in Kelly the Leatherhead striker rounded goalkeeper Wallington who had come off his line but with the goal at his mercy delayed his shot and Munro raced across the line to clear. It was a lucky let-off for City for had Leatherhead scored again it would almost certainly have been curtains for the First Division side.

After this incident City began to fight back and in the 54th minute SAMMELS beat Swannell with a diving header. Pace began to tell on the Tanners and the turning point of the game came

From the hall of fame. Dyke, Yeovil's goalkeeper, punches clear during a Sunderland attack – an incident during the famous Yeovil v First Division Sunderland Third Round tie in 1949 which the non-Leaguers won 2–1.

Copyright Photograph: *The Press Association*

Since the war Blyth Spartans of the Northern League have got farther in the F.A. Cup than any other non-League side – after drawing 1–1 away against Wrexham in the Fifth Round in 1978 they went on to lose the replay by a narrow 2–1 margin on Newcastle United's ground. In this photograph of the first game at Wrexham Terry Johnson puts the non-Leaguers one up.

One of the greatest penalty saves of all time... Dickie Guy playing for Wimbledon, then in the Southern League, saves from Peter Lorimer, the Leeds United striker, in a Fourth Round encounter in 1975 at Elland Road. The game ended in a goalless draw.

Copyright Photograph: *Wimbledon News*

Southern Leaguers Chelmsford City reached the Third Round in 1973 and attracted First Division Ipswich Town to their New Writtle Street ground, the part-timers losing 3-1. Here English international Trevor Whymark is in the thick of the action, his shot being saved by Chelmsford goalkeeper Taylor.

Copyright Photograph: *Chelmsford Weekly News*

One of the Cup sensations of 1980– the match-winning goal, scored by Peter MacKenzie for non-Leaguers Harlow Town that put out Second Division Leicester City at Harlow's Sportcentre in a Third Round replay. In the previous game at Leicester the part-timers held the League side to a 1–1 draw.

Copyright Photograph: *Harlow Gazette*

Tommy Skuse, Worcester City's outside left, opening City's account in the ninth minute against Second Division leaders Liverpool in the Third Round in 1959. A 15,000 crowd at St. George's Lane saw City gain a sensational 2–1 win.

Copyright Photograph: *Birmingham Post & Mail*

A Newcastle defender turns away as Isthmian Leaguers Hendon celebrate Rod Haider's goal in the Third Round at St. James's Park in 1974. The game ended in a 1-1 draw. Newcastle won the replay 4-0.

Copyright Photograph: *Hendon Times*

Isthmian Leaguers Wycombe Wanderers in action at Ayresome Park in a 1974/5 Third Round replay against First Division Middlesbrough. Boro beat the part-timers 1-0 after being held 0-0 at Loakes Park.

Copyright photograph: *Robert Mead, High Wycombe*

After conceding ground advantage non-Leaguers Leatherhead go two up with a Chris Kelly (No. 9) wonder goal against First Division Leicester City in the Fourth Round in 1975. But Leicester made a dramatic come-back to win 3–2.

Copyright Photograph: *Leatherhead Advertiser*

In a Third Round tie at St. James's Park in 1972 Hereford United, then Southern Leaguers, shook First Division Newcastle United with a 17th second goal scored by No. 10 Brian Owen. The game resulted in a 2–2 draw. The replay at Edgar Street caused the upset of the round, Hereford putting out their distinguished opponents 2–1 after extra time.

Copyright Photograph: *Hereford Times*

20 minutes later when Swannell, who had played a brilliant game, failed to hold a Worthington lob and EARLE dashed in to score.

This thrilling Cup-tie continued at top pace with Leatherhead visibly tiring. In the 80th minute Leicester, who had come back from the grave, netted the match-winner, WELLER slamming in the ball after Whitworth's cross had been headed on by Worthington.

One of the most thrilling Fourth Round Cup ties in recent years Leatherhead's gallant failure became the talk of the football world. After the match Jimmy Bloomfield, Leicester's manager, said that Leatherhead's performance had been "nothing short of a miracle".

Result: Leatherhead 2   Leicester City 3

Teams:
Leatherhead: Swannell; Sargent, Webb, Cooper, Reid, McGillicuddy, Woffinden, Lavers, Kelly, Smith, Doyle.
Leicester City: Wallington; Whitworth, Rofe, Earle, Munro, Cross, Weller, Sammels, Worthington, Birchenall, Glover.
Referee: Mr. D. R. G. Nippard, (Bournemouth).
Attendance: 32,490

Leatherhead (Contd)

CUP RUNS

1974/5

1st Round *23rd November*
Bishops Stort. . 0   Leatherhead ... 0

1st Round Replay *26th November*
Leatherhead ... 2   Bishops Stort. . 0

2nd Round - *14th December*
Leatherhead ... 1   Colchester Utd 0

3rd Round *4th January*
Brighton 0   Leatherhead ... 1

4th Round *25th January*
Leatherhead ... 2   Leicester 3
(at Leicester)

1975/6

1st Round *22nd November*
Leatherhead ... 2   Cambridge Utd 0

2nd Round *13th December*
Leatherhead ... 0   Tooting & Mit. 0

2nd Round Replay *16th December*
Tooting & Mit. 1   Leatherhead ... 1
(Abandoned after 57 mins *pitch unfit, ice)*

2nd Round Replay - *22nd December*
Tooting & Mit. 2   Leatherhead ... 1
(after extra time)

1976/7

1st Round *20th November*
Leatherhead ... 2   Northampton .. 0

2nd Round - *14th December*
Leatherhead ... 1   Wimbledon ... 3

1977/8

1st Round - *26th November*
Leatherhead ... 0   Swansea City .. 0

1st Round Replay *29th November*
Swansea City .. 2   Leatherhead ... 1

1978/9

1st Round - *25th November*
Leatherhead ... 2   Merthyr Tydfil 1

2nd Round - *16th December*
Leatherhead ... 1   Colchester Utd 1

2nd Round Replay - *19th December*
Colchester Utd . 4   Leatherhead ... 0

1980/1

1st Round - *22nd November*
Exeter City 5   Leatherhead ... 0

MACCLESFIELD

Founded: 1871

League: Northern Premier

Ground: Moss Rose

Colours: Royal blue shirts and white shorts

Macclesfield made a late start in the First Round post-war Cup appearances and did not get into the hat until the 1960/1 season when they had a discouraging start, being defeated by Fourth Division Southport 7-2 away from home. It was in the 1967/8 season that the Silkmen had their best Cup run to date, defeating Third Division Stockport County 2-1 at home in a First Round replay after holding their League opponents to a 1-1 draw away in the first encounter. The Silkmen went on to defeat non-Leaguers Spennymoor in the second Round thus qualifying to meet First Division Fulham at Craven Cottage in the Third Round where they went down 4-2 after giving a magnificent display of Cup-fighting football. The Silkmen have had no real Cup luck since then other than playing League sides Lincoln City, Scunthorpe and Bradford City in First Round contests plus the memorable occasion in 1975 when they appeared at Hillsborough to face then Division Three Sheffield Wednesday.

Macclesfield's first post-war appearance in the Cup ended in disaster away from home when they met Fourth Division Southport and suffered a 7-2 defeat. A near 8,000 crowd saw the League side take command and go into a 4-1 half-time lead. Macclesfield's goals came from a penalty and an 'own goal'.

At their next attempt at Cup honours in the First Round, in the 1964/5 season, the Silkmen did rather better. Drawn at home against Fourth Division Wrexham, a difficult side to beat in the Cup, the non-Leaguers went out by a narrow 2-1 margin after a ding-dong struggle.

Three seasons later, in 1967/8, came the Silkmen's best Cup run to date. Drawn away from home against Third Division Stockport at Edgeley Park the non-Leaguers put up a great Cup-fighting performance. Although the League side were a goal up at half-time against the run of the play the part-timers, led by Keith Goalen a local solicitor, fought tenaciously for the equaliser and got it in the 68th minute.

There was a capacity attendance of nearly 9,000 to watch the replay at Moss Rose when, on one of the most memorable nights that Macclesfield can remember, the Cheshire Leaguers put out their promotion-seeking opponents 2–1. The game opened on a sensational note, Stockport going into a three minute lead. Although the Macclesfield fans fell silent they came to life again seven minutes later when the non-Leaguers equalised. In the 25th minute the Silkmen scored in dramatic fashion what turned out to be the match-winner. County gave away a penalty but the Stockport goalkeeper saved Taberner's spot-kick. The referee ordered the kick to be retaken because the goalkeeper had moved and Brian Fidler who took the second kick hammered the ball into the net. Although Stockport threw everything into attack they were unable to secure the equaliser.

Macclesfield: Cooke; Berry, Forrester, Beaumont, Collins, Goalen, Goodwin, Taberner, Fidler, Young, Calder.

The Silkmen's great win took them into the Second Round and a home game against fellow part-timers Spennymoor of the Northern League whom they put out 2–0. For the first time in the club's history they had arrived at the Third Round, drawn away at Craven Cottage against then First Division Fulham, a magical game fully described in *Match Report*.

Macclesfield's next First Round encounter was in the following season, 1968/9, when they gained home advantage against pace-setting Fourth Division, Lincoln City. Any hopes of another Cup run were dashed as Lincoln went into a 3–1 half-time lead and then shut down the game in the second-half to prevent any further scoring.

In the following season, 1969/70, Macclesfield were again in the Cup hunt, drawing Fourth Division Scunthorpe at Moss Rose in the First Round. In the early stages Kevin Keegan, who was later to make his name with Liverpool and England, was injured and this upset the rhythm of the League side and they were lucky to get away with a 1–1 draw. Although the part-timers took a shock lead in the seventh minute in the replay at the Old Shell Ground, Scunthorpe struck back to win 4-2 after a half-time score of 2-2. Keegan scored two of Scunthorpe's goals.

Macclesfield were drawn away from home at the Valley Parade ground in the First Round of the 1970/1 season against Division Three Bradford City, so often the executioners of the non-League sides in the Cup. This occasion was to be no exception. In a game where the Silkmen twice came back from behind Bradford grabbed the match-winner four minutes from time to edge into the next round with a 3-2 win. However, the Silkmen once again demonstrated the slender margin separating the best sides in the Northern Premier League and those in the lower Divisions of the Football League.

The Silkmen did not appear again in the First Round until the 1975/6 season when they were drawn away at Hillsborough against one of the most famous Cup-fighting sides in the country, Sheffield Wednesday, then in the Third Division. Included in the Macclesfield team was Tony Coleman who was the player who scored Wednesday's last goal in Division One in April 1970. There was a crowd of 12,940, the best of the season, to watch the David versus Goliath encounter. The game was a typical Cup struggle but in the 26th minute the Owls went into the lead. Then just after the half-hour the Silkmen equalised through Eccleshare and half-time arrived with the part-timers on equal terms with their distinguished opponents. With less than ten minutes gone in the second half Wednesday scored twice and held their 3-1 lead until the final whistle.

Macclesfield: Mailey; Eccleshare, Mobley, Fish, Collins, Heys, Morris, Lloyd, Collier, O'Connor, Coleman.

MATCH REPORTS

THIRD ROUND F.A. CUP
27th January 1968
FULHAM 4   MACCLESFIELD 2

When the Silkmen stepped out on to the Craven Cottage pitch for this Third Round encounter with First Division Fulham it was the farthest point that the club had reached in the F.A. Cup. There was no question of the Macclesfield part-timers being over-awed by their surroundings for most of the side had had some League experience – there were several former Stockport County players, Frank Beaumont, John Collins, Dick Young and player-coach Keith Goalen; David Latham had previously played for Manchester United; goalkeeper John Cooke was on the books of Port Vale; right-back Sievwright had played for Oldham Athletic and Rochdale; defender and captain George Forrester had previously been on the books of former league club Accrington Stanley.

Included in the star-studded Fulham team were no fewer than five internationals, England's right-back George Cohen; Jim Conway who had had several games for Eire together with his Eire partner, centre-half John Dempsey; Allan Clarke the centre-forward Fulham obtained from Walsall and who later represented England and made his name with Leeds United and the legendary England star Johnny Haynes who had more than 500 appearances for Fulham.

As the game began the Silkmen, full of confidence, thrust at the Fulham defences and in the second minute of the game opened the scoring when after a Goodwin-Fidler movement TABERNER moved in to shoot past the bewildered Macedo.

Although this early blow rocked Fulham the League side quickly regained their confidence and within two minutes the Londoners were level when CLARKE moved in to rocket a low shot into the net before Cooke could move.

Macclesfield continued to hammer away at the shaky Fulham defence and in the 16th minute went ahead again when centre-forward Brian FIDLER, the club's leading goal scorer, snapped up a long kick from Cooke and beat Fulham defender Dempsey to lob the ball over Macedo as he came out.

The Macclesfield strikers were running rings round the Fulham defence and Macedo was often in action. Fulham began to come more into the game as half-time approached and Clarke headed in but the 'goal' was disallowed owing to offside. Macclesfield were well worth their half-time lead.

Half-time; Fulham 1   Macclesfield 2

As the Macclesfield side came out after the interval the chant of "Silkmen, Silkmen" struck up again as the 7,000 Macclesfield supporters, with their blue and white scarves in evidence from one end of the ground to the other, hoped to see the non-Leaguers continue where they had left off.

The result eventually turned on a controversial penalty awarded in the 55th minute when Clarke and Cooke went up together as the ball bobbed around in the Silkmen's penalty area. Despite Macclesfield's protests the referee awarded a penalty and CLARKE, who took the kick himself, easily beat Cooke.

With 13 minutes left for play and the Silkmen hoping for a replay Johnny HAYNES put Fulham in the lead for the first time. This gave the League side the encouragement they had been looking for and ten minutes later GILROY made the score 4-2 with a hook shot. The scoreline was a flattering result for a First Division side that had rarely matched Macclesfield's basic soccer skills; a fine achievement in what had been the greatest game in the history of the part-timers in the Cup.

Result: Fulham 4   Macclesfield 2

Teams:
Fulham: Macedo; Ryan, Dempsey, Brown, Callaghan, Conway, Haynes, Earle, Clarke, Gilroy, Barrett.
Macclesfield: Cooke; Sievwright, Forrester, Beaumont, Collins, Goalen; Goodwin, Taberner, Fidler, Young, Latham.
Referee: Mr. R. F. Prichard, (Salisbury).
Attendance: 23,642

Macclesfield (Contd)

CUP RUNS

1960/1

1st Round - *5th November*
Southport 7   Macclesfield 2

1964/5

1st Round - *14th November*
Macclesfield 1   Wrexham 2

1967/8

1st Round - *9th December*
Stockport 1   Macclesfield 1

1st Round Replay - *13th December*
Macclesfield 2   Stockport 1

2nd Round - *6th January*
Macclesfield 2   Spennymoor 0

3rd Round - *27th January*
Fulham 4   Macclesfield 2

1968/9

1st Round - *16th November*
Macclesfield 1   Lincoln City 3

1969/70

1st Round - *15th November*
Macclesfield 1   Scunthorpe 1

1st Round Replay - *18th November*
Scunthorpe 4   Macclesfield 2

1970/1

1st Round - *21st November*
Bradford City ... 3   Macclesfield 2

1975/76

1st Round - *22nd November*
Sheffield Wed ... 3   Macclesfield 1

MAIDSTONE UNITED

Founded: 1897

League: Alliance Premier

Ground: The Stadium

Colours: Amber shirts, black shorts

Maidstone's first appearance in a post-war First Round contest was delayed until the 1974/5 season when they reached the Second Round via a First Round replay success against Southern Leaguers Nuneaton Borough. A tough away encounter against Swindon at the County Ground opposing a team that traditionally does well in the Cup produced a not unexpected 3-1 defeat for the Stones.

Four seasons later Maidstone had a highly successful Cup run. After beating fellow non-Leaguers Wycombe Wanderers at The Stadium Stones again had home advantage in the Second Round — against Third Division Exeter City. A stirring 1-0 victory took the part-timers into the Third Round against Charlton Athletic at The Valley. This was the game that put the Stones into the history books, a crowd of over 13,000 applauding the minnows as they held their League opponents to a 1-1 draw. Maidstone's tiny ground held a capacity crowd of nearly 11,000 for the replay, an historic night which resulted in a 2-1 win for Charlton after a titanic struggle.

The Stones again fought their way to the Third Round in the 1980/81 season when, via the scalps of Kettering (after two replays) and Third Division Gillingham (also after two replays), they were hosts to Third Division Exeter City. Exeter gained their revenge for City's 1978 triumph by despatching the part-timers 4-2.

When Maidstone went to Nuneaton for their First Round contest in 1974/5 they stunned Borough when they opened the scoring in the sixth minute. Borough recovered and were leading 2-1 at the 80th minute when in a storming finish Stones drew level to force a replay. When the teams met again Stones were not extended against a below-form Borough and had a comparatively easy entry into Round Two, winning 2-0.

Maidstone drew a hard away tie against Division Three Swindon Town, valiant Cup fighters in their own right. It was the first meeting between the two clubs although both were original entrants in the F.A. Amateur Cup in 1893/4 and became full members of the Football Association in 1909, the year of its inauguration. It was the first time that Maidstone had played a Second Round F.A. Cup tie in their 77 years' history. The 10,000 crowd saw Swindon generally in command, only Maggs in the Stones goal keeping the League's side score down to 1–0 at half-time, the non-Leaguers finally losing 3–1.

The start of the Stones' memorable 1978/9 season saw them drawn at home in the First Round against fellow non-Leaguers and Cup heroes, Wycombe Wanderers. Maidstone scored the only goal in the 64th minute from a free kick. There was a touch of luck about it because if the goalkeeper had not touched the ball on its way into the net the point would have been disallowed. Maidstone drew a Second Round home tie against Third Divison Exeter City. Included in the Maidstone team was Peter Silvester who had been signed by Stones from Cambridge United and who had seen previous League experience with Reading, Southend and Norwich plus two Round Five appearances. Although Exeter had most of the play Maidstone ran out 1–0 winners with a goal from Ken Hill and earned a plum draw away from home against Second Division Charlton Athletic, a tie that took a replay before the issue was settled, both games being fully described in *Match Report*.

In the 1980/81 season Maidstone were again on the Cup trail, drawing fellow Alliance Premier Leaguers Kettering Town away from home in the First Round. Despite strong Kettering pressure half-time was reached with the scoresheet blank but after the interval Stones took control and went ahead in the 57th minute. When it looked almost certain that Maidstone would hold on Kettering's substitute equalised to take the Poppies to a replay at The Stadium. This encounter produced a goalless draw after extra time and the tie began to look as if a marathon might be developing. The second replay was also at Maidstone and the game was 2–1 in Stones favour with five minutes left when suddenly the notorious Maidstone floodlights failed and plunged the ground into darkness. The club's engineers had to spend a feverish 25 minutes before the lights were restored and in the remaining time Maidstone added another goal to their tally to emerge 3–1 victors. The win gave them a Second Round joust with their near neighbours, Third Division Gillingham at Priestfield.

The Stones little realised that the game against Gillingham would again result in a long running affair. Neither defence was ready to submit and despite strong pressure from the Gills, especially towards the end, Maidstone's famous goalkeeper Dickie Guy was in command. In the replay at Maidstone Guy was again the hero and produced two class saves that kept out Gillingham and sent the game into extra time. This failed to yield a goal and after three and a half hours' effort the teams had to meet again at Priestfield to decide the issue. Under the floodlights Maidstone again enhanced their reputation as Cup fighters when they despatched their elite neighbours with a clear-cut 2–0 victory. The first goal came from Newson just after half-time and the second a splendidly taken goal by Ovard. Over 24,000 spectators had seen the three games, the outcome of which gave Maidstone the right to meet another Third Division side, Exeter City, at home in the Third Round, fully recorded as a *Match Report*.

MATCH REPORTS

THIRD ROUND F.A. CUP
9th January 1979
CHARLTON ATHLETIC 1   MAIDSTONE UNITED 1

It was a proud day for Maidstone United manager Barry Watling when he saw his side go on to the pitch for their Third Round encounter with Charlton Athletic at The Valley, the first time the Southern Leaguers had reached the Third Round in the club's history. Two players on whom special attention was riveted were Mike Flanagan, the England 'B' International, one of the most dangerous strikers in the Second Division and Dickie Guy, the Maidstone goalkeeper who has gone down in football history as the man who stopped a Lorimer penalty.

Maidstone, unbeaten in their last thirteen games, at once took the attack into the Charlton half. In the thirteenth minute the Southern Leaguers took a dramatic lead when COUPLAND took a pass from Edwards, moved inside Berry and then smashed the ball home via a post.

Half-time: Charlton Athletic 0   Maidstone United 1

After the interval Maidstone continued their non-stop attack. When all seemed lost for Charlton FLANAGAN jinxed his way through the Maidstone defence and hammered in a fierce shot from 10 yards which left Guy stranded. In a dramatic end to the game there was an incident that has rarely been seen on a football field – two of the Charlton strikers, Derek Hales and Mike Flanagan, were both sent off for fighting each other!

Result: Charlton Athletic 1   Maidstone United 1

Charlton:	Wood, Shaw, Campbell, Gritt, Shipperley, Berry, Brisley, Hales, Flanagan, Madden, Powell, (Peacock).
Maidstone:	Guy, Kinnear, Merrick, Hill, Edwards, Budden, Aitken, Fusco, Coupland, Silvester, Gregory (Wallace).
Referee:	Mr. B. Martin, (Nottingham).
Attendance:	13,457

THIRD ROUND REPLAY
15th January 1979
MAIDSTONE UNITED 1   CHARLTON ATHLETIC 2

There was a capacity crowd of nearly 11,000 – a ground record – with hundreds outside as the battling Southern Leaguers faced their Second Division opponents on Maidstone's tiny ground in the replay. Again there was drama but of a different kind that spoiled the earlier encounter – with only two minutes left to play with the League side leading 2–1 the lights failed and the referee took the players off for 19 minutes until repairs were completed.

During the early Maidstone attacks Coupland and Gregory both had chances, Gregory putting a header wide when well-placed.

Eventually Charlton settled down and in the 25th minute scored through left-back David CAMPBELL.

Half-time: Maidstone United 0   Charlton Athletic 1

In the second half Charlton demonstrated their superiority, controlling the midfield through Peacock and Brisley with Powell in good form on the left. In the 53rd minute Flanagan's stand-in, Martin ROBINSON, volleyed in a Powell cross that had been headed on by Shipperley. Maidstone pressed on and had their reward three minutes from time through slack marking in the Charlton defence which enabled COUPLAND to put a powerful header past Athletic's goalkeeper Johns.

Result: Maidstone United 1   Charlton Athletic 2

Teams:
Maidstone: Guy, Kinnear, Edwards, Hill, Aitken, Merrick, Gregory, Coupland, Fusco, Budden, Silvester, (Sub: Hutton).
Charlton: Johns, Shaw, Campbell, Gritt, Shipperley, Berry, Brisley, Peacock, Robinson, Madden, Powell.
Referee: Mr. B. Martin, (Nottingham).
Attendance: 10,600

THIRD ROUND F.A. CUP
3rd January 1981
MAIDSTONE 2   EXETER CITY 4

Third Division Exeter City were out to avenge their 1–0 defeat in the Second Round at the hands of The Stones two seasons previously and did exactly that. After a quiet start Maidstone gave City a shock when Ovard unleashed a power drive from 25 yards that struck the City crossbar. But as the game developed City began to look impressive and in the 34th minute opened the scoring through PULLAR. The Stones allowed City too much space and had not Dickie Guy, the famous non-League goalkeeper, been on top form City might have gone in at the interval with more than just a single goal to show for their efforts.

Half-time: Maidstone 0   Exeter City 1

Exeter came out after the interval intent on goals and stormed into the attack. Within a minute City had increased their lead, poor marking by the Maidstone defence allowing prolific goalscorer KELLOW to move in.

Three minutes later the Stones hauled themselves back into the game with a beautifully-taken goal. WOON, moving on to a free kick taken by Thompson, had time to smash the ball into the net from close range as Bond, the City goalkeeper, groped for the ball.

Goals were coming fast and furious and within minutes Exeter had gone 3–1 in the lead when PULLAR beat Guy with a well-placed shot. City went into a 4–1 lead in the 74th minute when Peter ROGERS moved in fast to beat Guy and his co-defenders.

Still pressing forward the Stones got their reward in the closing stages when OVARD secured a well-deserved goal to reduce the deficit.

Result: Maidstone 2   Exeter City 4

Teams:
Maidstone: Guy, Thompson, Hill, Hutton, Kinnear, Hamberger, Wiltshire, Newson, Ovard, Woon, Daubney. (Sub: Shield).
Exeter: Bond, M. Rogers, Hatch, Forbes, P. Roberts, L. Roberts, P. Rogers, Pullar, Delve, Pearson, Kellow. (Sub: Pratt).
Referee: Mr. A. Robinson, (Waterlooville).
Attendance: 6,347

CUP RUNS

1974/5

1st Round *23rd November*
Nuneaton Bor. ..2 Maidstone 2

1st Round Replay *26th November*
Maidstone ....2 Nuneaton Bor. ..0

2nd Round *14th December*
Swindon Town .3 Maidstone 1

1978/9

1st Round *25th November*
Maidstone ....1 Wycombe W. 0

2nd Round *16th December*
Maidstone ....1 Exeter City 0

3rd Round *9th January*
Charlton Ath. ...1 Maidstone 1

3rd Round Replay *15th January*
Maidstone ....1 Charlton Ath. ...2

1980/81

1st Round *22nd November*
Kettering Town .1 Maidstone 1

1st Round Replay *26th November*
Maidstone ....0 Kettering Town 0
(after extra time)

1st Round 2nd Replay *1st December*
Maidstone ....3 Kettering Town 1

2nd Round *13th December*
Gillingham ....0 Maidstone 0

2nd Round Replay *16th December*
Maidstone ....0 Gillingham 0
(after extra time)

2nd Round 2nd Replay *22nd Dec.*
Gillingham ....0 Maidstone 2

3rd Round *3rd January*
Maidstone ....2 Exeter City 4

NORTHWICH VICTORIA

Founded: 1874

League: Alliance Premier

Ground: Drill Field

Colours: Green and white shirts, white shorts

The Vics had not enjoyed much Cup limelight in the post-war years until the 1976/7 season when they set the football world alight with a remarkable run which took them to the Fourth Round, thus emulating their feat of 1884 when they also reached that stage in the Cup. After beating League clubs Rochdale (after two replays), Peterborough and Watford in successive rounds, the Vics were eliminated in the Fourth Round 3-1 by Oldham Athletic. This stimulating run gave the Vics a taste for Cup glory and they had another successful Cup run in 1979/80 when, after putting out Alliance Premier Leaguers Nuneaton Borough (after a replay), they held Fourth Division Wigan Athletic 2-2 in the Second Round and finally succumbed by a narrow 1-0 margin in the replay. The following season, again in the First Round, the Vics drew an interesting tie against well-placed Third Division Huddersfield Town and surprised their League opponents by holding them to a 1-1 draw. It was a different story in the replay, Town trouncing the part-timers 6-0.

Vics first post-war appearance in the First Round was in the 1955/6 season when they lost 3-2 away against fellow non-Leaguers Boston Utd. In the 1961/2 season the Vics were again in the First Round and again drawn away – against Fourth Division Southport against whom they lost 1-0 before a 7,100 crowd. Vics began their sensational 1976/7 season with an away tie against Fourth Division Rochdale at Spotland. After a goalless first-half Rochdale went into a 1-0 lead after 60 minutes but the Vics equalised in the closing stages. The replay at Drill Field, watched by the biggest crowd for 20 years, resulted in a goalless draw after extra time. Maine Road, Manchester was the venue for the second replay and the scene of a shock result. Nearly 5,000 spectators saw Vics' goalkeeper John Farmer, formerly

Gordon Banks' deputy at Stoke City, give a magnificent performance that helped the non-Leaguers to record a notable 2-1 victory. The score stood at 1-1 until nine minutes from the end when Collier snatched the goal that took the Vics into the Second Round.

This time the Vics were matched against Third Division Peterborough United, once a non-League side to be reckoned with in the Cup battles, at home at Drill Field. Although Posh adapted well to the wintry conditions and took the lead in the 22nd minute it was all of no avail since three minutes later the referee abandoned the game because of fog. The attendance, 6,898, was the highest at Drill Field since 1950.

The Vics had learned some lessons from this brief encounter with Posh and when the tie was resumed gave their supporters one of the greatest nights in the club's history, trouncing their distinguished visitors 4-0. The Vics were in a 1-0 lead at half-time after Phil Smith had scored a well-worked goal in the 25th minute. Peterborough realised that the game was slipping from their grasp when the Vics went 2-0 up in the 62nd minute through a Les Wain penalty conversion. In the 82nd minute it was curtains for Posh as Vics scored their third through Swede. A minute from time, to complete the glory night, Smith made it four and his personal tally two.

Vics: Farmer, Eccleshare, Hamlett, K. Jones, Nieman, Wain, King, P. Jones, Collier, Swede, Smith.

Although Vics' manager Paul Ogden, with seven Merseysiders in his team, would dearly have loved a Third Round plum draw against Everton or Liverpool he had to be content with a home game against Fourth Division Watford. The Vics provided the Cup shock of the day when after trailing twice they hit back to gain a sensational 3-2 victory, fully described in *Match Report* as is also the Vics' great Fourth Round encounter with Second Division Oldham Athletic.

The Vics drew a difficult away tie against fellow Alliance Premier Leaguers Nuneaton Borough in the First Round of the 1979/80 season. Northwich were leading 3-2 with two minutes to go when Nuneaton levelled the score. In the replay at Drill Field Borough were no match for an on-form Northwich who went through to the next round with a clearcut 3-0 victory, their reward being a home time against

Fourth Division Wigan Athletic, themselves former 'giant-killers' of the Northern Premier League.

After many postponements the game was played on Christmas Eve. Wigan were winning 3–0 when fog caused the game to be abandoned in the 65th minute. In the replayed game the Vics found themselves facing an on-form Wigan at the Drill Field. In the early stages the Alliance Premier Leaguers had to soak up tremendous pressure as the League side went into a 2–0 lead. The non-Leaguers came back into the game when they scored from a penalty in the 74th minute. In the dying moments of the game, with the Vics storming into the Wigan area, the part-timers equalised when Paul Mayman scored following a corner.

There was a large attendance of 11,298 at Springfield Park for the replay, the prize for the winners being a Third Round tie with Second Division Chelsea. The blank scoresheet at the end of the first-half was a fair reflection of the first 45 minutes. With only two minutes to go before extra time Wigan substitute Brownbill put an end to Northwich dreams when he back-headed into the net.

The following season, 1980/1 the Vics again got through to the First Round, drawing highly-placed Third Division Huddersfield Town at Drill Field. Although Town scored in the ninth minute and looked set to gain an easy passage into the next round, the part-timers drew on the skills of ex-Liverpool star Brian Hall who had won both a winner's and a loser's F.A. Cup medal and the experience of ex-Everton John Anderson to get them back into the game. This they did for having held Town to their single goal lead at half-time the part-timers hit back for John Denham to score a brilliant equaliser four minutes from time to force a replay at Huddersfield. This did not go well for the Vics, Huddersfield celebrating their lucky let-off with a 6–0 victory before a 'gate' of nearly 10,000.

MATCH REPORTS
THIRD ROUND F.A. CUP
8th January 1977
NORTHWICH VICTORIA 3   WATFORD 2

This was a history-making day for the Vics – reaching the Third Round to draw Fourth Division Watford at home and then beating the League side to put the part-timers in the Fourth Round for the first time since 1884. But before the glory moment there were some shocks for the non-Leaguers as Watford dominated the early stages of the game.

Two fine saves from Vics' goalkeeper Farmer prevented Watford going into an unassailable lead – once when he had to dive at Jenkins' feet to prevent a certain goal and shortly afterwards when he stopped a well-placed header from Keith Mercer, playing a dominant part in Watford's attack.

The 14th minute heralded the long-expected Watford goal, a well-directed pass from Prichett finding Keith MERCER on the left, the striker racing down the wing to draw Farmer before slotting the ball home. Watford continued on the attack but in the 25th minute, against the run of the play, the Vics equalised, SWEDE eluding two Watford defenders before firing in an unstoppable shot. Before half-time the League side regained the initiative, BOND, in the 37th minute, putting Watford in the lead for the second time.

Half-time: Northwich Victoria 1   Watford 2

Only three minutes into the second half the Vics found themselves on equal terms. As he was going through WAIN was brought down in the area and the Northwich striker, taking the kick himself, easily beat Rankin. It was the turning point of the game and Watford thereafter found themselves under attack until the final whistle.

Watford's goal had a series of hairbreadth misses but it seemed possible that the League side might survive for a replay. Nine minutes from the end however the Vics scored the goal they richly deserved, CORRIGAN, who had had a hand in the first goal, scoring the winner, a shot from close range. The crowd invaded the pitch in their excitement but play resumed after a few moments.

Watford had little hope of the equaliser and the final whistle blew with the Northwich crowd celebrating a famous victory.

Result: Northwich Victoria 3   Watford 2

Teams:
Northwich Victoria: Farmer, Eccleshare, Nieman, P. Jones, Hamlett, K. Jones, Wain, Corrigan, Smith, King, Swede, (Sub: Collier).
Watford: Rankin, Geidmintis, Pritchett, Bond, Horsfield, Garner, Joslyn, Downs, Coffill, Mercer, Jenkins, (Sub: Mayes).
Referee: Mr. H. P. Hackney, (Barnsley).
Attendance: 8,989

FOURTH ROUND F.A. CUP
29th January 1977
NORTHWICH VICTORIA 1   OLDHAM ATHLETIC 3

This game was the climax of the Vics' endeavours as they removed one League side after another to make more Cup progress than ever before in the history of the Club. The tie was played on Vics' favourite neutral ground, Manchester City's Maine Road, against Second Division Oldham Athletic.

The part-timers made a shaky start and never recovered their poise throughout the first half. On a hard ground with the sun streaming into his eyes Vics' goalkeeper Farmer had a nightmare start; in the third minute of the game 18-year-old VALENTINE put Oldham in front with a shot that went in at the near post and Farmer may not have seen much of the ball.

Oldham played attractive football and their speed and ball control constantly had the Vics in trouble. In the 17th minute, with the Vics' nerves still on edge, Athletic went 2–0 up, HALOM rushing in to capitalise on a mistake by Farmer when he dropped the ball. Northwich occasionally got their line going only to find former Everton player Hurst and the other Athletic defenders in good form and the attacks fizzled out.

Half-time: Northwich Victoria 0   Oldham Athletic 2

The second half was a different story, the Vics having overcome their nervousness and beginning to play with cohesion and spirit. Within three minutes of the resumption the Vics pulled a goal back through COLLIER. The part-timers, sensing the possibility of another glory game, surged forward into the Oldham half. But despite the fury of the non-Leaguers' attacks Oldham went further ahead in the 64th minute when during a breakaway HALOM made the game safe for the League side.

Result: Northwich Victoria 1   Oldham Athletic 3

Teams:
Northwich Victoria: Farmer, Eccleshare, Hamlett, K. Jones, Nieman, Wain, King, Corrigan, Collier, Smith, Swede. (Sub: P. Jones).
Oldham Athletic: Platt, Wood, Hicks, Hurst, Whittle, Bell, Robins, Chapman, Halom, Irving, Valentine. (Sub: Groves).
Referee: Mr. G. Courtney, (Spennymoor).
Attendance: 28,635

CUP RUNS

1955/6

1st Round *19th November*
Boston Utd. 3   Northwich Vics . 2

1961/2 *4th November*
Southport 1   Northwich Vics . 0

1976/7

1st Round – *20th November*
Rochdale 1   Northwich Vics . 1

1st Round Replay – *22nd November*
Northwich Vics . 0   Rochdale 0
(after extra time)

1st Round, Second Replay – *29th Nov.*
Northwich Vics . 2   Rochdale 1
(at Maine Road)

2nd Round – *11th December*
Northwich Vics . 0   Peterborough 1
(abandoned after 25 minutes)

2nd Round – *14th December*
Northwich Vics . 4   Peterborough 0

3rd Round – *8th January*
Northwich Vics . 3   Watford 2

4th Round – *29th January*
Northwich Vics . 1   Oldham 3

1979/80

1st Round – *24th November*
Nuneaton 3   Northwich Vics .3

1st Round Replay – *26th November*
Northwich Vics .3   Nuneaton 0

2nd Round – *5th January*
Northwich Vics . 2   Wigan Athletic .2

2nd Round Replay – *7th January*
Wigan Athletic .. 1   Northwich Vics . 0

1980/81

1st Round – *22nd November*
Northwich Vics . 1   Huddersfield 1

1st Round Replay – *25th November*
Huddersfield 6   Northwich Vics 0

NUNEATON BOROUGH

Founded: 1937

Ground: Manor Park

League: Alliance Premier

Colours: Blue and white striped shirts; white shorts

Nuneaton began their post-war Cup exploits as late as the 1949/50 season but did so in style reaching the Third Round via two non-League 'scalps' before going out to League opponents Exeter City 3-0 away from home. Borough again reached the dizzy heights of the Third Round in 1966/7, first having to overcome Wealdstone and tough Cup opponents Third Division Swansea before meeting Second Division Rotherham at Manor Park. This tie produced one of Nuneaton's greatest-ever Cup performances, holding the League side 1-1. In the replay at Millmoor before a crowd of nearly 23,000 Borough went down fighting by a narrow 1-0 margin. In addition to these achievements Borough have reached the Second Round a further three times in post-war years, in 1953/4 when they forced Queen's Park Rangers to a replay before losing 2-1, in 1976/7 when they received a 6-0 buffeting from Lincoln City and in 1977/8 when fellow non-Leaguers Tilbury gave Borough's Cup hopes a 2-1 jolt at Manor Park. Other League sides who have met Borough in the post-war Cup games have included Watford, whom the part-timers dismissed from the Cup 3-0 in the First Round in 1953, Brentford, Exeter City, who provided a three-game marathon in 1967, Torquay, Oxford Utd and Crewe.

Borough began their search for Cup glory in the 1949/50 season when they drew then East Counties League side King's Lynn at Manor Park, the start of an historic season. With Nuneaton in the grip of Cup fever club officials anticipated that the ground record of 8,995 might be beaten and it was, 12,554 spectators cramming into Manor Park to see Borough pull off a 2–1 win against unbeaten Lynn. In the Second Round Nuneaton were again lucky with the draw, entertaining Mossley of the Cheshire League at Manor Park before a crowd of nearly 11,000. There was no score at half-time and a disorganised Nuneaton side, reduced to nine men because of injury, kept their goal intact to force a replay. Despite further injuries Borough were the better side in the return match at Mossley and ran out 3-0 winners.

Borough's luck deserted them when the draw for the Third Round was made, drawing an away tie against Exeter City, Third Division South, at St. James's Park. A crowd of 14,365 saw a game that was largely one-way traffic towards the Borough penalty area and at the final whistle Exeter had beaten the non-Leaguers 3-0. At the end of the game Borough's prolific goal-scorer Plant was transferred to Second Division Bury.

Borough: Barber, Hudson, Carter, Kelly, Thompson, Bond, Slack, Hackland, Plant, Gilmour, Campbell.

Nuneaton had another great Cup season in 1953/4. Drawn at Manor Park in the First Round against Watford, Third Division South, Borough made club history by beating League oppostion for the first time and by a handsome 3-0 margin. A record crowd of 12,673 saw Borough take the initiative and go into a first half 2-0 lead. Watford improved in the second half as they fought to get back into the game but in the 78th minute it was curtains for the League side when the part-timers scored number three. Borough drew formidable Queen's Park Rangers, Third Division South, in the Second Round away at Loftus Road before a crowd of 18,000, QPR's biggest 'gate' of the season. After a goalless first-half Nuneaton continued on the offensive and in the 62nd minute went ahead. Borough held on to their lead until three minutes from the end when Rangers equalised to enable the League side to force a replay at Manor Park. The ground record was again broken (13,062) for the next encounter when Nuneaton gained the honours but Rangers the victory – by a narrow 2-1 margin. Rangers built up a two goal lead although Borough had most of the play in the first 20 minutes. Eight minutes from time Nuneaton reduced the deficit but they could not grab the equaliser despite a storming finish. Borough's team in the game against Watford and the first of two exciting duels with Rangers:

Barber, Smith, Snowball, Kernick, Hughes, Whitcroft, Morrow, Catleugh, Davies, Wright, Jessop.

In the replay Perry took the place of the injured Jessop. Borough had to go to Griffin Park in the First Round of the

1954/5 competition to meet Brentford, Third Division South. The 13,000 spectators saw plucky Borough open the scoring in the 11th minute and retain their lead to half-time but after the interval the Bees fought back and ran out 2-1 winners.

Nuneaton had another glory season in 1966/7 when for the second time in the post-war era they fought their way to the Third Round. They commenced their inspiring run with an away tie in the First Round against Isthmian Leaguers Wealdstone, Amateur Cup holders. Although honours were even in the first-half Borough scored two late goals to put them in the Second Round for the first time for 13 years. Borough gained home advantage when the draw was made, against struggling Third Division Swansea, always a force to be reckoned with in the Cup and who had beaten Southern Leaguers Folkestone 7-2 in the First Round. A crowd of 18,031 saw Nuneaton pull off a sensational 2-0 victory. Shrugging aside the difference in status Borough roared into the attack and had the ball in the Swansea net in the first minute only to have the referee disallow the 'goal'. It was end-to-end football but when Swansea attacked Borough's defenders quickly dealt with the League side's international line-up which included Ivor Allchurch. Manor Park erupted half-way through the first-half when inside left Tommy Crawley put Borough one up. Midway through the second-half the same player had the ball in the net again but the 'goal' was disallowed after which Swans' right-half Coughlin nodded the ball over his own goal-line to put the Southern Premier Leaguers two up. Borough's splendid win was rewarded with a home tie in the Third Round against Second Division Rotherham United who were held to a 1-1 draw whilst in the replay the League side squeezed through by a lone goal. Both matches are described in *Match Report*.

Borough were again in the First Round in the following season, 1967/8, when they drew a home game against Fourth Division Exeter City. A crowd of 12,359 saw Borough in command but Exeter's defence stood firm and the match finished a goalless draw. Both captains, Johnny Watts of Nuneaton and John Newman of Exeter City were former Birmingham City players, Newman having filled City's right-half position in the 1956 Cup Final. In the replay at Exeter it was the same story of defences on top although in this game Exeter were in command instead of the non-

Leaguers. There were no goals at the end of 90 minutes and the game went into extra time but again with no decision. Both games were in charge of world famous referee Mr. Clive Thomas. The second replay was staged at Bristol City's ground at Ashton Gate and it was third time lucky for Exeter who scored the only goal of the game. Over 24,000 spectators had watched the three games.

Borough: Crump, Jones, Hope, Watts, Aston, Hill, Ashe, Cutler, Richards, Allen, Smith. Sub. L. Wright.

First game: Mick Keeley for Allen.

After their marathon against Exeter Nuneaton had to wait until the 1971/2 season before their next appearance in the First Round, an away game against Third Division Torquay United. The League side scored the only goal of the game in the 18th minute.

In the following season Nuneaton were again in the First Round draw, being matched away from home against fellow non-Leaguers Telford United (formerly Wellington Town) of the Premier Division of the Southern League. A hard game resulted in Borough being removed from the Cup by a narrow 3-2 margin.

Borough subsequently missed a season but in the 1974/5 they were back in First Round contention, gaining home advantage against fellow non-Leaguers Maidstone United, Premier Division, Southern League. After a terrific struggle both sides came out of it with two goals each. At the replay at London Road Common, Maidstone had a comparatively easy task against an off-form Borough and won 2-0.

Nuneaton continued their run of meeting fellow Southern League sides when in 1975/6 they drew a home game against tough F.A. Cup fighters Wimbledon. The Dons had most of the game, had a 'goal' disallowed, and scored the only goal of the game four minutes after half-time.

The next season, 1976/7, Borough had to travel to meet Crook Town of the Northern Premier League in the First Round. After taking a 2-0 lead Borough's goalkeeper put through his own goal but two further Nuneaton goals in the closing stages gave the Southern Premier Leaguers a comfortable 4-1 win. Borough's Second Round tie took them away from home to Lincoln City where they had a nightmare game, City piling up a 6-0 score including two penalties.

Nuneaton were again on the Cup trail in the 1977/8 season

when they drew a First Round tie at Manor Park against Third Division Oxford United and brought off a sensational 2-0 victory. Before a crowd of nearly 8,000 Borough were a goal up within two minutes and inspired by this success continued to throw attack after attack against the luckless League side. In the second-half a 59th minute penalty converted by Borough's Brendan Phillips effectively put paid to any further Oxford interest in the Cup.

Nuneaton: Knight, Stephens, Thomas, Cross, Peake, Lang, Philips, Fleet, Vincent, Lewis, Smithers. Sub. Owen.

After this giant-killing act much was expected of Borough in the Second Round when they again had home advantage and drew Isthmian Leaguers Tilbury. After Nuneaton had had the better of the opening exchanges Tilbury were presented with a 'gift' goal and although Borough were on terms by the interval it was Tilbury who snatched the match-winner during a break-away.

Nuneaton kept up their sequence of First Round appearances in the 1978/9 season when they drew a home tie against Fourth Division Crewe Alexandra. Crewe went into a two-nil lead by half-time and although Borough made several spirited attacks after the interval the Crewe defenders held out.

Borough were again in the First Round in the 1979/80 season drawing a home game against fellow Alliance Premier Leaguers Northwich Victoria, the resourceful Cup-fighting side from Lancashire. Honours were even at half-time with the score-line 1-1. In a fluctuating second half the Vics went ahead through a penalty, Nuneaton equalised, and again the Lancastrians hurled players forward and restored their lead. In the closing stages of the game there was a dramatic turn of events as Borough's Eamonn Pugh burst through to make the score 3-3 and at the same time to get his hat-trick. Borough were disappointing in the replay at Drill Field going down 3-0.

In the 1981/2 competition Boro drew an away game in the First Round against Northern League side, doughty Cup fighters Bishop Auckland. The Alliance Premier Leaguers had an off day and were no match for Auckland. The Bishops led 1-0 at half-time and although Nuneaton equalised early in the second half Auckland scored a further three to gain a comprehensive 4-1 victory.

MATCH REPORTS
THIRD ROUND F.A. CUP
28th January 1967
NUNEATON BOROUGH 1   ROTHERHAM UNITED 1

This great Cup tie, one of the finest F.A. Cup encounters in Borough's history, before a crowd of 22,114 at Manor Park, produced all the drama and excitement of a Third Round game. Borough held their Second Division opponents to a 1–1 draw and with any luck might have gone into the Fourth Round.

Nuneaton's captain for the day was right-winger Norman Ashe who had played for Rotherham three seasons previously.

In the early exchanges the eager Rotherham forwards swamped the Nuneaton defences and Crump was called into action to save several dangerous situations. It was not entirely one-way traffic for both Richards and Ashe went close for Borough. Drizzling rain which had set in shortly before the game began turned into a downpour and the players had to battle it out on an extremely muddy pitch.

In the 18th minute Nuneaton had a shock when Rotherham inside-left had the ball in the net but the referee disallowed the 'goal' because of a handling offence. Nuneaton responded briskly and in the next minute set the Manor Park ground alight when inside-right CUTLER glided the ball into the net through a crowd of players following a rebound from a Rotherham defender from a Billy Hails' shot.

Rotherham responded as expected to this setback and mounted a series of forceful raids on the Nuneaton goal. Malcolm Allen had a superb game in the left-half position for Borough.

Half-time: Nuneaton Borough 1   Rotherham United 0

The second half had only just begun when Rotherham drew level. A Massey shot was deflected by a Borough defender to Rotherham centre-forward Galley on the line who flicked the ball to David CHAMBERS who headed in out of Crump's reach.

Half way through the second half Nuneaton's free-scoring Crawley broke through and as a goal appeared imminent Rotherham goalkeeper Hill dashed out and both players collapsed in a heap. Crawley, with a knee injury, was carried off on a stretcher and Hill, suffering from concussion, collapsed on the touchline and had to be carried to the dressing room and took no further part in the game. Galley took over as goalkeeper for Rotherham.

In an intense bout of attacking by the Yorkshire visitors Fred Crump distinguished himself in the Nuneaton goal. In the 77th minute Nuneaton made loud appeals for a penalty as centre-forward Richards appeared to be brought down in the penalty area but the referee waved on play.

Result: Nuneaton Borough 1   Rotherham United 1

Teams:
Nuneaton Borough: Crump, Jones, Wilson, Davis, Watts, Allen, Ashe, Cutler, Richards, Crawley, Hails. Sub. Sweeney.
Rotherham United: Hill, Wilcockson, Clish, Rabjohn, Haselden, Tiler, Massey, Williams, Galley, Chappell, Chambers.
Referee: Mr. W. Crossley, (Lancaster).
Attendance: 22,114 (Ground record)

THIRD ROUND F.A. CUP REPLAY
31st January 1967
ROTHERHAM UNITED 1   NUNEATON BOROUGH 0

Nuneaton, the last non-League side left in the 1966/7 F.A. Cup competition, went out bravely. In a spirited replay, during which the Borough looked every bit as good as their Second Division opponents, United's goalkeeper Hill several times saved his side.

A capacity crowd of nearly 23,000 packed the Millmoor ground. Rotherham's pace dictated the early exchanges but once Borough got into their stride the League side was frequently in danger. Cutler narrowly missed putting Borough in the lead.

Half-time: Rotherham United 0   Nuneaton Borough 0

Four minutes after half-time luck deserted the Borough as Rotherham scored a much-disputed goal. Rotherham right-back Wilcockson lobbed the ball goalwards and with the United forwards rushing in Borough goalkeeper Crump made a half clearance; in the subsequent scramble, with Crump down, Rotherham inside-left CHAPPELL prodded the ball home. The referee gave a goal but was immediately surrounded by protesting Nuneaton players who alleged that Crump had been held as the goal was scored. The referee refused the appeal and the goal was allowed to stand. Nuneaton applied themselves to the task of getting the equaliser and frequently the only man between them and at least one goal was Rotherham's goalkeeper Hill. At the end of the match the sporting Rotherham side acknowledged Nuneaton's gallant fight by lining up and cheering the players off the field.

Result: Rotherham United 1   Nuneaton Borough 0

Teams:
Rotherham United: Hill, Wilcockson, Clish, Rabjohn, Haselden, Tiler, Massey, Williams, Galley, Chappell, Chambers.
Nuneaton Borough: Crump, Jones, Wilson, Davis, Thompson, Allen, Ashe, Cutler, Richards, Crawley, Hails. Sub. Sweeney.
Referee: Mr. W. Crossley, (Lancaster).
Attendance: 22,930

CUP RUNS

1949/50

1st Round – *26th November*
Nuneaton 2   King's Lynn 1

2nd Round – *10th December*
Nuneaton 0   Mossley 0

2nd Round Replay – *17th December*
Mossley 0   Nuneaton 3

3rd Round – *7th January*
Exeter 3   Nuneaton 0

1953/4

1st Round – *21st November*
Nuneaton 3   Watford 0

2nd Round – *12th December*
QPR 1   Nuneaton 1

2nd Round Replay – *17th December*
Nuneaton 1   QPR 2

1954/5

1st Round – *20th November*
Brentford 2   Nuneaton 1

1966/7

1st Round – *26th November*
Wealdstone 0   Nuneaton 2

2nd Round – *7th January*
Nuneaton 2   Swansea Town ..0

3rd Round – *26th January*
Nuneaton 1   Rotherham 1

3rd Round Replay – *31st January*
Rotherham 1   Nuneaton 0

1967/8

1st Round – *9th December*
Nuneaton 0   Exeter City 0

1st Round replay – *13th December*
Exeter City 0   Nuneaton 0
(after extra time)

1st Round, Second replay – *18th Dec.*
Nuneaton 0   Exeter City 1
(at Ashton Gate, Bristol)

1971/2

1st Round – *20th November*
Torquay Utd 1   Nuneaton 0

1972/3

1st Round – *18th November*
Telford Utd 3   Nuneaton 2

1974/5

1st Round – *23rd November*
Nuneaton 2   Maidstone Utd .2

1st Round Replay – *26th November*
Maidstone Utd ..2   Nuneaton 0

1975/6

1st Round – *22nd November*
Nuneaton 0   Wimbledon 1

1976/7

1st Round – *20th November*
Crook Town 1   Nuneaton 4

2nd Round – *11th December*
Lincoln C 6   Nuneaton 0

1977/8

1st Round – *26th November*
Nuneaton 2   Oxford Utd 0

2nd Round – *17th December*
Nuneaton 1   Tilbury 2

1978/9

1st Round – *25th November*
Nuneaton 0   Crew 2

1979/80

1st Round – *24th November*
Nuneaton 3   Northwich Vics .3

1st Round Replay – *26th November*
Northwich Vics .3   Nuneaton 0

1981/2

1st Round – *21st November*
Bishop Auck. 4   Nuneaton 1

OXFORD UNITED
(formerly Headington United)

Founded: 1896

League: Third Division (formerly Southern)

Ground: Manor Road

Colours: Yellow shirts with blue stripe; blue shorts.

Before they graduated to League status United played under the name of Headington United, honoured members of the Southern League. Their Cup exploits as non-Leaguers, when they fought their way to the Fourth Round in the 1953/4 season and again in 1960/1 when they reached the Third Round, undoubtedly put the seal on their election to the fourth Division, as it did subsequently for other non-League sides such as Peterborough United, Hereford, Wigan, etc. In their remarkable Cup run in 1953/4 Headington United were beaten 4-2 by Bolton Wanderers after having defeated League sides Millwall (after a replay) and Stockport County on their way to the heights. Their Third Round encounter in the 1960/1 season when they were beaten away from home by First Division Leicester City came via the 'scalps' of two non-League clubs. Other League sides that United met during the post-war period and before their election to the League were Norwich City and Brentford.

Not only was the 1953/4 season memorable for producing United's finest Cup run ever as non-Leaguers but it was the first time in their history that the club had got as far as the First Round. Their opponents were Eastern Counties League amateurs Harwich and Parkeston, the previous season's Amateur Cup finalists and United looked like making an early exit when Harwich built up a 2–0 half-time lead. The second-half belonged to Headington who scored three times without reply to make the final score 3–2. This victory led to a Second Round encounter with Third Division South, Millwall, away at The Den. Although Millwall opened the scoring the non-Leaguers had built up a fantastic 3–1 lead with 25 minutes to go. But a great victory just eluded United, Millwall pulling back two goals, the last three minutes from time, to force a replay at Manor Road. Local football history was made when a 7,000 'gate' saw the non-Leaguers pull off a sensational 1-0 victory, a 20th minute header from Ken Smith proving the decisive goal which took United into the prestige-making Third Round. Their opponents were Stockport City, Third Division North, away from home.

There was a crowd of 15,650 at the Edgeley Park ground to see Harry Thompson's men take on the League side. The part-timers brought off a goalless draw to force a replay at Manor Road. For this memorable replay, watched by 9,955, Headington were at full strength although Stockport made several positional changes because of injuries. A thrilling first-half produced no goals but in the 20th minute after the resumption Peart scored the match-winner for the non-Leaguers. United's defence held firm and the non-Leaguers triumph over powerful League opponents was one of the shock results of the round.

Headington: Ansell, Ramshaw, Croker, Hudson, Craig, Crichton, Steel, Peart, Smith, Duncan, Maskell.

Headington made further history when they went into the draw for the Fourth Round, yet another non-League side in the last 32, and set to meet mighty First Division Bolton Wanderers at Manor Road. This game is fully described in *Match Report*.

After this triumph Headington were again in the First Round in the next season, drawing a hard tie away from home against Norwich City, Third Division South. There was a crowd of 18,827 at Carrow Road to see United forge ahead in the 11th minute, only for Norwich to equalise before half-time. At that stage Headington had matched the resources of the League side but in the second-half the Canaries slipped into gear to score three more and with the part-timers adding a goal almost on time the final scoreline read 4-2.

Three seasons were to elapse before Headington again appeared in the First Round – in the 1958/9 season when they faced Margate, then in the Kent League, at Manor Road. Both sides were evenly matched and with the game almost over and the score reading 2-2, with Headington having taken the lead twice, the Southern Leaguers scored the match-winner nine minutes from the end. For their Second Round encounter Headington drew a difficult away tie with all-conquering Peterborough United, then still in the Midland League. There was a big 'gate' of 16,855 at the London Road ground to see Posh go into a 2-0 lead before half-time. In the last 15 minutes of the game four goals were scored including one from Billy Rees, formerly Cardiff, Spurs, Orient and Welsh international for Headington. The final tally read 4-2. It was the last occasion that Headington appeared in the First Round under that name.

In the 1960/1 season, in their first First Round turn-out as Oxford United, the Southern Leaguers were drawn away against Amateur Cup holders Hendon, the start of another epic season for United. Oxford, unbeaten leaders of the Southern League, scored in the sixth minute but Hendon, no pushovers, equalised and had a 'goal' disallowed early in the second half. The amateurs then went ahead but United got on terms to force a replay. There were 10,600 spectators at the replay under Oxford's floodlights, the Southern Leaguers making the early running to go 2-0 ahead. Hendon got one back, United restored their lead to make it 3-1, Hendon narrowing the gap in the closing stages with another goal. This win again saw Oxford in the Second Round, drawing Western League side Bridgwater at Manor Road. Bridgwater were not an easy side to overcome and until the 89th minute the two teams were locked in a 1-1 deadlock. Then up popped Kyle, the Southern Leaguers' centre-half, to head in the vital goal that once again took them into the Third Round, drawn away against First Division Leicester City, an exciting game which Leicester won 3-1 and fully reported in *Match Report*.

Again in the First Round in the 1961/2 competition Oxford had to visit Griffin Park to play Third Division South, Brentford no friends in the past of non-Leaguers in the Cup. Arthur Turner's team did well in the early stages causing the League side to concede corner after corner. But eventually Brentford turned on the pressure and emerged easy 3-0 winners. It was United's last appearance in the Cup as a non-League club, their well-merited election to the Fourth Division taking place in 1962/3.

MATCH REPORTS

FOURTH ROUND F.A. CUP
30th January 1954
HEADINGTON UNITED 2   BOLTON WANDERERS 4

This was one of the greatest moments in the United's history, a home tie against distinguished First Division opponents Bolton Wanderers. Excitement ran high in the university town before the match and in anticipation of a ground record a temporary stand was erected to accommodate the maximum number of spectators at Manor Road.

There were three internationals in the Bolton side.

The icy pitch prevented Bolton from showing their artistry and many passes went adrift. Territorially Headington had as much play as the First Division side.

In the 24th minute Bolton went into the lead when from a corner kick a goalmouth melee ensued and as the ball ran loose LOFTHOUSE snapped it up to score. Headington, stung by this reverse, set their attack moving but came up against a rock-like Bolton defence, in which centre-half Barrass played an outstanding game. Despite Headington's pressure Bolton scored again in the 36th minute, this time through a great drive from PARRY.

Half-time: Headington United 0   Bolton Wanderers 2

The second half opened with Headington's left-half Crighton narrowly missing with a free kick.

When play switched to the other end Lofthouse was brought down and Parry took the free kick for MOIR to head Bolton's third. Headington undiscouraged by this setback hit back and soon reduced the deficit with a goal from PEART who netted from close range. Headington continued to attack and both Steel and Duncan went close as the Southern Leaguers surged around the Bolton goal. It was while the Wanderers' defence was at full stretch dealing with this onslaught that they broke out and scored again. A free-kick was lofted into the penalty area where STEVENS accurately placed the ball wide of the Headington goalkeeper.

In the 76th minute Ken SMITH shot on the turn to score a great goal for the non-Leaguers to make the final score 4–2. Although beaten Headington's display did much to enhance the status of the club and Southern League football generally.

Result: Headington United 2   Bolton Wanderers 4

Teams:
Headington United: Ansell, Ramshaw, Croker, Hudson, Craig, Crighton, Steel, Peart, Smith, Duncan, Maskell.
Bolton Wanderers: Hanson, Ball, T. Banks, Wheeler, Barrass, Bell, Holden, Moir, Lofthouse, Stevens, Parry.
Attendance: 16,670

THIRD ROUND F.A. CUP
7th January 1961
LEICESTER CITY 3   OXFORD UNITED 1

In meeting this strong First Division opposition in the Third Round of the Cup, Oxford United put the seal on a highly successful Cup season, the first since changing their name from the famous Headington United to Oxford.

Oxford took 3,000 supporters to Filbert Street where a crowd of 25,600 saw Oxford captain Atkinson win the toss. On a muddy pitch the fast-moving Leicester attack quickly moved to the Oxford territory, Riley, the Leicester outside right initiating several dangerous raids.

Both defences played excellent football. Leicester looked for an early goal but Oxford's pivot Kyle, a dominant figure in the middle, kept City's strikers at bay.

In the 28th minute Leicester scored. The movement started with Riley who slipped WALSH a pass 30 yards from goal and the inside right's shot ripped into the net. Six minutes later the home side notched their second. Again the manoeuvre started with Riley who slipped through the Oxford defence, centred to Walsh for under-23 international LEEK to head in. Leicester turned on the pressure and United goalkeeper Medlock brought off several magnificent saves.

Half-time: Leicester City 2   Oxford United 0

The Cup-tie thrills continued in the second half. Under floodlights the Leicester City forwards swarmed to the attack but Oxford's defence remained steady under pressure. Once Medlock earned a big ovation when he tipped a Keyworth header over the bar. After the game had been in progress an hour Leicester added to their score when RILEY left the Oxford defence standing still as he hit the ball over the goalkeeper's head into goal.

Then came a tremendous Oxford rally. Corner after corner was conceded as Leicester were forced on the defensive. In the 78th minute Oxford got a richly deserved goal as Knight broke through the Leicester defence to enable JONES to score. The game finished with Oxford still pressing, a grand finish by the Southern League club. Oxford were loudly cheered off the ground.

Teams:
Leicester City: Banks, Chalmers, Norman, McLintock, King, Appleton, Riley, Walsh, Leek, Keyworth, Wills.
Oxford United: Medlock, Beavon, Adams, Atkinson, Kyle, Denial, Knight, McIntosh, Luke, Jones, Love.
Referee: Mr. A. Hawcroft, (Kilnhurst).
Attendance: 25,601 (receipts £6,100)

CUP RUNS

(As Headington United)

1953/4

1st Round *21st November*
Harwich & P. ...2   Headington 3

2nd Round *12th December*
Millwall 3   Headington 3

2nd Round Replay *17th December*
Headington 1   Millwall 0

3rd Round - *9th January*
Stockport 0   Headington 0

3rd Round Replay - *14th January*
Headington 1   Stockport 0

4th Round - *30th January*
Headington 2   Bolton W. 4

1954/5

1st Round *20th November*
Norwich 4   Headington 2

1958/9

1st Round *15th November*
Headington 3   Margate 2

2nd Round - *6th December*
Peterborough 4   Headington 2

(As Oxford United)

1960/1

1st Round *5th November*
Hendon 2   Oxford United ..2

1st Round Replay *9th November*
Oxford United ..3   Hendon 2

2nd Round - *26th November*
Oxford United ..2   Bridgwater 1

3rd Round - *7th January*
Leicester City 3   Oxford United 1

1961/2

1st Round - *4th November*
Brentford 3   Oxford United ..0

ELECTED TO 4th DIVISION 1962/3

PETERBOROUGH UNITED

Founded: 1923

League: Formerly Midland, now Fourth Division

Ground: London Road

Colours: Blue shirts, white shorts

Before they gained League status in 1960/1 Peterborough were one of the greatest non-League Cup-fighting sides in the country and there can be no doubt that it was because of those feats that Posh were eventually elected to the higher echelons in British football. The then non-Leaguers started their post-war Cup run in the 1946/47 season when they were drawn appropriately against another famous non-League Cup-fighting side Yeovil and defeated them after a replay to go on to draw Northampton Town in the Second Round, the League side needing two replays before they disposed of Posh in a 8-1 debacle.

In the 1953/4 season Posh fought their way to the Third Round for the first time since the war being defeated 3-1 by then First Division Cardiff City at Ninian Park. Peterborough went on to even greater heights in 1956/7 when, via the scalps of Yeovil and League sides Bradford City and Lincoln City (whom they beat in a Third Round replay 5-4) they took on Second Division Huddersfield Town away from home in the Fourth Round to be defeated 3-1.

Two seasons later, in 1958/9, Peterborough thrilled the soccer world by again appearing in the Third Round drawn away against Second Division Fulham. The encounter at Craven Cottage resulted in a 0-0 draw, Posh going down in the replay by a slender 1-0 margin.

In 1959/60 Peterborough again demonstrated their fitness for League status, again reaching the Fourth Round after inflicting defeats on League sides Shrewsbury, Walsall and Ipswich. their opponents in the Fourth Round being First Division Sheffield Wednesday away at Hillsborough, the League side narrowly defeating Posh 2-0 before a crowd of over 51,000. This impressive run finally convinced eveyone that Peterborough should be in the League and it was the last F.A. Cup game as non-Leaguers for Posh were rightly elected to the Fourth Division for the start of the 1960/61 season.

There was something symbolic about United's start to their

memorable post-war Cup history when they drew famous non-League Cup fighters Yeovil Town of the Southern League in the First Round of the 1946/7 season away from home at Huish. A thrilling game ended in a 2-2 draw with Yeovil forcing a replay 18 minutes from the end with a penalty. There was Cup-tie fever at Peterborough for the replay at London Road when after a goalless first-half Posh scored the only goal of the match in the 56th minute.

Peterborough were set to entertain Northampton Town, Third Division South, in the Second Round, an exciting game ending in a 1-1 draw to take the League side to a replay. The struggle continued on an ice-bound pitch, Posh scoring first in the 19th minute and holding on to their lead until half-time. Posh were besieged in the second-half and in the 70th minute the Cobblers got the equaliser. In the closing stages and during extra time the Peterborough defence held firm and a further replay was necessary. This was staged at Coventry and Peterborough's defence did not match their earlier performances. Northampton eclipsed the Midland Leaguers 8-1.

After missing a season Posh were back on First Round duty in 1948/9 when they had a home against Third Division South, Torquay United. In the 25th minute Torquay scored the only goal of the match.

When Peterborough were again in the First Round, in the 1952/3 season, by coincidence they again had to entertain at London Road their previous League opponents Torquay United. There were 12,938 spectators on the ground to see Posh gain a memorable victory and revenge for the 1948/9 defeat. After a goalless first-half the United strikers clicked into gear, scored their first in the 55th minute and got the ball in the net again a minute later but this effort was disallowed. In the 80th minute Torquay equalised but with only three minutes left for play Posh scored again to make the final score 2-1. In goal for Posh was player-manager Jack Fairbrother, the former Newcastle United star.

In the Second Round for the third time in its history the Midland Leaguers again had the luck of the draw being matched at home against Third Division South leaders Bristol Rovers. Before a crowd of 15,280 Posh fully extended their League opponents who were lucky to win by a lone goal.

Again in the First Round in the following season, 1953/4,

United were drawn against Athenian League amateurs Hitchin Town away at Top Field. Hitchin, one of the original entrants in the F.A. Cup competition in 1871, saw a lively Posh side leading 2-0 within seven minutes and to go through to the next round 3-1. In the Second Round Posh drew struggling Third Division South, Aldershot at London Road. The attendance, 16,717, broke the ground record. After a goalless first-half the Midland Leaguers were two up. After this setback Aldershot turned on a sustained bombardment for the rest of the game, pulling one back in the 75th minute but denied the equaliser by a resolute Posh defence.

The Midland Leaguers' reward for this great victory was a Third Round away encounter against First Division Cardiff City. Six special trains left Peterborough to watch the Midland Leaguers take on the Welshmen at Ninian Park before a crowd of 38,000. It was the first time that United had reached the Third Round other than in 1928 when the now defunct Peterborough and Fletton Utd went down 4-3 to Birmingham. In the Peterborough team were four former First Division players, Fairbrother, Anderson – both of whom had won Cup Finalist's medals – Sloan, the former Irish international and Hair. There was a sensational opening, United taking the lead in the fifth minute, George Hair thundering in a shot, Howells the City 'keeper unable to hold the ball and Martin following up to shoot into the net. Cardiff fought back strenuously for the equaliser and got it in the 14th minute through centre-forward Welsh international Trevor Ford. The game continued to be end-to-end, half-time being reached with the score still 1-1. For the first 20 minutes of the second-half Cardiff were in command although United occasionally threatened from breakaways. It looked as if the stalemate would continue when in the 81st minute Ford volleyed in number two for City. Four minutes from the end City broke out again for Northcott to score to bring the final tally to 3-1. The *Peterborough Citizen and Advertiser* summed up this moment in the history of the club when it said: 'All will recall January 9th 1954 as the day when the gallant 5,000 responded to a dream and travelled across the heart of England to watch their beloved United'.

Teams. Cardiff: Howells, Rutter, Sullivan, Baker, Mont-

gomery, Blair, Thomas, Nugent, Ford, Northcott, Edwards.
Peterborough: Fairbrother, Moody, Hall, Anderson, Rigby, Sloan, Campbell, Martin, Taft, Matthews, Hair.

Again in the First Round in the 1955/6 season United had an attractive home fixture against Third Division leaders Ipswich Town. The ground record was smashed with a crowd of 20,671 including several thousand from Ipswich, the highest Cup attendance of the day. At half-time the teams were level 1-1 Peterborough also having a 'goal' disallowed. In the second-half the Midland Leaguers gradually took over control and added two further goals to make the final score 3-1, one of the finest Cup victories ever witnessed at London Road.

In the Second Round United were drawn away from home to struggling Third Division South side Swindon Town. United were the sixth non-League side to visit Swindon's ground since the war in the early rounds of the Cup and each was defeated, in some cases heavily. There were eight thousand Posh fans among the 23,983 crowd who watched United put up a purposeful display against the League side. In the 12th minue Posh were ahead and they held the lead until after half time when Swindon equalised in the 69th minute to earn a replay at London Road.

There was a crowd of nearly 17,000 for the resumed game, a high turnout for a mid-week match. Posh had the better of the early exchanges and it was against the run of the play when Swindon scored in the 21st minute. Early in the second-half United equalised and the score was still 1-1 at the end of 90 minutes. Five minutes into extra time Swindon scored a surprise goal, the ball richochetting into the net to give the League side a 2-1 victory.

Then came the dream season of 1956/7 when United achieved the almost impossible of reaching the Fourth Round for the first time in the club's history. In the First Round they were matched against Southern Leaguers Yeovil away on the famous Huish slope. United manager George Swindon had the brainwave of taking his players for training to a local ground that had a marked resemblance to Huish. A 10,570 crowd, including 2,000 from Peterborough, saw Posh move quickly to the attack and score in the second minute. Five minutes from half-time the Southern Leaguers equalised but there was no stopping United who added two further goals to emerge 3-1 winners.

In the Second Round United again had the luck of the draw, playing hosts to Bradford, Third Division North. Bradford, formidable Cup fighters, had lost only one away Cup game since the end of the war, came out on to the pitch to a welcome from nearly 19,000 spectators. From the outset United stamped their authority on the game, were soon two goals to the good and in the 54th minute put the issue beyond doubt when the non-Leaguers scored again to make the final tally 3-0. United's reward was a Third Round home game against Second Division Lincoln City.

The game against Lincoln, which broke the previous ground record with a 22,000 all-ticket attendance, revived memories of 1895 when Peterborough Town, making their first appearance in the F.A. Cup met City and were defeated 13-0! An inside forward playing in the team of that year, Jim Stallebrass, watched the exciting game of 1957. Continuous pressure by United kept the Imps on the defensive but there were no goals up to half-time. Although the Second Division side continued to struggle after the resumption it was they who opened the scoring in the 58th minute with a Watson header. United counter-attacked and within seven minutes were level through Emery and three minutes later the same player scored again to send the Posh supporters wild with delight. Although Posh seemed home and dry Lincoln scored a sensational equaliser a minute from time when Troops scored a hotly disputed penalty to force a replay at Sincil Bank to provide the non-Leaguers with another history-making game.

This replay provided Peterborough with one of the greatest Cup victories in the club's annals. Lincoln made three forward changes from the side that drew at London Road. Posh set a fast pace that continued throughout the game and eventually into extra time. In the eighth minute the ball spun out of the City's goalkeeper's hands for Andy Donaldson, former Middlesborough centre-forward, to tap it into an empty net. Four minutes later Donaldson scored again; City got one back to make the half-time score 2-1. Lincoln improved in the second-half and scored their anticipated equaliser two minutes from time through Neal. During extra time United ripped into the Lincoln defence and in the space of ten minutes took the score from 2-2 to an unforgettable 5-2 through goals by Emery, Smith and Donaldson, his third of the match. Lincoln were by no means finished however and in an amazing fight-back scored twice through Northcott and Bannan (penalty) to make the final score an amazing 5-4 in favour of Posh.

Teams: Lincoln City. Downie, Graham, Troops, Middleton, Emery (T), Neal, Munro, Bannan, Northcott, Watson, Finch.
Peterborough: Walls, Douglass, Barr, Shaw, Rigby, Cockburn, Hails, Emery (D), Donaldson, Smith, Hogg.
Attendance: 18,216.

When the names came out of the hat for the Fourth Round Posh found they had an away game on their hands against Second Division Huddersfield Town, fully described in *Match Report*.

In 1957/8 United drew a home First Round tie against Torquay United, Third Division South, the third occasion in nine seasons that the two teams had met in the Cup. The one way traffic towards the Torquay area delighted the 17,800 crowd who were treated to a 3-0 lead by the non-Leaguers at half-time. But in the second-half Posh frittered away their lead to allow Torquay to draw level to force a replay at Plainmoor. Although for long periods of the resumed game Posh held territorial advantage they went down by a lone goal scored in the 16th minute.

It was now expected by the football world that Posh would be in contention in the First Round of the Cup and beyond and in the next season, 1958/9, the giantkillers drew a home game against fellow non-Leaguers Kettering Town, Southern League, in the First Round to begin another fantastic run. The game at London Road drew 17,800 spectators, the third highest Cup 'gate' of the day, who had a shock when the Poppies went ahead in the eighth minute. Posh equalised before half-time and a goal each after the interval produced a 2-2 final scoreline and a replay at Rockingham Road. It was a thrilling replay before a crowd of 11,400 and again the score at 90 minutes was 2-2, with Posh having the advantage of a Kettering 'own goal'. Peterborough dominated extra time and netted the match-winner once again to go into the Second Round.

For this tie Posh had the luck of the draw, matched against Southern Leaguers Headington United (now Oxford United of Division Three) at London Road. There was another fine attendance, 16,855, to see a thrilling encounter that produced a convincing 4-2 win for Posh. Peterborough were comfortably on top in the early stages, going into a 2-0 half-time lead and adding a further goal in the 74th minute. Headington got one back, Posh added to their score with a penalty and the Southern Leaguers further reduced the deficit in the closing stages to make the score look respectable. Headington's exit brought Peterborough a rewarding Third Round tie against then Second Division Fulham at Craven Cottage.

January 10th 1959 was the day when the name of Peterborough echoed throughout the soccer world as they held star-studded Fulham to a 0-0 draw. The Londoners included in their side such famous English internationals as Graham Leggat, Jim Langley and Eddie Lowe; Jimmy Hill, of BBC fame, was also in the Fulham side. Among the 31,000 spectators on the frozen Craven Cottage ground were over 10,000 Peterborough fans. When half-time arrived the scoresheet was blank despite ceaseless pressure from Posh. Both goalkeepers were on top form and in the dying moments of the game, as United mounted a series of sharp raids, only fine defensive work by the Fulham back division, Cohen, Langley and Bentley plus goalkeeper Macedo kept out the Posh strikers.

There was a great crowd of 21,600 to welcome Fulham to London Road for the replay which began with Fulham on the attack and in the eighth minute having the bad luck of having Langley injured and off the pitch for most of the game. Posh attacked strongly and it was against the run of the play when Fulham scored the only goal of the game in the 18th minute through Johnson. After the interval Peterborough were constantly on the attack, Fulham's goal having a charmed life, Macedo, who played brilliantly, once taking the ball off of Emery's head as he was about to score. Shots rained in on the Fulham goal, the ball striking the crossbar and the uprights but stubbornly refusing to go into the Fulham net. The hard-pressed Fulham rearguard held firm and despite a further Posh rally in the dying minutes went off with their 1-0 lead intact. Teams for both games:

Peterborough. Walls, Stafford, Walker, Banham, Rigby, Chadwick, Hails, Emery, Rayner, Smith, McNamee.
Fulham. Macedo, Cohen, Langley, Lowe, Bentley, Lawler,

Leggat, Hill, Cook, Haynes, Johnson.

Peterborough had another magical Cup run in the following year, 1959/60 which was to be, rightly and deservedly, their last season as non-Leaguers. For the First Round they drew Third Division Shrewsbury Town, once a Midland League side themselves, at home at London Road. There was a crowd of 16,321 to see a Cup thriller end in Peterborough's favour 4–3.

Shrewsbury went in at half-time with a 1–0 lead and added to their score five minutes after the interval. These reverses inspired Posh who reduced the deficit ten minutes later and then equalised mid-way through the half. Shrewsbury returned to the attack and with only 13 minutes left for play again went into the lead. Still Peterborough attacked and amid tremendous excitement drew level for the second time. With the crowd willing on the part-timers Peterborough threw everything into the attack and in an epic finish Jim Rayner, two minutes from time, made the final score 4–3 to give the game a fairy-tale ending. It was one of the greatest moments in Peterborough's great Cup sagas.

For the Second Round Posh had to travel to meet Walsall, top of the Fourth Division. The game turned out to be a great Cup battle played in front of a record crowd of 20,600, Fellows Park ground record having stood at 20,000 since 1948. United made a bad start and were a goal down in less than a minute but Posh soon counter-attacked, a Smith 'goal' was disallowed and the part-timers were on terms four minutes before half-time. Walsall had had to reshuffle their defence following an injury to their right-half and frequently got in a tangle. Posh scored twice to take the score to 3–1 before Walsall came back in the 70th minute to score again to make it 3–2, the final score.

In the Third Round Ipswich were beaten on their own ground 3–2 by Posh, a shock result that reverberated round the football world to give them entry once again to the Fourth Round and a meeting with the giants, this time Sheffield Wednesday, then in the First Division, at Hillsborough. Although Wednesday got the better of Posh 2–0 the non-Leaguers left the field with their heads high and later received their reward with election, which had national acclaim, to the Fourth Division. Both games are fully reported as *Match Reports*.

MATCH REPORTS
FOURTH ROUND F.A. CUP
26th January 1957
HUDDERSFIELD TOWN 3   PETERBOROUGH 1

Peterborough's prowess in the Cup in the 1956/7 season fired the imagination of soccer fans throughout the country. Cup fever was intense in Peterborough days before the game and on the great day some 12,000 supporters made a mass exodus to Yorkshire. Apart from the car cavalcade of fans by road British Rail laid on no fewer than 20 specials.

Huddersfield Town were then a Second Division club only 12 months removed from the First Division. In the side were famous names such as leader Dave Hickson, ex Aston Villa and Everton, the right wing pair of Kevin McHale and Dennis Law, then a promising 16-year-old and right half and skipper Len Quested. Not since they defeated Folkestone in the Cup 24 years previously had Huddersfield encountered non-League opposition.

Such was the interest in the game that a crowd limit of 50,000 was fixed and some 48,735 supporters were at Leeds Road for what was undoubtedly the glamour tie of the Round. On the day Posh were slightly slower and less confident than they had been against Lincoln. The ground was heavy and did not suit United's style as much as it did Huddersfield's.

The Town secured a vital goal in the third minute when LAW scored from eight yards.

Huddersfield's right wing pair gave the United defenders a hard time and Norman Rigby had a difficult day trying to keep track of Hickson who continually switched to the wings. United persisted in playing the ball close and had little luck with the commanding Town defence, splendidly generalled by Quested. When occasionally Emery ran through, the Town defence opened up giving an indication that a more open game would have produced better results for the non-Leaguers.

A let-off for Huddersfield came when Billy Hails was brought down. The referee awarded a free kick on the edge of the penalty area but it was a hairsbreadth decision and United supporters loudly appealed for a penalty. From the kick Shaw moved the ball over the heads of the lined-up defenders but the ball went out of play.

Half-time: Huddersfield Town 1   Peterborough United 0

In the 67th minute Huddersfield went further ahead when from a high cross HICKSON easily headed in. United mounted a great fight back and thrilled the great crowd at Leeds Road when they reduced the deficit from a penalty in the 82nd minute. As Dennis Emery was dribbling through he was upturned and the referee had no hesitation in awarding a spot kick. Right half SHAW took the kick and his shot flashed into the net past Fearnley. Peterborough stormed into the attack in an attempt to snatch the equaliser but the Town defence held firm. In a breakaway in the 87th minute Huddersfield scored again through a left-footed shot by SIMPSON to give Huddersfield a 3-1 victory.

Although United had not achieved the greatness of the Lincoln replay they gave a first-class display of fighting Cup tie football and earned a great ovation from the crowd as they left the field.

Result: Huddersfield Town 3   Peterborough United 1

Teams:
Huddersfield Town: Fearnley, Conwell, Gibson, Quested, Cockerill, Connor, McHale, Law, Hickson, Simpson, Metcalfe.
Peterborough United: Walls, Douglass, Barr, Shaw, Rigby, Cockburn, Hails, Emery, Donaldson, Smith, Hogg.
Referee: Mr. T. Cooper, (Bolton).
Attendance: 48,735

THIRD ROUND F.A. CUP
9th January 1960
IPSWICH TOWN 2   PETERBOROUGH UNITED 3

Peterborough's performance in this Third Round tie when they came back after being twice in arrears, played with a weakened defence after left back Jim Walker had been injured in the 42nd minute and endured the first 45 minutes with driving snow blowing into their faces, was an impressive one indeed. The Posh fully justified their claim to be giant-killers and deserved their position as the then recognised aristocrats of non-League football.

From the start Peterborough played with great zest but the Second Division side came more into the picture as the game progressed and in the 20th minute scored through MILLWARD following a goalmouth scramble.

In the 41st minute United equalised when, after a great run down the right wing, McNamee sent over a cross for Jim RAYNER to convert to the joy of the Posh supporters.

Half-time: Ipswich Town 1   Peterborough United 1

The snow died down when the second half began to give Ipswich a slight advantage. Although Peterborough's injured back, Walker, resumed he was a passenger on the wing and United had to rearrange their defence. Immediately after the restart Ted PHILLIPS put Ipswich in front for the second time. Undeterred United swarmed to the attack chasing every ball and generally giving Ipswich an uncomfortable time. The League side rarely got going, the Peterborough tackling being strong and unyielding.

In the 54th minute the non-leaguers got the equaliser when EMERY scored as the goalkeeper came out.

The dying moments of the game brought Peterborough a famous

victory. Three minutes to go and Ray Smith, benefitting from an Ipswich mistake, gave a pass to EMERY for the inside forward to put the ball into the net amid breathless excitement among the Posh supporters. This remarkable victory, which again brought the soccer spotlight on Peterborough, earned the Posh the reward of an away tie with First Division Sheffield Wednesday at Hillsborough.

Result: Ipswich 2   Peterborough United 3

Teams:
Ipswich Town: Bailey, Malcolm, Carberry, Pickett, Nelson, Elsworth, Owen, Millward, Crawford, Phillips, Leadbetter.
Peterborough United: Daley, Stafford, Walker, Banham, Rigby, Chadwick, Hails, Emery, Rayner, Smith, McNamee.
Referee: Mr. J. W. Hunt, (Portsmouth).
Attendance: 26,000

FOURTH ROUND F.A. CUP
30th January 1960
SHEFFIELD WEDNESDAY 2   PETERBOROUGH 0

This was another of Peterborough's great Cup achievements – in the Fourth Round for the second time in four seasons, taking 15,000 fans to Hillsborough in 15 trains and dozens of special buses and running out on the pitch to the roar of 51,144 spectators, all ready to pay tribute to one of the country's most outstanding non-League Cup fighters.

There were wintry conditions at Hillsborough; the pitch was coated with snow and in addition fog, ice and rain produced a murk that necessitated the use of the floodlights from the kickoff. Because of a clash of colours the Posh turned out in Arsenal colours while Wednesday were in all-white strip.

From the outset Wednesday took command of the midfield – but they were matched by a resolute Posh defence – Daley in goal, the back division of Stafford and Walker and the half back line of Banham, Rigby and Chadwick.

With the accent on defence the Posh attack had a frail look about it and Springett, the England international goalkeeper, was rarely in action.

Although the Owls had dictated the play the Posh put on a notable defensive display and when the teams went off the field at half time with the scoresheet blank, Peterborough received a warm ovation from the crowd.

Half-time: Sheffield Wednesday 0   Peterborough United 0

Posh were first to attack when the second half began but later on the game became one way traffic in the direction of the Posh goal area. Even so there was little to choose between the two teams at that stage.

In the end Wednesday's guile produced its reward. Alan Finney, the Wednesday captain, carried out his usual switch to the right wing and in the 75th minute, when the Wednesday supporters had almost given up hope, Finney made the move that led to Wednesday opening the scoring. Moving along the right his cross was met by Bobby CRAIG whose rising shot finished up in the top corner of the net.

This unexpected success gave Wednesday the necessary inspiration they needed and they stormed into the Peterborough area. Within three minutes Wednesday had scored again, Finney again operating on the right to give CRAIG his second goal.

Peterborough had come within an ace of giving the First Division side a shock and were unlucky not to have forced a replay. Dour, defensive play by one of the great non-League Cup fighting sides had been matched against the might and skills of a great First Division team.

Result: Sheffield Wednesday 2   Peterborough United 0

Teams:
Sheffield Wednesday: Springett, Johnson, Megson, McAnearey, Swan, Kay, Wilkinson, Fantham, Griffin, Craig, Finney.
Peterborough United: Daley, Stafford, Walker, Banham, Rigby, Chadwick, Hails, Emery, Rayner, Smith, McNamee.
Referee: Mr. J. Finney, (Hereford).
Attendance: 51,144 (receipts: £7,210)

Peterborough Utd (Contd)
CUP RUNS

1946/7

1st Round – *30th November*
Yeovil T. 2   Peterborough 2

1st Round Replay – *5th December*
Peterborough 1   Yeovil T. 0

2nd Round – *14th December*
Peterborough 1   Northampton 1

2nd Round Replay – *19th December*
Northampton 1   Peterborough 1

2nd Round, 2nd Replay – *23rd Dec.*
Northampton 8   Peterborough 1
(at Coventry)

1948/9

1st Round – *27th November*
Peterborough 0   Torquay Utd 1

1952/3

1st Round – *22nd November*
Peterborough 2   Torquay Utd. 1

2nd Round – *6th December*
Peterborough 0   Bristol Rovers ...1

1953/4

1st Round – *21st November*
Hitchin 1   Peterborough 3

2nd Round – *12th December*
Peterborough 2   Aldershot 1

3rd Round   *9th January*
Cardiff 3   Peterborough 1

1955/6

1st Round   *19th November*
Peterborough 3   Ipswich 1

2nd Round   *10th December*
Swindon 1   Peterborough 1

2nd Round Replay   *14th December*
Peterborough 1   Swindon 2
(After extra time. Score at
90 minutes: 1 1)

1956/7

1st Round – *17th November*
Yeovil 1   Peterborough 3

2nd Round – *8th December*
Peterborough 3   Bradford 0

3rd Round – *5th January*
Peterborough 2   Lincoln 2

3rd Round Replay – *9th January*
Lincoln 4   Peterborough 5
(After extra time. Score at
90 minutes: 2-2)

4th Round – *26th January*
Huddersfield 3   Peterborough 1

1957/8

1st Round – *16th November*
Peterborough 3   Torquay 3

1st Round Replay – *20th November*
Torquay 1   Peterborough 0

1958/9

1st Round – *15th November*
Peterborough 2   Kettering 2

1st Round Replay – *20th November*
Kettering 2   Peterborough 3
(After extra time. Score at
90 minutes: 2-2)

2nd Round – *6th December*
Peterborough 4   Headington 2

3rd Round – *10th January*
Fulham 0   Peterborough 0

3rd Round Replay – *24th January*
Peterborough 0   Fulham 1

1959/60

1st Round – *14th November*
Peterborough 4   Shrewsbury 3

2nd Round – *5th December*
Walsall 2   Peterborough 3

3rd Round – *9th January*
Ipswich 2   Peterborough 3

4th Round – *30th January*
Sheffield Wed. ..2   Peterborough 0

ELECTED TO 4th DIVISION 1960/61

RHYL

Founded: 1876

League: North-West Counties (Div. 1)

Ground: Belle Vue

Colours: All white, blue facings

To begin their long run of post-war appearances in the First Round of the Cup, Rhyl were drawn at home in the 1948/9 season against Midland Leaguers Scarborough and suffered a 2-0 defeat. Their two most successful Cup runs were in 1956/7 when they joined the big battalions in the Third and Fourth Round (in the Third Round sensationally beating Second Division Notts County 3-1 and succumbing in the Fourth Round to Second Division Bristol City 3-0) and in 1970/1 when they lost 6-1 to Swansea in the Third Round away at Vetch Field after beating League sides Hartlepool Utd and Barnsley. Twice previously they had reached the Second Round when they were defeated by Norwich City and Bristol City. Other League clubs Rhyl have encountered in Cup struggles have included Rochdale, Bradford City, Halifax, Bradford Park Avenue (then a League side), Carlisle, Chesterfield, Grimsby, Oldham and Hull. Between 1948 and 1962 Rhyl appeared for 15 consecutive seasons in the First Round of the Cup, a record for a non-League side.

It was Midland League side Scarborough whose appearance at Belle Vue in the First Round of the 1948/9 season heralded Rhyl's long and distinguished record of post-war Cup games, some against clubs from the higher echelons. Managed by Frank Taylor, the former Wolves and England full-back, Scarborough took control and won 2–0.

The following season, 1949/50, Rhyl had a better draw, again at home, but this time against a League side, Rochdale from Third Division North. Rochdale kept a tight grip on the game and ran out comfortable 3–0 winners.

Rhyl drew a First Round tie with their old rivals Scarborough away from home in the 1950/1 season, thus reviving memories of Rhyl's defeat at Belle Vue by the Midland Leaguers in 1948. This time Rhyl had better luck, leading 1–0 at half-time and going on to win 2–1. The Second

Round brought Norwich City, then in Third Division South, to Belle Vue, the tie producing a record crowd of over 9,000 to watch the Canaries who included Eire international right-winger Johnny Gavin in their side. The only goal of the game was scored by Norwich in the fourth minute as a result of a bad back pass, a disallowed goal adding to the Lilywhites' misfortunes.

Luck deserted the Lilywhites in the following season, 1951/2, when they had to travel to the north-east to meet Hartlepool Utd, Third Division North in a First Round encounter. There was a 'gate' of 13,037, against a 'norm' of eight or nine thousand, a compliment to the part-timers. In the 10th minute Rhyl had the ball in the net but the 'goal' was disallowed and 'Pools went on to a 2-0 victory.

In 1952/3 Rhyl had a First Round tie against Bradford City, Third Division North. The game attracted a crowd of 11,500 to the Valley Parade Ground to watch Bradford win easily 4-0. Bradford included in their side Welsh international Ivor Powell and Brian Close, the Yorkshire and England cricketer.

Rhyl were in the hat again in 1953/4 for the First Round draw, away from home to Halifax Town, Third Division North. Over 10,000 were at The Shay to watch what turned out to be a defensive battle with the scoresheet blank at the end of the game. The replay at Belle Vue saw Rhyl add a glorious chapter to its Cup-fighting history. The Lilywhites had a tremendous task on their hands as the League side went into a 2-0 half-time lead. Then Rhyl picked themselves up and scored twice to force extra time. Rhyl startled the football world when despite evident fatigue they scored twice and although Halifax reduced the deficit towards the end Rhyl, with the scoreline 4-3 in their favour, celebrated a famous victory.

The great win over Halifax gave Rhyl a Second Round tie against Bristol City, Third Division South, at Belle Vue. A crowd of over 10,000 saw City two up at half-time, the turning point of the game coming when Rhyl missed a penalty early in the second-half. City then took command and scored again to make the final tally 3-0.

In the following season, 1954/5, Rhyl again fought their way to the First Round, drawn away to Yorkshire League side Selby Town. A goal ahead at half-time, Selby went on to win 2-1, ex-Arsenal inside forward Horsfield playing a leading part in the Yorkshire side's victory.

In a First Round encounter in the next season, 1955/6, the Cheshire League side had attractive visitors at Belle Vue in Bradford Park Avenue, then a League side in the Third Division North. Three 'gift' goals gave the League side a comfortable passage into the next round.

The 1956/7 season was a time of great rejoicing for Rhyl, when the club's name went into the football history books on reaching the Fourth Round. This memorable season was heralded in at the First Round stage with a home game against Midland Leaguers, Scarborough, the third First Round Cup encounter between the two clubs since the end of the war. Although two down on the half-hour Rhyl battled back, first to equalise and then to snatch the match-winner in the 82nd minute to make the final score 3-2. In the last minute of the game Rhyl gave away a penalty and in a tense moment Rhyl supporters watched their goalkeeper Hanson bring off a wonder save. Rhyl earned a Second Round tie with famous Northern League amateurs Bishop Auckland at Belle Vue and after the Lilywhites had gained a one nil half-time lead they went on to win 3-1, Auckland's consolation goal coming from a penalty. Rhyl's reward was a Third Round away game against Second Division Notts County, Cup-winners in 1894. Rhyl's 3-1 win, the sensation of the round, is fully described in *Match Report*.

For their Fourth Round game, which made history for Rhyl, the first time the club had advanced so far in the Cup, the non-Leaguers drew Bristol City, of the Second Division, away at Ashton Gate. A crowd of 29,438 saw City open in style when following a Wally Hinshelwood cross Etheridge scored with a header in the second minute. Four minutes later City centre-forward Atyeo scored number two and it looked at that stage that the non-Leaguers might be swamped. But City never again reached such a high note and Rhyl began to have more of the game, missed several chances and Jeff Williams had a 'goal' disallowed. Half-time came with City leading 2-0, Atyeo scoring again early in the second half to make the final score 3-0 and a repeat of the result of the two clubs' earlier encounter. Although this put an end to Rhyl's Cup progress for that season they had done sufficient to make them a toast among the non-League fraternity. Teams:

Bristol City: Anderson, Bailey, Thresher, White, Peacock,

Burden, Hinshelwood, Williams, Atyeo, Etheridge, Watkins.

Rhyl: Hanson, Spruce, Reynolds, Roberts, Rogers, Donaldson, Hughes, Russell, J. Williams, H. Williams, Meakin.

Continuing their successful post-war First Round encounters Rhyl were again in the hunt in the 1957/8 season but they were unlucky with the draw, having to travel to meet Third Division North, Carlisle United, a traditionally poor prospecting ground for the non-League sides. A crowd of over 13,000 saw the part-timers force six corners in the first ten minutes, lose their left-back injured at an early stage and after a goalless first-half go down 5-1.

Rhyl had no more luck the following season, 1958/9, when they drew lowly-placed Third Division Chesterfield in the First Round away from home at Saltergate. Over 11,000 supporters saw Rhyl get the ball in the net after only ten minutes but the 'goal' was disallowed. After a goalless first-half Chesterfield piled on three goals late in the game whilst Rhyl had a further 'goal' disallowed.

Rhyl's opponents in the First Round of the 1959/60 season were Third Division Grimsby Town at home at Belle Vue. Although Rhyl lost by a narrow 2-1 margin they had the unhappy distinction of scoring all three goals. Rhyl's captain Reynolds gave Grimsby the lead when he put through his own goal, Rhyl got back on terms only for the Lilywhites' centre-half Mills, in the closing stages, to chip the ball into his own net whilst under Grimsby pressure.

The ill-luck that had dogged the Lilywhites' performances in the two previous seasons struck again in 1960/1 when the non-Leaguers faced Fourth Division Oldham Atheltic at Belle Vue. Although the part-timers dictated the pace of the game throughout it was Oldham who scored the only goal of the match. Twice the Lilywhites had the ball in the Oldham net but on both occasions the 'goals' were disallowed.

In the First Round again in the 1961/2 season Rhyl faced Third Division Hull City at Boothferry Park. The Third Division side were two goals to the good by half-time and added three further goals after the interval to win 5-0.

In the First Round for the 15th consecutive time since the war Rhyl were again away from home in the 1962/3 season, drawn against Third Division Barnsley at Oakwell. Barnsley ran out easy 4-0 winners.

Rhyl had to wait until the 1970/1 season before their next

appearance in the First Round – when they were again to have a highly successful season, winning through to the Third Round and hitting the national headlines. Their First Round draw was against Fourth Division Hartlepool Utd and the Lilywhites celebrated their return to Cup-fighting at this level by snatching a magnificent 1–0 victory.

Rhyl's reward was a Second Round draw against Third Division Barnsley, at home at Belle Vue, and after something of a marathon the part-timers succeeded in avenging their 1962 defeat. The first encounter ended in a goalless draw and in the replay at Oakwell a dour struggle developed. After a goalless first half the game ended on a dramatic note, Barnsley scoring four minutes from time and the Lilywhites equalising a minute later. The game went into extra time but there was no further scoring. Rhyl had the honour of appearing at Old Trafford for the second replay to face Barnsley at the famous Manchester United stadium which on the night provided only 3,009 spectators to see the non-Leaguers gain a famous victory. After a blank scoresheet at half-time Rhyl scored twice in the second half, one by Eurwyn Davies and the other by Laurie Davies, to administer the coup de grace to Barnsley.

In the Third Round for the second time since the war the North Wales side had no luck with the draw, having to travel to meet Third Division Swansea City at Vetch Field. It was not Rhyl's day and the professionals ran out easy winners by a 6–1 margin, including a Rhyl 'own goal'. One interesting facet of the game was that two brothers were at opposite ends of the field, Tony Millington in goal for Swansea and Grenville Millington for Rhyl.

Attendance: 15,014.

Teams: Swansea: Millington (g), Screen (A), Gomersall, Williams (A), Nurse, Hole, Allchurch, Thomas, Hill, Gwyther, Evans.

Rhyl: Millington (g), Congerton, Weston, Seaton, Evans (J), Smart, Davies (L) Davies (E), Allen, Metcalf, Evans (D).

Rhyl reappeared in the First Round reckoning in the 1972/3 season when they had a hard tie against Third Division Chesterfield at the Saltergate ground. Rhyl, then Cheshire League champions, were hoping to gain revenge for their 3–0 beating in 1958 but they were doomed to disappointment, the League side running out 4–2 winners.

MATCH REPORT
THIRD ROUND F.A. CUP
5th January 1957
NOTTS COUNTY 1   RHYL 3

This was one of the greatest victories in the history of the Rhyl part-timers. There was a 16,000 crowd (including 2,000 Rhyl supporters) at Meadow Lane, the attendance being affected by Forest also being at home in the Cup.

County brought in 18-year-old Peter Bircumshaw who had his first game in the senior side. It was 30 years previously that Rhyl had last played in the 3rd Round – beaten 2–1 at Darlington, then in Division Two. It was County's fourth meeting with a non-League side since the war and it was the first time for 44 years that a non-League side had accounted for the Magpies (Bristol Rovers, then in the Southern League, beating them 2–0 on 11th January, 1913).

It was an unforgettable moment as the Rhyl Silver Prize Band marched round the ground playing "Men of Harlech" and "We'll keep a welcome", the leeks in their place of honour in the centre of the pitch, the Red Dragon flying and the sound of the Welsh National Anthem . . . a moment of history for the part-timers as they moved into the Fourth Round for the first time in their history.

For long periods of the first half County were outclassed by the quick-moving Rhyl front-line. Rhyl concentrated on fast, open football and chased every ball, but Linton gave a fine display in the Notts goal to keep the non-Leaguers out. A free-kick in the 20th minute led to Rhyl opening the scoring. WILLIAMS was bundled off the ball as he was going through and, taking the free-kick himself, lobbed the ball over the Notts defenders into the net.

Eight minutes from the interval County scored the equaliser. From a free kick Wills centred for Wylie to flick in a header. Rhyl goalkeeper Hanson punched out to BIRCUMSHAW who scored while the Rhyl goalkeeper was off balance. This goal gave fresh heart to County who attacked strongly but the Rhyl defence stood firm.

Half-time: Notts County 1   Rhyl 1

In an exciting second half played under floodlights Rhyl out-manoeuvred their League opponents. In the 60th minute the Lilywhites were awarded a penalty for obstruction, H. Williams being impeded as he was going through. Billy Hughes took the kick and the ball flew into the top corner of the net. But a Rhyl player had moved and the kick was ordered to be retaken. HUGHES again took the kick and placed his shot in the same place. The experience of Rhyl's ex-League players (particularly former Irish international Billy Hughes) stood them in good stead as the tension built up.

In the closing stages Rhyl continued to have the upper hand and eight minutes from time settled the issue when H. Williams lobbed the ball to an unmarked Graham MEAKIN who headed in to score Rhyl's third. The North Wales contingent on the ground their banner "Rhyl for the F.A. Cup" waving furiously, went wild with excitement. Rhyl continued to mount attack after attack, Jeff Williams, Russell and Meakin, all having shots at goal. It was a sensational victory for the non-Leaguers.

Result: Notts County 1   Rhyl 3

Teams:
Notts County: Linton, Southwell, Cruickshank, McGrath, Russell, Loxley, Lane, Wylie, Wills, Carver, Bircumshaw.
Rhyl: Hanson, Spruce, Reynolds, Roberts, Robers, Donaldson, Hughes, Russell, J. Williams, H. Williams, Meakin.
Referee: Mr. H. Webb, (Leeds).
Attendance: 16,231

Rhyl (Contd)

CUP RUNS

1948/9
1st Round – *4th December*
Rhyl .... 0 Scarborough 2

1949/50
1st Round – *26th November*
Rhyl .... 0 Rochdale 3

1950/51
1st Round – *25th November*
Scarborough ..... 1 Rhyl 2
2nd Round – *9th December*
Rhyl .... 0 Norwich City 1

1951/2
1st Round – *24th November*
Hartlepool .... 2 Rhyl 0

1952/3
1st Round – *22nd November*
Bradford City ... 4 Rhyl 0

1953/4
1st Round – *21st November*
Halifax .... 0 Rhyl 0
1st Round Replay – *26th November*
Rhyl .... 4 Halifax 3
(after extra time. Score at 90 mins: 2-2)
2nd Round – *12th December*
Rhyl .... 0 Bristol City 3

1954/5
1st Round – *20th November*
Selby .... 2 Rhyl 1

1955/6
1st Round – *19th November*
Rhyl .... 0 Bradford Pk A... 3

1956/7
1st Round – *17th November*
Rhyl .... 3 Scarborough 2
2nd Round – *8th December*
Rhyl .... 3 Bishop Auck. 1
3rd Round – *5th January*
Notts County .... 1 Rhyl 3
4th Round – *26th January*
Bristol City .... 3 Rhyl 0

1957/8
1st Round – *16th November*
Carlisle .... 5 Rhyl 1

1958/9
1st Round – *15th November*
Chesterfield .... 3 Rhyl 0

1959/60
1st Round – *14th November*
Rhyl .... 1 Grimsby 2

1960/1
1st Round – *5th November*
Rhyl .... 0 Oldham 1

1961/2
1st Round – *4th November*
Hull .... 5 Rhyl 0

1962/3
1st Round – *3rd November*
Barnsley .... 4 Rhyl 0

1970/71
1st Round – *21st November*
Rhyl .... 1 Hartlepool Utd. 0
2nd Round – *11th December*
Rhyl .... 0 Barnsley 0
2nd Round Replay – *15th December*
Barnsley .... 1 Rhyl 1
(After extra time. Score at 90 mins: 1-1)
2nd Round, second replay – *21st Dec.*
Barnsley .... 0 Rhyl 2
(at Old Trafford)
3rd Round – *2nd January*
Swansea .... 6 Rhyl 1

1972/3
1st Round – *18th November*
Chesterfield .... 4 Rhyl 2

RUNCORN

Founded: 1918

League: Alliance Premier

Ground: Canal Street

Colours: Green and yellow striped shirts and green shorts

Runcorn, the go-ahead and high-riding Alliance Premier League side which only a few years ago was making modest progress in the Cheshire County League, has recently been hitting the Cup headlines and is now recognised as one of the leading non-League teams in the country. Beginning their post-war First Round Cup runs in 1946 when the non-Leaguers were beaten 4-0 away from home by Third Division Carlisle United they have since appeared seven times at that stage and have reached the Second Round no fewer than three times. One of their most outstanding Cup successes was in the 1967/8 season when they beat Fourth Division Notts County, the oldest club in the Football League, by a single goal at home at Canal Street. Another triumph against League opposition in the Cup was in 1977/8 when they defeated Fourth Division Southport 1-0 after a replay.

The Linnets' first taste of First Round Cup football after the war came in the 1946/7 season when they were drawn away from home against Third Division Carlisle United. A 'gate' of 13,680 saw the non-Leaguers put up a tough first-half battle to restrict Carlisle's first-half lead to a single goal. Runcorn tired towards the end of the game and Carlisle scored three more to make the final tally 4–0.

The following season Runcorn were again in the First Round, drawn at home against then Midland Leaguers Scunthorpe United. An attendance of 7,739 saw Scunthorpe have the better of the first half, scoring first and going in at half-time leading 2–1. It was a different story in the second half, Runcorn piling on the pressure to equalise in the 65th minute. The Linnets added two more, as well as missing a penalty, to make the final score 4–2.

Runcorn again had the luck of the draw in the Second Round which they reached for the second time in the club's history. Drawn against Third Division Barrow at Canal Street the non-Leaguers put up a magnificent fight before a crowd of 8,314 to lose by only a lone goal. This defeat cost the non-Leaguers a Third Round trip to Chelsea.

The Linnets were again in the First Round in the following season, 1948/9 when they were drawn against well-placed Third Division North, York City, a thousand Runcorn supporters swelling the 'gate' of 9,558. On a fog-enshrouded ground Runcorn's defenders held the City attack and went in at half-time with the scoresheet goalless. A disputed penalty gave York the lead after the resumption, Runcorn equalised but the League side scored again to make the final score 2-1.

This ended the Linnets First Round appearances for a number of seasons but in 1967/8 they reappeared to gain one of the most dramatic victories in the club's history when they took on and defeated Fourth Division, Notts County 1-0 at Canal Street. It was the shock Cup result of day. The match is reported in full in *Match Report*.

For their Second Round encounter the Linnets were drawn away at Haig Avenue against Third Division Southport. A 'gate' of 13,353 saw Billy Bingham's side go into a 2-0 half-time lead and to score again midway through the second-half. The Linnets put on a brave rally towards the end when striker Alan Ryan scored twice in the 84th and 89th minutes to make the score respectable. Southport also managed a late goal to bring the final tally to 4-2.

Runcorn had to wait another six seasons before again getting to the First Round, a home game in the 1973/4 season against Third Division Grimsby Town. Although Town won 1-0 their victory was against the run of the play, the Northern Premier Leaguers attacking throughout the game with Grimsby falling back and defending for long periods.

There was a break of another three seasons before Runcorn again got into their First Round stride, drawn away in the 1977/8 season against old adversaries Fourth Division Southport with whom the Linnets had an old score to settle – Southport having beaten them in the Second Round in 1968. Up to half-time defences were in control with the scoresheet blank but five minutes into the second-half the non-Leaguers opened the scoring. Southport equalised and then went into a 2-1 lead in the 77th minute. The Linnets stormed back and scored a late goal to make the final score

2-2 to force a replay at Canal Street. The replay at Runcorn saw the League side generally in command in the first-half. In the second-half the non-Leaguers took control and six minutes from the final whistle Liverpool schoolteacher Barry Whitbread headed in the winner to give Runcorn a dramatic victory.

In the Second Round Runcorn had to travel to the Victoria Ground to meet lowly-placed Fourth Division Hartlepool United. Although the non-Leaguers battled hard and restricted the League side to a narrow 2-1 half-time lead the full-time professionals ran out 4-2 winners. Attendance: 6,112

The Linnets again fought their way to the First Round in the 1978/9 competition, drawing an away game against Third Division Chester at Sealand Road. With Runcorn desperately unlucky not to have opened the scoring early in the game the score read 0-0 at 90 minutes with a goalless draw appearing to be the likely result. Then in injury time came two dramatic goals. First Chester scored what looked like the winner only for Runcorn to race to the other end for the equaliser and a creditable draw. But the replay at Canal Street was a disaster for the non-Leaguers. With Alan King, their captain, out through injury Runcorn were no match for their League opponents and were handed out a 5-0 thrashing.

Runcorn next appeared in the First Round in the 1981/2 season when they were drawn to face famous F.A. Cup fighters Burnley at Turf Moor. Third Division Burnley, who won the Cup in 1914, still retain memories of their unhappy encounter with then non-League Wimbledon in 1975 when they were put out of the Cup in the Third Round. This game could easily have gone the same way for the non-Leaguers posed plenty of problems for the League side. At the end honours were even with a 0-0 draw with Runcorn's goalkeeper Brian Parker having an outstanding game.

Burnley at the Canal Street ground was a memorable occasion for the Alliance Premier Leaguers and an exciting game was watched by over 5,000. Although Burnley were a goal ahead in the 14th minute a Seddon header put Runcorn level and this is how it remained until the 80th minute when Burnley edged ahead and Runcorn's Cup dreams were over for another season.

MATCH REPORT
FIRST ROUND F.A. CUP
9th December 1967
RUNCORN 1   NOTTS COUNTY 0

This Cup defeat of Fourth Division Notts County, the oldest side in the Football League, by non-Leaguers Runcorn ranks as one of the epics in the then Cheshire Leaguers' history. On a snow-covered pitch before a sizeable crowd of over 6,000 the Linnets soon settled down and began to play good football despite the conditions. County were generally at sixes and sevens. Runcorn were making all the running in the early stages and in the 20th minute reaped their reward when centre forward Alan RYAN, much in demand by the League clubs, dashed in as County goalkeeper Rose failed to clear a Herring shot, and rammed the ball in the net. It was Ryan's 39th goal of the season. He had scored in every one of the four previous qualifying rounds. In one of their rare raids Bradd got the ball in the net for County but the 'goal' was disallowed because of offside. Runcorn's defenders were well in control and County seldom got as far as the Linnets' penalty area. Runcorn all but added a second just before half-time.

Half-time: Runcorn 1   Notts County 0

After the interval the Magpies stepped up their attacks but all attempts to secure the equaliser foundered at the hands of the capable Runcorn rearguard. Bryan Pendlebury, in the Runcorn goal, played a brilliant game. In the closing stages it was Runcorn who looked dangerous as they stormed into the County goalmouth, twice nearly adding to their tally.

This was County's first defeat in the Cup by non-League opposition since 1964 when they were defeated by Bath City. Runcorn's well-deserved triumph took them into the Second Round for the second time since the war.

Result: Runcorn 1   Notts County 0

Teams:
Runcorn: Pendlebury, Stanley, Houghton, Phoenix, Oxtoby, Denton, Tongue, Herring, Ryan, Moss, Bateson, (Sub: Gorrie).
Notts County: Rose, Ball, Gibson, Thompson, Needham, Smith (K), Weaver, Farmer, Smith (J), Bradd, Elliott, (Sub: McGovern).
Referee: Mr. G. W. Hill, (Leicester).
Attendance: 6,246

CUP RUNS

1946/7

1st Round – *30th November*
Carlisle Utd. 4   Runcorn 0

1947/8

1st Round – *29th November*
Runcorn 4   Scunthorpe 2

2nd Round – *13th December*
Runcorn 0   Barrow 1

1948/9

1st Round – *27th November*
York City 2   Runcorn 1

1967/8

1st Round – *9th December*
Runcorn 1   Notts County 0

2nd Round – *6th January*
Southport 4   Runcorn 2

1973/4

1st Round – *24th November*
Runcorn 0   Grimsby Town ..1

1977/8

1st Round – *26th November*
Southport 2   Runcorn 2

1st Round Replay – *28th November*
Runcorn 1   Southport 0

2nd Round – *17th December*
Hartlepool Utd .4   Runcorn 2

1978/9

1st Round – *25th November*
Chester 1   Runcorn 1

1st Round Replay – *28th November*
Runcorn 0   Chester 5

1981/2

1st Round *21st November*
Burnley 0   Runcorn 0

1st Round Replay – *24th November*
Runcorn 1   Burnley 2

SCARBOROUGH

Founded: 1879

League: Alliance Premier

Ground: Athletic Ground

Colours: All red with white trimmings

Twice in the Third Round of the Cup in the post-war era, seven times in the Second and reaching the First Round on a host of occasions Borough have been one of the most consistent non-League performers in the competition. Their 'glory' games were in the 1975/6 season when they were narrowly beaten 2-1 at home in the Third Round by Third Division Crystal Palace and two seasons later when their Third Round contest against Second Division Brighton ended in a 3-0 defeat. They were defeated in the Second Round in 1948/9, 1964/5 (after a replay), 1972/3, 1973/4 and 1978/9 against League opponents Gateshead (then Third Division North), Doncaster Rovers, Doncaster Rovers again, Port Vale and York City. Other League sides who have clashed with Borough in the Cup have included Mansfield, Bradford City, Bradford Park Avenue (then in Third Division North), Crewe, Workington (then Fourth Division) Hartlepool Utd, Oldham Athletic, Preston North End, Darlington, Rochdale and Halifax.

Scarborough began their post-war Cup runs in the 1948/9 season when they were drawn away from home in a First Round encounter against Cheshire Leaguers Rhyl whom they defeated 2-0. Thus Borough repeated the triumph of 18 years previously when Rhyl were shot out 6-0 on the Athletic Ground. In the Second Round Borough again had an away engagement, against Gateshead, Third Division North. Borough were no match for the Tynesiders who had a comfortable 3-0 victory.

In the First Round of the 1950/1 season Scarborough were again drawn against Cup rivals Rhyl at home at the Athletic Ground. Rhyl were anxious to avenge their 2-0 defeat in 1948 and before a 'gate' of 8,257, the second highest attendance in Borough's history, they beat Borough 2-1, getting the match-winner in the dying minutes.

In the 1952/3 competition Scarborough drew a home First Round tie against Mansfield Town, Third Division North. A top form Town recorded their highest score since 1949, swamping the part-timers 8-0.

Again in the First Round in the 1953/4 season Scarborough found themselves opposed by well-known northern Cup-fighters Wigan Athletic, then in the Lancashire Combination, away from home at Springfield Park. A 'gate' of 13,500 saw Wigan go into a 1-0 half-time lead and then notch three more after the interval.

In the following season, 1954/5, an away First Round encounter between the part-timers and York City, Third Division North, attracted a 'gate' of 10,155 to Bootham Crescent. The two clubs had met three times previously in F.A. Cup encounters. Four former York players, Brenan, Patrick, Barber and Ware, were in the Borough side. Borough gave the League side a fright when they went one up in the 24th minute and held their lead up to the interval. In a fluctuating second half York equalised, only for Borough to again snatch the lead and then finally to go down fighting after city had scored two more.

Scarborough's First Round opponents in 1955/6 were Workington, Third Division North, away from home at Borough Park. Although Borough kept the 'Reds' score down to 1-0 at the interval the League side leapt into a 4-0 second half lead. Undeterred Borough scored two late goals to make the score respectable.

In a First Round tie in the 1956/7 season Scarborough drew their old Cheshire League rivals Rhyl away from home, a thrilling struggle ending in a win for Rhyl 3-2 with Borough missing a penalty two minutes from time.

In the First Round of the 1957/8 competition the then Midland Leaguers were set a hard task when they had to travel to Valley Parade to meet Bradford City, strongly placed in Third Division North. Borough fielded a rearranged side and the non-Leaguers were easy prey for an on-form City, going down 6-0.

Two seasons later, in 1959/60 Borough were again bound for Bradford in a First Round tie, their opponents being Bradford Park Avenue, another Third Division North outfit. Borough fared little better than they had against City, going down 6-1 to give Avenue their best Cup win since they defeated Manchester City 8-2 in 1946.

In the 1960/1 season Scarborough again had to visit their bogey town Bradford for a First Round encounter against Bradford City, Third Division, at the Valley Parade ground. The part-timers were anxious to wipe out the memory of their 6-0 defeat in 1957 and put up a fine defensive display to keep the scoresheet blank. In the replay at the Athletic Ground Borough were a goal to the good within 90 seconds and the non-Leaguers kept their lead until a few minutes from half-time when City equalised. In the second-half Borough again found the net but the referee disallowed the 'goal' and the game went into extra time, City scoring twice to make the final score 3-1.

In the 1962/3 season Borough were drawn away from home to Fourth Division Crewe Alexandra in the First Round and put up a fine performance to hold the League side to a 1-1 draw at the Gresty Road Ground. Borough were unlucky to lose the replay by the odd goal. Borough produced an early sensation when they scored within three minutes but Crewe equalised and both sides added a further first-half goal to make it 2-2 at the interval with no further scoring by the end of the 90 minutes. The game went into extra time Crewe scoring again to run out 3-2 winners.

Borough fought their way to the First Round again in 1964/5 when they dramatically dismissed their old opponents from the Fourth Division Bradford City by a lone goal at the Athletic Ground. This victory was sweet revenge for the non-Leaguers who had had several Cup defeats inflicted on them by the Paraders. It was no surprise when Borough went ahead in the 25th minute from Johnny Edgar and Scarborough held this lead until the end of the game despite some hair breadth escapes in the second-half. The North Eastern Leaguers went into Round Two for the first time since 1948 drawing another away game, Fourth Division Doncaster Rovers at Belle Vue before a crowd of 10,535. The result was a goalless draw, honours being even in the first-half and Borough having the edge after the interval. In the replay Borough went down 2-1, Doncaster scoring twice, once from a penalty, after a goalless first half. Borough scored ten minutes from the end.

Borough were again in the First Round in the following season, 1965/6, drawn away from home at Moss Lane in a non-League affair against Cheshire Leaguers Altrincham. Altrincham went on a goal spree, winning 6-0, the Robins' inside-left Jack Swindells scoring five of the goals.

Scarborough had to wait four seasons before they were again in the First Round, in 1970/1, when they were drawn at home against Fourth Division Workington. The League side had built up a 3-1 lead shortly after the interval but in the closing stages Borough scored from a penalty.

Next season, 1971/2, Borough were again in the First Round drawing an away game against Fourth Division Hartlepool United. On a snow-covered Victoria Ground the League side built up a 6-0 lead which they held until three minutes from the end when Borough scored.

There were better things in store for Borough in the following season, 1972/3 when they again reached the First Round, to be drawn against Third Division Oldham Athletic away from home at Boundary Park. This was a tough proposition for few non-Leaguers have had any joy playing Oldham in the Cup on their own ground. Borough stormed into the Latics' half from the kick-off, scored a vital early goal and held on to the lead until ten minutes into the second-half when Oldham's captain scored a face-saving equaliser. In the replay Borough brought off a famous victory when they put out the Latics 2-1 after having conceded an early goal. With the half-time score 1-1 with Oldham having had a 'goal' disallowed both sides challenged for the match-winner and Borough got it in the 50th minute. Ground advantage again came Scarborough's way in the Second Round drawn against Fourth Division Doncaster Rovers who had beaten the non-Leaguers 2-1 eight seasons previously. Borough again lost 2-1.

In the First Round in the following season, 1973/4, Borough again drew Fourth Division opposition in Crewe Alexandra. The tie was fought out away from home at the Gresty Road ground and history repeated itself, the game ending in a goalless draw, Crewe having a 'goal' disallowed. In the replay at Borough the League side went into a sixth minute lead but by half-time the non-Leaguers were back in the game and went 2-1 up, one of their goals coming from a penalty. In the second-half Borough were content to hold on to their advantage.

Scarborough: Garrow, Fountain, Hewitt, Dunn, Dodds, Fagan, Donoghue, Barmby, Leask, Lee, Todd.

For their Second Round tie Scarborough lost ground advantage, drawn away from home against Third Division

Port Vale. After a blank scoresheet at half-time Borough surprised their hosts by taking a deserved lead but two late goals by Vale put an end to further Cup progress.

Borough had to wait until the 1975/6 season before again appearing in the First Round but it was to be a memorable season. Borough's opponents at the Athletic Ground were fellow Northern Premier Leaguers Morecambe and the game was notable for having three 'goals' disallowed, two from the Shrimps, and one from Borough. The goals that counted were two late efforts by Borough once again to put them into Round Two. Scarborough secured a plum draw against famous Cup fighters Preston North End, then in the Third Division, at the Athletic Ground and Borough were to record one of their greatest Cup victories. A crowd of 4,100 saw the battling non-Leaguers take the initiative and adapt better to the snow-covered pitch. In the 24th minute Scarborough took the lead through Ayre. Preston were on terms three minutes later and towards the end of the first half went into a 2-1 lead. Borough were on terms in the 70th minute through a Woodall back header and in a sensational finish Marshall scored in the last minute to give the non-Leaguers a well-deserved 3-2 win, the shock Cup result of the day.

Scarborough: Barnard, Fountain, Barker, Dunn (H), Ayr, Dunn (H. A.), Jackson, Barmby, Woodall, Hewitt, Marshall. (Sub: Abbey).

This great win put Scarborough into the Third Round draw for the first time since 1938, the same year that Preston had last won the F.A. Cup. Borough's opponents, at the Athletic Ground, were Third Division Crystal Palace. Full details of this exciting game, which Scarborough narrowly lost 2-1, are given in *Match Report*.

Scarborough reappeared in the First Round in the 1976/7 competition when they drew a home game against Fourth Division Darlington whom they held to a 0-0 draw. It was a slightly different story at the replay at Feethams, the Quakers going into a 2-0 half-time lead and scoring a further two goals in the second-half. Borough managed a consolation goal towards the end.

Season 1977/8 brought more glory and more headlines as Borough once again battled their way through to the Third Round for the second time since the war. And they did it via the 'scalps' of two League clubs. The First Round duel was fought against Fourth Division Rochdale at the Athletic Ground where a near 5,000 crowd saw Borough pull off a magnificent 4–2 victory against the League side. For their second Round encounter Scarborough drew an away tie against lowly-placed Crewe Alexandra who had twice before been beaten by the non-Leaguers, in 1962 and 1973, both after replays and history was to repeat itself. Before a 'gate' of over 4,000, Crewe's best of the season, the first game produced a scoreless draw. In the replay at the Athletic Ground, a game that pulled in 7,000, the non-Leaguers put on a 'giant-killing' performance, beating the League side 2–0 with a goal in each half. Borough richly deserved their Third Round tie against promotion-seeking Second Division Brighton away at Goldstone described in *Match Report*.

The following season, 1978/9, Borough were in First Round Cup action again, away from home against fellow non-Leaguers Chorley of the Cheshire County League. This turned out to be a harder game than Borough had anticipated but their narrow 1–0 win was enough to take them into the Second Round. Their opponents were Fourth Division York City, away from home at Bootham Crescent. The two sides had met previously in the First Round in 1954 when City had won a thrilling encounter 3–2 but this time the result was more decisive, York winning by three clear goals.

Once again on First Round Cup duty in the 1979/80 season Borough took 2,000 supporters to Halifax where the Northern Premier Leaguers were set to face a Fourth Division side whose colours had been lowered on several occasions by non-League outfits. This time the story was different with Halifax proving too strong for the part-timers. The League side went 2–0 ahead in the first-half and defended their lead until the final whistle.

In the following season, 1980/1, the Alliance Premier Leaguers were again in the First Round, drawn away at Turf Moor against Third Division Burnley, once F.A. Cup winners, but having a reputation for not faring too well when matched against non-Leaguers. Borough put the League side under pressure in the first half but without being able to find the Burnley net. It was not until the 77th minute that the League side finally broke down the gallant Scarborough defence to gain a narrow 1–0 victory.

MATCH REPORTS
THIRD ROUND F.A. CUP
3rd January 1976
SCARBOROUGH 1 CRYSTAL PALACE 2

This was the first time that Borough had appeared in the Third Round since before the war and they faced a Palace side that had suffered three successive League defeats. It was the 24th time that Borough, three years away from its Centenary, had been in the competition proper and the tie brought back memories of their 1930 achievement when they had reached the Third Round for the first time and had drawn 1-1 against Luton before a crowd of 11,000 and then lost the replay 5-1. It was at that time that the Scarborough manager, Colin Appleton, was playing for the club before moving on to his 12-year spin with Leicester City with whom he played in two F.A. Cup finals against Spurs and Manchester United.

Among the part-timers playing in the Scarborough side against Palace were Geoffrey Barnard in goal, who had played nearly three hundred games for Scunthorpe before moving to the Northern Premier League side and who had played in the Cup against such sides as Newcastle United, Sheffield Wednesday and West Bromwich Albion, and leading goal scorer John Woodall who had been transferred for a £1,000 fee from Rotherham United.

There was a crowd of some 8,000 at the Athletic ground to see Borough put up a sterling performance to give Palace a scare.

The somewhat sluggish Palace defence were soon under pressure as the speedy Scarborough forwards swept forward and Woodall, the Northern Premier League centre-forward gave Hammond, the Palace goalkeeper, a few early frights. Once Hammond had to rush out from his charge to take the ball from Woodall as Evans lay on the ground. After twenty minutes, and much against the run of the play, Palace got the ball in the net through Evans but the 'goal' was disallowed. Two minutes from the break TAYLOR put Palace one up with a deflected shot.

Half-time- Scarborough 0 Palace 1

After the interval Palace continued to create chances with some efficient football but Scarborough redressed the balance in the 60th minute when they pulled off Barmby and brought on as substitute a second Harry Dunn, Harry A. Dunn. In the 69th minute Scarborough scored a fine goal, Harry A. Dunn drifting in a dangerous cross and ABBEY getting to the ball first in a goalmouth scramble to head a brilliant goal past the Palace goalkeeper. Palace piled on the pressure and in the 80th minute EVANS nodded in a well-directed header.

Result: Scarborough 1 Crystal Palace 2

Teams:
Scarborough: Barnard, Fountain, Hewitt, H. Dunn, Ayre, Marshall, Jackson, Barmby, Woodall, Abbey, Hilley, (Sub: H. A. Dunn).
Crystal Palace: Hammond, Wall, Cannon, Holder, Jump, Evans, Chatterton, M. Hinshelwood, Kemp, Swindlehurst, Taylor, (Sub: Whittle).
Referee: Mr. L. Hayes, (Doncaster).
Attendance: 8,000

THIRD ROUND F.A. CUP
7th January 1978
BRIGHTON 3 SCARBOROUGH 0

There was a crowd of nearly 24,000 at the Goldstone ground to watch the redoubtable Northern Premier Leaguers make a tilt at on-form Third Division Brighton in this Third Round encounter. From the beginning Albion seized midfield control and with a 4-2-4 formation, with two orthodox wingers, gave notice that they were going for goals. In the early stages local joiner, David Chapman, in the Scarborough goal, had to deal with two dangerous headers from Teddy Maybank. Peter Ward was in a particularly lethal mood and Borough had to detach three men to mark him.

In the 37th minute Albion took the lead through Peter WARD who scored his first goal in 11 matches, a glancing header from an O'Sullivan chip going just inside the post. Two minutes later Brighton added to their lead through POTTS who smashed the ball past Chapman from close range.

Half-time: Brighton 2 Scarborough 0

After the interval Scarborough came more into the picture and Brighton did well to stop Harry A. Dunn as he was heading for goal. Borough continued on the attack and forced two corners in quick succession.

In the 72nd minute Brighton put matters beyond doubt when HORTON scored from a free-kick after Ward had been brought down just outside the penalty area. A few minutes later with Albion again piling on the pressure the Borough's defence was at full stretch and Marshall had to bring down Maybank in the area to save a certain goal. From the resultant penalty Horton placed the ball wide.

Result: Brighton 3 Scarborough 0

Teams:
Brighton: Steele, Potts, Williams, Horton, Winstanley, Lawrenson, Towner, Ward, Maybank, Clark, O'Sullivan, (Sub: Mellor).
Scarborough: Chapman, Marshall, Smith, H. Dunn, Deere, Fountain, Donoghue, H. A. Dunn, Woodall, Smith, Gill, (Sub: Barnby).
Referee: Mr. T. D. Spencer, (Wootton Bassett).
Attendance: 23,748

Scarborough (Contd)

CUP RUNS

1948/9
1st Round – *4th December*
Rhyl 0   Scarborough 2

2nd Round – *11th December*
Gateshead 3   Scarborough 0

1950/1
1st Round – *25th November*
Scarborough 1   Rhyl 2

1952/3
1st Round – *22nd November*
Scarborough 0   Mansfield 8

1953/4
1st Round – *21st November*
Wigan 4   Scarborough 0

1954/5
1st Round – *20th November*
York 3   Scarborough 2

1955/6
1st Round – *19th November*
Workington 4   Scarborough 2

1956/7
1st Round – *17th November*
Rhyl 3   Scarborough 2

1957/8
1st Round – *16th November*
Bradford City ... 6   Scarborough 0

1959/60
1st Round – *14th November*
Bradford Pk. A. 6   Scarborough 1

1960/1
1st Round – *5th November*
Bradford City ... 0   Scarborough 0

1st Round Replay – *9th November*
Scarborough 1   Bradford City ... 3
(After extra time. Score at 90 mins: 1–1)

1962/3
1st Round – *3rd November*
Crewe 1   Scarborough 1

1st Round Replay – *7th November*
Scarborough 2   Crewe 3
(After extra time. Score at 90 mins: 2–2)

1964/5
1st Round – *14th November*
Scarborough 1   Bradford City ... 0

2nd Round – *5th December*
Doncaster 0   Scarborough 0

2nd Round Replay – *9th December*
Scarborough 1   Doncaster 2

1965/6
1st Round – *13th November*
Altrincham 6   Scarborough 0

1970/71
1st Round – *21st November*
Scarborough 2   Workington 3

1971/2
1st Round – *20th November*
Hartlepool 6   Scarborough 1

1972/3
1st Round – *18th November*
Oldham Ath. 1   Scarborough 1

1st Round Replay – *22nd November*
Scarborough 2   Oldham Ath. ... 1

2nd Round – *9th December*
Scarborough 1   Doncaster 2

1973/4
1st Round – *24th November*
Crewe 0   Scarborough 0

1st Round Replay – *28th November*
Scarborough 2   Crewe 1

2nd Round – *15th December*
Port Vale 2   Scarborough 1

1975/6
1st Round – *22nd November*
Scarborough 2   Morecambe 0

2nd Round – *13th December*
Scarborough 3   PNE 2

3rd Round – *3rd January*
Scarborough 1   Crystal Palace .. 2

1976/7
1st Round – *20th November*
Scarborough 0   Darlington 0

1st Round Replay – *22nd November*
Darlington 4   Scarborough 1

1977/8

1st Round – *26th November*
Scarborough 4   Rochdale 2

2nd Round – *17th December*
Crewe 0   Scarborough 0

2nd Round Replay – *21st December*
Scarborough 2   Crewe 0

3rd Round – *7th January*
Brighton 3   Scarborough 0

1978/9

1st Round – *25th November*
Chorley 0   Scarborough 1

2nd Round – *16th December*
York City 3   Scarborough 0

1979/80

1st Round – *24th November*
Halifax 2   Scarborough 0

1980/1

1st Round – *22nd November*
Burnley 1   Scarborough 0

STAFFORD RANGERS

Founded: 1876

League: Alliance Premier

Ground: Marston Road

Colours: Black and white shirts; black shorts

Rangers were comparative latecomers to the post-war First Round Cup scene but they have since made good their earlier lack of success. On the losing end of a First Round encounter in 1972/3 away against Fourth Division Crewe Alexandra, Stafford reached the heights in the following season when they battled to the Fourth Round, beating League sides Stockport County, Halifax and Rotherham on the way. One of the few non-League sides ever to reach the rarified strata of the Fourth Round Stafford drew Third Division Peterborough at home although Rangers, for crowd reasons, elected to play the tie on Stoke City's ground, going down 2-1 after a thrilling contest. Rangers have subsequently reached the Second Round twice, in the 1975/6 season, when they were defeated by Third Division Halifax 3-1 and in 1979/80 when they were beaten 2-0 away from home by famous cup-fighting side Third Division Blackburn Rovers. Other League sides who have drawn Rangers in First Round battles have included Carlisle, Hull City, Walsall, and York City.

In their first First Round post-war game Rangers had to travel to meet Fourth Division Crewe Alexandra and lost by a lone goal in the 41st minute with the linesman flagging for offside.

Rangers' magical Cup run of the 1974/5 season opened with a First Round game against Fourth Division Stockport County away at Edgeley Park. The Northern Premier Leaguers did well to force a replay with the scoresheet blank. In the replay at Marston Road Rangers began their 'giantkilling' exploits with a brilliant 1–0 victory to put the part-timers in the Second Round for the first time in the club's 98 years' history.

Victory over Stockport gave the Rangers a home game against lowly-placed Third Division Halifax Town in the

Second Round. Halifax had the better of the first-half, having a goal disallowed in the third minute and scoring mid-way through the half to give them a 1-0 half-time lead. Then Rangers took up the running, equalising three minutes after the resumption and scoring the match-winner in the last minute of the game.

For their history-making Third Round appearance Rangers drew a home fixture against Fourth Division Rotherham United. A record-breaking 8,532 crowd saw Rotherham in the ascendency in the early stages. Half-time arrived with the scoresheet blank. Throughout the second-half Rangers played powerful, aggressive football and the League side were glad to settle for a draw. The successful replay and the subsequent Fourth Round battle against Third Division Peterborough United are both fully reported in *Match Reports*.

Rangers were again in the First Round in the next season, 1975/6, when they were drawn away from home at The Windmill against fellow non-Leaguers AP Leamington of the Southern League. A record crowd of 3,200 saw Rangers achieve a narrow 3-2 victory to go into the Second Round for the second season running.

By coincidence Rangers drew their old adversaries Third Division Halifax at the Marston Road ground in the Second Round. Although the sides changed over at half-time with the scoresheet blank the second-half belonged to Halifax who went through 3-1.

Then in the 1976/7 season with Rangers again in the First Round it was the long arm of coincidence that decreed that Stafford's opponents at Marston Road should once again be Halifax. This game ended in a goalless draw and in a keenly-contested replay at The Shay ground the League side squeezed into the next round with a 1-0 win.

Rangers' now regular appearances in the First Round continued in the 1977/8 season but they were not to get any farther. The non-Leaguers drew a difficult tie against Third Division Carlisle United at Brunton Park and although they were able to hold off their League opponents to go in at half-time with the scoresheet blank two second-half goals by United barred any further Cup progress for the part-timers.

Still hungry for Cup success Rangers again strode through the qualifying rounds in the next season, 1978/9, to reappear in the First Round but luck deserted them and they had to travel to meet Third Division Hull City at Boothferry Park. Luck also deserted Rangers during the game for after having held up the League side with a goalless first-half it seemed odds-on on a replay with only six minutes left for play when Rangers conceded an 'own goal'. Hull capitalised on this and added a second a minute later. Even then Rangers fought back fiercely and scored a consolation goal a minute from time.

Again in the Cup hunt in the 1979/80 season Rangers drew Midland Combination team Moor Green in the First Round, and beat them 3-2. The Second Round produced an interesting tie for Rangers → against famous F.A. Cup winners Blackburn Rovers away at Ewood Park. Although the Alliance Premier Leaguers put up a gallant fight they were a goal down at half-time. In the second half the part-timers harassed the frequently hesitant Blackburn defence but they were unable to get the equaliser and Rovers added another in injury time to gain a Third Round tie against Fulham.

Rangers had a difficult task in the First Round of the 1980/1 season when they were set to meet Third Division Walsall at Fellows Park. A goal down at half-time the part-timers found the going hard against an on-form Saddlers and in the second half the League side scored two late goals to make the final score 3-0.

Rangers were again in the Cup limelight in the 1981/2 season when they drew a home game in the First Round against Fourth Division York City. Stafford had an unbelievable start, a goal up in three minutes and City's equaliser half-way through the first-half was against the run of the play. York went ahead in the 55th minute of an evenly-contested second half and held on to their lead to defeat the non-Leaguers 2-1.

MATCH REPORTS
THIRD ROUND F.A. CUP REPLAY
7th January 1975
ROTHERHAM UNITED 0   STAFFORD RANGERS 2

Rangers gave a brilliant performance before a 11,000 Millmoor crowd to notch up one of the best-ever performances by a non-League club in the Cup when they beat the high-riding Fourth Division side 2–0 to achieve the honour of being the first Northern Premier League side to reach the Fourth Round of the Cup. Man-of-the-match for Rangers was Mick Cullerton, their former Port Vale and Derby County striker and leading goal-scorer who had scored in each of the previous Cup encounters against League opposition, ably supported by Jim Sargeant and Colin Chadwick. Back in the Rotherham side was their leading goal-scorer Trevor Womble.

In the early stages it was Rotherham who took the initiative and in the tenth minute got the ball in the net but the referee refused to allow the 'goal'. This was the signal for Rangers to take the play into the Rotherham half and within three minutes the Northern Premier Leaguers scored a memorable goal from Stuart CHAPMAN, Rangers midfield player, who latched on to a loose ball, steadied himself and lashed in a vicious 25-yards shot which left Rotherham goalkeeper McDonagh standing. Cullerton was having a brilliant game, creating space and contriving generally to bamboozle the Rotherham defenders. In the 28th minute he fooled the Rotherham defence and sent over a cross aimed for Chadwick whose header struck the Rotherham goalkeeper but was hooked out by Derrett.

Half-time: Rotherham 0   Stafford Rangers 1

In the second half Rangers, sensing victory, stormed into the attack and from one save by Arnold two defenders missed his clearance to give Cullerton a chance to rush in and lob the ball over the advancing Rotherham goalkeeper but was foiled by Derrett kicking the ball off the goal line. In order to try to preserve their lead Rangers pulled back the entire team to defend their goal area but 16 minutes from the end, during a breakaway, Rangers' Cup hero CULLERTON scored the second goal that effectively put Rotherham out of the Cup. Involved in the movement was Sargeant who intercepted a Rotherham pass and volleyed the ball to Cullerton who tricked both the Rotherham defender and the goalkeeper and calmly steered the ball into the net. It was Cullerton's seventh goal of the competition that season.

It was, without doubt, Rangers' greatest moment and they earned a place in the history books of those little clubs who have earned glory in the Third and Fourth Rounds of the Cup. It was the first occasion that Rotherham had been beaten in the Cup at Millmoor by non-League opposition.

Result: Rotherham 0   Stafford Rangers 2

Teams:
Rotherham United: McDonagh, Derrett, Leng, Swift, Delgado, Spencer, Finney, Womble, Wigg, Goodfellow, Crawford, (Sub: Woodhall).
Stafford Rangers: Arnold, Ritchie, Cooke, Sargeant, Seddon, Morris, Chapman, Cullerton, McLeish, Jones, Chadwick, (Sub: Keyes).
Referee: Mr. David Lloyd.
Attendance: 11,262

FOURTH ROUND F.A. CUP
25th January 1975
STAFFORD RANGERS 1   PETERBOROUGH 2
(At Stoke City's ground)

Stafford Rangers had the luck of the draw for their history-making Fourth Round tie against Third Division Peterborough United who themselves had several times appeared in the record books (as a non-League side) for their Cup performances against teams from the higher divisions. Near-neighbours, First Division Stoke City, offered the non-Leaguers the use of the Victoria Ground for the game and this was gratefully accepted by Rangers who had strong links with Stoke – the wife of Roy Chapman, Rangers' manager being the secretary to the Stoke manager and Stafford defender Bob Ritchie the brother of Stoke City's famous striker, John Ritchie. As a result of their previous wins against League opposition Stafford were brimming over with confidence when they took the field before a record crowd of 31,000.

The Northern Premier Leaguers were in no way over-awed by either the First Division environment or the tough League opposition for they boasted several players themselves with League experience, including Bob Ritchie, Stoke and Arsenal, David Cook, Wolves and Stockport, Ben Seddon, Tranmere Rovers, Mick Morris, Port Vale, Stuart Chapman, Port Vale, Roger Jones, Walsall, Mick Cullerton, Port Vale, and Ian McLeish, Sunderland, Dundee United and Luton Town.

Immediately after the kick-off the non-Leaguers surged into the attack and Peterborough goalkeeper Eric Steele was in action when he managed to get a leg to a power drive from Seddon. Jim Sargeant broke through the Peterborough defence but was upended as he got near the 'Posh' penalty area. Mick CULLERTON took the 20-yard free kick and the Rangers' supporters went wild as his kick was deflected off a Peterborough defender into the net. For the next quarter of an hour Peterborough were penned back into their own half as the jubilant Rangers pressed forward but gradually the League side came back into the game. In the 27th minute came the turning point when, as a result of a defensive error, a shot from Nixon which rebounded into play was not properly cleared and NIXON followed up to put the 'Posh' on terms. This reverse upset the rhythm of the non-Leaguers and Peterborough began to take over midfield control. Two minutes before the interval, after Chadwick was booked, Peterborough continued to surge forward and GREGORY, with a fine solo effort, deceived two Rangers' defenders and fired in a low shot that went into the back of the net.

Half-time: Stafford Rangers 1   Peterborough United 2

As soon as the second half began Rangers all but got the equaliser when following a Morris corner Roger Jones headed in and was just wide of the mark. The professionals closed up the game and gave the Rangers' strikers little chance to get through. It was a magnificent attempt by Rangers to endeavour to emulate the example of Yeovil, Walthamstow Avenue and Blyth Spartans – the only non-League sides to reach the Fifth Round since the war – but the dream faded in an atmosphere of glory.

Result: Stafford Rangers 1   Peterborough 2

Teams:
Stafford Rangers: Arnold, Ritchie, Cooke, Sargeant, Seddon, Morris, McLeish, Chapman, Jones, Cullerton, Chadwick, (Sub: Keyes).
Peterborough: Steele, Bradley, Lee, Walker, Turner, Carmichael, Murray, Gregory, Nixon, Hill, Robson, (Sub: Oakes).
Referee: Mr. R. Kirkpatrick, (Leicester).
Attendance: 31,000

Stafford Rangers (Contd)
CUP RUNS

1972/3
1st Round – *18th November*
Crewe Alex. 1   Stafford R. 0

1974/5
1st Round – *23rd November*
Stockport 0   Stafford R. 0

1st Round Replay – *26th November*
Stafford R. 1   Stockport 0

2nd Round – *14th December*
Stafford R. 2   Halifax 1

3rd Round – *4th January*
Stafford R. 0   Rotherham 0

3rd Round Replay – *7th January*
Rotherham 0   Stafford R. 2

4th Round – *25th January*
Stafford R. 1   Peterborough 2
(at Stoke)

1975/6
1st Round – *22nd November*
Leamington AP 2   Stafford R. 3

2nd Round – *13th December*
Stafford R. 1   Halifax 3

1976/7
1st Round – *20th November*
Stafford R. 0   Halifax 0

1st Round Replay – *23rd November*
Halifax 1   Stafford R. 0

1977/8
1st Round – *26th November*
Carlisle Utd 2   Stafford R. 0

1978/9
1st Round – *25th November*
Hull City 2   Stafford R. 1

1979/80
1st Round – *24th November*
Stafford R. 3   Moor Green 2

2nd Round – *17th December*
Blackburn Rov. 2   Stafford R. 0

1980/1
1st Round – *22nd November*
Walsall 3   Stafford R. 0

1981/2
1st Round – *21st November*
Stafford R. 1   York City 2

SUTTON UNITED

Founded: 1898

League: Isthmian

Ground: Gander Green Lane

Colours: Amber shirts with brown stripe; amber shorts

Sutton have made only sporadic First Round appearances since 1945/6 and then mostly against non-league opposition — with one important exception, the 1969/70 season when after beating non-Leaguers in the First, Second and Third Rounds they drew a magic home game in the Fourth Round against mighty Leeds United, then champions of England.

Sutton's first post-war appearance in the First Round was in the 1945/6 season when they were matched against fellow Isthmian Leaguers Walthamstow Avenue in a two-leg tie which United lost 11-3 on aggregate. Both teams were later to give distinguished performances in the Cup and to reach the Fourth Round.

It was not until the 1963/4 season that the club had a taste of League opposition, against Fourth Division Aldershot who won 4-0.

Sutton's glory season of 1969/70 was built on defeats of non-Leaguers Dagenham, Barnet and Hillingdon and although Leeds predictably ended the U's run in the Fourth Round it was the game of the century for the amateurs and in the wider context one of the finest examples of the glamour of the little clubs battling it out in the Cup against the top clubs in the land.

Sutton's 1945/6 First Round contest against Walthamstow Avenue under the two-leg scheme (the system was dropped the following year) saw Avenue win 4-1 at Gander Green Lane and then pile up a 7-2 win on their own ground to go through to the next round on a 11-3 aggregate. In the final qualifying round Sutton had travelled to semi-professional Southern League Gillingham and won by the remarkable score of 9-3. United scorers included Charlie Vaughan (later to turn pro with Charlton) and Wally Hinshelwood (father of Martin and Paul). In the First Round of the 1946/7 season Sutton drew an away game against fellow non-Leaguers Barnet, losing 3-0. Then in 1960/1 they were once again contenders in the First Round battles, drawn at home against Southern Leaguers Romford. The U's managed to hold the semi-professionals to a 2-2 draw but in the replay at Romford the Isthmian Leaguers were demolished 5-0.

Sutton's first post-war League opponents in the First Round were Fourth Division Aldershot at home in the 1963/4 season. A crowd of over 6,000 was at Gander Green Lane in the hope of seeing Sutton, Amateur Cup finalists the previous season, make further progress in the Cup but they were doomed to disappointment, Aldershot turning in a competent performance to win 4-0.

The 1966/7 season saw Sutton again in the First Round draw and having to travel to meet Southern Leaguers Bath City, a hard side to beat on their own ground in the Cup. This was confirmed when City scored the only goal of the match to sink the U's for another season.

The fairy-tale season that put Sutton on the football map in the 1969/70 season opened modestly enough with an away encounter against fellow Isthmian Leaguers Dagenham, no pushovers in the Cup. U's scored the only goal of the match early in the first half and then spent the rest of the game defending their lead as Dagenham threatened to equalise. The draw for the next round again proved unkind for Sutton with another away tie - against Southern Leaguers Barnet. The U's owed it to a resolute defence that they were able to leave Underhill with a 2-0 win to become the first amateur side to reach the Third Round since Barnet themselves, then in the Athenian League, in 1964/5. Barnet's 15 corners to the U's three was the measure of Sutton's fine rearguard action with two breakaway goals to give them victory.

Instead of one of the First Division glamour clubs for their Third Round tie the U's had to be content with Southern League opposition, Hillingdon Borough away from home. On a frostbound pitch the Southern Leaguers had the lion's share of the play but like Barnet before them they could make little impression on the U's defence and at the end of the 90 minutes the scoresheet was blank. The well-organised, unyielding Sutton defence included goalkeeper Roffey, Gradi, Pritchard and Powell, all on top form. Don Revie, the Leeds and England manager was at the Leas Stadium to run the rule over the two sides since, because the game had had to be postponed owing to the state of the pitch, Leeds already knew that they had to face either the U's or Hillingdon. It also gave the England manager the chance to see Boro's player-manager Jimmy Langley in Southern

League colours – a player who once wore an England shirt at Hampden Park before a crowd of 134,000.

U's put up a sparkling performance at Gander Green Lane in the replay, running out 4–1 winners before a 8,000 crowd. With Langley out through injury Boro were disorganised and although the Southern Leaguers held out until half-time they looked a spent force in the second-half. Soon after the second period had begun the England amateur-international packed U's began giving Boro a footballing lesson, Mellows, released by his teachers' training college for the game, scoring the first in the 47th minute and followed by further goals from Bladon (2) and Howard against a consolation goal for Boro by Terry. Sutton thoroughly deserved their Fourth Round clash with mighty Leeds United, fully described in *Match Report*.

Sutton: Roffey, Brooks, Clarke, Powell, Faulkner, Gradi, Mellows, Bladon, Drabwell, Pritchard, Howard.

Five seasons were to elapse before Sutton were again in the First Round hunt, gaining a home fixture in 1975/6 against Fourth Division Bournemouth. The two sides were evenly matched and this was reflected in the final scoreline, one goal each. In the replay at Dean Court the Cherries ran out winners by a lone goal, the U's being unable to penetrate Bournemouth's stout defence.

Sutton's next First Round appearance was in 1981/2 when they were drawn away to fellow Isthmian Leaguers Bishop's Stortford with a chance to avenge the last minute defeat that Stortford had inflicted on the U's in the 1980 F.A. Trophy final at Wembley. Sutton went into a 2–1 half-time lead but Stortford grabbed the equaliser in the 78th minute to force a replay at Gander Green Lane.

After being a goal down for most of the replay the U's made a dramatic last-ditch recovery, equalising in the 76th minute and scoring the match-winner two minutes later through captain John Rains who had had to leave his sick bed to play. Attendance: 2,100.

Sutton were matched in the Second Round against Third Division Swindon Town away at the County Ground. Sutton took a shock lead in the 19th minute through top scorer Mickey Joyce, Swindon equalising ten minutes later. When a replay seemed certain Swindon made it 2–1 in the dying seconds of the game.

MATCH REPORT
FOURTH ROUND F.A. CUP
24th January 1970
SUTTON UNITED 0   LEEDS UNITED 6

The greatest game in Sutton's history as over 14,000 spectators packed the tiny, tree-lined Gander Green Lane ground to watch, in carnival spirit, the U's take on mighty Leeds United, the champions of England. In atmosphere the game had everything – famous internationals in the star-studded Leeds side, £165,000 Allan Clarke, then Britain's costliest footballer, Mick Jones, Jackie Charlton, Paul Reaney, Norman Hunter, Billy Bremner, Peter Lorimer, Johnny Giles – a £1 million side opposed by eleven amateurs, Mr. Jim Finney in charge of proceedings, Don Revie on the bench, the TV cameras perched precariously on a makeshift gantry – an unbelievable fairy-tale occasion.

The Isthmian Leaguers did well to hold their distinguished opponents to a 3–0 lead at half-time, the U's defence working overtime as the Leeds attackers constantly surged into Sutton's penalty area with Dave Roffey making some fine saves, despite a couple of errors that led to Leeds' goals. John Faulkner, who shortly after the match was transferred to Leeds, had an inspired game, splendidly carrying out his main task of shadowing England international Mick Jones. Occasionally a Sutton raid in the Leeds half would relieve the hard-pressed defenders but in the main it was one way traffic. Leeds' first goal came in the 15th minute when CLARKE put the finishing touches to a Giles-Hunter move down the left flank.

Five minutes before half-time Leeds put paid to Sutton's chances of getting back in the game with two goals, the first by LORIMER who pushed the ball through Roffey's legs in the 41st minute and another by CLARKE just on half time.

Half-time: Sutton United 0   Leeds United 3

Whereas the professionals had forced their first corner in the fourth minute of the game the U's had to wait until the start of the second half before they obtained their first. Clarke had the ball in the net shortly after the resumption but the referee disallowed the 'goal'. There were two Sutton attacks of note in the second half – one when Larry Pritchard's shot hit the bar with Harvey beaten and the second when Faulkner headed into goal only for the point to be disallowed because of a foul on a Leeds defender.

Further goals by CLARKE, bringing his tally to four and LORIMER, with his second, brought the Leeds total to six. Mick Jones also had the ball in the net but again the 'goal' was disallowed.

Although one-sided it was a memorable game for the non-

Leaguers and when the final whistle blew the whole of the Leeds team, in a fine sporting gesture, lined up to cheer the Sutton heroes off the pitch.

Result: Sutton United 0   Leeds United 6

Teams:
Sutton: Roffey, Brookes, Clarke, Powell, Faulkner, Gradi, Mellows, Bladon, Drabwell, Pritchard, Howard, (Sub: Waughman).
Leeds: Harvey, Reaney, Cooper, Bremner, Charlton, Hunter, Lorimer, Clarke, Jones, Giles, Madeley, (Sub: Bates).
Referee: Mr. J. Finney, (Hereford).
Attendance: 14,000

Sutton Utd (Contd)

CUP RUNS

1945/6

1st Round (First Leg) – *17th November*
Sutton 1   Walthamstow 4

1st Round (Second Leg) – *24th Nov.*
Walthamstow 7   Sutton 2
(Walthamstow won on 11–3 aggregate)

1946/7

1st Round – *30th November*
Barnet 3   Sutton Utd. 0

1960/61

1st Round – *5th November*
Sutton 2   Romford 2

1st Round Replay – *9th November*
Romford 5   Sutton 0

1963/4

1st Round – *16th November*
Sutton 0   Aldershot 4

1966/7

1st Round – *26th November*
Bath City 1   Sutton 0

1969/70

1st Round – *15th November*
Dagenham 0   Sutton 1

2nd Round – *6th December*
Barnet 0   Sutton 2

3rd Round – *6th January*
Hillingdon 0   Sutton 0

3rd Round Replay – *12th January*
Sutton 4   Hillingdon 1

4th Round – *24th January*
Sutton 0   Leeds Utd 6

1975/6

1st Round – *22nd November*
Sutton 1   Bournemouth 1

1st Round Replay – *26th November*
Bournemouth 1   Sutton 0

1981/2

1st Round – *21st November*
Bishops Stort. ... 2   Sutton 2

1st Round Replay – *24th November*
Sutton 2   Bishops Stort. ... 1

2nd Round – *15th December*
Swindon 2   Sutton 1

THANET UNITED
(formerly Margate)

Founded: 1929

League: Southern (Southern Division)

Ground: Hartsdown Park

Colours: White shirts and blue shorts

Margate (now re-named Thanet United) have appeared consistently in the First Round draw ever since their first post-war First Round encounter in 1955/6 against Third Division South, Walsall held to a 2-2 draw at home and were heavily defeated 6-1 in the replay. They have fought their way through to the Second Round on no fewer than four occasions, in 1956/7 against Millwall, in 1959/60 against Crystal Palace against whom they forced a replay, in 1961/2 against Notts County and another replay, and in 1967/8 against Peterborough United. But their crowning glory was reserved for the 1972/3 season when they entertained First Division Spurs at Hartsdown Park — and were beaten 6-0 — after having defeated Swansea 1-0 at home in the First Round and Walton and Hersham of the Isthmian League away from home in the Second Round. Other League opponents in the Cup have included Bournemouth (1961/2, First Round, Margate gaining a sensational 3-0 win away from home), Brentford, Northampton and Aldershot.

Margate's first post-war appearance in the Cup, in the 1955/6 season, was an attractive home fixture against Walsall, Third Division South, at Hartsdown Park. The former Kent Leaguers held the League side to a 2-2 draw, Walsall leading 2-1 until the closing minutes when Margate equalised. The near-10,000 crowd at the replay saw Margate open the scoring and to go in at half-time with their 1-0 lead intact. In the second-half Walsall went on a goal spree, knocking in six goals.

The next season, 1956/7, saw Margate again in the First Round, drawn at home against Dunstable Town of the Metropolitan League, the Kent League side winning a one-sided affair 3-1. In the Second Round for the first time since 1936 Margate had an away game against Millwall, Third

Division South at The Den. There was a bumper 'gate' of 15,982, more than at the First Division match at nearby Charlton. Millwall secured a comfortable 4–0 win.

In the 1957/8 season Margate again won through to the First Round and had the luck of the draw – at home against Crystal Palace, Third Division South. Palace scraped through by a narrow 3–2 margin.

To begin their successful 1959/60 Cup season when they once again reached the Second Round Margate, in their first season in the Southern League (Division One), drew fellow Southern Leaguers, Kettering (Premier Division) away from home. Kettering were not at their best and could only manage a 1-1 draw. In an exciting replay at Hartsdown, Margate were on top in the first-half and went 2–0 in the lead but Kettering rallied after the interval and scored twice to equalise. With only five minutes to go Kearns, the former West Ham and Norwich centre-forward, scored the match-winner for Margate and notched his hat-trick. The Kent side was matched in the Second Round against Fourth Division Crystal Palace, their conquerors in the First Round in 1957/8, at home at Hartsdown. There was a record 'gate' of 8,200 at the match. Margate pounded away at the Palace goal without success and had to be content with a 0–0 draw.

As a bonus for both teams the largest crowd that Margate had ever played before in the Cup, 29,300, assembled at Selhurst Park to watch the return game. Margate's defence stood firm and it was not until after an hour's play that Palace went one up. Palace were in control for the rest of the game and scored two further goals, ironically through former Margate centre-forward Johnny Roche. Margate put up a magnificent defence, with 36-year-old former Wolves and Notts County centre-half Ray Chatham and David Laing, who once played in a Scottish Cup final, being outstanding.

Margate: Prodger (the Kent batsman), Wells, Joyce, Worthington, Chatham, Laing, Peters, Foan, Kearns, Yeomans, Tucker.

The 1961/2 season was a dramatic one for the Kent side. In the First Round they were drawn against Division Three leaders Bournemouth away from home at Dean Court before 12,405 spectators. At the interval the scoresheet was blank. After the change of ends the non-Leaguers got into their stride and in the 66th minute were a goal ahead, adding two further goals late in the game. It was the Cup shock of the day.

Margate: Hughes, Parry, Joyce, John, Harrop, Smith, Fraser, Roche, Jones, Blackburn, Hills.

In the Second Round Margate drew a home game with the oldest football league club in the world, Third Division Notts County. The Cup fever in the town helped to draw a 'gate' of nearly 8,000. Margate dictated the play from the start and their domination lasted for three-quarters of the game, including the magical moment, in the 33rd minute, when Barnett put the non-Leaguers ahead, a lead they held to half-time. It was against the run of the play when four minutes from time County equalised.

Margate: Hughes, Parry, Joyce, John, Harrop, Smith, Fraser, Roche, Blackburn, Barnett, Hills.

Once having been let off the hook County were more decisive in the replay at Meadow Lane. Watched by a crowd of 12,302 County built up a 3-0 lead before Margate were able to snatch a consolation goal.

The following season, 1962/3, Margate drew a hard First Round tie against Third Division Millwall at The Den. Millwall ran up a 3-0 lead, Margate closing the gap with a consolation goal ten minutes from the end. The tie drew a 'gate' of 14,041.

Again in the First Round in 1963/4 Margate were given a difficult task at Griffin Park against Third Division Brentford. In the Bees' line-up there were players of the calibre of centre-forward Billy McAdams, capped 14 times for Ireland, Welsh international Dai Ward and John Dick, ex West Ham and a Scottish international. Surprisingly Margate dominated the first half and led 1-0 at the interval. Brentford showed their skills in the second-half and went into a 2-1 lead although Margate deservedly equalised six minutes from time. At the replay at Hartsdown although Margate had the better of the play in the first half the Bees had the edge after the interval and went on to win 2-0.

Margate's next appearance in the First Round was in the 1967/8 season when they drew a difficult away game against fellow Southern Leaguers and renowned Cup 'giantkillers' Yeovil. The Somerset side found Margate in devastating form on the slope and returned to Hartsdown with a splendid 3-1 win under their belts. For their Second Round tie Margate had ground advantage when they drew Third Division Peterborough United but the non-Leaguers were no match for their League opponents and were knocked out of the Cup by four clear goals.

In the following season, 1968/9, Margate again fought their way to the First Round to find themselves drawn away from home against Third Division Northampton Town. After the Cobblers had gone into a 2-0 lead Margate pulled a goal back to make the half-time score 2-1 but after the interval Northampton scored again to make the final score 3-1.

Again in the First Round in the 1969/70 season Margate drew a home game against Fourth Division Aldershot but the Southern Leaguers took a pounding. Despite scoring first and holding the League side to a 1-1 draw at half-time a goal blitz struck the Southern Leaguers in the second-half and they went down 7-2.

Margate did not do much better in the following season when again they earned a place in the First Round, drawing an away game against Isthmian Leaguers Dagenham. Margate made no further progress in the Cup, the amateurs defeating them 2-0.

The greatest trouncing Margate have received was in the 1971/2 season when, drawn away against Third Division Bournemouth at Dean Court the League side won by a cricket score - a record 11-0 win that saw Ted MacDougall, later to win fame with Norwich and England, score nine to go into the history books as an F.A. Cup record.

Better things were to come in the 1972/3 season when for the first time in 37 years Margate reached the Third Round. In the First Round they were drawn at home against Third Division Swansea City. There was only a small crowd at Hartsdown braving a freezing temperature to see the non-Leaguers bundle the Welshmen out of the Cup 1-0, one of the shock Cup results of the round. Only a faultless display by City's Welsh international goalkeeper Millington prevented Margate scoring further goals.

Margate had to travel for the Second Round encounter which brought them into contact with Isthmian Leaguers Walton and Hersham. There was little difference between the two teams and it was not until the last five minutes of the game that Margate scored. Thus Margate were in the Third Round with a magical home game against mighty Spurs, fully described in *Match Report*.

MATCH REPORT
THIRD ROUND F.A. CUP
13th January 1973
MARGATE 0 TOTTENHAM HOTSPUR 6

This was one of the greatest days in Margate's history when the humble Southern Leaguers faced mighty Spurs at Hartsdown in the Third Round before a capacity crowd of 8,500. When Martin Peters led out the Spurs side there was a million pounds worth of talent on the Hartsdown pitch, including famous names such as Scottish international Alan Gilzean, English international Martin Chivers, Mike England in the centre-half spot and Jimmy Pearce. Although Spurs went immediately into the attack the Margate defence held up well marshalled by Eddie Clayton, an old Spurs player himself, and ably supported by Davie Houston, Ray Summers, Dave Paton and Norman Fusco. The Southern Leaguers managed to contain the fast moving Spurs attack until the 25th minute when Martin CHIVERS scored the first goal with a deflected drive.

Irish international Pat Jennings in the Spurs goal had little to contend with but he was tested when Fusco drove in a hard shot which the Spurs goalkeeper was lucky to save. In the 34th minute Perryman was taken off as a result of the leg injury that he had received earlier and was substituted by Jimmy Pearce.

Half-time: Margate 0 Spurs 1

Immediately the second half began Spurs piled on the pressure and despite Paton's challenge Martin CHIVERS drove in number two from close in. The Southern Leaguers had scarcely recovered from this blow when Spurs came up with number three, Jimmy PEARCE scoring following a brilliant run by Ralph Coates.

Only occasionally did Margate find any attacking rhythm although Clayton continued to supply inspiration to his side. Spurs notched number four in the 76th minute when Gilzean gave a perfect pass for PETERS to hammer home from close range. Seven minutes later Cyril KNOWLES headed the fifth when he beat three of the Margate defenders to send a terrific shot into the back of the net. Margate were now outpaced and their goal fell again three minutes from the end when John PRATT completed a run down the left wing to send an angled shot past Brodie.

Result: Margate 0 Tottenham Hotspur 6

Teams:
Margate: Brodie, Summers, Butterfield, Fusco, Paton, Houston, Baber, Clayton, Barry, Brown, Walker, (Sub: Ferry).
Tottenham Hotspur: Jennings, Evans, Knowles, Pratt, England, Naylor, Gilzean, Perryman, Chivers, Peters, Coates, (Sub: Pearce).
Referee: Mr. B. J. Homewood, (Sunbury-on-Thames).
Attendance: 8,500

Margate (Contd)

CUP RUNS

1955/6

1st Round – *19th November*
Margate 2   Walsall 2

1st Round Replay – *24th November*
Walsall 6   Margate 1

1956/7

1st Round – *17th November*
Margate 3   Dunstable 1

2nd Round – *8th December*
Millwall 4   Margate 0

1957/8

1st Round – *16th November*
Margate 2   Crystal Palace ...3

1959/60

1st Round – *14th November*
Kettering Town .1   Margate 1

1st Round Replay – *19th November*
Margate 3   Kettering Town 2

2nd Round – *5th December*
Margate 0   Crystal Palace ...0

2nd Round Replay – *9th December*
Crystal Palace ...3   Margate 0

1961/2

1st Round – *4th November*
Bournemouth 0   Margate 3

2nd Round – *25th November*
Margate 1   Notts County ...1

2nd Round Replay – *30th November*
Notts County ...3   Margate 1

1962/3

1st Round – *3rd November*
Millwall 3   Margate 1

1963/4

1st Round – *16th November*
Brentford 2   Margate 2

1st Round replay – *20th November*
Margate 0   Brentford 2

1967/8

1st Round – *13th December*
Yeovil 1   Margate 3

2nd Round – *6th January*
Margate 0   Peterborough U. 4

1968/9

1st Round – *16th November*
Northampton 3   Margate 1

1969/70

1st Round – *15th November*
Margate 2   Aldershot 7

1970/71

1st Round – *21st November*
Dagenham 2   Margate 0

1971/2

1st Round – *20th November*
Bournemouth .. 11   Margate 0

1972/3

1st Round – *18th November*
Margate 1   Swansea 0

2nd Round – *9th December*
Walton & H 0   Margate 1

3rd Round – *13th January*
Margate 0   Tottenham 6

TOOTING & MITCHAM UNITED

Founded: 1887 (as Tooting Graveney)
1932 amalgamated with Mitcham Wanderers
League: Isthmian

Ground: Sandy Lane

Colours: Black and white shirts, black shorts

Tooting have gone down into Cup history more than anything else perhaps as a result of their magical 1958/9 season when after having disposed of League opponents Bournemouth and Northampton they entertained mighty First Division Notts Forest in the Third Round at Sandy Lane and to the astonishment of the football world held them to a 2-2 draw. Although the gallant amateurs were beaten 3-0 at the City ground in the replay before a crowd of 35,000 they had done enough for their name for ever to be associated with 'giantkilling' deeds in the Cup. But it was in the 1975/6/season that they went one better, reaching the Fourth Round to be defeated 3-1 at the Valley Parade ground by Fourth Division Bradford City, beating several non-Leaguers and Swindon Town (after a replay) on the way. Other League clubs that the Lilywhites have engaged in either First or Second Round post-war ties have included Millwall, Brighton, Q.P.R., Crystal Palace, and Northampton.

When Tooting drew Third Division South, Millwall away at The Den in the 1948/9 season they were able to claim two 'firsts' – it was the club's first appearance in the First Round of the Cup and their first competitive game against a League side. Tooting had the misfortune of having a 'goal' disallowed and after having mounted a superb defence saw Millwall snatch the match-winner 12 minutes from the end.

After missing a season the Lilywhites were back in First Round contention in the 1950/1 season when they were hosts to Brighton, Third Division South, at Sandy Lane. In a game of fluctuating fortunes Tooting opened the scoring in the 12th minute before a crowd of over 10,000, the teams were on terms at half-time, and added a further goal each after the interval. In the last five minutes of the game Brighton scored the match-winner to bring the final score to 3-2.

Tooting had to wait until the 1956/7 season before reappearing in the First Round, drawing a home tie against fellow non-Leaguers Bromsgrove Rovers playing in the Birmingham League. The first-half ended with Tooting holding a 1-0 lead. After the resumption Rovers had a 'goal' disallowed and then equalised but United secured a place in the next round when they scored the match-winner seven minutes from time. For their first-ever appearance in the Second Round the Lilywhites again had the luck of the draw attracting Third Division South, Queen's Park Rangers to Sandy Lane. The game was only ten minutes old when United got the ball in the net but the 'goal' was disallowed. Shortly afterwards Rangers scored to gain a 1-0 half-time lead and netted again in the later stages to make the final score 2-0.

The 1958/9 season made history for Tooting when they went forward into the Third Round to gain a plum draw against First Division Notts Forest. For their First Round game they drew Bournemouth, Third Division South, at Sandy Lane, the amateurs stunning the football world by beating the League side 3-1. The Isthmian League champions held a 1-0 half-time lead and scored again shortly after the restart. Although the Cherries pulled back a goal they went futher in arrears in the closing stages when Tooting notched another to make the final scoreline 3-1.

One of Tooting's best Cup performances came in the Second Round when they were opposed to Fourth Division Northampton Town at home at Sandy Lane. Although Northampton snatched a seven minute lead the amateurs were on terms at the interval and in the 70th minute Paddy Hasty, Tooting's Irish international centre-forward, scored the match-winner. Hasty got the ball in the net again but the point was disallowed. Tooting thus secured a place in the Third Round for the first time in the club's history, drawn at home against First Division Notts Forest and the amateurs' great achievement in holding their illustrious opponents to a 2-2 draw has become a legend in non-League football. The game is fully reported in *Match Report*.

The largest crowd that the amateurs had ever played before, 42,000 greeted Tooting as they came out on the City Road pitch for the memorable replay on 24th January 1959. The professionals dominated the play from the start to run out comfortable 3-0 winners. In the 29th minute the first of

Forest's goals was scored by Dwight and in the 38th minute Wilson added another to give Forest a 2-0 half-time lead. In the closing stages Forest resumed their attack and left winger Imlach gave them their third goal. The sides were the same as for the opening encounter except that for the amateurs Wally Pearson kept goal instead of Secker.

Tooting missed four seasons before reappearing in the First Round in 1963/4, drawn at home at Sandy Lane against Southern Leaguers Gravesend, and losing 2-1.

The amateurs had a long wait of 11 seasons before they were again seen in the First Round, drawing ground advantage over Third Division opponents and near neighbours Crystal Palace. A 10,000 crowd at Sandy Lane saw Palace, with at least half a million pounds worth of talent in their side, put up a pedestrian performance and lucky to scrape through on a 2-1 margin.

The Isthmian Leaguers had another glory season in 1975/6, on a par with their classic 1958/9 season, although on this occasion they reached the Fourth Round for the first time in the club's history. There was little hint of the titanic struggles to come when the amateurs drew Southern Leaguers Romford away from home at the Brooklands ground. A hard match resulted in a 1-0 win for the amateurs, Alan Ives, the former England amateur international, scoring the vital goal in the first-half. In the Second Round luck deserted Tooting, drawn away against fellow Isthmian Leaguers Leatherhead. In an end-to-end contest the defenders came out on top and at the final whistle the scoresheet was blank. The replay at Sandy Lane was played on an icy pitch and the game stood at one all when the referee abandoned proceedings in the 57th minute.

When the tie was resumed Tooting again had to contend with a lively Leatherhead side who took a 17th minute lead, Tooting drawing level with a 54th minute penalty and scoring the match-winner in extra time. Tooting went into the Third Round for the second time since the war after a tie that had lasted 267 minutes.

Tooting were hoping for a glamour club in the Third Round draw but found themselves away from home facing lowly-placed Swindon Town. It was a great day for Tooting's 26-year-old Ronnie Howell who had once played League football for Swindon and also for their manager Roy Dwight who was one of the Notts Forest strikers in the

1958/9 Third Round contest against Tooting. A crowd of nearly 10,000 saw Tooting fall back before a Swindon onslaught which gave Town two shock goals in the fifth and sixth minutes, the first from Peter Eastoe, who had been signed from Wolves for a club record of £80,000, and the second when midfield player Dixon placed a powerful header out of reach of Tooting's ex-Aston Villa goalkeeper Dunn. Irish international Anderson almost made it three but his 'goal' was disallowed. The fire seemed to go out of the Swindon attack and after the break the League side appeared to be content to rely on their 2-0 lead. As the game neared its end Tooting were buzzing and staged one of the most sensational finishes ever recorded in a Cup game featuring non-League and League opposition. In the 88th minute Tooting centre-forward Glover scored a scrambled goal after two shots had been charged down and almost on time Casey scored a great equaliser. It was a dramatic finish to a game that Swindon seemed to have under control from the start and spoke volumes for a team of part-timers with the crowd against them that they fought back to force the League side to a replay. This resulted in a magnificent 2-1 win for the non-Leaguers with Tooting drawing a Fourth Round game away from home against Bradford City. Both matches are fully reported in *Match Report*.

After their triumphs of the previous season the Isthmian League 'giantkillers' were again in the First Round in 1976/7 drawing Southern Leaguers Dartford at Sandy Lane. Leading 2-1 at half-time through two penalty goals the Isthmian Leaguers dominated the second-half and the Southern Leaguers, who had gone 14 games without defeat, were finally beaten 4-2. Tooting did not have a good draw in the Second Round being matched against redoubtable Cup fighters Kettering, Southern League, managed by ex-Wolves Derek Dougan and having played 29 games without defeat. In an end-to-end thriller Kettering scored the only goal of the game in the 81st minute.

Tooting were back in the First Round fray in the 1977/8 season when they drew a home tie against Fourth Division Northampton Town. Town secured a 1-0 half-time lead which was neutralised seven minutes into the second-half when veteran captain Billy Smith scored from 25 yards. Midway through the second-half Northampton scored again and then pulled men back to defend their lead.

MATCH REPORTS

THIRD ROUND F.A. CUP
10th January 1959
TOOTING AND MITCHAM 2   NOTTINGHAM FOREST 2

Tooting and Mitcham, the gallant amateurs from the Isthmian League, could rightly feel when this game ended that only a hotly disputed penalty saved their First Division opponents, Nottingham Forest, from defeat. The first escape for Forest was when Holden lobbed the ball upfield for Paddy Hasty to crash a power drive against the bar over the head of the advancing Forest goalkeeper.

Tooting opened the scoring after 20 minutes. After a mix-up in the Forest goal area Albert GRAINGER headed the ball into an empty net.

Secker played a fine game in the Tooting goal, dealing capably with shots from Gray and Quigley and although playing in his first Cup tie showed little or no nerves.

A great roar went up from the 14,000 crowd when Tooting notched their second goal. From 35 yards out Ted MURPHY, who had taken up a clearance from Forest right-back Whare, sent the ball speeding past a well-beaten Forest goalkeeper. Tooting deserved their half-time lead.

Half-time: Tooting and Mitcham 2   Nottingham Forest 0

On resuming Tooting continued to play good football but after eight minutes Forest came back into the game with an incredible goal. MURPHY intercepted a Forest pass and casually tapped the ball to Secker but the ball bounced through the goalkeeper's hands into the net. Forest piled on the pressure playing top-class football on the ice-covered Sandy Lane pitch.

Secker dived full-length to save from Quigley and soon afterwards was knocked out as he collided with a Forest forward in saving his goal but recovered afterwards. Then came the major sensation of the afternoon. With only 13 minutes left for play the ball bounced into the Tooting penalty area and the ball appeared to hit Murphy's right shoulder but the referee at once signalled for a penalty and GRAY scored from the spot.

Result: Tooting and Mitcham 2   Nottingham Forest 2

Tooting and Mitcham:	R. Secker, J. Harlow, G. Edwards, G. Holden, B. Bennett, E. Murphy, A. Grainger, A. Viney, P. Hasty, A. Slade, D. Flanagan.
Nottingham Forest:	Thomson, Whare, McDonald, Whitefoot, McKinlay, Burkitt, Dwight, Quigley, Wilson, Gray, Imlach.
Referee:	Mr. R. G. Warnke, (Coventry).
Attendance:	14,300

THIRD ROUND F.A. CUP REPLAY
6th January 1976
TOOTING AND MITCHAM 2   SWINDON TOWN 1

On a snow covered pitch Tooting played themselves to a standstill and went off the pitch at the end of the game with a glorious 2-1 win under their belts to earn a Fourth Round tie for the first time in their history.

In the 34th minute Tooting took a 1-0 lead at the time when Stroud, the Swindon midfield player, was off the field with a dislocated elbow. Berrecloth was responsible for making the goal, setting up a dazzling run down the right wing crossing for JUNEMAN to sweep the ball into the net from 20 yards. Swindon were demoralised at this reverse and only Eastoe, playing competent football in the centre, seemed capable of turning the tide for the League side. Half-time came with Tooting holding their 1-0 lead intact.

Half-time: Tooting and Mitcham 1   Swindon Town 0

In the second half Swindon began to get more into the game and six minutes after the resumption were given a soft equaliser. Swindon had been hammering away and under the pressure Bobby GREEN, the Isthmian Leaguers' left back, turned the ball towards his own goal but Dunn was off his line and the crowd had the mortification of seeing the ball trickle over the Tooting goal line. This goal gave Swindon new heart and the League side began to put on intense pressure with Eastoe causing Tooting's defenders a good deal of trouble.

With eight minutes to go before extra time and with Swindon hanging on for a further half hour's play Tooting delighted their 7,500 crowd when Alan IVES swept the non-Leaguers to victory. Green set up the movement when he robbed Syrett of the ball and moved it on to Ives on the left wing. The winger raced 20 yards up the line, tricked defender Taylor and then hammered the ball past Barron who was advancing from his goal.

Result: Tooting and Mitcham 2   Swindon Town 1

Teams:
Tooting and Mitcham: Dunn, Berrecloth, Smith, Grubb, Green, Casey, Howell, Ford, Juneman, Glover, Ives.
Swindon Town: Barron, Taylor, Trollope, Stroud, Burrows, McLaughlin, Moss, Dixon, Eastoe, Syrett, Anderson.
Referee: Mr. A. J. Hamil, (Wolverhampton).
Attendance: 7,500

FOURTH ROUND F.A. CUP
24th January 1976
BRADFORD CITY 3 TOOTING AND MITCHAM 1

This was an historic day for non-Leaguers Tooting who were appearing in the Fourth Round, the last 32 clubs in the country, for the first time in their history. It was an incredible achievement that the part-timers should have got so far and they might have been expected to have at least held Bradford, lowly placed in the Fourth Division, to a draw but although they dominated the play for most of the first-half they eventually went down 3–1. For the first twenty minutes of the game the crowd at Valley Parade were entertained to the sight of Tooting roaring into the Bradford penalty area and only good luck and some capable goalkeeping by Bradford's goalkeeper, Downsborough, kept out the part-timers.

Bradford took a 1–0 lead against the run of the play in the 23rd minute through HUTCHINS who picked up a weak clearance and sent a powerful shot swerving into the net past Dunn. Casey and Howell continued to work industriously in midfield feeding through passes to the Tooting strikers.

Half-time: Bradford City 1 Tooting and Mitcham 0

Tooting should have been level in the second half when Ron Howell, whose cool nerve was a feature of his earlier playing career at Spurs, Millwall, Cambridge United and Swindon, was skilfully trying to get round a defender in the penalty area and was brought down. The referee refused to award a penalty and gave a free-kick outside the area. Bradford went further ahead in the 63rd minute again through HUTCHINS. Two minutes later the gallant part-timers pulled one back when JUNEMAN smashed the ball into the net through a crowd of defenders from a pass by Howell. John Dunn, whose League and Cup experiences with Chelsea, Torquay United, Aston Villa and Charlton Athletic stood him in good stead during the final attacks from Bradford, kept the City strikers at bay until almost the end of the match when centre-half MIDDLETON scored number three. It was the end of the Cup trail for Tooting who were acclaimed by the 12,000 crowd as they left the field, the highest attendance at Valley Parade since the Third Round of the F.A. Cup in 1974 against non-League Alvechurch.

Result: Bradford City 3 Tooting and Mitcham 1

Teams:
Bradford City: Downsborough, Todd, Cooper, Johnson, Middleton, Fetwell, McGinley, Ingram, Cooke, Hall, Hutchins.
Tooting and Mitcham: Dunn, Berrecloth, Smith, Grubb, Green, Casey, Howell, Ford, Juneman, Glover, Ives.
Referee: Mr. R. N. Perkins, (Stafford).
Attendance: 12,152

Tooting & Mitcham (Contd)
CUP RUNS

1948/9
1st Round - *27th November*
Millwall 1   Tooting & M. ...0

1950/1
1st Round   *25th November*
Tooting & M. ...2   Brighton 3

1956/7
1st Round - *17th November*
Tooting & M. ...2   Bromsgrove R. ..1
2nd Round - *8th December*
Tooting & M. ...0   QPR 2

1958/9
1st Round - *15th November*
Tooting & M. ...3   Bournemouth 1
2nd Round   *6th December*
Tooting & M. ...2   Northampton 1
3rd Round   *10th January*
Tooting & M. ...2   Notts. Forest 2
3rd Round Replay - *24th January*
Notts. Forest 3   Tooting & M. ...0

1963/4
1st Round - *16th November*
Tooting & M. ...1   Gravesend 2

1974/5
1st Round   *27th November*
Tooting & M. ...1   Crystal Palace ...2

1975/6
1st Round - *22nd November*
Romford 0   Tooting & M. ...1
2nd Round - *13th December*
Leatherhead 0   Tooting & M. ...0
2nd Round Replay - *16th December*
Tooting & M. ...1   Leatherhead ......
(Abandoned after 57 mins - pitch unfit ice)
2nd Round Replay - *22nd December*
Tooting & M. ...2   Leatherhead 1
(After extra time)
3rd Round - *3rd January*
Swindon 2   Tooting & M. 2
3rd Round Replay - *6th January*
Tooting & M. ...2   Swindon 1
4th Round - *24th January*
Bradford City ...3   Tooting & M. ...1

1976/7
1st Round - *20th November*
Tooting & M. ...4   Dartford 2
2nd Round - *11th December*
Kettering 1   Tooting & M. ...0

1977/8
1st Round   *26th November*
Tooting & M. ...1   Northampton 2

WALTHAMSTOW AVENUE

Founded: 1901

League: Isthmian

Ground: Green Pond Road

Colours: Pale and deep blue hoops, blue shorts

One of the greatest amateur sides of all time, Walthamstow Avenue have an F.A. Cup record second to none among the non-Leaguers. Avenue's outstanding feat was to hold mighty First Division Manchester United to a 1-1 draw at Old Trafford in the Fourth Round in the 1952/3 season, having progressed to that stage by eliminating League clubs Watford and Stockport County in earlier rounds. Although Avenue lost the replay 5-2 at Highbury they did enough that season to put themselves among the elite of the non-League Cup fighters.

Apart from that memorable season Walthamstow have reached the Second Round no fewer than five times — in the 1945/6 season when Brighton beat them 5-2 on aggregate in a two-leg competition, in 1948/9 when beaten by Oldham 3-1, in 1953/4 when Ipswich snatched a narrow 1-0 win, in 1954/5 when Darlington ran out 3-0 winners after Avenue had accounted for Q.P.R. 4-0 in a second replay at Highbury in the First Round and in 1967/8 when Bournemouth ran out 3-1 winners at Green Pond Road. Other League sides that Avenue have encountered on First Round Cup duty have included Northampton, Mansfield, Crystal Palace and Coventry.

Avenue began their post-war appearances in the First Round in 1945/6 when the two-leg system was in operation, drawn against Athenian League side Sutton United. The first 'leg' was played away at the Borough Sports Ground resulting in an easy 4-1 win for Avenue whilst in the second 'leg' Avenue overan United to the tune of 7-2 thus giving the Isthmian Leaguers a comprehensive 11-3 win on aggregate. For the Second Round Avenue drew Brighton and Hove Albion, Third Division South. The first 'leg' was fought out at Green Pond Road before a crowd of nearly 10,000, a hard-fought game resulting in a 1-1 draw. Although Avenue were

2-1 in the lead at half-time in the second 'leg' Brighton, using a seven man striking force after the resumption, raced into a 4-1 victory to give them a 5-2 win on aggregate.

Walthamstow were next in the First Round in the 1948/9 season when they drew a home tie against fellow amateurs, Cambridge Town. After an evenly-contested first-half with the score 1-1, Avenue had a slight edge after the interval, squeezing into the next round with a 3-2 win. Avenue's reward was a Second Round home game against Oldham Athletic, Third Division North. In the 10th minute Avenue went one up and retained their lead until the 70th minute when Oldham equalised. The game went into extra time and within four minutes Athletic went ahead. With only two minutes left an Oldham victory seemed inevitable but Avenue scored a dramatic equaliser to force a replay. When the game was resumed, at Oldham before a crowd of over 26,000, Avenue found themselves facing an on-form Oldham and were 3-0 down as the final whistle approached. Avenue snatched a consolation goal in the closing stages.

In the 1949/50 season Avenue's Cup luck deserted them when they found themselves paired with Northampton Town, Third Division South, away from home. The Cobblers were set to avenge a 6-1 defeat at Walthamstow's hands in 1936. Northampton were three up at half-time and finally won 4-1 with Avenue reduced to ten men in the closing stages.

In the following season, 1950/51, with Avenue again in the First Round, the amateurs had to journey north to meet Mansfield Town, Third Division North, at Field Mill. Freddie Steele, Mansfield's player-manager and former England international, scored the only goal of the game.

Walthamstow's greatest season of all, when the team won renown as 'giantkillers', was in 1952/3 when against all the odds Avenue forced their way through to the Fourth Round. Their First Round contest was an all-amateur clash at Green Pond Road against fellow Isthmian Leaguers Wimbledon. Although the Dons went into a 2-0 lead Avenue hit back with a goal by Trevor Bailey, the England and Essex cricketer, and then equalised in the 62nd minute to gain a well-deserved replay. At Plough Lane Walthamstow outplayed their hosts to go through to the next round with a comfortable 3-0 victory.

This excellent performance earned Avenue a Second

Round draw against Watford, Third Division South, at Green Pond Road. This tie resulted in a 1-1 draw. There was a thrilling finish at the replay at Vicarage Road, Watford having held on to a 11th minute lead until two minutes from time when the amateurs equalised. In extra time the amateurs had the better of the exchanges, missed a penalty and then went on to win 2-1 with a late goal. The draw for the Third Round, which Avenue had reached for the first time since the war, paired them with Stockport County, Third Division North, at Green Pond Road.

For this memorable game Avenue included four amateur internationals in their team, Gerula of Poland in goal, Stratton, Saunders and Lewis, one-time England captain. Before a crowd of nearly 10,000 Avenue had some anxious moments before they began to put the Stockport defenders under pressure. In the 23rd minute Avenue took the lead through Lucas and in the 36th minute the amateurs scored again, Lucas again being the marksman. After the interval, with the amateurs still leading 2-0 Walthamstow pulled back men in attempting to hold on to their lead but County reduced the deficit. They were unable to grab the equaliser and Avenue's shock 2-1 win reflected a competent, all-round performance.

Walthamstow: Gerula, Young, Stratton, Harper, Brahan, Saunders, Bailey, Lucas, Lewis, Hall, Camis.

Among the elite in the Fourth Round Avenue went on to attain Cup glory as a result of their death-or-glory performances against mighty First Division Manchester United at Old Trafford with a replay at Highbury, both matches being covered in *Match Report*.

In the following season Avenue were again in the Cup hunt, securing a First Round tie against Gillingham, Third Division South, at Green Pond Road. Over 9,000 saw the amateurs again give a 'giant-killing' performance as they disposed of the professionals by a lone goal. Within two minutes Avenue had found the net but the 'goal' was disallowed. Then in the 17th minute Vic Groves scored the only goal of the game for Avenue and in the closing stages the amateurs' goalkeeper Stan Gerula became the hero of the afternoon when he saved a penalty.

In the Second Round Avenue were drawn away from home at Portman Road against Third Division South leaders Ipswich. The game was a special occasion for Tommy Garneys, the Ipswich leader, who formerly played for Walthamstow reserves before moving on to League football. Avenue put on a scintillating performance and were 2–0 in the lead at half-time. But Ipswich fought back, pulled back a goal through a penalty and equalised 10 minutes from time.

A packed Green Pond Road ground saw Avenue narrowly knocked out of the Cup at the replay. After early pressure by Ipswich the amateurs settled down and got the ball in the net but the 'goal' was disallowed. It then looked odds-on on extra time until the League side snatched the winner three minutes from time.

Avenue again popped up in the First Round in the following season, 1954/5, when they drew professional neighbours Third Division South, Queen's Park Rangers away from home at Loftus Road. Rangers went into a 2–0 half-time lead but Avenue hit back after the restart, pulled back a goal and were on level terms in the 54th minute.

Avenue were a goal down within two minutes in the replay at Green Pond Road and by half-time Rangers had built up a 2–0 lead as they had in the first encounter. After an hour's play Avenue's fortunes changed when they scored an easy goal and three minutes from time they were on terms. The game went into extra time but there was no further scoring and a second replay became necessary with Highbury the venue.

There was a crowd of 11,939 at Arsenal's ground to watch the marathon continue on a mud-churned pitch. After a goal-less first half, during which the Rangers burned themselves out against the Gerula, Clarke, Farrer defensive combination, the fireworks began. Efficiently led by Jim Paris, the Walthamstow line carried out ceaseless raids against the Q.P.R. goal and in the 51st minute went into the lead with a Julians header. In less than two minutes the amateurs struck again, Denzil Flanagan, whose runs down the left wing were a feature of the game, giving a cross to Paris who scored easily. In the 57th minute Walthamstow went into a 3–0 lead when Anderson saw his shot deflected into the net by the Rangers' goalkeeper. Avenue kept up their attack and in the 73rd minute Anderson scored again to make the final score 4–0. It was a great victory for the amateurs who had totally out-manoeuvred their League opponents.

Avenue: Gerula, Clarke, Farrer, Harper, Brahan, Lucas, Anderson, Julians, Paris, Bee, Flanagan.

When Avenue drew Darlington, Third Division North at Green Pond Road in the Second Round there were thoughts that the amateurs might again reach the Third Round. It was not Avenue's day however and a crowd of 8,000 saw the League side register an easy 3-0 victory.

In the 1956/7 First Round competition Avenue faced Crystal Palace, Third Division South, before a 17,837 crowd at Selhurst Park. Although Avenue had most of the game in the early stages Palace opened the scoring in the 17th minute with a second-half goal making matters safe.

In the following season, 1957/8, Avenue drew a First Round tie away from home against Coventry City, then in the Third Division South. Although the A's had more of the game in the first-half and were unlucky not to have scored, City turned the tables after the restart and scored the only goal of the match on the hour and also had a 'goal' disallowed. The 'gate' was over 19,000.

Walthamstow had to wait until the 1959/60 season before they reappeared in the First Round, drawing a home game against Third Division Bournemouth. Avenue shot into a 1-0 lead in the 15th minute and at half-time were two up after scoring from a penalty. After the interval Avenue unwisely relaxed, allowing Bournemouth to draw level and then to snatch victory in the last 30 seconds to make the final score 3-2.

In the First Round again in the following season, 1960/1, Avenue were matched against former foes Queen's Park Rangers away at Loftus Road. Avenue held up the League side for half an hour before Rangers went into a 1-0 lead only for Avenue to equalise from a penalty to go in at half-time on terms. Both sides scored in the second-half and with the score 2-2 and with only a minute left for play a replay looked certain. Rangers staged a final rally and scored the match-winner through Bedford who completed his hat-trick. Rangers thus obtained revenge for the beating they received from Avenue six seasons previously.

Walthamstow's record of consecutive appearances in the

First Round continued into the next season, 1961/2, when they drew a home tie against Southern League semi-professionals Romford. Captaining Romford was Malcolm Allison and also appearing in the Southern League side were former Spurs stars goalkeeper Ted Ditchburn and Charlie Withers. Although the amateurs secured a 1-0 half-time lead it was a game of fluctuating fortunes, Romford in an inspired second-half spell going into a 2-1 lead with Avenue drawing level in the 85th minute. Then disaster struck Walthamstow. In the closing seconds Romford were awarded a hotly-disputed penalty, Allison took the kick and scored but the referee ordered it to be retaken. Allison coolly placed his shot the other side of the 'keeper to put Avenue out of the Cup.

There was a break in Avenue's Cup exploits until the 1967/8 season when they drew West Midland Leaguers Kidderminster Harriers in a First Round clash at Green Pond Road. After both sides had scored a penalty Avenue went into a 2-1 lead just before the interval and there was no further scoring. The match was played in blizzard conditions, a snow squall near the end forcing the referee to take the teams off for ten minutes. For the Second Round Avenue were drawn at home against Third Division Bournemouth, their opponents of the 1959/60 season when the League side won 3-2. This time the outcome was no different, Avenue losing 3-1.

MATCH REPORTS
FOURTH ROUND F.A. CUP
31st January 1953
MANCHESTER UNITED 1   WALTHAMSTOW AVENUE 1

This was a fairy-tale encounter – the Amateur Cup holders versus the reigning First Division champions fought out before a crowd of over 34,000 at the famous Old Trafford ground.

A gale blew across the pitch for most of the first half as United stormed into Avenue's penalty area. Walthamstow's Polish international goalkeeper Stan Gerula was in brilliant form, handling everything that came his way from the on-form United strikers.

Gerula was ably supported by his fellow Avenue defenders, notably Derek Saunders, captain and centre-half and the two backs Young and Stratton.

In this blood-tingling atmosphere only once did Walthamstow yield – in the 40th minute when E. LEWIS put the First Division champions in the lead.

Half-time: Manchester United 1   Walthamstow Avenue 0

In the second half Walthamstow had the wind at their backs and the Isthmian Leaguers had more of the game. But in the 72nd minute Avenue had a lucky let-off when United's centre-forward Lewis, operating on the left wing, took the ball forward to unleash a power shot from 10 yards only to hit the woodwork.

Three minutes later the ground erupted when against the odds Avenue equalised. From a Harper free kick Lucas laid on a precision pass for J. LEWIS, unmarked in the penalty area, to lash the ball into the corner of the net with United's goalkeeper Wood well beaten.

This set the match alight and Walthamstow, gathering courage and hope by the minute, surged into the attack. Harper, taking another free kick, tried to repeat the move that had brought the goal but this time Lewis shot over the bar.

The remaining minutes were played out in high tension, the game see-sawing from end to end with both sides having chances. But in the end United settled for a draw to make Avenue the talk of the football world – the modest Isthmian League side moral victors at Old Trafford and taking the mighty League side to a replay.

Result Manchester United 1   Walthamstow Avenue 1

Manchester United:	Wood, Aston, Byrne, Carey, Chilton, Cockburn, Berry, Downie, E. Lewis, Pearson, Rowley.
Walthamstow Avenue:	Gerula, Young, Stratton, Harper, Saunders, Hall, Bailey, Lucas, J. L. Lewis, Fielder, Camis.
Referee:	Mr. P. Rhodes, (Yorkshire).
Attendance:	34,748

FOURTH ROUND F.A. CUP REPLAY
5th February 1953
WALTHAMSTOW AVENUE 2   MANCHESTER UNITED 5

Highbury was the scene of this memorable replay when nearly 50,000 fans watched the Davids of the amateur world challenging the Goliaths of the First Division. Walthamstow started well with their half-back line Harper, Saunders and Hall setting up an attack which ended with United goalkeeper Wood dealing with a sharp drive from Trevor Bailey. Within a space of four minutes however United established a 3–0 lead. First centre-forward Rowley engineered a movement that led to PEARSON heading in. Two minutes later United went further ahead when from a Berry flag-kick E. LEWIS placed the ball low into the corner of the net to give Gerula no chance. These reverses unbalanced Avenue and before they could settle down United scored again when ROWLEY beat Gerula with a power drive. Avenue fought back and returning to the attack Jim Lewis and his fellow forwards surged into the United half, Bailey going close with one determined attack. United went further ahead when BYRNE scored from the penalty spot after a foul on Pearson. Walthamstow redeemed the situation slightly just before half-time when the amateurs were awarded a penalty for a foul on J. Lewis. LEWIS took the kick himself and beat Wood.

Half-time: Manchester United 4   Walthamstow Avenue 1

In the second half Walthamstow staged a great rally, the forwards storming into the United goalmouth spurred on by the cheers of the great Highbury crowd.

Walthamstow's reward came following a free kick when Jim LEWIS headed in to send the crowd wild with delight. The United attacks became fewer as the United wing-halves Carey and Cockburn began to concentrate on holding Lewis and Lucas rather than prompt their own forwards. Walthamstow kept the attack going until the final whistle and once Trevor Bailey narrowly missed scoring during a fierce assault on the United goal.

United added a further goal in the closing stages, however, when a dropping shot from ROWLEY curled into the net out of Gerula's reach to make the final score 5–2.

Result: Walthamstow Avenue 2   Manchester United 5

Teams:
Walthamstow Avenue: Gerula, Young, Stratton, Harper, Saunders, Hall, Bailey, Lucas, J. Lewis, Fielder, Camis.
Manchester United: Wood, Aston, Byrne, Carey, Chilton, Cockburn, Berry, E. Lewis, Rowley, Pearson, Pegg.
Referee: Mr. P. Rhodes, (Yorkshire).
Attendance: 49,119

CUP RUNS

1945/6

1st Round (1st leg) - *7th November*
Sutton 1   Walthamstow 4

1st Round (2nd leg)   *24th November*
Walthamstow 7   Sutton 2
(Walthamstow won on 11-3 aggregate)

2nd Round (1st leg) - *8th December*
Walthamstow 1   Brighton 1

2nd Round (2nd leg) - *15th December*
Brighton 4   Walthamstow 1
  (Brighton won on 5-2 aggregate)

1948/9

1st Round - *27th November*
Walthamstow 3   Cambridge T......2

2nd Round - *11th December*
Walthamstow 2   Oldham 2
   (after extra time.
    Score at 90 mins: 1-1)

2nd Round Replay - *18th December*
Oldham 3   Walthamstow 1

1949/50

1st Round - *26th November*
Northampton 4   Walthamstow 1

1950/51

1st Round - *25th November*
Mansfield 1   Walthamstow 0

1952/3

1st Round   *22nd November*
Walthamstow 2   Wimbledon 2

1st Round Replay - *26th November*
Wimbledon 0   Walthamstow 3

2nd Round - *6th December*
Walthamstow 1   Watford 1

2nd Round Replay - *10th December*
Watford 1   Walthamstow 2
      (after extra time)

3rd Round - *10th January*
Walthamstow 2   Stockport 1

4th Round - *31st January*
Manchester U. .. 1   Walthamstow 1

4th Round Replay - *5th February*
Walthamstow 2   Manchester U. ..5

1953/4

1st Round - *21st November*
Walthamstow 1   Gillingham 0

2nd Round - *12th December*
Ipswich 2   Walthamstow 2

2nd Round Replay - *16th December*
Walthamstow 0   Ipswich 1

1954/5

1st Round - *20th November*
QPR 2   Walthamstow 2

1st Round Replay - *25th November*
Walthamstow 2   QPR 2
      (after extra time)

1st Round, 2nd Replay - *29th November*
Walthamstow 4   QPR 0
      (at Highbury)

2nd Round - *11th December*
Walthamstow 0   Darlington 3

1956/7

1st Round - *17th November*
Crystal Palace ... 2   Walthamstow 0

1957/8

1st Round - *16th November*
Coventry City ... 1   Walthamstow 0

1959/60

1st Round - *14th November*
Walthamstow 2   Bournemouth 3

1960/1

1st Round - *5th November*
QPR 3   Walthamstow 2

1961/2

1st Round - *4th November*
Walthamstow 2   Romford 3

1967/8

1st Round - *9th December*
Walthamstow 2   Kidderminster ...1

2nd Round - *6th January*
Walthamstow 1   Bournemouth 3

WEYMOUTH

Founded: 1890

League: Alliance Premier

Ground: Recreation Ground

Colours: Terra cotta and blue shirts; light blue shorts

Weymouth are one of the most consistent performers of the non-League sides in the F.A. Cup battling it out season after season, often drawn against highly-placed League clubs to emphasise the Alliance Premier League's challenge for recognition. The 1949/50 season was an unforgettable one for The Terras, reaching the Third Round for the first time in the club's history and then realising the ambition of every non-League club, an away tie against First Division Manchester United at Old Trafford where they went down 4-0. Then in 1961/2, after beating Barnet, Newport County and Morecambe, a Fourth Round away tie against Preston North End where the part-timers were beaten 2-0 after a first game had been abandoned because of fog. In other post-war seasons Weymouth have reached the Second Round on no fewer than seven occasions, being defeated at that stage by Yeovil, Bristol Rovers (twice), Orient, Southend, Southampton and Swansea (after a replay).

Other League sides that the Terras have encountered in the post-war era in the Cup have included Aldershot, Colchester United, Shrewsbury, Torquay, Bournemouth, Northampton, Cambridge United, Peterborough, Gillingham, Swindon and Coventry.

The Terra's first appearance in the post-war First Round Cup games was in the 1948/9 season, the first time they had managed that stage of the Cup for over 20 years. They drew a home game against strongly fancied Southern Leaguers Chelmsford but Weymouth, at that time in the Western League, pulled off a fine 2–1 victory. Chelmsford, who were led by former Stoke and England international Frank Soo, had the ball in the net in the fading moments but the 'goal' was disallowed. In the Second Round the Terras were drawn at home to another Southern League side, Yeovil, when a new ground record of 12,000 (which still stands) was established. Yeovil won easily 4-0.

The Terras began their memorable 1949/50 Cup run – the season in which they appeared at Old Trafford in the Third Round – with a First Round home game against Aldershot, Third Division South. A crowd of 9,500 saw Weymouth earn a 2-2 draw. At the replay at Aldershot Weymouth made history when they defeated the League side 3-2. It was the first time ever that the Terras had beaten a League side away from home in the Cup.

In the Second Round the Terras were on their own ground for a meeting with fellow non-Leaguers Hereford United of the Southern League. Hereford scored an early goal, the Terras quickly equalised and netted the match-winner before half-time to give them a 2-1 victory. Weymouth went on into the Third Round to secure a fairy-tale away game at Old Trafford against Manchester United, going down fighting before a crowd of nearly 39,000, the game fully covered in *Match Report*. Three cup records were established by Weymouth that season – it was the first time the Terras had met a First Division side in the F.A. Cup; the victory over Aldershot was the first win in the Cup over a League side away from home, and it was the first time they had reached the Third Round.

The Terras came down to earth when they next appeared in the First Round, in the 1951/2 season, drawn away from home against Brush Sports, the Loughborough works side operating in the Birmingham League. Played at Brown's Lane, formerly used by the defunct Midland League side Loughborough Corinthians, Weymouth, who had joined the Southern League, won a tough, thrilling game 3-2 once again to enter the Second Round draw. Again the Terras had to travel, drawn to play Third Division South, Bristol Rovers at Eastville before a crowd of 28,000, the biggest Cup 'gate' of the day. On a mud-churned pitch Rovers won 2-0 scoring both their goals in the first half hour.

Weymouth were again in the First Round in the following season, 1952/3, matched against Colchester United, Third Division South at home at the Recreation Ground. Despite going into arrears with an 'own goal' Weymouth scored the equaliser in the 40th minute. From then on defences were in control and the Terras forced the League side to a replay at Layer Road. Although the Terras were in command for the first half of the replay the League side began to dominate the game and finally gained an easy 4-0 victory.

Keeping up their sequence of First Round appearances the Terras were again in the hunt in the following season, 1953/4, an all-Southern League affair matched against Bedford Town. A crowd of 6,000 saw the Terras take control to win comfortably 2-0. The Terras were drawn away from home against Third Division South, Leyton Orient in the Second Round and there were 14,313 spectators at Brisbane Road to see a full-strength Orient take on the part-timers. The Terras were below form and the League side romped home 4-0.

After missing a season the Terras were again on First Round duty in 1955/6, having the luck of a home game against fellow non-Leaguers Salisbury of the Western League. After establishing a 3-0 lead the Terras seemed to be coasting home but the Western Leaguers pulled back two goals and Weymouth had to hang on to win 3-2. The Second Round brought a home game against Third Division South Southend United. The game brought together in opposition Weymouth captain Willie Fagan and Southend captain Kevin Baron, both of whom had played in the 1950 Liverpool Cup Final team. There were early shocks for the Third Division side as the Terras twice got the ball in United's net but on both occasions the 'goals' were disallowed. Twenty minutes from the end Southend scored the only goal of the match.

The next season, 1956/7, saw the Terras gain a sensational 1-0 victory in the First Round over Shrewsbury Town, Third Division South before a crowd of 7,000. Shrewsbury at that time had one of the strongest defences in the Third Division but their defences were breached in the 69th minute when the Terras' captain and inside forward John Henderson scored from a penalty to see the part-timers once again in the Second Round. Weymouth's opponents were Southampton, Third Division South leaders, away at The Dell. The fourth highest Cup crowd of the day, 21,664, saw the Saints squeeze into the next round with a narrow 3-2 victory.

Reappearing in the First Round in the 1958/9 season the Terras were set to entertain Third Division South, Coventry City at The Rec. A crowd of over 7,000 saw the Terras score first after 15 minutes but were gradually overwhelmed 5-2.

In the First Round in the 1960/1 competition the Terras

were hosts at The Rec to Third Division Torquay United. Weymouth went ahead midway through the first-half with a penalty goal but the League side came back to win 3-1.

The following season, 1961/2, produced another dazzling run for the Southern Leaguers when they clawed their way to the Fourth Round for the first time in the club's history. First they had a First Round encounter against Barnet, then amateurs playing in the Isthmian League, at home at The Rec. All the first-half belonged to the Terras but their meagre return was a penalty goal scored by Colin Court. After the Weymouth goalkeeper left the field in the 75th minute through injury Barnet piled on the pressure but could not get the equaliser. The Terras' Cup luck held when they were drawn at home for the Second Round against Third Division Newport County. There was a crowd of 6,000 at The Rec to see the Southern Leaguers record a memorable 1-0 victory over the League side. Colin Court scored the match-winner in the closing stages.

Weymouth's opponents in the Third Round were Lancashire Combination leaders Morecambe away from home at Christie Park before 9,383 spectators. Cup fever gripped Morecambe and an exciting, evenly-balanced game ensued, Weymouth scoring the only goal of the match in the 48th minute through Ronnie Fogg who put the Terras in the Fourth Round for the first time in the club's history. The tie was a personal triumph for both Weymouth player-manager Frank O'Farrell, the former Preston and Eire international and ex-Hull City goalkeeper Billy Bly who played with a broken finger.

Weymouth: Bly, Sheppard, Stocker, Anderson, Hobson, O'Farrell, Court, Jones, Fogg, Allan, Beven.

This fine performance earned the Terras an away draw against Second Division Preston North End. Over 1,200 Weymouth supporters made the long journey to Deepdale only to find the ground enshrouded in fog with the floodlights trying to pierce the gloom. The referee began the game but in the 16th minute abandoned proceedings. When the teams got back to the dressing rooms it was discovered that Billy Bly was missing and when the trainer was despatched to find him he was found still on his goalline looking for the missing Preston forwards! Official attendance was 18,000 despite the fog. The replay, which Preston won 2-0 is fully described in *Match Report*.

Weymouth were next in the First Round in the 1963/4 season when they were drawn at The Rec against fellow Southern Leaguers Bedford Town. With an injuries-affected side the Terras were hard pressed to hold the powerful Bedford side and did well to emerge with a 1-1 draw. At the replay at The Eyrie where an evenly-balanced game was dominated by the defences Weymouth were removed from the Cup with a second-half goal.

In the First Round again in the following season, 1964/5, the Terras drew an away tie against Western League side Welton Rovers. This was no pushover for the Terras as they came up against determined opposition and could only manage a 1-1 draw. An exciting replay at The Rec saw the Southern Leaguers scrape through 4-3. The Second Round took the Terras to Eastville to meet Third Division Bristol Rovers. Weymouth matched the Rovers for skill in the first-half and were able to go in at half-time on level terms with the score 1-1. But the second-half belonged to Rovers who scored three times to make the final tally 4-1.

Back in the First Round in the following season, 1965/6, Weymouth had a tough draw away against Third Division Bournemouth at Dean Court. A 11,000 crowd saw the Southern Leaguers put up a great defensive battle against the League side to emerge with a creditable 0-0 draw. At the replay at The Rec Bournemouth went ahead in the fourth minute and although the Terras equalised three minutes later Bournemouth went on to secure an easy 4-1 win to put paid to the Southern Leaguers' hopes.

Weymouth had to wait until the 1967/8 season before they were next in the First Round when they drew a home game against Third Division Orient. It was the start of a marvellous run which took the Terras into the First Round for five successive seasons. Managed by Stan Charlton, who had spent ten years with Orient, Weymouth had the best of the first-half against their League opponents. But the second half belonged to Orient and two late goals were enough to put the Terras out of the Cup.

The following season, 1968/9, saw an all-Southern League clash develop in the First Round at home between the Terras and famous giant-killers Yeovil. It was a hard game, the Terras taking a 1-0 lead through a penalty and finally winning 2-1 with the visitors having a 'goal' disallowed. The Second Round brought another home game at The Rec against Fourth Division Swansea. A ding-dong struggle saw the Swans move into a 1-0 lead in the 35th minute, have a 'goal' disallowed with no further scoring during the first half. Midway through the second period Weymouth scored a dramatic equaliser through Ray Gough. Swansea had to settle for a draw and a replay at Vetch field. After gaining midfield control Swansea were able to hold the Swans to a goalless first-half and it seemed odds on that extra time would be played when Swansea killed off the Terras with two late goals.

In the 1969/70 season Weymouth, again contestants in the First Round, were drawn away from home against Fourth Division Northampton Town. A hard-fought game ended in a goalless draw. The Terras had high hopes of making further Cup progress in the replay at The Rec but it was not to be, Northampton running out 3-1 winners. After the Cobblers had scored their first goal through ex-Worcester City striker Fairbrother the Southern Leaguers then conceded a penalty to make the half-time score 2-0. Weymouth pulled back a goal midway through the second half but three minutes from time Northampton made sure of their place in the next round with a further goal.

The following season, 1970/1, Weymouth had a disastrous First Round encounter away from home against Fourth Division Southend United. The Southern Leaguers had no answer to the lively Southend attack conceding three goals in the first half and four in the second.

Undeterred Weymouth were back in the First Round in the 1971/2 season drawing Fourth Division and former Southern Leaguers Cambridge United away from home at the Abbey Stadium. The Terras more than redeemed their dismal performance against Southend and were the equal of their League opponents in the first-half which ended with the scoresheet blank. Five minutes after the interval the non-Leaguers went into the lead. Cambridge hit back with two late goals to give them a 2-1 edge to put an end to the Terras' hopes.

Weymouth missed a season before getting back among the First Round challengers, finding themselves opposed at The Rec by fellow Southern Leaguers Merthyr Town. A great tussle developed which ended in Merthyr going forward with a lone second half goal.

The First Round of the 1974/5 season gave Weymouth an away tie against renowned Cup fighters Third Division Peterborough United, a game that was to develop into a marathon. The first game ended in a 0–0 draw, an interesting contest notable for some fine defensive work by Peterborough as the Southern Leaguers several times threatened to take the lead. The replay at The Rec was a highly dramatic affair. Three times Weymouth took the lead and three times Peterborough came back from the brink. The experienced Weymouth side, containing no fewer than seven players with League football behind them, took an 18th minute lead with Posh getting the equaliser before half-time. After the interval the Terras again took the lead which they held until seconds to go when Peterborough, pushing every man forward, again got on terms. It was the same story in extra time, the Terras forging ahead again only for Peterborough to score a last-gasp equaliser in the dying seconds. It was a particularly happy occasion for Tony Hobson, one of the gallant Weymouth defenders, who was making his 975th appearance for the club.

In the second replay the Southern Leaguers kept Peterborough pegged back for most of the first half at the end of which there was a blank scoresheet. It was not until the 66th minute that the deadlock was broken with a Peterborough goal. This was the signal for Posh to develop an all-out attack on the Southern Leaguers and they scored two further goals in rapid succession to make the final score 3–0.

Again in the First Round in the following season, 1975/6, Weymouth gained home advantage against Third Division Gillingham. There were no goals in the first half despite some great attacking football by the Southern Leaguers. Gillingham's disappointment was a disallowed 'goal' because of offside. In the second half the Gills scored twice to put the Terras out of the Cup.

In the 1976/7 season First Round contest Weymouth again had a marathon encounter – this time against Isthmian Leaguers Hitchin, with a Second Round tie against Swindon Town at stake. The first game was an end-to-end affair with both sides notching a first-half goal and settling for a draw. In the first replay, at Top Field, an exciting game ended in a 2–2 draw after extra time. As in the first battle Hitchin took the lead with Weymouth equalising with two minutes to go.

It was then Weymouth's turn to take the lead but with only minutes remaining poor covering by the Southern Leaguers' defence enabled the amateurs to snatch the equaliser.

Aldershot was the venue for the next attempt at resolving the issue and again a Cup thriller emerged. Weymouth had high hopes of going thorough when they went into a 2-0 first-half lead but again the amateurs caught up. Then it was Hitchin's turn to go into the lead but with a quarter of an hour left to play Weymouth equalised. The game went into extra time but neither side could produce the winning goal so after 330 minutes play stalemate continued. The third replay took place at Salisbury when Hitchin finally put the Terras out of the Cup by a 3-1 margin. The Terras' consolation goal came in the closing stages from a penalty. It had taken seven hours' play to resolve the issue.

The Terras next appeared in the First Round in the 1977/8 season when they drew a difficult away tie against high-riding Third Division Gillingham. The part-timers took a shock lead in the 25th minute after some consistent attacking, the Gills had a 'goal' disallowed and the non-Leaguers went in at half-time with their lead intact. Midway through the second half however Weymouth had a man sent off and shortly afterwards Gillingham were on terms. The Terras gave a plucky display on their own ground in the replay but faced an on-form Gillingham and lost the game in the 65th minute when the Gills scored the only goal of the match.

Weymouth were again in the First Round in the following season, 1978/9, when they drew another away tie, against Fourth Division Aldershot. The Terras had to withstand some ferocious Aldershot attacks but in one of their few raids in the first half took a surprise lead in the 32nd minute. Aldershot retaliated strongly but Weymouth retained their lead up to half-time. Weymouth kept up their resolute defence throughout the second half and it was cruel luck for the Southern Leaguers when Aldershot equalised two minutes from time. Hopes were high that Weymouth would produce a giant-killing performance in the replay at The Rec but after the Terras had forced no fewer than six corners in the first seven minutes Aldershot got themselves back into the game and after taking a 17th minute lead scored again ten minutes from time to make the game safe.

Weymouth's lack of Cup luck continued into the 1980/81

season when, after having missed a season, they reappeared in the First Round to find themselves matched away from home against Third Division Swindon. The Terras gave a magnificent fighting performance and although Swindon opened the scoring midway through the first half the Terras equalised soon afterwards and went off at half-time on level terms. A minute after the interval the County Ground was stunned when Weymouth went ahead from a penalty and continued to storm into the attack, forcing three corners in quick succession. Swindon were back on terms midway through the half with a 'soft' goal and against the run of the play scored the match-winner in the last five minutes, an unstoppable shot from the Swindon captain from 25 yards. It was Swindon's lucky day.

The Terras were again in the Cup hunt in the 1981/2 season when they drew a First Round tie at home against Fourth Division Northampton Town. A disappointing game ended in a 0–0 draw. In the replay at Northampton the Terras were two down in the opening minutes, a blow from which they did not recover. By half-time the Cobblers had gone 5–0 in the lead. In the second half Weymouth fought back and reduced the deficit in the 73rd minute although the Cobblers restored their lead soon afterwards. Even then Weymouth did not give up and in a final flurry two minutes from the end scored again to make the final tally 6–2.

MATCH REPORTS
THIRD ROUND F.A. CUP
7th January 1950
MANCHESTER UNITED 4   WEYMOUTH 0

Before an Old Trafford crowd of nearly 40,000 the part-timers from Weymouth, led by their famous player-manager Paddy Gallacher, ex Third-Lanark and Blackburn Rovers (who had won a Scottish Cup finalist's medal in 1935) gave a plucky display of Cup-tie football against their star-studded opponents. United had eight of their 1948 Cup-winning side on the field and the side included six internationals, Aston, Cockburn, Rowley, Pearson (England), Carey, capt. (Ireland) and Delaney (Scotland).

United did the 'giantkillers' the honour of taking the field without their usual accompaniment and when the Terras came out the band struck up United's signature tune, "March of the Gladiators". Weymouth were recording two 'firsts' – the first time that the side had met a First Division team in the F.A. competition and the first time that they had reached the Third Round.

When the game began United soon switched to the attack with Mitten, Bogan and Pearson having scoring chances. Weymouth's mid-field play was attractive and was comparable with that of their distinguished opponents. Gallacher drew some applause for his approach work and Haynes and Sammy McGowan, the "G.O.M. of Weymouth football", with over 500 appearances to his credit, combined well on the right wing.

United pressure was almost continuous with only Lucas and the valiant Weymouth defence between United's forwards and a lot of goals. It was not until the 32nd minute that United scored when ROWLEY added the finishing touch to a Delaney centre.

It was a tremendous tribute to the Weymouth defence that they had held the powerful United attack for over half an hour and it remains one of the greatest achievements in the Weymouth club's history.

Three minutes later United went further ahead when a pass intended for Grant was intercepted by PEARSON who beat two defenders before slipping the ball past Lucas. At the other end Carey cleared off the line when Grant seemed set to score.

Half-time: Manchester United 2   Weymouth 0

In the second half United maintained their pressure, with Lucas again defending magnificently. In the 51st minute right winger DELANEY notched number three for United from a corner kick. In the 88th minute ROWLEY scored his second and United's fourth. Weymouth defended stoutly to the end and at the final whistle left the field to a tremendous ovation. It was a moment of Cup glory for the Southern Leaguers.

Result: Manchester United 4   Weymouth 0

Teams:
Manchester United: Feehan, Carey (capt.), Aston, Cockburn, Chilton, McGlen, Delaney, Bogan, Rowley, Pearson, Mitten.
Weymouth: Lucas, Marsden, Ransom, Grant, Brawley, Lawes, McGowan, Haynes, Johnston, Gallacher (capt.); Jones.
Referee: Mr. G. Salmon, (Stoke-on-Trent).
Attendance: 38,284

FOURTH ROUND F.A. CUP
29th January 1962
PRESTON NORTH END 2   WEYMOUTH 0

For their memorable Fourth Round encounter Weymouth were drawn away from home to famous Cup fighters, Preston North End, then in the Second Division. The fog, which had brought the first encounter to an end after only 14 minutes play, had disappeared for the replay under floodlights.

Weymouth had their share of the attacking and for a spell North End were forced on the defensive. In the 15th minute Biggs, eight yards out, looked certain to score for Preston but hooked the ball over the cross bar. Then Spavin, Preston's inside left, fired in a shot that had the Weymouth goalkeeper diving full length to hold. Two minutes before half-time North End went into the lead when DAWSON, the former Manchester United centre-forward, headed a rebound past Bly.

Half-time: Preston North End 1   Weymouth 0

On resuming Preston set up a non-stop attack and goalkeeper Bly was constantly in action. In the 57th minute Preston scored again with an unstoppable THOMPSON shot. The left winger gained possession at the half-way mark, raced towards goal, sold the dummy to left back Stocker and unleashed a thunderbolt shot that hurled past Bly into the net. Weymouth continued to attack, Fogg, the Southern League's most persistent forward, testing Kelly, the North End's goalkeeper on several occasions. In the last ten minutes Weymouth mounted a series of raids against the North End goal and Fogg twice almost beat Kelly. The final whistle blew with the Southern Leaguers still on the attack.

It was a glorious finish and the North End fans generously accorded the part-timers a great ovation as they left the field. Particularly singled out for the applause was Billy Bly, Weymouth's veteran goalkeeper, whose last Cup game, after 22 years on the Wembley trail, ended in a glorious farewell.

Result: Preston North End 2   Weymouth 0

Teams:
Preston North End: Kelly, Cunningham, Ross, Wylie, Singleton, Smith, Wilson, Biggs, Dawson, Spavin, Thompson.
Weymouth: Bly, Sheppard, Stocker, Anderson, Hobson, O'Farrell, Court, Jones, Fogg, Nugent, Bevan.
Referee: Mr. R. T. Langdale, (Darlington).
Attendance: 26,034

CUP RUNS

1948/9

1st Round – *27th November*
Weymouth 2   Chelmsford 1

2nd Round – *11th December*
Weymouth 0   Yeovil 4

1949/50

1st Round – *26th November*
Weymouth 2   Aldershot 2

1st Round Replay – *30th November*
Aldershot 2   Weymouth 3

2nd Round – *10th December*
Weymouth 2   Hereford 1

3rd Round – *7th January*
Manchester U. .. 4   Weymouth 0

1951/2

1st Round – *24th November*
Brush Sports 2   Weymouth 3

2nd Round – *15th December*
Bristol R. 2   Weymouth 0

1952/3

1st Round – *22nd November*
Weymouth 1   Colchester 1

1st Round Replay   *27th November*
Colchester 4   Weymouth 0

1953/4

1st Round – *21st November*
Weymouth 2   Bedford 0

2nd Round   *12th December*
Leyton Orient ... 4   Weymouth 0

1955/6

1st Round   *19th November*
Weymouth 3   Salisbury 2

2nd Round   *10th December*
Weymouth 0   Southend 1

1956/7

1st Round   *17th November*
Weymouth 1   Shrewsbury 0

2nd Round   *8th December*
Southampton 3   Weymouth 2

1958/9

1st Round   *15th November*
Weymouth 2   Coventry 5

1960/1

1st Round – *15th November*
Weymouth 1   Torquay 3

1961/2

1st Round – *4th November*
Weymouth 1   Barnet 0

2nd Round – *25th November*
Weymouth 1   Newport C. 0

3rd Round – *6th January*
Morecambe 0   Weymouth 1

4th Round – *27th January*
Preston NE 0   Weymouth 0
(abandoned after 14 minutes – fog)

4th Round Replay – *29th January*
Preston NE 2   Weymouth 0

1963/4

1st Round – *16th November*
Weymouth 1   Bedford 1

1st Round replay – *21st November*
Bedford 1   Weymouth 0

1964/5

1st Round – *14th November*
Welton Rovers .. 1   Weymouth 1

1st Round Replay – *18th November*
Weymouth 4   Welton Rovers .. 3

2nd Round – *5th December*
Bristol Rovers ... 4   Weymouth 1

1965/6

1st Round – *13th November*
Bournemouth 0   Weymouth 0

1st Round Replay   *17th November*
Weymouth 1   Bournemouth 4

1967/8

1st Round   *9th December*
Weymouth 0   Orient 2

1968/9

1st Round – *16th November*
Weymouth 2   Yeovil 1

2nd Round   *7th December*
Weymouth 1   Swansea 1

2nd Round Replay   *10th December*
Swansea 2   Weymouth 0

Weymouth (Contd)

1969/70

1st Round - *15th November*
Northampton 0   Weymouth 0

1st Round Replay   *19th November*
Weymouth 1   Northampton 3

1970/71

1st Round - *21st November*
Southend 7   Weymouth 0

1971/2

1st Round - *20th November*
Cambridge 2   Weymouth 1

1973/4

1st Round   *24th November*
Weymouth 0   Merthyr 1

1974/5

1st Round - *23rd November*
Peterborough 0   Weymouth 0

1st Round Replay   *4th December*
Weymouth 3   Peterborough 3
(After extra time. Score at 90 mins: 2-2)

1st Round 2nd Replay - *9th December*
Peterborough 3   Weymouth 0

1975/6

1st Round   *22nd November*
Weymouth 0   Gillingham 2

1976/7

1st Round   *20th November*
Weymouth 1   Hitchin Town ...1

1st Round Replay   *23rd November*
Hitchin 2   Weymouth 2
(After extra time. Score at 90 mins: 1 1)

1st Round Second Replay   *29th Nov.*
Weymouth 3   Hitchin 3
(After extra time - score at 90 mins: 3-3)
At Aldershot
1st Round Third Replay - *2nd December*
Weymouth 1   Hitchin 3
At Salisbury

1977/8

1st Round   *26th November 1977*
Gillingham 1   Weymouth 1

1st Round Replay   *30th November*
Weymouth 0   Gillingham 1

1978/9

1st Round   *25th November*
Aldershot 1   Weymouth 1

1st Round Replay   *29th November*
Weymouth 0   Aldershot 2

1980/1

1st Round   *24th November*
Swindon 3   Weymouth 2

1981/2

1st Round   *21st November*
Weymouth 0   Northampton 0

1st Round Replay   *24th November*
Northampton 6   Weymouth 2

WIGAN ATHLETIC

Founded: 1932

League: Third Division, formerly Northern Premier League

Ground: Springfield Park

Colours: Royal blue and white stripes

Before Wigan Athletic were deservedly elected to the Fourth Division in 1978/9 they were one of the most powerful non-League Cup-fighting sides in the country. Three times they forced their way to the Third Round in post-war Cup battles – in the 1953/4 season when they held mighty First Division Newcastle United to a 2-2 draw at St. James's Park before being defeated 3-2 in an exciting replay at Springfield Park, in the 1970/71 season at Maine Road when only a Colin Bell goal enabled First Division Manchester City to beat the part-timers and in 1977/8 when they again faced First Division opposition — Birmingham City at St. Andrew's where they lost 4-0. These fighting displays put Wigan well and truly in the ranks of the giantkillers. In reaching those Third Round peaks the non-leaguers hit the headlines in beating League sides Peterborough United, once a great non-League Cup-fighting side themselves, York City and Sheffield Wednesday.

Apart from those successes the Latics reached the Second Round on five occasions post-war and have claimed the League scalps of Southport (then in the Third Division North), Doncaster Rovers, Halifax and Shrewsbury. Other League clubs who played non-League Wigan in post-war First Round encounters included Barnsley, Mansfield, Stockport County, Chester, Tranmere Rovers, Port Vale, Grimsby and Huddersfield.

Wigan began their post-war Cup runs in fine style in the 1953/4 season when after reaching the First Round for the first time they got to the Third Round to gain a glamour tie with First Division Newcastle United. Their First Round hurdle was a home game against former Midland Leaguers Scarborough and a 13,500 crowd at Springfield Park saw the then Lancashire Combination leaders pull off a comfortable 4–0 victory. Wigan again had the luck of the draw in the Second Round, home against then Southern Leaguers

Hereford United. Another inter-League tussle, the game drew a 'gate' of 27,500 to see Wigan triumph 4-1, to take them into a Third Round encounter with Newcastle United. Wigan pulled off a fantastic 2-2 draw at St. James's Park and in the replay at Springfield Park went down by a narrow 3-2 margin after a fighting finish. Both games are described in *Match Report*.

After their breathtaking performances of the previous season the Latics were again in the First Round in the next season, 1954/5 when they had to travel to meet Barnsley, then Third Division North. There was a crowd of 17,767 to see the Latics narrowly beaten 3-2.

Wigan were again in the First Round in the 1956/7 season when they had a home game against Goole Town. Despite Latics going in at half-time with a 1-0 lead Goole came back to win 2-1 in one of the shock results of the day.

The Latics had a better run in the following season, 1957/8, when they drew League opposition in the First Round against Southport, Third Division North, away from home. The tie attracted 14,270, the largest 'gate' at Haig Avenue since 1931. In less than 20 minutes the non-Leaguers were leading 2-0 and although Southport got a goal back they were unable to force the equaliser. For the Second Round Wigan had the luck of the draw, set to entertain Mansfield Town, Third Division North, at Springfield Park. There was a crowd of 16,900 to see Mansfield go into a ninth minute lead with the non-Leaguers getting a much-deserved equaliser early in the second half. The replay at Mansfield brought the League side a 3-1 victory.

In the First Round in the 1962/3 competition Athletic had to travel to Redheugh Park to meet Gateshead, then in the North Eastern League. Although Wigan scored in the sixth minute Gateshead gained control and won 2-1.

The Latics were again in the First Round in the 1964/5 season when they drew an away tie against Fourth Division Stockport County. A crowd of 11,570 at Edgeley Park saw the non-Leaguers go into a 1-0 half-time lead but County grabbed two second half goals to run out 2-1 winners.

In the following season, 1965/6, the Latics returned to the First Round, matched against Fourth Division Doncaster Rovers at Belle Vue. Over 10,000 saw Wigan score midway through the first half, and have two 'goals' disallowed. In the second half Rovers went into a 2-1 lead, the non-Leaguers drawing level ten minutes from time to force a replay at Springfield Park. The replay was a fairy-tale affair. Lyon, the hero of the game, was carried off injured in the 18th minute but returned to score a hat-trick in the part-timers' 3-1 shock win. Wigan had no luck in the Second Round, away to Fourth Division Chester, at Sealand Park. A crowd of 16,285 saw a goalless first-half, Wigan scoring first in the fourth minute of the second period with Chester pulling the game round with two late goals to win 2-1.

Wigan were in the First Round again in the 1966/7 season, drawing an away tie against Fourth Division Tranmere Rovers at Prenton Park. A 10,000 crowd saw Wigan take a 1-0 half-time lead but the non-Leaguers conceded a penalty in the 65th minute from which Tranmere equalised. A thrilling replay at Springfield Park attracted a 'gate' of 14,304. Rovers scored the only goal of the game in the 56th minute.

After missing two seasons Wigan were next in the First Round in 1969/70, drawing a home game against Fourth Division Port Vale, the start of a marathon contest. Drawing the largest Cup crowd of the day to Springfield Park (12,622), Wigan scored in the 56th minute but eight minutes from time, Vale, unbeaten in the League, notched the equaliser. The replay at Vale Park resulted in a 2-2 draw after extra time, to give Wigan the opportunity of playing on one of the country's most famous grounds. Old Trafford, in the second replay. A crowd of 16,453, including over 9,000 Wiganers, saw the non-Leaguers hold the Fourth Division side to a 0-0 at full time and it was not until the 328th minute since the two sides first met that Vale scored a soft goal that gave them victory. After the match Sir Matt Busby, Manchester United's famous manager, congratulated the Wigan players.

Wigan were again in the First Round in the next season, 1970/71, when they drew an away game against fellow Northern Premier Leaguers South Shields. A hard game ended in a 1-1 draw, the replay drawing a 10,592 crowd to Springfield Park where Latics won 2-0. This victory gave Wigan a Second Round home tie against renowned Cup fighters Fourth Division Peterborough United. A crowd of 17,100, the largest Cup attendance of the day, went wild as the Latics set up a 1-0 half-time lead. In the second half 'Posh' got on level terms but gave away a penalty a minute from time. Jim Fleming converted the spot kick to give the non-Leaguers a 2-1 win to take them into the Third Round for the first time in 17 years. Their reward was a plum draw against First Division Manchester City at Maine Road, fully reported in *Match Report*.

After their stirring display the previous season Wigan were again in the First Round in 1971/2 when they had a home game against powerful Third Division Halifax Town, the Latics bringing off a magnificent 2-1 victory. This produced a Second Round encounter against formidable Cup fighters Third Division Wrexham away at the Racecourse Ground. There was a 'gate' of 12,895 to see Athletic go in at half-time with the scoresheet blank. Thirteen minutes from the end Wrexham scored four to give the game a sudden death ending for the non-Leaguers.

Continuing their run of First Round appearances, which was to last until their election to the Fourth Division, the Latics were drawn away in 1972/3 to Third Division Grimsby Town. A crowd of 11,568 at Blundell Park saw an exciting tie, Grimsby taking a first-half lead, Wigan equalising and the Mariners snatching victory with a goal six minutes from time.

The next season, 1973/4, Wigan were matched away against Third Division Huddersfield Town at Leeds Road. Town's highest 'gate' of the season, 9,557, saw the League side manage a goal in each half to put out Wigan for another season.

In the First Round in 1974/5 Wigan found themselves drawn away from home for the third consecutive season, matched against Fourth Division Shrewsbury Town at Gay Meadow. Wigan went into a thrilling 1-0 lead in the 74th minute only for Shrewsbury to draw level in injury time. The fairy-tale replay at Springfield Park, before a crowd of 11,860, resulted in a magnificent victory for the Northern Premier Leaguers, coming back from being a goal down to win 2-1 despite being reduced to ten men when Billy Sutherland was stretchered off. Ground advantage again went Wigan's way in the Second Round when they were drawn at Springfield Road against Fourth Division leaders Mansfield Town. Wigan had a 'goal' disallowed, Mansfield scored against the run of the play a minute from the interval and in the second half a Mansfield defender put through his own goal to give the Latics another chance. At the Field Mill Ground a 'gate' of 11,209 saw the Latics make a fight of it but go down 3–1. It was a coincidence that 16 years previously when Wigan and Mansfield had met in the Cup the results were exactly the same – a 1–1 draw in the first game and a 3–1 victory for Mansfield in the replay.

After their stirring encounters with the League clubs Wigan took on non-League opposition in Matlock Town, Northern Premier League, at home in the First Round of the 1975/6 competition. Wigan coasted to a 4–1 win. Wigan's reward was an away Second Round game against renowned Cup fighters Third Division Sheffield Wednesday at Hillsborough. Although the Latics were under pressure during the early stages they held off the League side's challenge to go in at half-time with the scoresheet blank. But the non-Leaguers were a goal down in the 55th minute. Wednesday increasing their lead to 2–0 before the final whistle.

The next season, 1976/7, Wigan again drew fellow Northern Premier Leaguers Matlock in the First Round but this time it was away at the Causeway Ground, the Gladiators avenging their previous defeat by beating the Latics 2–0.

In their last season as non-Leaguers, 1977/8, the Latics had ground advantage when they drew Fourth Division York City in the First Round. The part-timers took a shock sixth minute lead when their experienced striker Wilkie scored the only goal of the game. Wigan's reward in the Second Round was a home game, played before 13,871 spectators, against Third Division Sheffield Wednesday. Although the first-half belonged to Wednesday the non-Leaguers held out until half-time. It was a different story after the interval as Athletic took command, Whittle scoring the only goal of the match in the 74th minute.

For their memorable Third Round game against First Division Birmingham City, away at St. Andrew's, Wigan put up a better performance than the 4–0 scoreline suggests. The 29,202 crowd was fascinated by the sight of England international Trevor Francis battling it out against the non-Leaguers. It was Francis who opened the scoring in the fourth minute with Bertschin adding another before half-time. It was not all one-way however, Mick Moore, Wigan's most dangerous striker, constantly probing City's defences. Six minutes after the interval Francis scored number three with Bertschin completing the scoring. The Midlanders gave

Wigan a rousing cheer at the end of the game.

Birmingham City: Montgomery, Calderwood, Styles (A), Towers, Howard, Gallagher, Connolly, Francis, Bertschin, Hibbitt, Dillon. Sub. Page.
Wigan: Brown, Morris, Hinnigan, Gore, Ward, Gillibrand, Whittle, Moore, Wilkie, Wright, Worswick. Sub. Styles.

Having beaten two League sides and then given a good account of themselves against Birmingham City the football world was at last convinced that the Latics could no longer be denied a place in the Football League and in 1978/9 the Northern Premier Leaguers took their rightful place in the Fourth Division.

MATCH REPORTS
THIRD ROUND F.A. CUP
9th January 1954
NEWCASTLE UNITED 2   WIGAN ATHLETIC 2

This great game at St. James's Park produced the Cup shock of the day – mighty Newcastle United humbled by part-timers Wigan Athletic. Only some fine solo efforts by United's inside-left and English international Jackie Milburn saved the Magpies from a humiliating defeat. There was a 'gate' of over 52,000.

United gave a workmanlike performance in the first-half and there was no indication of the surprises to come. Broadis gave Athletic defenders a hard time for the first half hour. In the 27th minute Newcastle scored a 'gift' goal. Following a Broadis-Monkhouse movement BROADIS received an unexpected pass from a Wigan defender as the Latics fell back under pressure and the Newcastle striker slipped the ball past Lomas.

During repeated attacks on the Wigan goal Lomas, Athletic's 27-year-old part-timer, brought off a number of spectacular saves, including several 'thunderbolts' from Milburn.

Half-time: Newcastle United 1   Wigan Athletic 0

After the interval Wigan continued their raids and the First Division side began to look shaky. In the 53rd minute the Lancashire Combination leaders scored a well-deserved equaliser when inside-left LYON converted a Lomax pass.

Wigan increased their pace as Newcastle went on the defensive and in the 75th minute electrified their supporters when a 15 yards drive from inside-right LIVESEY flashed into the net.

Wigan's lead was short-lived however. From the kick-off Jackie MILBURN gained possession and after beating three Wigan defenders scored from 18 yards.

Six minutes from time Wigan almost pulled off a sensational victory. Hindle got the ball into the Newcastle net but the 'goal' was disallowed because of offside.

Result: Newcastle United 2   Wigan Athletic 2

Teams:
Newcastle United: Simpson, Batty, McMichael, Scoular, Brennan, Stokoe, Walker, Broadis, Monkhouse, Milburn, Mitchell.
Wigan Athletic: Lomas, Lindsay, Parkinson, Lynn, Mycock, Banks, Butler, Livesey, Lomax, Lyon, Hindle.
Referee: Mr. J. T. Williams, (Woodthorpe, Notts).
Attendance: 52,222

THIRD ROUND F.A. CUP REPLAY
13th January 1954
WIGAN ATHLETIC 2   NEWCASTLE UNITED 3

There was a great crowd of 26,000 at Springfield Park for this fabulous replay against Latics' First Division opponents. Jimmy Scoular won the toss for Newcastle and Athletic kicked off on a heavy ground. Play was end to end with Newcastle marginally in control. The Wigan defenders held firm under this pressure but yielded in the 13th minute when KEEBLE, unmarked, headed in wide of Lomas. With Scottish international centre-half Brennan on top form the Wigan attackers found it difficult to break through. Newcastle continued to have the edge despite the occasional Wigan breakaway and in the 34th minute scored again through WHITE. Two minutes later Wigan staged a remarkable rally and LOMAX reduced the arrears with a splendid goal.

Half-time: Wigan Athletic 1   Newcastle United 2

Wigan attacked strongly in the second half and there was a loud appeal for a goal when following a difficult lob from Lyon Newcastle's goalkeeper Simpson appeared to have fallen over the line with the ball in his hands. But the referee would have none of it despite Wigan's appeals. The Wigan raids continued and Hindle got in a shot and Simpson once again appeared to go behind his line. But the referee waved away appeals for a goal.

The Wigan rally flagged and in the 71st minute United added a further goal. Milburn sending over a cross for BROADIS to head in. This did not subdue Wigan and the part-timers reduced the deficit in the 81st minute with a goal by LOMAX.

Result: Wigan Athletic 2   Newcastle United 3

Wigan Athletic:	Lomas, Lindsay, Parkinson, Lynn, Mycock, Banks, Butler, Livesey, Lomax, Lyon, Hindle.
Newcastle United:	Simpson, Cowley, McMichael, Scoular, Brennan, Casey, White, Broadis, Keeble, Milburn, Mitchell.
Referee:	Mr. J. T. Williams, (Woodthorpe, Notts.).
Attendance:	26,000

THIRD ROUND F.A. CUP
2nd January 1971
MANCHESTER CITY 1   WIGAN ATHLETIC 0

This was the game of the century for Wigan, eclipsing if anything the fabulous Third Round games against Newcastle United 17 years previously. It was a fairy-tale occasion for the Northern Premier Leaguers as they came out on to the Maine Road ground to the roar of 46,000 spectators, including thousands of Wiganers – a nostalgic moment for Athletic's manager and right-half Gordon

Milne, who had often played on the ground as a member of the legendary Liverpool half-back line of Milne, Yates and Stevenson.

It was also a great occasion for City's famous manager, Joe Mercer, who was able to renew his old friendship with Milne who in his League club days had played for Preston, Liverpool and England. Wigan's talented team included striker Derek Temple, formerly Everton, Preston and England (who scored Everton's winning goal against Sheffied Wednesday in the 1966 Cup final), goalkeeper Dennis Reeves, formerly Wrexham and Chester, right-back Alan Turner, ex-Bradford Park Avenue; Billy Sutherland, left-back, formerly with Rangers; Doug Coutts, ex-Aberdeen; Jim Fleming, ex-Luton and Hearts and Graham Oates, formerly Scunthorpe, Blackpool and Grimsby. This line-up added up to an enormous amount of League experience and posed no small threat to City. Facing the part-timers were such stars as Joe Corrigan, City's legendary goalkeeper, Mike Doyle, Tommy Booth, Mike Summerbee, Colin Bell and England centre-forward Francis Lee as well as Tony Book who once wore the shirt of Southern Leaguers Bath City.

When City kicked off they little realised that instead of the goal harvest that their fans were expecting they were to scrape through by a single goal. Mike Summerbee was quickly in the picture and the Wigan defence had difficulty in checking his lively runs down the wing. During these early City raids Athletic's defenders smartly back-pedalled and were helped out by the front men.

Half-time: Manchester City 0   Wigan Athletic 0

In the second half City put sustained pressure on Wigan and the part-timers desperately defended to keep out the lively City attackers. In the 70th minute Lee, who was affected by an injury sustained the previous week, went off and was replaced by Carrodus with Summerbee moving into the middle. Two minutes later City scored the only goal of the game, Colin BELL crashing in a low shot which sailed past Reeves and put the part-timers out of the Cup. It was a fine display by the non-Leaguers and at the end of the game the whole of Maine Road rose to salute them.

Result: Manchester City 1   Wigan Athletic 0

Teams:
Manchester City: Corrigan, Book, Mann, Doyle, Booth, Oakes, Summerbee, Bell, Lee, Young, Jeffries. (Sub: Carrodus).
Wigan Athletic: Reeves, Turner, Sutherland, Milne, Coutts, Gillibrand, Temple, Todd, Davies, Fleming, Oates.
Referee: Mr. P. Partridge, (Middlesborough).
Attendance: 46,212

Wigan Athletic (Contd)
CUP RUNS

1953/4
1st Round - *21st November*
Wigan 4   Scarborough 0

2nd Round - *12th December*
Wigan 4   Hereford Utd. ... 1

3rd Round - *9th January*
Newcastle Utd. .. 2   Wigan 2

3rd Round Replay - *13th January*
Wigan 2   Newcastle Utd. .. 3

1954/5
1st Round - *20th November*
Barnsley 3   Wigan 2

1956/7
1st Round - *17th November*
Wigan 1   Goole 2

1957/8
1st Round - *16th November*
Southport 1   Wigan 2

2nd Round - *7th December*
Wigan 1   Mansfield 1

2nd Round Replay - *11th December*
Mansfield 3   Wigan 1

1962/3
1st Round - *3rd November*
Gateshead 2   Wigan 1

1964/5
1st Round - *14th November*
Stockport C. 2   Wigan 1

1965/6
1st Round - *13th November*
Doncaster R. 2   Wigan 2

1st Round replay - *17th November*
Wigan 3   Doncaster R. 1

2nd Round - *11th December*
Chester 2   Wigan 1

1966/7
1st Round - *26th November*
Tranmere R. 1   Wigan 1

1st Round Replay - *28th November*
Wigan 0   Tranmere R. 1

1969/70
1st Round - *15th November*
Wigan 1   Port Vale 1

1st Round Replay - *18th November*
Port Vale 2   Wigan 2
(after extra time - at 90 minutes 1-1)

1st Round Second Replay - *24th Nov.*
Wigan 0   Port Vale 1
(at Old Trafford)
(after extra time - at 90 minutes 0-0)

1970/1
1st Round - *21st November*
South Shields 1   Wigan 1

1st Round Replay - *23rd November*
Wigan 2   South Shields ... 0

2nd Round - *11th December*
Wigan 2   Peterborough ... 1

3rd Round - *2nd January*
Manchester City 1   Wigan 0

1971/2
1st Round - *20th November*
Wigan 2   Halifax Town ... 1

2nd Round - *11th December*
Wrexham 4   Wigan 0

1972/3
1st Round - *18th November*
Grimsby 2   Wigan 1

1973/4
1st Round - *24th November*
Huddersfield 2   Wigan 0

1974/5
1st Round - *23rd November*
Shrewsbury 1   Wigan 1

1st Round Replay - *25th November*
Wigan 2   Shrewsbury 1

2nd Round - *14th December*
Wigan 1   Mansfield 1

2nd Round Replay - *16th December*
Mansfield 3   Wigan 1

1975/6
1st Round - *3rd November*
Wigan 4   Matlock 1

2nd Round – *13th December*
Sheffield Wed. .. 2   Wigan 0

1976/7
1st Round – *20th November*
Matlock 2   Wigan 0

1977/8
1st Round – *26th November*
Wigan 1   York City 0
2nd Round – *17th December*
Wigan 1   Sheffield Wed. ..0
3rd Round – *7th January*
Birmingham 4   Wigan 0

ELECTED TO FOURTH DIVISION 1978/9

WIMBLEDON

Founded: 1889 (as Wimbledon Old Centrals)

Ground: Plough Lane

League: Fourth Division, formerly Southern

Colours: Yellow and blue shirts, blue shorts

The Dons, before their election to the Football League in 1977/8, were one of the greatest non-League Cup-fighting sides in the country, always to be feared in the great Cup battles and whose name will be enshrined in football history. The Dons began their thrilling post-war First round Cup appearances in 1947/8 against a League club, Mansfield Town, Third Division North, although subsequently they were often opposed by fellow non-Leaguers interspersed with occasions when there was a meeting with the giants.

The Dons' greatest season ever was in 1974/5 when after defeating non-Leaguers in the First and Second Rounds they were drawn away at Turf Moor against First Division Burnley and caused one of the greatest upsets ever in Cup football by beating them 1-0. Thence to Elland Road in the Fourth Round for the epic game against First Division star-studded Leeds United, a 0-0 draw and the penalty save that has become a legend — when Dickie Guy of Wimbledon saved a Lorimer penalty 'special' to give the non-Leaguers another chance. Then the memory of the 45,700 crowd at the Crystal Palace ground for the replay and the deflected goal that gave Leeds victory by the narrowest of margins.

Only two seasons later the Dons were in the Third Round again, holding First Division Middlesbrough to a goalless draw at Plough Lane before going out at Ayresome Park in the replay to a second-half penalty goal. These were stirring times and the other League sides who were drawn against the Dons in the Cup, Colchester United, Bristol City, Bristol Rovers, Peterborough and Brentford always knew that they had a fight on their hands.

In their post-war First Round encounter in 1947/8 the Dons, then in the Isthmian League, drew a home game against Mansfield Town, Third Division North. A crowd of nearly 10,000 watched a stern struggle with one dramatic incident just before half-time when Jones, Mansfield's former Welsh international, missed a penalty. Although Mansfield were reduced to ten men in the second half they scored the only goal of the game.

The Dons had to wait until the 1952/3 season for their next First Round appearance when they were drawn away from home against Amateur Cup holders Walthamstow Avenue. Although the Dons were two goals in the lead at one stage Walthamstow rallied to get on level terms and force a replay. The resumed game was a disappointment for the Dons. Avenue adapted better to the muddy conditions and gained an easy passage into the next round with a 3-0 win.

It was not for ten years that the Dons were again seen in the First Round, in the 1962/3 season, but it was an impressive re-entry to Cup football at this level. Drawing Third Division Colchester United at home at Plough Lane the Dons beat the professionals 2-1 to give one of their greatest performances in 72 years of Cup football. From the kick-off Colchester stormed into the Dons' area to secure their first corner in a matter of seconds, a pattern that was to continue throughout the game with United gaining 20 corners before the end. Against the run of the play Wimbledon scored first in the 27th minute, Colchester had a 'goal' disallowed and in the 76th minute the Dons made it 2-0. Facing the threat of defeat United threw everything into the attack and reduced the deficit towards the end but they had left it too late to grab the equaliser.

Wimbledon: Kelly, Rudge, Coote, Ardrey, Law, Murphy, Brown, Hamm, Reynolds, Moore, Williams.

The Dons' luck ran out when the draw was made for the Second Round tie, the part-timers having to travel to the West Country to meet Third Division Bristol City. A crowd of 13,778 were at Ashton Gate to see City establish a 2-0 half-time lead. In the second-half the game swung in favour of the Isthmian League champions who reduced the deficit in the 60th minute when City put the ball in their own net. In the closing stages the Dons mounted raid after raid against the City defenders but were unable to force a replay. The game was refereed by Jim Finney who controlled the Spurs v Burnley Cup Final in 1962.

Wimbledon were again in the First Round in the following season, 1963/4, by right of being Amateur Cup winners, drawn away against Southern Leaguers Bexley United. The

Southern Leaguers could not match the Dons' skills and were badly beaten 5–1. For their Second Round encounter the Dons drew Cup battlers Bath City of the Southern League at Plough Lane. A fluctuating game ended in a 2–2 draw. In the replay at Bath the Dons had no answer to a City side strong in defence and attack and the Southern Leaguers brought off an easy 4–0 win to gain a home tie against First Division Bolton Wanderers in the Third Round.

Season 1965/6 saw the Dons, now in the Southern League, once again in the First Round and drawn at home against fellow Southern Leaguers Gravesend. The Dons, playing five of the team who had helped to win the Amateur Cup two seasons previously, had an easy 4–1 win. Wimbledon again had the luck of the draw in the Second Round, matched against another Southern League club, Folkestone Town. The Dons were unexpectedly defeated 1–0, the only goal of the match being an 'own goal' credited to the Dons' goalkeeper.

Three seasons later the Dons reappeared in the First Round to find themselves matched against another non-League side, Grantham, then in the Midland League.

Grantham scored first through an 'own goal' in the first-half, The Dons equalised in the second half only for Grantham to snatch the winner soon afterwards.

Wimbledon again reached the First Round in the following season, 1967/8, drawn at home at Plough Lane against fellow Southern Leaguers Romford. On a snow-covered pitch the Dons mastered the conditions better than their rivals and ran out 3–0 winners. The Dons' reward was a Second Round tie at Plough Lane against Third Division Bristol Rovers. Wimbledon were no match for the League side and went out 4–0.

The Dons missed a season before again bidding for Cup success in the First Round in 1969/70. Drawn away from home against fellow Southern Leaguers Hillingdon Borough the Dons had an off day and lost 2–0 to put an end to their Cup ambitions for another year.

Fighting their way to the First Round in the following season, 1970/1, Wimbledon had a difficult pairing away from home against famous Cup fighters Fourth Division Peterborough United. Midway through the first-half 'Posh' were two goals ahead and although the Dons reduced the deficit Peterborough scored again before the end to make the final score 3-1.

After a break of two seasons Wimbledon's name again appeared in the First Round draw having to travel to meet fellow Southern Leaguers King's Lynn. A closely-contested game ended in a win for Lynn by a lone goal.

The next season 1974/5 added another glorious page to Wimbledon's Cup history. It was a trail that was to lead to Burnley and Leeds United but began modestly enough in the First Round when the Dons, after fighting their way through the qualifying rounds, were set to meet fellow Southern Leaguers Bath City at Plough Lane. The Dons were seeking to avenge their defeat by Bath in the Second Round in 1963 and in this they succeeded but only by a narrow 1-0 margin. In the Second Round the Dons again had ground advantage, drawing fellow Southern Leaguers Kettering and beating them 2-0 after a tough battle.

This win gave Wimbledon the right to meet mighty First Division Burnley in the Third Round at Turf Moor to gain a sensational 1-0 victory and a place in Cup lore. Then came the equally sensational Fourth Round with the Dons matched against First Division Leeds United at Elland Road, the part-timers forcing a 0-0 draw with the game seeing high drama when the Dons goalkeeper Dickie Guy saved a Lorimer penalty kick. From there the Dons took Leeds to Crystal Palace for the replay and only a deflected shot gave Leeds the lone goal that put Wimbledon out of the Cup. These three exciting games are fully described in *Match Report*.

After their remarkable deeds the previous season the Dons were back in First Round business in 1975/6, when they drew an away tie against fellow Southern Leaguers Nuneaton Borough. Although the Dons were in control for most of the game the scoresheet was blank at half-time but a 49th minute goal took Wimbledon into the next round. This was against fellow Londoners Fourth Division Brentford at Plough Lane. The Bees scored twice in the first-half and held their lead until the end.

The Dons again fought their way to the First Round in 1976/7 which was to prove another glory season. The Dons had a fairly modest encounter in the First Round, drawing Isthmian Leaguers Woking at home at Plough Lane. After a goalless first-half the game went Wimbledon's way, the Dons scoring the only goal of the match in the 72nd minute. Dickie Guy, Wimbledon's famous goalkeeper, had a special reason for keeping his goal intact for it was his 500th game for the club.

For their Second Round game the Dons drew tricky opposition in Leatherhead away from home. The Isthmian Leaguers, no mean Cup fighters, had already put Northampton out of the Cup in the previous round. At one stage the Dons were 2–0 in the lead, Leatherhead made a fight of it by pulling a goal back but the Dons scored again almost on time to make the final score 3–1 to gain a fairy-tale home tie in the Third Round against First Division Middlesbrough. 'Boro's reputation for dour, uncompromising football is such that only a moderate crowd, 8,539, turned out to watch the minnows of the Southern League do battle against the giants. The first-half was a fairly negative affair but the game came to life in the 34th minute when Roger Connell got the ball in the net only for the 'goal' to be disallowed. Half-time arrived with the scoresheet blank, 'Boro seeming content to keep their goal intact although David Armstrong occasionally shone in sporadic Middlesbrough attacks. In the second-half it was the mixture as before with 'Boro playing defensively and seemingly content to settle for a draw. The Dons almost clinched it in the 75th minute when Roger Connell hammered in a powerful drive that the 'Boro goalkeeper just managed to turn around the post. The final whistle blew with the scoresheet still blank, the moral victory being with the Dons for having contained their First Division opponents and forcing a replay at Ayresome Park, an exciting contest fully described in *Match Report*.

Wimbledon: Guy, Tilley, Bryant, Donaldson, Edwards, Bassett, Cooke, Aitken, Connell, Marlowe, Holmes.

This was the last season that the Dons appeared in the Cup as non-Leaguers, their exploits having deservedly secured election to the Fourth Division in the 1977/8 season.

MATCH REPORTS
THIRD ROUND F.A. CUP
4th January 1975
BURNLEY 0   WIMBLEDON 1

This was the dream draw that every non-League club hopes and prays for but rarely gets – a mighty David and Goliath encounter that ended with the incredible scoreline Burnley 0 Wimbledon 1 to create one of the biggest sensations in the F.A. Cup in its long history. Wimbledon manager, Allen Batsford, and his coach, Brian Hall, worked out a plan for containing the experienced First Division side and to make sure that Leighton James was given as little room to operate as possible. The game opened as expected, Wimbledon defending stoutly as Burnley's front men ripped into the attack. Wimbledon, with a combination of efficient football, courage and cool composure, began to rattle their First Division opponents. Bassett had a crack at goal with a 20 yards shot which went wide and left-back Edwards sent a speculative lob into the Burnley penalty area which put goalkeeper Stevenson under pressure. Wimbledon's strikers, centre-forward Roger Connell, Micky Mahon, who was a member of the Colchester United team which had beaten Leeds United three years previously and Kieron Somers were in good form and gave the Burnley defenders problems.

It was Dickie Guy who had not missed a first team match for four years and was approaching his 300th consecutive game who was one of the heroes of the day. In the 27th minute it looked a certainty that a Ray Hankin header would flash into the net but Guy brilliantly turned the ball round the post. Three minutes later Newton volleyed in a rocket-like shot and it was inconceivable that Dickie Guy could stop it but he did so at the second attempt. It was an astonishing performance by the non-Leaguers and Ian Cooke, the skipper, had much to be proud of when he took his team off at half-time with the scoresheet blank.

Half-time: Burnley 0   Wimbledon 0

Some of the fire seemed to go out of the Burnley attack in the early stages of the second half and it was in the 49th minute when Wimbledon history was made. Ian Cooke moved swiftly past Jim Thomson to try a shot which the Burnley goalkeeper, Alan Stevenson, charged down. The ball was not cleared and ran along the edge of the penalty area where both Roger Connell and Micky Mahon were waiting. Connell mistimed his kick but MAHON made no mistake with a hard shot into the corner of the net that left Stevenson helpless. Soon afterwards Somers tried to make it number two as he burst through the Burnley defence but his shot went wide of the post. In the 73rd minute with Burnley throwing in everything in the attempt to get the equaliser Dickie Guy made the save of the match, a reflex action save from a cannonball shot from Fletcher at point blank range. As Burnley continued to throw in one desperate attack after another it was Guy who stood between them and a replay at Wimbledon but it was not to be and the final whistle blew with the Dons having achieved the unbelievable and joining the ranks of those few non-League sides that have put some of the elite from the First Division out of the Cup. Their reward – a visit to Elland Road to meet League champions Leeds United in the Fourth Round.

Result: Burnley 0   Wimbledon 1

Teams:
Burnley: Stevenson, Newton, Thomas, Ingham, Waldron, Noble, Flynn, Hankin, Fletcher, Collins, James, (Sub: Morris).
Wimbledon: Guy, Stockley, Bryant, Donaldson, Edwards, Bassett, Cooke, Rice, Connell, Somers, Mahon.
Referee: Mr. R. B. Lee, (Cheadle).
Attendance: 19,683

FOURTH ROUND F.A. CUP
25th January 1975
LEEDS UNITED 0   WIMBLEDON 0

This was a fairy-tale draw which will be the talk of the soccer world down the years – League champions and European Cup quarter finalists Leeds United versus Wimbledon of the Southern League. It was a game that captured the imagination of the sporting world everywhere and was reflected in the attendance, no fewer than 46,000, with the gates being closed before the kick-off. It was the biggest crowd of the season at Elland Road. The fairy-tale quality of the encounter was reflected in the two sides, Leeds United packed with internationals, star-studded names such as Paul Reaney, Billy Bremner, Paul Madeley, Peter Lorimer, Johnny Giles, Frank and Eddie Gray having a brilliance that compared oddly with the down-to-earth composition of the Dons, printers, hairdressers, clerks, etc. with only Micky Mahon having League experience when he played for Colchester. That was the scene when Wimbledon skipper, Ian Cooke, a former public school rugby player who had spent 13 years with the Dons, led his side out at Elland Road to the cheers of the 46,000 plus spectators to face the mighty Leeds side.

The Dons were not overawed by the occasion and quickly settled down to meet the First Division challenge. Leeds began in a desultory manner and this cautious approach was evident right through the first-half and well into the second before they made a real effort to overcome their Southern League opponents. On the other hand Wimbledon almost took a shock lead in the 11th minute as defender Billy Edwards put in a cross which Cooke dummied and Kieron Somers was right up with the action and quickly slammed in a left-foot shot which just went the wrong side of the post. After a quarter of an hour Leeds came more into the game and Frank Gray and McKenzie tried to force their way through but were blocked by the well-marshalled and competent Wimbledon defence.

As it dawned on Wimbledon that this was going to be no runaway affair for the First Division side the Dons began to go over to the attack, Bremner being beaten time and time again in the tackle, Lorimer was kept under control and even the impeccable Madeley being harried into poor ball distribution. The action on the Leeds flank was rather more effective, Frank Gray and Eddie Gray combining well to pose some problems for Wimbledon but it was the only bright spot in a colourless first-half display by the champions. At half-time Wimbledon received a tremendous ovation as they went into the dressing-room.

Half-time: Leeds United 0   Wimbledon 0

The ordinariness of the first-half when Leeds seemed unable to raise their game continued throughout the early stages of the second half with the drama and colour of a Cup tie missing. Leeds were playing with their usual patience, trying to build up their attacks from midfield but coming up against an unyielding Dons' defence. The Yorkshiremen were strangely out of gear.

With a quarter of an hour's play to go it suddenly dawned on Leeds that if they did not raise their game they would be left with a trip to Wimbledon for a replay. The Leeds goal-scoring machine at last broke into action and there was some dramatic moments before the final whistle. Dickie Guy, who had had a comparatively quiet afternoon, faced a terrific bombardment from the Leeds strikers and gave a dramatic solo performance. Once Yorath gave Donaldson the slip and Guy made an incredible save, the Leeds striker's shot being thrust aside out of harm's way by a right-fisted punch.

Then, in the 83rd minute, came the most dramatic moment of all when Eddie Gray moved confidently down the wing into the Wimbledon box and was bundled off the ball by Bassett. The relief round the Leeds ground was audible as the referee pointed to the spot and so sure was the Leeds captain, Bremner, that Lorimer would score, as he usually did from the penalty spot, that he ran over to Bassett to commiserate with him. Then the incredible happened. Lorimer moved up to the ball and instead of blasting in a cannonball shot moved the ball to Guy's right and saw the Wimbledon keeper make an incredible save. Lorimer and the whole of the Leeds team and their supporters were dumbfounded – it was one of the most famous penalty saves in the history of the F.A. Cup and Dickie Guy's name will always be associated with Cup football as a result. It was still not over as Leeds, finally convinced that a draw was on the cards attacked in force but the incredible Wimbledon defence and in particular Dickie Guy were more than a match for them.

Result: Leeds United 0   Wimbledon 0

Teams:
Leeds United: Harvey, Reaney, F. Gray, Bremner, McQueen, Madeley, McKenzie, Yorath, Lorimer, Giles, E. Gray.
Wimbledon: Guy, Stockley, Bryant, Donaldson, Edwards, Bassett, Cooke, Rice, Connell, Somers, Lucas, (Sub: Aitken).
Referee: Mr. Dennis Turner, (Cannock).
Attendance: 46,000

FOURTH ROUND F.A. CUP REPLAY
10th February 1975
WIMBLEDON 0   LEEDS UNITED 1

For this never-to-be-forgotten replay Wimbledon switched the venue of the tie to the Crystal Palace ground at Selhurst Park and in the circumstances it was the correct decision for there was a fantastic 46,000 crowd, the same as at Leeds, to watch the 'giant-killers' do battle with mighty Leeds United. It was a night to remember. The packed Crystal Palace ground, flood-lights gleaming down on the pitch to illuminate one of the most incredible sights ever seen on a soccer ground, the part-timers of Wimbledon against the international-studded Leeds United, League champions and set for European honours.

Wimbledon started with tremendous zest and Leeds were lucky that they were not two goals down in the first five minutes. In the opening seconds Somers connected with a Mahon cross which had Harvey beaten but Yorath, replacing the injured McQueen, was on hand to clear off the line. Again Wimbledon raced into the attack and Harvey had to make an acrobatic dive to save a hard shot from Rice. As at Elland Road the Leeds defence was extremely jittery and midfield control had been surrendered to Wimbledon as Bremner strove unsuccessfully to get into the game. Towards half-time Leeds began to settle down and Eddie Gray and McKenzie strove to calm the raw nerves of the champions. At half-time Wimbledon went off the pitch to a tremendous ovation.

Half-time: Wimbledon 0   Leeds United 0

When the second half began Leeds piled on the pressure and Duncan McKenzie, in good form, laid on the ball for Alan Clarke who hammered the ball into the roof of the net. However, the linesman had already flagged for offside. It was a narrow escape for the Dons.

Then tragedy struck for the Southern Leaguers. It was not a potentially dangerous situation when Johnny Giles got the ball 20 yards out and sent in a speculative shot that Guy would have collected easily; at the last minute the ball hit Dave

BASSETT, the Dons' defender who had given away the penalty at Elland Road, and the ball was deflected into the net just wide of Dickie Guy. It was a goal that could hardly have pleased Leeds and yet it was the one that mattered. It was the first goal that had been scored against Wimbledon in 765 minutes' play in nine F.A. Cup ties.

Despite this tragedy the Dons quickly picked themselves off the floor and began to batter at the Leeds goal for the equaliser, Mahon moving the ball skilfully up front, Wimbledon still looked capable of securing the equaliser and Cooke all but managed it ten minutes from the final whistle. Billy Bremner who had had a good deal of stick throughout the night from the crowd, rushed over to the Wimbledon players and shook hands with each one as they moved off the pitch, 'giant-killers' every one, to one of the greatest ovations ever heard at Selhurst Park.

Result: Wimbledon 0   Leeds United 1

Teams:
Wimbledon: Guy, Stockley, Bryant, Donaldson, Edwards, Bassett, Rice, Cooke, Connell, Somers, Mahon, (Sub: Aitken).
Leeds United: Harvey, Reaney, Gray, F. Bremner, Yorath, Madeley, McKenzie, Clarke, Jordan, Giles, Gray, E. (Sub: Cherry).
Referee: Mr. Dennis Turner, (Cannock).
Attendance: 45,701

THIRD ROUND F.A. CUP REPLAY
11th January 1977
MIDDLESBROUGH 1   WIMBLEDON 0

On an ice-covered pitch at Ayresome Park it was a different story from the dour defensive display that Boro had put on at Plough Lane. Jack Charlton, 'Boro's manager, had done some hard talking to his squad who stormed through the Dons' defences and brought some spectacular saves from Wimbledon hero Dickie Guy. It was a case of defending almost throughout the entire match and it is to the tremendous credit of the Dons' back division, in particular Dave Donaldson, Geoff Byrant and Billy Edwards, that kept Middlesbrough to a meagre 1–0 victory with the only goal coming from a penalty.

In the opening stages of the game the red shirts of 'Boro swept down into the Wimbledon goal area and brought out the best in the Dons' embattled defenders. It was exciting, exhilarating Cup football with the Dons intent on preserving their great Cup record. When the whistle blew for half-time a great shout went up from the 23,000 crowd as they saluted the brave battle by the Southern Leaguers in keeping their goal intact despite continuous pressure from the First Division giants.

Half-time: Middlesbrough 0   Wimbledon 0

In the second half Middlesbrough continued as they had left off with continuous assaults on the Dons' goal area and with the non-Leaguers putting up a classic defensive display. It was in the 56th minute that their coolness gave way, right back Kevin Tilley bringing down 'Boro left-winger, David Armstrong, in the penalty box. Even so Wimbledon protested strongly at the penalty decision and Roger Connell had his name taken in the process. David ARMSTRONG himself strode up to take the penalty kick and this time Dickie Guy could not repeat his glorious save he made at Leeds against Lorimer and the ball cannoned into the Wimbledon net. It was Armstrong who had put out Wycombe in the Third Round replay at Ayresome Park two seasons previously with a last minute goal and on this occasion he was to repeat the performance for it was the only goal of the match.

Wimbledon picked themselves up off the floor after this reverse and in the last twenty minutes of the game began to move into the Middlesbrough half with Roger Connell and Glenn Aitken both having chances. When the final whistle blew the Dons were cheered off the pitch after having given a brave battling display against one of the strongest teams in the First Division.

Result: Middlesbrough 1   Wimbledon 0

Teams:
Middlesbrough: Cuff, Craggs, Cooper, Souness, Boam, Maddren, McAndrew, Mills, Brine, Wood, Armstrong. (Sub: Boersma).
Wimbledon: Guy, Tilley, Bryant, Donaldson, Edwards, Bassett, Cooke, Aitken, Connell, Marlowe, Holmes. (Sub: Leslie).
Referee: Mr. D. Turner, (Cannock).
Attendance: 23,000

CUP RUNS

1947/8

1st Round - *29th November*
Wimbledon 0   Mansfield 1

1952/3

1st Round   *22nd November*
Walthamstow 2   Wimbledon 2

1st Round Replay - *26th November*
Wimbledon 0   Walthamstow 3

1962/3

1st Round   *3rd November*
Wimbledon 2   Colchester 1

2nd Round - *24th November*
Bristol City 2   Wimbledon 1

1963/4

1st Round - *16th November*
Bexley Utd 1   Wimbledon 5

2nd Round   *7th December*
Wimbledon 2   Bath City 2

2nd Round Replay - *12th December*
Bath City 4   Wimbledon 0

1965/6

1st Round   *13th November*
Wimbledon 4   Gravesend 1

2nd Round   *4th December*
Wimbledon 0   Folkestone 1

1966/7

1st Round   *26th November*
Grantham 2   Wimbledon 1

1967/8

1st Round   *9th December*
Wimbledon 3   Romford 0

2nd Round   *6th January*
Wimbledon 0   Bristol Rovers ... 4

1969/70

1st Round   *15th November*
Hillingdon 2   Wimbledon 0

1970/71

1st Round   *21st November*
Peterborough 3   Wimbledon 1

1973/4

1st Round   *24th November*
King's Lynn 1   Wimbledon 0

1974/5

1st Round - *23rd November*
Wimbledon 1   Bath City 0

2nd Round - *14th December*
Wimbledon 2   Kettering 0

3rd Round - *4th January*
Burnley 0   Wimbledon 1

4th Round - *25th January*
Leeds Utd. 0   Wimbledon 0

4th Round Replay - *10th February*
Wimbledon 0   Leeds Utd. 1
(at Crystal Palace)

1975/6

1st Round - *22nd November*
Nuneaton Boro . 0   Wimbledon 1

2nd Round - *13th December*
Wimbledon 0   Brentford 2

1976/7

1st Round - *20th November*
Wimbledon 1   Woking 0

2nd Round - *14th December*
Leatherhead 1   Wimbledon 3

3rd round - *8th January*
Wimbledon 0   Middlesbrough ... 0

3rd round Replay - *11th January*
Midlesbrough 1   Wimbledon 0

ELECTED TO FOURTH DIVISION
1977/8

WORCESTER CITY

Founded: 1902

League: Alliance Premier

Ground: St. George's Lane

Colours: Blue and white striped shirts, white shorts

City made a late start in the hunt for post-war Cup honours, not reaching the First Round until the 1950/1 season when they were beaten 4-1 at St. George's Lane by Third Division North side Hartlepool United. But City made up for lost time in their glory season of 1958/9 when after beating fellow Southern Leaguers Chelmsford after a replay, they overwhelmed Fourth Division Millwall 5-2 at The Lane and then made Cup history in the Third round, again at home, by beating mighty Liverpool 2-1 then setting the pace in the Second Division, to make it the greatest day in the club's history. Then in the Fourth Round another red letter day when Second Division Sheffield United visited the Lane only this time there was no fairy-tale ending, the League side ending City's run by two clear goals.

In other F.A. Cup contests City took Fourth Division Aldershot to two First Round replays in 1957/8 before going out 3-2 at Birmingham City's ground after extra time. In the 1960/1 season City again had the luck of the draw when they entertained Third Division Coventry City at St. George's Lane but were beaten 4-1. Eighteen years later City reappeared in the First Round beating Third Division Plymouth Argyle 2-0 at The Lane and then going out in the Second Round against Fourth Division Newport County by a narrow 2-1 margin after extra time in a replay.

City's first post-war First Round encounter was in the 1950/1 season when they were drawn at home against Third Division North, Hartlepool United. A crowd of 8,982 saw City go into a well-deserved 1–0 interval lead through a Jackman goal but Pool scored four times in the second half. City's goalkeeper Ron Baynham, who was later to play for First Division Luton and England, gave a fine display.

There was a gap of six seasons before City again appeared in the First Round, drawn away again Aldershot, Third

Division South. City did well to hold the League side to a goalless draw and at the replay at St. George's Lane there was a bumper crowd of 10,887 to watch a rugged game in which over 40 free kicks were awarded for a succession of fouls. None the less it was an exciting game which produced a terrific finish. Whilst City had opened the scoring Aldershot hit back to set up a 2-1 lead which they held up to the closing stages when, with seconds to go, Worcester grabbed the equaliser. The game went into extra time but there was no further scoring. In the second replay, staged at Birmingham's ground at St. Andrew's, a crowd of 22,926 saw Aldershot put City out of the cup by a slender 3-2 margin after extra time. This was City's longest-ever Cup run to date, 11 matches played including the qualifying games, five replays and a total audience of 81,518.

The following season, 1958/9, produced City's greatest Cup run to date with the club making history by reaching the Fourth Round. That season's First Round Cup battle began unspectacularly enough with an away tie against fellow Southern Leaguers Chelmsford when City did well to hold their opponents to a goalless draw. In the replay at St. George's Lane City reached the Second Round for the first time in their history with a splendid 3-1 victory.

City's Second Round contest at St. George's Lane against Fourth Division Millwall in December 1958 will be remembered as long as football is played at Worcester. Completely demoralising their League opponents City piled on the goals to record a famous 5-2 victory. The 12,525 spectators saw City take a first minute lead and then notch a further goal before half-time. City so completely dominated the proceedings that at one time they were leading 5-1, Millwall adding a second just before the end.

City's giant-killing feats continued in the Third Round when in a sensational game at St. George's Lane before a crowd of 15,011 the Southern Leaguers disposed of mighty Second Division Liverpool 2-1. The game, fully described in *Match Report*, ended on a high note when, as one morning newspaper described it: "Ten thousand whooping, ecstatic fans leaped the barriers ... and in 20 seconds the latest heroes of the F.A. Cup were hidden from view. Slowly a short stocky figure in the blue and white colours of Worcester emerged from the roaring mass of jubilant humanity. Inch by inch they carried him shoulder high from the ground. It was Roy Paul, 38-year-old hero of a host of sporting triumphs."

In the Fourth Round, with City again having the luck of home advantage, Second Division Sheffield United were welcomed to St. George's Lane. This time there was no giant-killing, United putting on a class performance to beat City comfortably 2–0. This game is also fully reported in *Match Report*.

After this highly successful Cup campaign, in which City were the toast of the football world, the Southern Leaguers were again in the First Round the next season, 1960/1. Drawn against Third Division Coventry City, a crowd of 7,751 at St. George's Lane saw Coventry build up a 2–0 half-time lead. Although City reduced the deficit from a penalty early in the second-half Coventry notched two more to run out comfortable 4–1 winners.

Eighteen long years were to elapse before City were again in the First Round, the Southern Leaguers invariably failing at the fourth qualifying round hurdle. But to make up for their long absence from Cup-fighting at this level they drew interesting Third Division opponents Plymouth Argyle to St. George's Lane and produced one of the Cup shocks of the day by disposing of them 2–0. A crowd of 8,253 at St. George's Lane saw City take a 13th minute lead through defender Malcolm Phelps. Malcolm Allison's team were finally knocked out of the Cup when Jimmy Williams scored City's second in the 89th minute.

City: Cumbes, Barton, Punsheon, Tudor, Phelps, Deehan, J. Williams, Stevens, B. Williams, Lawrance, Allner, (Sub: Martin).

City's Second Round opponents were Fourth Division Newport County away at Somerton Park. A fine display by City's back four with an impeccable performance from goalkeeper Jimmy Cumbes produced a goalless draw. In the replay at St. George's Lane a Malcolm Phelps header gave City a 1–0 half-time lead and when it seemed that the Southern Leaguers were through disaster struck in the 89th minute when a deflection off City defender Norman Pemberton went into the back of the net. With City demoralised Newport scored again in extra time through Howard Goddard to gain a plum draw against West Ham.

MATCH REPORTS
THIRD ROUND F.A. CUP
15th January 1959
WORCESTER CITY 2   LIVERPOOL 1

After a postponement due to a frozen pitch Worcester City, playing their Third Round tie with Liverpool in mid week before over 15,000 spectators – a ground record – harassed the Merseyside club into two blunders that cost them the game and brought Cup glory to the Southern Leaguers. At the end of the game thousands of ecstatic City fans leapt the barriers to carry ex-Manchester City and Welsh international Roy Paul shoulder high from the field. It was a day that will for ever be remembered in Worcester City's Cup annals.

From the commencement the Worcester side clicked into gear. They played the correct type of football on a ground that was still icy despite a covering of sand and salt. They quickly tackled whenever the Liverpool line moved forward and the half-back line, which included the City captain Roy Paul, constantly fed the quick moving Worcester forwards. Melville, at centre half, played the game of his life and the defence generally was rock-like with goalkeeper Kirkwood playing an outstanding game.

Both Worcester goals were the result of defensive errors by Liverpool. The first came after only nine minutes of play. Liverpool right-back Molyneux diverted a cross from City centre-forward Harry Knowles but the ball went out of reach of Scottish international 'keeper Younger and sent centre half White and 17-year-old Worcester outside left Tommy Skuse racing for possession. White got a foot to the ball but sent it to SKUSE who only had to steer it into the net. A tumultuous roar went up as Worcester took the lead. Up to half time Worcester continued the attack but generally defences were in command. Liverpool were rarely allowed to shoot for goal.

Half-time: Worcester City 1   Liverpool 0

Soon after the game was resumed Liverpool began to improve with its potentially dangerous left wing of England international Alan A'Court and Harrower, well supported by left half Twentyman. The Liverpool snap-shooting was good and Twentyman once rattled the crossbar with a 20 yards power drive. Knowles and Brown, the Worcester outside right, frequently switched positions and both Eddie Follan, the ex-Aston Villa forward, and Skuse kept the Liverpool defenders on their toes.

In midfield Twentyman and Wheeler were continually striving to set their forwards in action but the Worcester defence was on top and Kirkwood was seldom extended.

In the 81st minute Worcester put the matter beyond doubt when they scored their second, again as a result of a Liverpool defensive slip. Centre-half WHITE, whilst trying to clear a Knowles pass, lobbed the ball into his own goal as Younger rushed out. The crowd erupted as they realised that the Southern Leaguers were within an ace of defeating mighty Liverpool to gain a place in the Fourth Round.

A hotly disputed penalty gave Liverpool a consolation goal. While Kirkwood was clutching the ball on the ground and attempting to keep the Liverpool forwards away Melville was penalised for charging. TWENTYMAN scored from the spot kick, despite protests from Kirkwood who left his goal as the kick was taken.

At the end of the game the Worcester supporters swept onto the ground to carry Roy Paul, who had taken Manchester City to Wembley in 1955 and 1956, and goalkeeper Kirkwood triumphantly to the dressing room.

Result: Worcester City 2   Liverpool 1

Teams:
Worcester City: Kirkwood, Wilcox, Potts, Bryceland, Melville, Paul, Brown, Follan, Knowles, Gosling, Skuse.
Liverpool: Younger, Molyneux, Moran, Wheeler, White, Twentyman, Morris, Melia, Bimpson, Harrower, A'Court.
Referee: Mr. L. Tirebuck, (Halifax).
Attendance: 15,111

FOURTH ROUND F.A. CUP
24th January 1959
WORCESTER CITY 0   SHEFFIELD UNITED 2

Worcester City's ground record was again broken when 17,042 spectators crowded into the St. George's Lane ground to see the Southern League giantkillers take on Sheffield United. It was the first time in Worcester's history that they had secured a place in the Fourth Round.

A great roar broke out as Roy Paul led the Worcester team on to the field. From the kickoff it became evident that Sheffield were a polished, compact side and early in the game the home defence was caught napping as Pace went through on his own to test goalkeeper Kirkwood with a hard shot.

Both the Sheffield inside men Hamilton and Russell tried early shots at goal and in the ninth minute took the lead through outside right LEWIS. Lewis nearly repeated his success a few minutes later when his shot from 25 yards range hit the bar. Kirkwood was injured when he grabbed the ball on the rebound as Russell rushed in.

Sheffield's famous defenders, England goalkeeper Alan Hodgkinson, international left back Graham Shaw, right back Coldwell, with veteran Joe Shaw in the centre half berth gave nothing away and it was a long time before Worcester could get within shooting distance.

City eventually came into the picture and the Southern Leaguers centre forward Harry Knowles for once managed to get the better of Shaw to crash a shot against Hodgkinson. Just before half time United had a lucky break when a free kick, taken by Paul was ballooned over the bar from five yards.

Half-time: Worcester City 0   Sheffield United 1

After the interval Sheffield continued to play attractive football and after five minutes scored their second goal. Hoyland booted a high pass down the middle and SIMPSON brought the ball under control and glided it into the net. Brown and Knowles repeating the switch that had paid dividends in previous rounds enabled City to force several corners in quick succession. In one attack Follan got the ball past Shaw for Knowles to race in, Hodgkinson having to dive at the centre forward's feet to clear.

For Worcester Kirkwood in goal, centre half Melville and ex-Port Vale left back Potts, who once played in a Cup semi-final, were outstanding defenders.

Result: Worcester City 0   Sheffield United 2

Teams:
Worcester City: Kirkwood, Wilcox, Potts, Bryceland, Melville, Paul, Brown, Follan, Knowles, Gosling, Skuse.
Sheffield United: Hodgkinson, Coldwell, Shaw, (G). Hoyland, Shaw, (J). Summers, Lewis, Hamilton, Pace, Russell, Simpson.
Referee: Mr. C. W. Kingston, (Newport).
Attendance: 17,042

Worcester City (Contd)   CUP RUNS

1950/1
1st Round   *25th November*
Worcester City .. 1   Hartlepool 4

1957/8
1st Round   *16th November*
Aldershot 0   Worcester City ..0

1st Round Replay   *21st November*
Worcester City .. 2   Aldershot 2
(after extra time)

1st Round, 2nd Replay   *25th November*
Aldershot 3   Worcester City ..2
(after extra time)
(At St. Andrew's, Birmingham)

1958/9
1st Round   *15th November*
Chelmsford 0   Worcester City ..0

1st Round Replay   *20th November*
Worcester City .. 3   Chelmsford 1

2nd Round   *6th December*
Worcester City .. 5   Millwall 2

3rd Round   *15th January*
Worcester City .. 2   Liverpool 1

4th Round - *24th January*
Worcester City .. 0   Sheffield United 2

1960/1
1st Round - *5th November*
Worcester City .. 1   Coventry City ...4

1978/9
1st Round - *25th November*
Worcester City .. 2   Plymouth A. 0

2nd Round - *16th December*
Newport County 0   Worcester City ..0

2nd Round Replay   *18th December*
Worcester City .. 1   Newport County.2

WYCOMBE WANDERERS

Founded: 1884

League: Isthmian

Ground: Loakes Park

Colours: Light blue shirts, dark blue shorts

The Wanderers have been regular performers in the First Round of the Cup — once going as far as the Third — since their first post-war encounter at that level at Loakes Park in the 1955/6 season when they were hosts to Burton Albion. Although Wycombe have drawn a high proportion of non-League sides to oppose them in the First Round stakes they have occasionally drawn League opponents and in the 1973/4 season dismissed Fourth Division Newport County in the First Round. But it was the Wanderers' exploits in the 1974/5 season that put the Isthmian Leaguers on the football map. After a 3-1 home win against fellow part-timers Southern Leaguers Cheltenham the amateurs went on to beat Third Division Bournemouth 2-1 away from home. In the Third Round Wycombe drew a home tie against mighty First Division Middlesbrough and staggered the football world by holding Jack Charlton's team to a 0-0 draw. The replay produced another glory game for Wycombe who, before a crowd of 30,000, put up a valiant defence which fell only in the last seconds of the game to give their First Division opponents a lucky 1-0 victory.

Wycombe have also played League sides Northampton, Watford, Peterborough, Cardiff City and Reading in post-war First Round contests.

Appearing in the First Round in the 1955/6 season, their first post-war encounter at that level, Wycombe drew a home tie at Loakes Park against semi-professionals Burton Albion, then in the Birmingham League. A crowd of nearly 10,000 saw Wycombe beaten 3-1 by the Midlanders.

Wycombe's next appearance in the First Round was in 1957/8 when they drew an away game against Dorchester Town, semi-professionals of the Western League. In a see-saw game Wanderers were defeated 3-2.

In the following season, 1958/9, Wycombe were again in

the First Round drawing League opposition in Fourth Round Northampton Town away from home. Wycombe put up a fine Cup-fighting display before a 'gate' of 12,934, holding the League side to a goalless first-half and eventually going out 2–0.

The Wanderers were again in action in the First Round in the 1959/60 season when they were matched at home against Southern Leaguers Wisbech Town. The Wisbech line-up included three former English internationals, Jesse Pye, ex-Wolves, Billy Elliott, their captain, formerly of Sunderland and Bernard Streten, the ex-Luton goalkeeper plus Tommy McKenzie, the former Scottish international. As the game neared its end with the score at 2–2 it looked all set for a replay when the Wanderers set the game alight with a grandstand finish, scoring twice in the last four minutes to sweep the semi-professionals out of the Cup. It was a piece of history-making for the amateurs as they moved into the Second Round for the first time.

Wanderers drew an away tie in the Second Round against Fourth Division Watford. There was a crowd of 23,907 at Vicarage Road, the largest 'gate' at Watford since the visit of Manchester United seven years' previously and the second biggest Cup crowd of the day. Although the Wanderers put up a plucky display they were out-generalled by the League side who won 5–1.

Again in the First Round in the following season, 1960/1, Wycombe gained a home draw against Southern Leaguers Kettering. Wycombe had only ten fit men for most of the game and were knocked out 2–1.

In the First Round of the 1961/2 competition Wycombe drew a home tie against another Southern League side Ashford Town which ended in a goalless draw. In the replay at Ashford the Southern Leaguers took an early lead which they consolidated with two late goals to run out 3–0 winners.

In the First Round again the next season, 1962/3, but again away from home, the Wanderers were matched against Corinthian Leaguers Maidenhead United, securing a comfortable 3–0 victory after United had missed a penalty. The Second Round draw produced another difficult away game for Wycombe against another Southern League side Gravesend. The amateurs found themselves opposed to a top-form Gravesend who included in their side their capture from Leeds United, Bobby Cameron, who scored one of the goals in the Southern Leaguers 3-1 victory.

The Wanderers were next in the First Round in the 1965/6 season when their unlucky run of away games continued – this time against Southern Leaguers Guildford City at the Josephs Road ground. Although Wycombe secured a 1-0 half-time lead Guildford got back into the game and after a twice-taken penalty City equalised. Midway through the half Guildford went into a 2-1 lead which they held until the dying seconds when Wycombe scored a shock equaliser. Although the Wanderers kept the scoresheet blank at half-time in the replay at Loakes Park. Guildford scored the only goal of the game midway through the second-half to wreck Wycombe's chances of making further progress.

When Wycombe drew Southern Leaguers Bedford Town in the First Round in the 1966/7 season they could have had little idea that the contest would develop into a marathon that was not resolved until 6½ hours after the first kick-off. The first game at Loakes Park drew a crowd of nearly 8,000 to see a goalless first-half and Bedford opening the scoring with Wycombe equalising five minutes from time. Bedford held on to a 1-0 half-time lead in the replay but after the interval Wycombe attacked strongly to go 2-1 up, the Southern Leaguers being lucky to equalise in the closing stages. The game went into extra time, Wycombe going into the lead with Bedford again drawing level, a hotly-disputed penalty two minutes from the final whistle making the score 3-3. Angry scenes followed and the referee had to be escorted from the pitch.

A toss of a coin gave Wycombe the venue for the second replay and a crowd of 8,821 saw the amateurs hold the Southern Leaguers to a 1-1 draw at 90 minutes, the referee abandoning the game at the beginning of extra time because of incessant rain. The marathon continued at Bedford when the Eagles squeezed into the next round on a 3-2 margin, Wycombe contributing to their defeat with an 'own goal'. In the course of the 6½ hours' play some 32,000 spectators had watched the duel.

After this marathon Wycombe did not reappear in the First Round until the 1970/1 season when they managed a home tie against Athenian League amateurs Slough Town. A ding-dong struggle developed between the two amateur sides and resulted in a 1-1 draw with Wycombe having two 'goals' disallowed. The replay at Slough Stadium went against Wycombe, Slough scoring the only goal of the match early in the second-half from a penalty to put the Athenian Leaguers into the Second Round for the first time.

Wycombe did not reappear in the First Round until the 1973/4 season, the amateurs recording a remarkable 3-1 victory at Loakes Park over Fourth Division Newport County. Although Wycombe had the greater share of the play during the first-half their efforts failed to produce a goal and at half-time the scoresheet was blank. Midway into the second-half the amateurs went on a goal spree scoring three times to leave their League opponents groggy. Although Newport scored a consolation goal seven minutes from time they were no match for the amateurs who thoroughly deserved their 3-1 win.

Wycombe: Maskell, Williams, Grant, Wood, Bullock, Reardon, Horseman, Pritchard, Evans, Holified, Perrin, (Sub: Brothers).

After their amazing win against Newport, Wycombe again had the luck of the draw in the Second Round with a tie at Loakes Park against famous Cup-fighters and Fourth Division leaders Peterborough United. Before the game Wycombe tried a useful but unsuccessful propaganda exercise relating to their famous pitch and its drop of eleven feet from side to side plus the local story that a team of players with one leg shorter than the other would be unbeatable at Loakes Park! All to no avail as the Posh gained a 3-1 victory, with the teams level one all at half-time.

Wycombe's glory season was in 1974/5 when they were to battle through to the Third Round to take on First Division Middlesbrough, the first time in the club's 90 years' history that they had entertained a First Division side at Loakes Park. Their First Round draw was a more modest affair, however, against Southern Leaguers Cheltenham Town at home, both sides managing a penalty in the first-half of a cut and thrust game. It was in the second half that the Wanderers' superior class told over the Southern Leaguers, two goals in the first five minutes giving the amateurs a comfortable 3-1 win. Their reward was a home tie against Third Division Bournemouth. The League side were aware that they had a hard task on their hands, Wycombe having won the Isthmian League championship three times out of the last four and had not been beaten at home in over two years. In the event Bournemouth put up a weak performance but were able to withstand a second half Wycombe siege to force a replay at Dean Court. In the early stages the Cherries dominated the game, went into a nine minute lead which they held to half-time but then allowed the amateurs to take control. Towards the end Tony Horseman, Wycombe's veteran amateur international, scored the equaliser and then Wycombe made it 2-1 to earn the right to meet Jackie Charlton's high-flying First Division side Middlesbrough at Loakes Park, fully described in *Match Report*.

After this history-making encounter Wycombe came down to earth in the 1975/6 season when they had a First Round home tie against Southern Leaguers Bedford Town and had to settle for a 0-0 draw. It was a different story in the replay at Bedford where the Southern Leaguers were two goals up in the first half hour. In the second half Wycombe fought back and scored twice to take the game into extra time. There were no further goals. The second replay at Wycombe reversed the 1966 outcome, Wanderers gaining sweet revenge with a narrow 2-1 victory to give the amateurs a Second Round game away at Ninian Park against Third Division Cardiff City. It was the League side's first non-League opposition in the Cup since they met Southern Leaguers Cheltenham 37 years' previously. It was a familiar scene for Wycombe, drawing a large crowd - 11,607 - on a League side's ground. Although Wycombe had the edge in the first half it was then that Cardiff scored the only goal of the match, two minutes from the interval.

After their fine Second Round showing Wycombe found themselves back to basics in the First Round of the 1976/7 tie when they drew an away game against Southern Leaguers Waterlooville. After going two goals ahead in less than 20 minutes Wycombe seemed set for an easy win but in the second half the Southern Leaguers pulled back a goal although Wycombe managed to hang on. Wycombe had the luck of the draw in the Second Round set to entertain Third Division Reading at Loakes Park. A frostbound ground again produced the suggestion that the sloping pitch was akin to a ski run but it was Reading who took advantage of the conditions to go through to the next Round with a narrow 2-1 win.

Wycombe: Maskell, Birdseye, B. Davies, Mead, Phillips,

Fraser, Kennedy, Holified, Evans, Pearson, Priestley. (Sub: Horseman).

The Wanderers, exempted from the earlier rounds in recognition of their past Cup prowess, were hopeful of making further progress when they drew little-known Southern Leaguers Minehead away in the First Round in the 1977/8 season. But although Wycombe pressurised the Southern Leaguers for most of the game they failed to take their chances, were a goal down just before half-time and then let in Minehead to score their second a minute from time.

Wycombe rarely seem to do well against the Southern League sides and their luck was again out when they drew Maidstone away in the 1978/9 season. One goal settled the issue, a 64th minute free kick which if the Wycombe goalkeeper had not touched the ball on its way into the net would have been disallowed.

Wycombe had a shock set-back in the First Round of the 1979/80 season when they drew a home game against fellow Isthmian Leaguers Croydon who had reached this stage of the Cup for the first time. The Wanderers were shot out 3–0 after Croydon had set up a 2–0 half-time advantage.

Wycombe had no better luck in the following season 1980/1 when they drew League opposition in Bournemouth, Fourth Division, at Loakes Park. This contest produced an interesting confrontation between the two managers, Alec Stock of Bournemouth who over 30 years previously had masterminded non-League Yeovil's sensational win over Sunderland and Wycombe's Mike Keen who for 13 years played for QPR and Luton under Stock. There was no luck for the home manager however, the Cherries going into a 2–0 half-time lead and adding another in the second half.

In the First Round again in the 1981/2 season Wycombe were drawn against fellow Isthmian Leaguers Hendon away at Claremont Park. A battle royal developed between two sides both unbeaten for months. Wycombe edged ahead in the 21st minute but Hendon equalised in the 66th minute to force a replay. Loakes Park drew a crowd of over 2,500 to see Wanderers, the better side on the night, end Hendon's 15-match unbeaten record with two second-half goals.

In the Second Round Wanderers drew an away fixture against lowly-placed Barnet of the Alliance Premier League. The 2,015 attendance at Underhill saw Barnet go ahead in the 28th minute on a waterlogged pitch, have a 'goal' disallowed midway through the second half and make it 2–0 in the 89th minute.

MATCH REPORTS

THIRD ROUND F.A. CUP
4th January 1975
WYCOMBE WANDERERS 0   MIDDLESBROUGH 0

This was the game of a lifetime for Wycombe facing Jack Charlton's mighty Middlesbrough, joint leaders of the First Division, on the tiny sloping Loakes Park pitch in the Chiltern Hills. There was a capacity crowd of 12,000 in the tiny ground with others clinging to the gasometers and balancing precariously on the roofs of the nearby multi-storey car park. Middlesbrough put up a mediocre performance perhaps brainwashed by fears of the notorious slope. For most of the game Wycombe dominated the midfield with Mead, Phillips and Reardon playing the game of their lives, winning the ball and prompting the forwards, every one of whom played a hero's game. Middlesbrough relied especially on their two defenders Maddren and Boam and had they not have been on form Middlesbrough might have faced disaster.

Half-time: Wycombe Wanderers 0   Middlesbrough 0

After the interval the muddy pitch did nothing to help Middlesbrough out of their plight and throughout the remaining 45 minutes Wycombe laid siege to the 'Boro goal. Middlesbrough were outplayed by the amateurs and in this second 45 minutes did not produce a single shot at the Wycombe goal. Perrin, a local schoolteacher, who almost scored in the 47th minute, taunted the Boro defence throughout the game. Middlesbrough began to rely on a ten-men defence to keep out the amateurs, an unbelievable, incredible sight that may never again be seen at Loakes Park. Two defenders, Birdseye and Phillips, both came up to have a crack at the 'Boro goal and both went near, Phillips' header rocketing into the side netting. The justice was not there although the performance and the carnival spirit were and Jack Charlton had to take his team back to Middlesbrough to face the uncertainty of the replay at Ayresome Park.

Result: Wycombe Wanderers 0   Middlesbrough 0

Teams:
Wycombe: Maskell, Birdseye, Hand, Mead, Phillips, Reardon, Perrin, Kennedy, Searle, Holifield, Horseman, (Sub: Evans).
Middlesbrough: Platt, Craggs, Spraggon, Souness, Boam, Maddren, Brine, Hickton, Mills, Foggon, Armstrong, (Sub: Willey).
Referee: Mr. A. Porter, (Bolton).
Attendance: 12,000

THIRD ROUND F.A. CUP REPLAY
7th January 1975
MIDDLESBROUGH 1   WYCOMBE WANDERERS 0

This was the greatest game in Wycombe Wanderers history, an

unforgettable night as the amateurs held Middlesbrough right up to the final minute of the game when the First Division side snatched the match winner.

Against all the odds the Isthmian Leaguers took the game into the Middlesbrough half and Howard Kennedy made two attempts early on to pierce the 'Boro defences, first a free-kick which was beaten down by the massed defence and a hard volley from 25 yards out which made goalkeeper Jim Platt dive to save. It was not until halfway through the first half that Maskell had to go into action to keep out the League side. Then began the 'Boro onslaught on the Wycombe goal which brought John Maskell, the heroic Wycombe goalkeeper, into action to play the game of his life. Stalwart in defence too were Alan Phillips and Keith Mead; they had the main task of trying to check the Middlesbrough front line of Armstrong, Foggon, Hinton, Souness, the Scottish international, and Mills.

Half-time: Middlesbrough 0   Wycombe Wanderers 0

When the game recommenced Wycombe started off confidently and began attacking the Middlesbrough goal but 'Boro's attacking potential was always apparent and Maskell had to react quickly when Hickton moved in smartly to test the Wycombe goalkeeper.

Towards the end Middlesbrough began to click and the Wycombe goal underwent a sustained barrage, Maskell playing an incredible game with some acrobatic saves that will never be forgotten by the Teeside crowd. It was not until the final seconds of the game, after the barrage had lasted over ten minutes, that the Wycombe goal finally fell. The movement began with Craggs who picked up one of Wycombe's hasty clearances stroked the ball to Souness who passed to ARMSTRONG. The speeding 'Boro winger sliced through the remaining defenders and steered the ball wide of Maskell. The courageous part-timers had given a magnificent display of skill and courage on the First Division ground under the floodlights and when they went off the field they were given a great ovation by the 30,000 crowd. The Middlesbrough players formed a line to congratulate the Wycombe team as they went off the field. Afterwards the Middlesbrough manager, Jack Charlton, said that it was the greatest ovation to a visiting side that he could ever remember.

Teams:
Middlesbrough: Platt, Craggs, Spraggon, Souness, Boam, Maddren, Charlton, Mills, Hickton, Foggon, (Sub: Willey 60 mins.), Armstrong.
Wycombe: Maskell, Birdseye, Hand, Mead, Phillips, Reardon, Perrin, Kennedy, Searle, Holifield, Horseman, (Sub: Dylan 74 mins).
Referee: Mr. A. Porter, (Bolton).
Attendance: 30,128.

Wycombe (Contd) — CUP RUNS

1955/6
1st Round – *19th November*
Wycombe W. ....1 Burton A. 3

1957/8
1st Round – *16th November*
Dorchester T. ....3 Wycombe W. 2

1958/9
1st Round – *15th November*
Northampton ....2 Wycombe W. 0

1959/60
1st Round – *14th November*
Wycombe W. ....4 Wisbech 2

2nd Round – *5th December*
Watford ....5 Wycombe W. 1

1960/1
1st Round – *5th November*
Wycombe W. ....1 Kettering 2

1961/2
1st Round – *4th November*
Wycombe W. ....0 Ashford 0

1st Round Replay – *8th November*
Ashford ....3 Wycombe W. 0

1962/3
1st Round – *3rd November*
Maidenhead ......0 Wycombe W. 3

2nd Round – *24th November*
Gravesend ....3 Wycombe W. 1

1965/6
1st Round – *13th November*
Guildford C. ......2 Wycombe W. 2

1st Round Replay – *17th November*
Wycombe W. ....0 Guildford C. 1

1966/7
1st Round – *26th November*
Wycombe W. ....1 Bedford Tn. 1

1st Round Replay – *30th November*
Bedford Tn. ....3 Wycombe W. 3
(after extra time. Score at 90 mins: 2-2)

1st Round, 2nd Replay – *5th December*
Wycombe W. ....1 Bedford Tn. 1
(Abandoned after 90 mins.
Ground unfit)

1st Round, 3rd Replay – *8th December*
Bedford Tn. ....3 Wycombe W. 2

1970/71
1st Round – *21st November*
Wycombe W. ....1 Slough 1

1st Round Replay – *25th November*
Slough ....1 Wycombe W. 0

1973/4
1st Round – *24th November*
Wycombe W. ....3 Newport C. 1

2nd Round – *15th December*
Wycombe W. ....1 Peterborough 3

1974/5
1st Round – *23rd November*
Wycombe W. ....3 Cheltenham 1

2nd Round – *14th December*
Wycombe W. ....0 Bournemouth 0

2nd Round Replay – *18th December*
Bournemouth ....1 Wycombe W. 2

3rd Round – *4th January*
Wycombe W. ....0 Middlesbrough .0

3rd Round Replay – *7th January*
Middlesbrough ..1 Wycombe W. 0

1975/6
1st Round – *22nd November*
Wycombe W. ....0 Bedford Tn. 0

1st Round Replay – *24th November*
Bedford Tn. ....2 Wycombe W. 2
(After extra time)

1st Round 2nd Replay – *1st December*
Wycombe W. ....2 Bedford Tn. 1

2nd Round – *13th December*
Cardiff ....1 Wycombe W. 0

1976/7
1st Round – *20th November*
Waterlooville ....1 Wycombe W. 2

2nd Round – *11th December*
Wycombe W. ....1 Reading 2

1977/8
1st Round – *26th November*
Minehead ....2 Wycombe W. 0

1978/9
1st Round - *25th November*
Maidstone 1   Wycombe W. 0

1979/80
1st Round - *24th November*
Wycombe W. 0   Croydon 3

1980/1
1st Round - *22nd November*
Wycombe W. 0   Bournemouth 3

1981/2
1st Round - *21st November*
Hendon 1   Wycombe W. 1
1st Round Replay - *24th November*
Wycombe W 2   Hendon 0
2nd Round - *15th December*
Barnet 2   Wycombe W. 0

YEOVIL TOWN

Founded: 1921

League: Alliance Premier

Ground: Huish

Colours: White and green jerseys, white shorts.

Yeovil Town — the magical name among the non-Leaguers fighting great F.A. Cup battles — have reached the Third Round and further no fewer than six times since the war (nine times in all) with a never-to-be-forgotten season in 1948/9 when their name went into the history books. In that season, after disposing of two non-League sides in the First and Second rounds they beat Second Division Bury 3-1 at Huish in the Third Round, in the Fourth Round achieved a memorable victory against First Division Sunderland 2-1 after extra time (again on the famous slope) and gained lasting fame by reaching the Fifth Round, a post-war honour shared so far only by Colchester United (in their Southern League days) and Blyth Spartans. For their Fifth Round encounter Yeovil had a plum draw against international-studded Manchester United and although going down 8-0 had the distinction of attracting a massive 'gate' of 81,565.

Two other First Division clubs have met Yeovil since the war, both having to visit Yeovil's sloping pitch at Huish — Arsenal in the 1970/1 season, the Gunners winning 3-0 and Norwich City in 1979/80 who won by the same margin. Yeovil have met a large number of League clubs in the earlier rounds and have tasted the fruits of success against Southend United, Walsall, Crystal Palace, Bournemouth and Brentford.

The first of Yeovil's post-war Cup runs began in 1945/6 the season in which the competition was played on a two-leg basis. Yeovil were drawn against Bristol City, Third Division South and managed a 2–2 draw at Huish. There was a 'gate' of over 13,000 at Ashton Gate for the second leg when City ran out winners by three clear goals and won the tie on a 5–2 aggregate.

In the following season Yeovil drew a home tie against then Midland Leaguers Peterborough United. A hard game ended with honours even, a 2-2 draw in which Yeovil equalised ten minutes from the end with a penalty. It was Alec Stock's first year at Yeovil as player-manager. There was a 'gate' of 9,000 at Peterborough for the replay which saw Yeovil go out of the Cup by a lone goal.

To begin their history-making 1948/9 season Yeovil had a home draw in the First Round against Romford, then amateurs playing in the Isthmian League, registering a comfortable 4-0 victory. For their Second Round encounter Yeovil were drawn away from home at The Rec against Weymouth, then in Division One of the Western League, and the attendance of 11,000 broke the ground record. For the second Cup game in succession Yeovil won by four clear goals.

Yeovil, the only non-League side left in the Third Round, were at full strength for their encounter with Second Division Bury and provided the sensation of the day by defeating them 3-1 before a near-record crowd of 13,500. Yeovil were on top for long periods of the game and went ahead in the seventh minute from Hargreaves. In the 19th minute Bury equalised through centre-forward Massart although Yeovil regained their lead a few minutes before the interval with a goal by Wright. Midway through the second half excitement rose to fever pitch when the part-timers went into a 3-1 lead through a goal from Hamilton. When the final whistle blew the excited fans swarmed on to the pitch and chaired the Yeovil players to the dressing room. Yeovil thus entered the Fourth Round for the first time in the club's history and Sunderland were next on the list to brave the sloping ground at Huish.

Teams:
Yeovil: Hall, Hickman, Davis, Keeton, Blizzard, Collins, Hamilton, Stock, Bryant, Wright, Hargreaves.
Bury: Grieves, Griffiths (G), Griffiths (W), Jones, Hart, Bardsley, Whitworth, Dolan, Massart, Worthington, Bellis.

Yeovil went on to Cup glory when they pushed mighty Sunderland out of the Cup in an epic 2-1 victory and themselves went down fighting, even though defeated by an 8-0 margin against Manchester United at Maine Road in the next round – both these great games are fully described in *Match Reports*.

Following their record run Yeovil found themselves in the

First Round again, drawn at home against Romford, the previous season's Isthmian League Amateur Cup runners-up. Using tactics devised by their Scottish international player-manager, left half George Paterson, Yeovil were a goal ahead within five minutes and went on to win 4-1. Their opponents at Huish for the Second Round were fellow Southern Leaguers Gillingham, later to be elected to the League, and managed by Archie Clark, formerly of Everton and Arsenal. The 'gate' reached over 13,000. Yeovil scored first and went on to win 3-1.

Again drawing the national newspaper headlines after once again being in the Third Round draw Yeovil found themselves travelling to meet Second Division Chesterfield at Saltergate. Yeovil put up a plucky display before over 24,000 spectators and held up the League side for nearly half an hour when Chesterfield opened the scoring. Encouraged by this success Chesterfield surged forward and within five minutes were two goals ahead. The Southern Leaguers' hopes were kept alive when Mansley scored from a penalty to reduce the arrears. Chesterfield put the issue beyond doubt when they scored again in the 60th minute.

Yeovil: Dyke, Hickman, Davis, Haines, Blizzard, Paterson, Rae, Mansley, Foulds, Wright, Hamilton.

Yeovil were again in the First Round in the 1952/3 season when they were drawn at home against Brighton, Third Division South. The crowd of over 10,000 saw highly-placed Brighton's speed and stamina too much for the Southern Leaguers who lost 4-1.

The First Round draw of the 1953/4 competition brought Yeovil a home game against Norwich City, then Third Division South. It was the 13th time that Yeovil had appeared in the First Round but it was unlucky for the Southern Leaguers, a 12,000 crowd seeing two late Norwich goals put an end to the Somerset side's Cup hopes.

Yeovil drew a home tie against Aldershot, Third Division South, in the First Round of the 1955/6 season and the first game, before a 'gate' of 10,600 in what subsequently turned out to be a marathon, ended in a 1-1 draw. Yeovil were without their injured player-manager, ex-Portsmouth Ike Clarke but he was back for the replay at Aldershot, the game ending as before 1-1 despite extra time. It was a different story in the second replay, staged on Southampton's ground, where Yeovil were defeated 3–0.

The 1956/7 First Round contest produced a clash of non-League giants – on the Huish slope Yeovil were matched against Peterborough United, then Midland League champions. There was a crowd of over 10,000 to see the home side go down to a 3–1 defeat.

In 1957/8 Yeovil began another of their triumphant Cup runs which was to see them once again through to the Third Round. Their opponents in the First Round, away from home, (the first time Yeovil had been drawn away in the First Round since 1932) were fellow Southern Leaguers Guildford City. It took a replay before the issue could be resolved, the first encounter producing a 2–2 draw. Then in the replay a lone goal, snatched in the final minute, luckily got Yeovil into the next round. There they once again had the luck of the draw, set to entertain fellow Southern Leaguers Bath City at Huish. A crowd of nearly 12,000 saw Yeovil grab two vital goals within four minutes without reply.

The Third Round saw Yeovil away from home to Fulham at Craven Cottage. Yeovil played some splendid football during the first half and had the better of the exchanges with their Second Division opponents. Midway through the first half Yeovil's right back Robshaw moved up to unleash a terrific shot from 30 yards that ended up in the back of the Fulham net with Macedo well beaten. But the 'goal' was disallowed, a cruel stroke of luck for the non-Leaguers. In the second half the muddy conditions favoured the superior stamina of the League side and Fulham piled up a 4–0 lead which they held to the end. Two of Fulham's goals were scored by Jimmy Hill, of BBC fame.

Yeovil: Lawrence, Robshaw, Elder, Baldwin, Nagy, Elliott, Riseborough, Alexander, Travis, Torrance, McKay.

For the First Round of the 1958/9 season Yeovil were drawn away from home against Southend United, Third Division South. Before a crowd of 15,296 Yeovil put up a cast-iron defence to hold the League side to a goalless draw. In the replay at Huish the Southern Leaguers gained a memorable victory. Winning 1–0 they added a further chapter to their Cup history – it was the first time that the part-timers had won a replay against a League side. Yeovil scored the match-winner seven minutes from the end with an unstoppable shot from 18-year-old John Dennis.

In the next round Yeovil had an away tie against Colchester United, Third Division South and one-time non-League 'giant-killers'. Although Colchester struck first to hold a 1–0 half-time lead Yeovil equalised from the penalty spot to bring Colchester to Huish. There was a 10,000 crowd at the replay when Colchester dealt out a 7–1 drubbing.

Yeovil had visions of a hard game when, in the 1960/1 competition, they drew Walsall, Third Division, away from home. At that time Walsall, newly promoted from the Fourth Division, were unbeaten at home. The tie revived memories of the 1936/7 Second Round Cup encounter when Yeovil held Walsall to a 1–1 draw at Walsall and then lost the replay at Huish. At Fellows Park in this game Yeovil pulled off one of their greatest ever Cup victories away from home. During non-stop raids Yeovil netted twice in quick succession only for both 'goals' to be disallowed. But in the 37th minute Yeovil's aggression paid off when Taylor scored the only goal of the game. Yeovil had another hard task in Round Two when they had to travel to meet Third Division Bournemouth at Dean Court. A crowd of 15,932 saw the Cherries go into a 2–0 lead after half-time, Yeovil got one back to stay in the game but two minutes from the end Bournemouth scored again to make the final result 3–1.

In the 1961/2 competition Yeovil drew Notts County, Third Division, the oldest League club, at Meadow Lane. Although Yeovil never surrendered despite having to fight back from a goal down County were generally in command and won fairly comfortably 4–2. Attendance: 11,375.

The 1962/3 season produced a First Round tie for Yeovil at Huish against fellow Southern Leaguers Dartford. Yeovil were quickly two goals in arrears but got one back before the interval and later in the game not only equalised but went ahead to move into the next round on a 3–2 margin. Yeovil had the luck of the draw for the Second Round when they were drawn at Huish against Third Division Swindon Town. A crowd of 12,292 saw Swindon win 2–0.

The next League victim on the Huish slope, in 1963/4, was Third Division Southend United who had visited the Somerset club in the First Round in 1958/9 and had gone down 1–0. Southend were looking for revenge but Yeovil repeated the dose as before with a 1–0 win, the matchwinner being scored by Terry Foley. Round Two was another home draw for the Southern Leaguers who entertained

342

Third Division Crystal Palace at Huish before a crowd of 15,000. For long periods of the first half Palace were outplayed by the Southern Leaguers who went in at half-time with a 2–0 lead. Although Palace got one back in the second half the game was in injury time when Yeovil netted again to make the final score 3–1. The Southern Leaguers had thus repeated their success of 39 years previously when Palace were their victims at Huish.

For the Third Round tie Yeovil again had the luck of the draw, Huish being the venue for a meeting between the Southern Leaguers and Second Division Bury. Fifteen years previously Yeovil had humbled Bury 3–1 at Huish in the Third Round. This time the Division Two side were seeking revenge and got it with a 2–0 victory despite a great Yeovil second half rally.

Yeovil: Jones, Herrity, Harris, Albury, Lambden, Muir, Pounder, Foley, Hall, Taylor, Pound. Attendance, 12,055.

Yeovil were next in the First Round in the 1965/6 season when they had an away tie at Griffin Park against Division Three Brentford. Up to that point non-League sides had had very little luck against the Bees; only once in 11 post-war encounters up to 1965/6 had a non-League side recorded any success at all – when Margate drew two all at Griffin Park in 1963. Yeovil were no more successful than the rest, going down 2–1 before a 'gate' of 9,320.

Yeovil attempted some more giant-killing in the First Round of the 1966/7 competition when they entertained Third Division Oxford Utd at Huish but in the event went down 2–1.

Yeovil were again in the First Round in the following season, 1967/8, when they were drawn at Huish against fellow Southern Leaguers Margate. The visitors had a poor away record against Yeovil but on this occasion raised their game and won 3–1.

For the 1968/9 First Round tie Yeovil drew another Southern League side, hardened Cup fighters Weymouth, away from home and after a hard struggle lost 2–1.

Yeovil again fought their way into the First Round in the 1969/70 season when they were drawn at Huish against Third Division Shrewsbury. The League side won 3–2. In Yeovil's back division was Alan Herrity who was making his 400th appearance for the club.

In the following season Yeovil once again had a highly successful Cup run which again saw them into the Third Round where a joust with Arsenal made them the talking point of the football world. Yeovil's opponents in the First Round, at home at Huish, were non-League Aveley, an Essex village amateur side playing in the Second Division of the Athenian League.

Yeovil scored the only goal of the game.

The win against Aveley gave Yeovil the right to meet Fourth Division Bournemouth away from home. A crowd of 11,583 saw a weakened Bournemouth side struggle against the Southern Leaguers, intent on avenging the 3-1 deafeat in 1960 at Dean Court. It was a return to his home ground for Chris Weller, the Yeovil striker who formerly played for Bournemouth. A few minutes before half-time Myers scored the only goal of the game for Yeovil.

Yeovil: Clark, Herrity, Bayliss, Myers, Smith, Hughes, Housley, Weller, Grey, Thompson, Clance, (Sub: McClusky). Attendance 11,583.

This fine result over the Fourth Division side gave Yeovil a dream Third Round encounter at Huish against mighty First Division Arsenal, fully described in *Match Report*.

Yeovil had to wait until the 1972/3 season before they were again in the First Round, drawing a home tie against Third Division Brentford. After a goalless first half the Bees scored first on the resumption but Yeovil netted twice to go forward to the next round. This time their opponents, again at Huish, were fellow west countrymen Third Division Plymouth Argyle. A 'gate' of 10,577 saw the teams fairly evenly-matched in the first half with the scoresheet blank. Plymouth had a slight edge in the second half and scored twice to put Yeovil out of the Cup.

Yeovil were out of the First Round until the 1975/6 season when they drew Third Division Millwall at Huish, a contest that was to develop into something of a marathon. Millwall had had indifferent luck against non-League sides in the Cup and could hardly have relished the prospect of meeting the legendary west country Cup fighters on their sloping pitch. Yeovil held a 1-0 lead until 12 minutes from the end when Millwall equalised and were lucky to fight another day. The replay at The Den added to Yeovil's reputation when they held Millwall to a 2-2 draw after extra time. The Southern

Leaguers had a splendid game, twice coming back from behind.

In the second replay, at Aldershot, Millwall had the better of the first half exchanges and had the ball in the net twice but the referee disallowed both 'goals'. Millwall scored the only goal of the match in the 60th minute.

Yeovil were at home in the 1978/9 competition First Round tie against Isthmian Leaguers Barking making their first First Round appearance since 1924. The game promised to be a needle affair, with Yeovil up to that time having an unbeaten home record and the Isthmian Leaguers unbeaten away from home. In the end it was Barking's day – the amatuers scoring the only goal of the match in the first half.

Yeovil, again in the First Round in the 1979/80 season, had a hard away tie against Isthmian League champions Enfield but managed to win 1–0.

In the Second Round Yeovil drew Slough, at that time propping up the Premier Division of the Isthmian League, at Huish. Yeovil's second-half goal earned them a plum home draw in the Third Round against First Division Norwich City.

It was Yeovil's ninth appearance in Round Three and John Bond, the Norwich manager who had seen something of Yeovil's skills during his days at Bournemouth, was prepared for a do-or-die struggle. Robson helped to set up the first Norwich goal in the 23rd minute when Paddon hit the ball on the turn into the top of the net. Yeovil could make little impression against the powerful Norwich defence and half-time arrived with Norwich ahead. In the second half Yeovil attacked furiously and City were unsettled at the Town work-rate. The game really ended for Yeovil when goalkeeper Parker was injured. There were several stoppages while the goalkeeper was given treatment. It is doubtful whether he knew anything of the second goal which Robson headed in. City got number three through Fashanu almost on time. There was nearly five minutes of extra time which Yeovil utilised to continue trying to breach the Norwich stronghold.

Teams:
Yeovil: Parker, Battams, Payne, Jones, Harrison, Broom, Morrall, Scott, Green, Finnigan, Gold. (Sub: Williams).
Norwich: Keelan, Bond, Downs, Ryan, Brown, Powell,

Mendhan, Robson, Fashanu, Paddon, Peters. Attendance: 8,524.

Yeovil were drawn at home in the First Round of the 1980/81 season against Isthmian League side Farnborough Town. No goals had been scored up to the 72nd minute when Yeovil broke the deadlock only to have the stalemate restored five minutes later when Farnborough scored from a penalty. A replay seemed on the cards when four minutes from the end ex-Torquay United full back Steve Ritchie made it 2-1 for Yeovil.

In the Second Round for the 17th time post-war Yeovil were matched against Colchester United, away at Layer Road. Yeovil, determined on giving their former fellow Southern Leaguers a football lesson, buzzed around the box and in the 14th minute were rewarded when they went 1-0 in the lead. It was not until the 87th minute that the U's grabbed the equaliser to force a replay at Huish. "Down to the slope" said the headlines in one newspaper as Colchester prepared to brave both Yeovil's sloping pitch and their Cup tradition on their own ground. But there were to be no further battle honours that season, Colchester going through to the next round with two second half goals.

Yeovil's next attempt to scale the Cup heights came in the following season, 1981/2, when they were drawn away in the First Round against fellow Alliance Premier Leaguers Dagenham. Although Yeovil dominated the first-half they went in at half-time only one goal ahead for their efforts. Within a minute of the resumption the West Countrymen struck again and it looked curtains for Dagenham. But Yeovil let their opponents back into the game and midway through the half Dagenham scored twice to take them to Huish for a replay. This game had an unfortunate ending for Yeovil. In an even contest in which the defenders dominated the scene there were no goals and the game went into extra time. In the 112th minute Dagenham scored to end the stalemate.

MATCH REPORTS
FOURTH ROUND F.A. CUP
29th January 1949
YEOVIL 2   SUNDERLAND 1

Over 17,000 spectators were at Huish to see this memorable David and Goliath encounter when Yeovil entertained the famous First Division side.

The Yeovil side, looking smart in their new green shirts bearing the Borough coat of arms, were led on to the field by 10-year-old Rex Rainey, the club's mascot.

Yeovil began the game in great style and Mapson, in the Sunderland goal, was called upon to bring off early saves from Bryant and Hamilton. With Mapson out of position Hamilton put over a centre that rolled across the goalmouth.

With the great crowd roaring their encouragement Yeovil continued to attack and shots by Stock and Keeton went close. Another Hamilton centre enticed Mapson from his goal once again and only Sunderland's right-half Watson on the goal-line prevented Yeovil from scoring.

In the 26th minute, amid scenes of great enthusiasm, Yeovil scored through Alec STOCK. Hickman took a free kick, placed the ball to Wright who headed it to Stock for the inside-right to beat Mapson.

Half-time: Yeovil 1   Sunderland 0

Sunderland came more into the game in the second half. Both Duns and Turnbull led dangerous Sunderland raids but the Yeovil defence held together until the 15th minute after the resumption when Sunderland equalised. In bringing off a difficult save from Ramsden Yeovil goalkeeper Dyke dropped the ball in front of ROBINSON who scored easily. It was Robinson who, playing for Sheffield Wednesday, put Yeovil out of the Cup in 1939. Dyke, an amateur, was playing his first game for Yeovil, standing in for the injured Hall.

The game continued to be fought out at a great pace. Sunderland's £20,000 Shackleton, who up to then had rarely been in the picture, became more persistent.

Score at 90 mins: Yeovil 1   Sunderland 1

In the 14th minute of extra time Yeovil made Cup history when Bryant scored the winning goal. Intercepting a Shackleton pass Yeovil's inside left Wright moved the ball across to BRYANT who easily beat Mapson. There were scenes of unparalleled enthusiasm on the ground and five minutes before time the spectators dashed on the pitch after mistaking the whistle for a free kick for full time.

Long after the game had ended the crowd stayed on the ground and Alec Stock spoke over the public address system. In a never-to-be-forgotten night crowds packed the streets of Yeovil.

Result: Yeovil 2   Sunderland 1

Teams:
Yeovil: Dyke, Hickman, Davies, Keeton, Blizzard, Collins, Hamilton, Stock, Bryant, Wright, Hargreaves.
Sunderland: Mapson, Stelling, Ramsden, Watson, Hall, Wright, Duns, Robinson, Turnbull, Shackleton, Reynolds.
Referee: Mr. A. W. Smith, (Aldershot).
Attendance: 17,000

FIFTH ROUND F.A. CUP
12th February 1949
MANCHESTER UNITED 8   YEOVIL 0

There was a tumultuous welcome at Maine Road for the Yeovil part-time professionals. Six thousand Yeovil fans flowed into the city and excitement mounted as the rival supporters thronged through the streets wielding their rattles, bells and motor horns. A goodwill message came from Gloversville, U.S.A., founded by Yeovil emigrants during the depression at the start of the century.

Remarkable scenes took place before the start of the match. The clash between the Cupholders and the Southern League club fired the imagination of the Manchester fans and 20 minutes before the game was due to start the gates were closed. The youngsters were passed over the heads of the crowd so that they could sit on the touch-line. When the game began there were over 80,000 spectators inside and it was easily the biggest 'gate' of the day.

Facing six internationals in the United team – with Yeovil being dealt a severe blow with left winger Jack Hargreaves reported unfit – the gallant Southern Leaguers leapt into the fray and within the first minute Bobby Hamilton forced a corner. It was not long before United turned on the heat and after only six minutes the Cupholders opened their account, ROWLEY heading a simple looking goal. The harried Yeovil defence conceded a second goal after 12 minutes, ROWLEY again being the marksman.

After several brilliant saves by Hall, United notched their third. Twenty two minutes had gone when ROWLEY completed his hat-trick, beating Hall in a race for the ball and at the same time colliding with the Yeovil 'keeper.

BURKE notched United's fourth goal in the last minute of the first half, beating Hall at the second attempt.

Half-time: Manchester United 4   Yeovil 0

United added to their score two minutes after the interval, BURKE again being the scorer. Yeovil still put plenty of determination and spirit into the game but they could not match the Cupholders' speed and craft. In the 65th minute United went still further ahead, ROWLEY making the score 6–0.

In the 72nd minute MITTEN snapped up an easy chance with the Yeovil defence appealing for off-side. Two minutes from the end ROWLEY made it eight, bringing his personal tally to five.

One of the heroes of the game was yeovil goalkeeper Stanley Hall who for 70 minutes of the game played with a gash in the lower abdomen and had to have four stitches inserted at half time. Alec Stock's Yeovil heroes had been unable to stop the United power house and when they did attack Chilton, Carey and Aston provided an unshakeable defence.

Result: Manchester United 8   Yeovil 0

Teams:
Manchester United: Crompton, Carey, Aston, Cockburn, Chilton, McGlen, Delaney, Perason, Burke, Rowley, Mitten.
Yeovil: Hall, Hickman, Davies, Keeton, Blizzard, Collins, Hamilton, Stock, Bryant, Wright, Roy.
Referee: Mr. A. Bond, (London).
Attendance: 81,565 (Receipts: £7,141)

THIRD ROUND F.A. CUP
6th January 1971
YEOVIL 0   ARSENAL 3

The 14,500 spectators at the tiny Huish ground were hoping that Yeovil's notorious sloping pitch, 6 ft. from touch line to touch line, would help to overcome Arsenal's power and maybe add another fairy-tale chapter to the Southern Leaguers' history on the same lines as their famous victory over Sunderland. But it was not to be. The game had been postponed from the previous Saturday because of icy conditions and when the teams finally met the icebound pitch had given way to a firm green surface, the kind of pitch that served only to highlight Arsenal's skills. In the early stages of the game Arsenal gained possession time after time and took the attack into the Yeovil half and Town's goalkeeper Clark was often in action. By steady slog and a high work rate Yeovil were able to keep out their august First Division opponents but survived one appeal for a penalty for a possible offence by the Yeovil goalkeeper. Yeovil's back divisions put on a splendid performance but lacked height and Arsenal's two tall strikers, Kennedy and Radford, were constantly up front probing at Yeovil's defence. In the 36th minute Arsenal scored a goal that had been threatening from the kick-off, Paul Smith, who in fact had a splendid game, being late to intercept RADFORD who rose above the defenders to head in a well flighted ball from Sammels. Just before the interval Arsenal scored their second when Town goalkeeper Clark and Smith got in each other's way to give KENNEDY an easy goal.

Half-time: Yeovil 0   Arsenal 2

Throughout the second half Arsenal played possession football and it was only some fine work by the Yeovil back division that kept out their First Division opponents until late in the game. In their occasional incursions into the Arsenal half Yeovil strikers Grey, Weller and Clancy tried to break through but Arsenal skilfully marshalled their defence in which McLintock and Simpson were especially prominent and broke down the Yeovil attacks. Bob Wilson, in the Arsenal goal had very little to do and during the second half did not have to handle a single direct shot. Ten minutes from the end Arsenal scored their third goal following a run down the left wing by Armstrong who placed the ball on to the head of RADFORD who put the ball out of the reach of Clark. The result was never in doubt after Arsenal gained their 2–0 lead but it was a memorable game and Yeovil were by no means disgraced.

Result: Yeovil 0   Arsenal 3

Teams:
Yeovil: Clark, Herrity, Bayless, Myers, Smith, Hughes, Housley, Weller, Grey, Thompson, Clancy.
Arsenal: Wilson, Rice, McNab, Storey, McLintock, Simpson, Armstrong, Sammels, Radford, Kennedy, Graham, (Sub: Kelly).
Referee: Mr. W. J. Gow, (Swansea).
Attendance: 14,500 – receipts £12,500 (ground record)

CUP ROUNDS

1945/6
1st Round (1st leg) – *17th November*
Yeovil .... 2 Bristol City 2

1st Round (2nd leg) – *24th November*
Bristol City .... 3 Yeovil 0
(Bristol City won on 5-2 aggregate)

1946/7
1st Round – *30th November*
Yeovil .... 2 Peterborough 2

1st Round Replay – *5th December*
Peterborough .... 1 Yeovil 0

1948/9
1st Round – *27th November*
Yeovil .... 4 Romford 0

2nd Round – *11th December*
Weymouth .... 0 Yeovil 4

3rd January – *8th January*
Yeovil .... 3 Bury 1

4th Round – *29th January*
Yeovil .... 2 Sunderland 1
(after extra time. Score at
90 minutes: 1–1)

5th Round – *12th February*
Manchester U. .. 8 Yeovil 0

1949/50
1st Round – *26th November*
Yeovil .... 4 Romford 1

2nd Round – *10th December*
Yeovil .... 3 Gillingham 1

3rd Round – *7th January*
Chesterfield .... 3 Yeovil 1

1952/3
1st Round – *22nd November*
Yeovil .... 1 Brighton 4

1953/4
1st Round – *21st November*
Yeovil .... 0 Norwich 2

1955/6
1st Round – *19th November*
Yeovil .... 1 Aldershot 1

1st Round Replay – *23rd November*
Aldershot .... 1 Yeovil 1
(after extra time)

1st Round, 2nd Replay – *28th November*
Aldershot .... 3 Yeovil 0
(At Southampton)

1956/7
1st Round – *17th November*
Yeovil .... 1 Peterborough   3

1957/8
1st Round – *16th November*
Guildford .... 2 Yeovil 2

1st Round Replay – *21st November*
Yeovil .... 1 Guildford 0

2nd Round – *7th December*
Yeovil .... 2 Bath 0

3rd Round – *4th January*
Fulham .... 4 Yeovil 0

1958/9
1st Round – *15th November*
Southend .... 0 Yeovil 0

1st Round Replay – *20th November*
Yeovil .... 1 Southend 0

2nd Round – *6th December*
Colchester .... 1 Yeovil 1

2nd Round Replay – *11th December*
Yeovil .... 1 Colchester 7

1960/1
1st Round – *5th November*
Walsall .... 0 Yeovil 1

2nd Round – *26th November*
Bournemouth .... 3 Yeovil 1

1961/2
1st Round – *4th November*
Notts County ... 4 Yeovil 2

1962/3
1st Round – *3rd November*
Yeovil .... 3 Dartford 2

2nd Round – *24th November*
Yeovil .... 0 Swindon 2

1963/4
1st Round – *16th November*
Yeovil .... 1 Southend 0

2nd Round – *7th December*
Yeovil .... 3 Crystal Palace ... 1

3rd Round – *4th January*
Yeovil .... 0 Bury 2

Yeovil (Contd)

1965/6
1st Round – *13th November*
Brentford 2   Yeovil 1

1966/7
1st Round – *26th November*
Yeovil 1   Oxford Utd. 3

1967/8
1st Round – *13th December*
Yeovil 1   Margate 3

1968/9
1st Round – *16th November*
Weymouth 2   Yeovil 1

1969/70
1st Round – *15th November*
Yeovil 2   Shrewsbury 3

1970/71
1st Round – *21st November*
Yeovil 1   Aveley 0
2nd Round – *11th December*
Bournemouth 0   Yeovil 1
3rd Round – *6th January*
Yeovil 0   Arsenal 3

1972/3
1st Round – *18th November*
Yeovil 2   Brentford 1
2nd Round – *9th December*
Yeovil 0   Plymouth 2

1975/6
1st Round – *22nd November*
Yeovil 1   Millwall 1
1st Round Replay – *25th November*
Millwall 2   Yeovil 2
(after extra time)
1st Round 2nd Replay – *3rd December*
Yeovil 0   Millwall 1
(at Aldershot)

1978/9
1st Round – *25th November*
Yeovil 0   Barking 1

1979/80
1st Round – *24th November*
Enfield 0   Yeovil 1
2nd Round – *15th December*
Yeovil 1   Slough 0
3rd Round – *5th January*
Yeovil 0   Norwich City 3

1980/81
1st Round – *22nd November*
Yeovil 2   Farnborough 1
2nd Round – *13th December*
Colchester Utd. . 1   Yeovil 1
2nd Round replay – *17th December*
Yeovil 0   Colchester Utd .. 2

1981/2
1st Round – *21st November*
Dagenham 2   Yeovil 2
1st Round Replay – *25th November*
Yeovil 0   Dagenham 1
(after extra time)